Karl Barth and the
Future of Evangelical Theology

Used with permission from the Karl Barth Archiv, Basel, Switzerland.

Karl Barth
and the
Future of Evangelical Theology

Edited by
Christian T. Collins Winn
and
John L. Drury

Foreword by
William J. Abraham

CASCADE *Books* • Eugene, Oregon

KARL BARTH AND THE FUTURE OF EVANGELICAL THEOLOGY

Copyright © 2014 Wipf and Stock Publishers. All rights reserved. Except for brief quotations in critical publications or reviews, no part of this book may be reproduced in any manner without prior written permission from the publisher. Write: Permissions, Wipf and Stock Publishers, 199 W. 8th Ave., Suite 3, Eugene, OR 97401.

Cascade Books
An Imprint of Wipf and Stock Publishers
199 W. 8th Ave., Suite 3
Eugene, OR 97401

www.wipfandstock.com

ISBN 13: 978-1-60899-682-7

Cataloguing-in-Publication data:

    Karl Barth and the future of evangelical theology / edited by Christian T. Collins Winn and John L. Drury ; with a foreword by William J. Abraham.

    xxii + 290 pp. ; 23 cm. Includes bibliographical references and index.

    ISBN 13: 978-1-60899-682-7

    1. Barth, Karl, 1886–1968—Criticism and interpretation. 2. Theology, Doctrinal—History—20th century. 3. Evangelicalism. I. Collins Winn, Christian T. II. Drury, John L. III. Abraham, William J. (William James), 1947–. IV. Title.

BX4827.B3 K330 2014

Manufactured in the U.S.A.

Contents

Foreword | vii
William J. Abraham

Acknowledgments | xi

Introduction | xiii
Christian T. Collins Winn and John L. Drury

Abbreviations | xxiv

Part I: Reframing the Conversation

1 Karl Barth and Evangelicalism: The Varieties of a Sibling Rivalry | 3
   Donald W. Dayton

2 Karl Barth and Pietism | 20
   Eberhard Busch

3 Bringing an Elephant and a Whale into Conversation: Karl Barth and Pietism | 45
   Kimlyn J. Bender

Part II: Reconceiving Christian Experience and Practice

4 Christ in Us: The Hope of Glory or the Sentimentality of a "Bohemian Private Enterprise"? Barth, Pietists, and Pentecostals | 69
   Terry L. Cross

5 Karl Barth on Fellowship with Jesus Christ: The Calling of the Christian | 91
   James Nelson

6 Barth and Testimony | 102
   John L. Drury

7 Jesus's Earthly Father as Protector and Example for the Church: How Karl Barth's Theology Challenges the Contemporary Evangelical Masculinist Movement | 115
   Stina Busman Jost

8 "Thy Kingdom Come!" Karl Barth and the Promise of a Prophetic Evangelical Church | 130
   Christian T. Collins Winn and Peter Goodwin Heltzel

Part III: Renewing Christian Doctrine

9 "Speak, for Your Servant Is Listening": Barth, Prayer, and Theological Method | 149
   Joel D. Lawrence

10 Better News Hath No Evangelical than This: Barth, Election, and the Recovery of the Gospel from Evangelicalism's Territorial Disputes | 162
   Chris Boesel

11 God Says What the Text Says: Another Look at Karl Barth's View of Scripture | 191
   Frank D. Macchia

12 The Church as "Witness": Karl Barth and the Missional Church | 206
   Kyle A. Roberts

13 Jesus Christ as the One and Only Sacrament | 230
   Kurt Anders Richardson

14 Eschatology from Basel to Azusa Street: The Voices of Karl Barth and Pentecostalism in Dialogue | 254
   Peter Althouse

Contributors | 283

Index | 287

Foreword

William J. Abraham

I HAVE NEVER BEEN A Barthian. I have never lusted after being a Barthian. Indeed, I have at times considered Karl Barth to be a disaster for the intellectual life of Christianity in the twentieth century and now on into the twenty-first century.

To be sure, I know that Barth has worked wonders in restoring interest in and commitment to the doctrine of the Trinity. However, when I read the small print, I find his vision of the Trinity with its sophisticated vision of modalism thin and unconvincing. To be sure, I have rejoiced at his recovery of the significance of divine revelation for providing warrants for central Christian claims. However, when I read the details, I find the sophisticated fideism involved to be inhabited by conceptual muddle and fraught with extremely poor epistemological backing. To be sure, I have at times been overwhelmed by the sheer beauty and audacity of his thought, especially in those early essays, *The Word of God and the Word of Man*. However, working through all the dense and maddening prose of the *Church Dogmatics* and the prolix historical diversions in the small print leaves one exhausted and full of probing objections. They become suffocating and disastrous when deployed by insiders who expect critics to read further so that in time our worries will be allayed by the voice of the master.

So what am I doing writing a laudatory Foreword to a book on Karl Barth and Evangelicalism? This is not just a favor to wonderful friends and colleagues whose intellectual fecundity I never cease to admire. Nor is it that I consider the range and content of these essays to be first-rate in style and content (I do). The enthusiasm for this volume stems from the following considerations.

First, I do so because there is no future for Christian theology without working through rather than around the colossal contribution of Barth to

Christian theology. Barth will still be read when most theologians we know, not least our own good selves, will not even make it into the footnotes. From beginning to end he is a theologian's theologian. His personal biography, his stance against the Nazis, his immersion in the ministry of the church, and the like, draw us into the drama of his intellectual endeavors. He became a theologian almost by accident, so we can lay aside any drive to professional stability and stardom. When he took up the challenge of theology, he was all in from the start. The result was an extraordinary reappropriation and restatement of the Christian faith that bristles with energy and a host of intellectual virtues. He never yielded to the gloomy conservative instincts that can so readily mar those of us who are looking for fresh fish when we have been fed stones. His appreciation, say, for the legacy of Lotze (a legacy carried to America by Borden Bowne and then highjacked by Liberal Protestants in Methodism) and what it might have been is startling in its insight. In the end, it is his detailed and utterly fresh treatment of the whole gamut of Christian theology that matters. He returns us to the proper subject of theology—God and God's actions in creation and redemption. On this score, I indirectly owe a debt to Barth and the legacy he unleashed in the English-speaking world. These essays much more fulsomely display the fecundity of the Barthian legacy for us all.

Second, I do so because Barth's return to the deep resources of the faith is crucial to the welfare of the Evangelical tradition. Brought up in and then converted in Irish Methodism, I have never been tempted to disown the Evangelical tradition. I have long held that Evangelicalism is an essentially contested tradition. Its strength lies in part precisely in varied historical instantiations of the tradition and in the intense feuds that take place within it both synchronically and diachronically. Efforts to corral the evangelical tradition into the legacy of fundamentalism over the last generation are legion; they are now apace afresh in the move to canonize Carl F. H. Henry as the great hero of Evangelicalism whose work is to be the source and the benchmark for the future. In these circumstances it is vital that alternative sources and norms of intellectual propriety be taken up in conversation about the future of evangelical theology. On this score, Barth is an obvious choice as inspiration and intellectual partner. To be sure, this move will destabilize the tradition; it will evoke a new round of debate. Rather than lamented, this is exactly what is needed. Without the Barthian voice Evangelicalism will surely give birth to a new round of post-evangelical liberals and progressives who invariably give away the store. At crucial points, I think Barth did that himself; it is no accident that a raft of Death of God and secular theologians started out on Barthian territory. However, if I am right about this Barth's mistakes are deeply illuminating mistakes; it is up to Evangelical theologians to avoid them in the future. So right or wrong, engaging Barth is pivotal for the health of the Evangelical tradition. It is radically incomplete in itself; it needs nourishing partners in distress; and Barth is as good as any in filling this desideratum.

Third, I do so because wrestling with Barth's vision of divine revelation is the spur to the invention and pursuit of a new subdiscipline in theology and philosophy that I have dubbed the epistemology of theology. Barth's vision of divine revelation and its concomitant account of Holy Scripture are dense and nuanced. His deepest insight, as I see it, is that God is made known through God's acts. What he did with this insight and how it got mishandled among his children and grandchildren are another matter that need not detain us here. What matters is that he was on the money and that in articulating his vision he was interested not in some thin theism beloved of so many analytic philosophers but in a robust Trinitarian version of the Christian faith. Hence, Barth has to be a crucial canon for work in the epistemology of theology. What I mean by this is a new subdiscipline lying in the cracks between theology and philosophy that engages in fully critical investigation of the relevant warrants for Christian theological claims. What is at stake here is not just this or that set of material claims about how a theologian justifies or renders credible his or her version of Christianity, but rather the further investigation of how we should best conceive and execute this enterprise in the first place. No doubt Barthians will smell a rat here, complaining that this makes theology subject to alien philosophical categories that will undo their deepest insights. If they do, then let them bring their rat poison, as Barth himself tried to do in his own inimitable style. The rest of us, however, reserve the right to check the biochemistry of the rat poison for its efficacy. Serious Barthians, as opposed to the camp followers who want to wallow in their disguised dogmatism, will not take this line. They will come to the table without reserve and see how their proposals fare in the light of historical, conceptual, and material epistemological inquiry.

Acknowledgments

L IKE ANY WRITING PROJECT, this one would have been impossible without the many hands that have helped bring it to light. We would like to thank Brian Bauernfeind, Hilary Ritchie, Robert Alexander Simpson, Matthew Eddy, and Suzanne Cooley for their organizational and editorial assistance. The project would not have made it across the finish line without the invaluable editorial labor of Sara Misgen. Thanks also should go to the editorial team at Wipf and Stock for their patience and care. We would both also like to thank our families—Julie, Jonah, and Elijah Winn, and Amanda, Samuel, and Clara Drury—for their patience and love.

Introduction

Christian T. Collins Winn and John L. Drury

IN THE SUMMER OF 2007 the editors of the present volume met at the 50th Anniversary Celebration of the NCCC Faith and Order Commission held at Oberlin College. We immediately resonated with one another, both personally and professionally. One particularly potent point of resonance was a shared frustration with the framing of the dialogue between Karl Barth and evangelical theology. This topic had come up because earlier that summer Princeton Theological Seminary had sponsored a conference devoted to this dialogue.[1] Though there were many excellent papers given and rich discussion was fostered, nevertheless, the conference was still caught in a framework which has shaped the question of the relationship of Barth and evangelical theology over the past several decades.[2] That framework consists of the unexamined premise that American Evangelicalism ought primarily to be understood as a species of Protestant orthodoxy, especially of the Reformed variety, and that the defining task of evangelical theology is the preservation of Protestant orthodox theology. The dialogue between Barth and evangelical theology is often conducted under these constraints, a shared source of frustration for many.

The present volume seeks to offer an alternative to the dominant constraints, one that we believe will open up new avenues for fruitful conversation. In this endeavor, our motivating conviction is that dialogue between

---

1. Many of those papers were published in McCormack and Anderson, *Karl Barth and American Evangelicalism*.

2. This is not to say that the framework described here was intentionally adopted by the conference organizers. Rather, the framework described here is part of the larger academic "social imaginary" that has shaped the scholarship on the relationship of Barth and Evangelicalism, especially in North America, for the past several decades. The conference was simply caught up in this larger set of assumptions, because they were brought to the table by conference participants, etc.

Karl Barth and evangelical theology as framed by the question of orthodoxy is at best misleading and at worst wrong-headed. We believe that the vast majority of academic evangelical reception of Barth has been so framed. We also believe that the vast majority of Anglophone Barth scholarship, insofar as it engages the evangelical tradition, takes this faulty premise for granted.

What, then, is the alternative? How should one frame the dialogue between Karl Barth and evangelical theology? The reframing we propose requires a twofold revision, in which we reinterpret both partners to the dialogue. We begin with a revised understanding of evangelical identity. Rather than identifying American Evangelicalism with Protestant orthodoxy, we believe that it ought to be identified with the revivalist forms of Protestantism which arose in the post-Reformation era, what W. R. Ward has named "the Protestant evangelical awakening."[3] This refers to the broader transatlantic Protestant coalition that finds its roots in Pietism and Wesleyanism—as well as some strands of "new light" Puritanism—where the theological orientation is centered more on the virtues of love and hope, rather than on faith. This is not to say that these movements were not concerned with faith, or the question of theological knowledge. Nevertheless, they were far more interested in the practice of love, or the shape of the Christian life in relation to the neighbor, and in the question of hope, or what kind of transformation can be expected in this life.

As such, the defining task of the evangelical tradition is the promotion of a form of life. Questions of orthodoxy are thus a function of a set of practical commitments and its accompanying theology of the Christian life. Accordingly, the dialogue with Barth ought to consist primarily in the question of his relationship to characteristic evangelical practices. Questions of orthodoxy come in to play, but never abstracted from the form of life that constitutes their significance. The structure of this volume as a whole reflects this priority.

But the reframing we propose does not rest on a revisionist reading of Evangelicalism alone. A fresh look at Karl Barth is also necessary. We believe that Barth himself is fundamentally misunderstood when seen as a preserver of orthodoxy. The question is not whether he succeeded in this task, answers to which vary among both evangelical theologians and scholars of Barth. The more pressing question is whether this task defined him. Our answer: it did not. Rather, Barth too was driven by an attunement to the primacy of praxis—though he was attuned first and foremost to the primacy

---

3. See his *Protestant Evangelical Awakening* and *Early Evangelicalism: A Global Intellectual History, 1670–1789*. See also Noll, *Rise of Evangelicalism*, 13–25.

of *divine* praxis.⁴ Barth's theological revolution cannot be understood—let alone joined—when pictured as a preservation of orthodoxy.

This twofold revision of the conversation requires significantly more substantiation than can be supplied by a single volume, let alone its introductory essay. However, we can at least explain ourselves in some detail. So, in the following two sections, we articulate our revisionist readings of each dialogue partner in turn: first evangelical theology, then Karl Barth. This overture to the volume as a whole unfolds around a single, simple theme: the new birth.

Rethinking Evangelical Theology: The New Birth of the Christian

We begin with some clues to the wider misunderstanding of Evangelicalism that come from evangelicals' critiques and appropriations of Karl Barth. The vast majority of evangelical literature on Karl Barth (positive or negative) focuses on the doctrine of Scripture.⁵ This focus is a function of the assumption that the doctrine of Scripture is the defining feature of evangelical identity. Although the reading of Scripture plays a central role in the evangelical tradition, doctrines of Scripture do not provide an illuminating means of identifying Evangelicalism. At this point we need not contest the truth of these doctrines of Scripture. In fact, one could, for example, affirm the doctrine of inerrancy yet reject it as the defining feature of evangelical identity. Such identification betrays a foundationalism that conceals more than it reveals.

---

4. More to come on this below, but for now, consider this striking passage: "What has that metaphysics of being to do with the God who is the basis and Lord of the Church? If this God is He who in Jesus Christ became man, revealing Himself and reconciling the world with Himself, it follows that the relationship between Him and man consists in the event in which God accepted man out of pure, free compassion, in which He drew him to Himself out of pure kindness, but first and last in the eternal decree of the covenant of grace, in God's eternal predestination. It is not with the theory of the relationship between creaturely and creative being, but with the theory of this divine praxis, with the consideration and conception of this divine act, of its eternal decree and its temporal execution, that theology, and therefore theological ethics, must deal" (*CD* II/2, 531).

5. This claim is so obvious even to a casual reader of the literature that it needs no substantiation. But perhaps this is as good a place as any to list a handful of the most influential evangelical engagements with Barth: Van Til, *Christianity and Barthianism*; Runia, *Karl Barth's Doctrine of Holy Scripture*; Henry, *God, Revelation and Authority*; and Ramm, *After Fundamentalism*.

In addition to these sources is the famous—and highly symbolic—encounter between Barth and Carl F. H. Henry during Barth's American tour in 1962. Henry, who at the time was editor of *Christianity Today*, had the opportunity to ask Barth any number of theological questions and chose to focus his question on the doctrine of inerrancy. For a discussion of this encounter, see Worthen, *Apostles of Reason*, 15–17.

It is not that evangelicals are committed to a particular view of Scripture on which is built a set of practical concerns and commitments. Rather, a form of life with its implicit practical concerns and commitments requires a set of conceptual commitments regarding Scripture. One may contest how to best articulate these conceptual commitments and remain firmly within the evangelical tradition. But one who contests, let alone rejects, these practical commitments undergoes a deep alienation from the movement. Case in point: one who can sign off on inerrancy but lacks a personal testimony to conversion or way of describing a living faith experience will have difficulty getting a teaching job at an evangelical Christian college.

This phenomenon is inexplicable in terms of a more foundationalist interpretation of evangelical theology (i.e., that Evangelicalism is constituted primarily by adherence to key doctrines). Such phenomena are better explained when one takes evangelical identity as centered in the experience and event of new birth. This is the common theme that runs through German Pietism, the Anglo-American Awakenings, Holiness Revivalism, Pentecostalism, and contemporary Evangelicalism—the traditions that the present volume seeks to postulate as productive partners for dialogue with Barth. "New birth" is a term that can encompass both the experience of conversion as well as the ongoing experience of grace, the latter of which is expressed through cultivating a diverse array of practices. The centrality of new birth to Evangelicalism is particularly evident in its polemical relations with those outside the tradition. The dividing point comes over the question of regeneration and whether this is something that has actually taken place in one's life—and continues to do so. Nearly all the practical commitments of Evangelicalism center on the event of new birth, and the subsequent cultivation of the new life. One is either moving towards the new birth, or testifying to it in one of its many manifestations.

A focus on the centrality of new birth better explains the dynamics and emergence of Evangelicalism. Early German Pietism, one of the key streams that flow into Evangelicalism, arose in response to a nominal, confessional orthodoxy.[6] In Philipp Jakob Spener's programmatic text, the *Pia Desideria* (1675), he argued that many theologians seemed to think that true theology consisted more in argumentation than in the fruit of new life.[7] The theologians who first felt the wrath of these Pietists were themselves orthodox. Describing them, rather unfortunately, as unregenerate, the same epithet was later used for Enlightenment rationalists, many of whom the orthodox equally polemicized against, though for different reasons. Within the early

---

6. See Roger E. Olson and Christian T. Collins Winn, *Reclaiming Pietism*.

7. See Spener, *Pia Desideria*, 44–57.

stages of evangelical history, particularly the eighteenth century, a triangle was formed between Protestant orthodoxy, Pietism, and Enlightenment. Any two corners of the triangle would align themselves against the third. So orthodoxy and Enlightenment resisted the conversionism of the evangelicals. Pietism and Enlightenment joined forces against the heteronomy and confessional restrictiveness of orthodoxy. And orthodoxy and Pietism were allied in their defense of the supernatural against the Enlightenment. It is this third alliance that in the Anglo-American world has contributed to the confusion about Evangelicalism. The common enemy of "liberalism" led many to conflate revivalist Evangelicalism and Protestant orthodoxy.[8] But the experience of new birth and its accompanying practices remains definitive for evangelicals over against both liberalism and orthodoxy.

When the alternative genealogy of Evangelicalism, one shaped more by the dynamics of "new birth" as understood in Pietism and Wesleyan revivalism, is taken into account, evangelical theology looks and feels different. The question of doctrine does not recede, but it is reframed. Concern with elucidating theological themes that are framed by questions of praxis and experience—such as "new birth," regeneration, sanctification, pneumatology, prayer, social ethics, ecclesiology, hope, and certain forms of eschatology—become more important, while more classical themes like justification, atonement, and Scripture are themselves engaged in new ways. Admittedly, not all of these themes are engaged in the present volume, but what is offered is done so as a first draft of an emerging dialogue.

Rethinking Karl Barth: The New Birth of All Creation

When we approach Karl Barth from this revised understanding of Evangelicalism, we begin to see things that have been overlooked—the reality of new birth displaces the doctrine of Scripture as the framework for dialogue, and a different set of convergences and divergences comes into the foreground. In fact, the standard criticism gets turned upside down. Whereas Barth is criticized for being too subjectivistic in his epistemology by those who consider Evangelicalism to be a species of Protestant orthodoxy, when he is brought into dialogue with a Pietist understanding of Evangelicalism he is often attacked for being too objectivistic in his soteriology.[9]

---

8. For a discussion of the wider historiographical confusion, see Hart, *Deconstructing Evangelicalism*, 48–61.

9. In chapter 1 below, Donald Dayton presents this point as evidence of the confusion over just what the term *evangelical* actually means.

Notwithstanding the truth—or lack thereof—of these criticisms of Barth, the significance of this antinomy in evangelical reception of Barth betrays the extent to which there is a fundamental misunderstanding of the heart of Barth's theology. For the heart of Barth's mature theology is neither epistemology nor soteriology as such, but the living Christ himself.[10] "Jesus Christ as attested to us in Holy Scripture is the one Word of God whom we must hear and whom we must trust and obey in life and in death."[11] "The risen and living Jesus Christ is the one Word of God."[12] Jesus Christ, crucified and risen, is the revelation of God, the true witness to the covenant between God and humanity fulfilled in his own life of obedience unto death. Thus the risen Christ himself occupies the center of all theological knowledge, for he is in fact the center of all theological reality. This living Christ displaces all competitors, even well-meaning religious ones, among which is to be included a well-crafted Christology![13] Accordingly, neither a metaphysical doctrine of Scripture nor a personal experience of conversion may occupy the center of theological reflection. Both are relegated to the periphery surrounding the living center of Jesus Christ himself. They are not denied, but rather relocated to their proper place. And so Barth disrupts both an orthodox objectivism and a pietist subjectivism from the perspective of his Christocentric actualism.

It is precisely Barth's Christocentric actualism that both attracts and repels evangelicals. Evangelicals share Barth's sense and taste for living, vibrant faith in a living, active God. It is this livingness that immediately resonates with evangelicals. What evangelical is not immediately drawn in by passages like the following?

> The definition that we must use as a starting-point is that God's being is *life*. Only the Living is God. Only the voice of the Living is God's voice. Only the work of the Living is God's work; only the worship and fellowship of the Living is God's worship and fellowship. So, too, only the knowledge of the Living is knowledge of God. We recall in this connexion the emphatic Old and New Testament description of God as "the living God." This is no metaphor. Nor is it a mere description of God's relation to the

---

10. Although this can perhaps be said of Barth's theology from its inception, it comes most clearly into view in the later volumes of his *Church Dogmatics*. For the most striking instances of Barth's particular brand of Christocentrism, see his revisions of the doctrines of election (*CD* II/2), humanity (*CD* III/2) and reconciliation (*CD* IV/1–3).

11. Barth, *CD* IV/3.1, 3. Barth is here quoting the Barmen Declaration as his *Leitsatz* for §69, but he has changed the pronoun from an abstract "which" to a personal "whom."

12. *CD* IV/1, 347.

13. See *CD* IV/3.1, 173–80.

world and to ourselves. But while it is that, it also describes God Himself as the One He is.[14]

But it is this same livingness that perpetually disrupts the evangelical desire for assurance, whether in personal experience, ecclesial practice, or apologetic argument. When one or more of these modes of assurance are thematized, a fundamental rift with Barth is felt. Hence evangelicals are not wrong to be uneasy about Barth, though the cause of this unease is usually misdiagnosed.

The key to rethinking Karl Barth as a conversation partner for evangelical theology is to understand his own doctrine of new birth. For in fact the event of new birth is also at the center of Barth's theology! The difference between them is the location of this event. For the evangelical tradition, the new birth takes place here and now in the life of the believer. Of course, this event is grounded in the atoning work of the cross of Christ. But, in contrast to certain forms of Protestant orthodoxy and the concern with election and atonement, the accent lies on the present event of conversion.

For Karl Barth, the new birth takes place in the resurrection of Jesus Christ from the dead. The event of new birth is irreducible to either a self-enclosed event in the past or an inward event in the life of a Christian. Rather, it is the very living-again of Jesus Christ, which both took place once for all and continues to take place. In him occurred the new birth of all creation, and in him occurs the new birth of many creatures invited to join him in his self-attestation. Here we are recapitulating the movement of thought in *CD* IV/1–3, especially the great transitional sub-sections on Christ's resurrection, i.e., §59.3, §64.4, and §69.4.[15] But there is no substitute for Barth's own words. So consider the following characteristic passage, to which many more could be added:

> The determination given the world and man by this event [of Christ's resurrection] is a total one. The reconciling work of Jesus Christ is not just accomplished, but has gone out into the reconciled world as a shining light.... The love with which God loved the world cannot remain external. The world is now the world loved by Him in His only-begotten Son. Man is now the man justified and sanctified in Him, and called by Him.... And the death to which he has fallen victim is now the death from which he is delivered, which he can have behind him and under

---

14. Barth, *CD* II/1, 263.

15. For further explication and substantiation of our interpretation of Barth's doctrine of Christ's resurrection, see Collins Winn, *"Jesus Is Victor!"*, and Drury, *The Resurrected God*.

him, since Jesus Christ, and he too as elect in Him, is risen from the dead to new life. He is now the son of God, since the eternal Son of God has come to his side as his true Brother, and is revealed and confirmed in his proximity, and as it were hand in hand with him. . . . He is now the heir of eternal life and as such already has a share in his inheritance, because Jesus as the One who lives eternally has not merely associated with him but addressed him in His resurrection as one with him.[16]

So, is Barth's theology too subjectivistic or too objectivistic? Yes! Barth's Christocentric actualism, here crudely summarized, explodes any sort of subject/object scheme used to assess his theology. For Barth focuses relentlessly on the living God in his communion with the living human being, as this comes to be and be known in Jesus Christ. And as we have said, it is this very livingness that both attracts and repels evangelicals. Perhaps this twofold response betrays incoherence in Barth's theology. But it is just as likely that it betrays an antinomy in evangelical theology. Either way, by rethinking both conversation partners along these lines, a new and more fruitful dialogue can take place.

Outline of the Volume

The volume is divided into three sections. In the first section, "Reframing the Conversation," contributors offer thoughtful considerations of Barth's complex relationship with Evangelicalism, especially when the latter is conceived along Pietist lines. Donald Dayton begins the conversation by noting "the essentially contested nature" of the descriptor "Evangelicalism." The conversation with Barth unfolds along different lines depending on which definition one chooses to adopt. His own choice, not surprisingly, is for a definition shaped more by Pietism and the Anglo-American Awakening movements of the eighteenth and nineteenth centuries. Though published in 1985, Dayton's argument remains relevant today.

Of course, swapping out a Protestant Orthodoxy–inflected definition of Evangelicalism for a Pietist one creates new challenges for a dialogue between Barth and Evangelicalism—challenges that some might argue are far more problematic. But as Eberhard Busch shows in his contribution, Barth's relationship to "actually existing" Pietism was far more nuanced and dialectical than often understood. Busch traces Barth's lifelong engagement with Pietism and Pietist themes and describes Barth as a "friendly critic, or critical friend," who sought to do justice to Pietist themes, though often from a

16. *CD* IV/3.1, 301-2.

very different angle. Finally, Busch helps us see the kinds of questions that Barth's theology raises for a Pietistic Evangelicalism. Kimlyn Bender continues along this vein by tracking and teasing out the "family resemblances" that he detects between Barth and Evangelicalism. His sketch highlights a shared Christocentrism, a pneumatological theology of Scripture, and a "believers church" ecclesiology with mission at the center.

The second section, "Reconceiving Christian Experience and Practice," is comprised of reflections that engage concepts which might be described as distinctly evangelical. Terry Cross opens with a consideration of Barth's theology of experience—a descriptor that many Barth readers might consider a misnomer. However, through a careful engagement with Barth's later theology, Cross argues that Barth articulated a persuasive "heart theology" that resonates deeply with Pietist, Wesleyan, and Pentecostal concerns. James Nelson continues this line of inquiry through a consideration of Barth's theology of vocation, or calling. Despite some criticisms that Barth's soteriology leaves no room for the personal appropriation or response of the believer—a notion of considerable importance in evangelical circles—Nelson shows that Barth's conception of vocation is far more nuanced, including both subjective and objective dimensions.

John Drury follows this with a consideration of the evangelical practice of "testimony," bringing it into dialogue with Barth's conception of witness. Delving into the structural similarities between the two, Drury then argues that testimony/witness offers a better theological understanding of the dynamics and authority of Scripture than what is usually offered in evangelical reflections on Scripture.

Stina Busman Jost, implicitly drawing on the deep history of evangelical feminism, raises questions about current "masculinizing" trends among evangelicals. She argues that a faithful church is one that serves as witness rather than as origin of the gospel of Jesus Christ. To this end, she offers a consideration of Barth's theology of Joseph—in distinction from Mary—as a resource for how evangelicals should conceptualize the church. Collins Winn and Heltzel follow this through a consideration of Barth's ecclesiology and theology of prayer as sources for a socially engaged church. Their argument is that Barth's conception of the church as a parabolic witnessing community that calls out to God "Thy kingdom come!" offers a vision of the church that is necessarily engaged in a prophetic social witness.

In the final section, "Renewing Christian Doctrine," contributors engage key doctrinal themes with an eye towards the concerns of the volume as a whole. Joel Lawrence opens this section with a reflection on the central place of prayer in Barth's theological method. As Lawrence notes, this dimension of Barth's theology is widely misunderstood and overlooked and he recommends Barth's approach to current evangelical discussions about the nature and task of theology. Chris Boesel follows this with a careful consideration of the doctrine of election. Boesel helpfully contextualizes the present volume by arguing that whether Evangelicalism is conceived as Reformed orthodoxy or as Pietism is ultimately of secondary importance—what matters is faithfulness to the "good" news of Jesus Christ. In Boesel's estimation, Evangelicalisms of various stripes often obscure the goodness of the news about Jesus, while Barth's theology of election goes a long-way towards bringing that goodness back into view.

Frank Macchia offers a careful reappraisal of Barth's often maligned theology of Scripture. His account shows how Barth's theology offers a dynamic and pneumatocentric approach to Scripture which does justice to the historical and ineluctably human nature of the text of the bible. Kyle Roberts follows with a consideration of Barth's ecclesiology in relationship to a more recent phenomenon in ecclesiology: the "missional theology movement." Roberts offers a reconsideration of the genealogy of missional theology, one which places Barth more at the center of the story. In so doing, Roberts hopes to commend Barth as a resource for current evangelical reflections on the nature of the church.

Kurt Anders Richardson's contribution offers a full-scale discussion of Barth's controversial "sacramental" theology. As Richardson shows, Barth's late, decisive move towards "believer's baptism" was no left turn. Rather, it was in continuity with some of the deepest impulses of Barth's thought. Peter Althouse concludes the section, bringing Barth's eschatology into dialogue with concerns in Pentecostalism. He bridges the conversation through an appeal to the Blumhardts, two nineteenth century Pietist figures who had an important influence on Barth's theology, revealing some unexpected continuities between the respective eschatologies of Barth and Pentecostals which point to future avenues for research and dialogue.

The reconceptualization offered here of the dialogue between Barth and evangelical theology opens up new possibilities. For Evangelicalism this offers the potential to deepen evangelical theological commitments, but also potential and useful correctives to evangelical theology. Furthermore, it fosters continued reconsideration of evangelical identity, one which embraces the Pietist, Wesleyan, and Pentecostal dynamics of the tradition. For Barth studies, this dialogue puts Barth in a new light, surfacing key elements in Barth's theology which have often been overlooked or misunderstood. Barth becomes a "critical friend" for evangelical theology as it seeks to articulate a theological vision that is both faithful to the gospel of God's reconciliation of the world in Jesus Christ, and able to engage and meet the continuing challenges which face the churches. Our hope is that the present volume constructively contributes to this important task.

Bibliography

Collins Winn, Christian T. *"Jesus Is Victor!": The Significance of the Blumhardts for the Theology of Karl Barth*. Eugene, OR: Pickwick, 2009.

Drury, John L. *The Resurrected God: Karl Barth's Trinitarian Theology of Easter*. Philadelphia: Fortress, 2014.

Hart, D. G. *Deconstructing Evangelicalism: Conservative Protestantism in the Age of Billy Graham*. Grand Rapids: Baker Academic, 2004.

Henry, Carl F. H. *God, Revelation, and Authority*. 6 vols. Waco, TX: Word, 1976–83.

McCormack, Bruce L., and Clifford B. Anderson, eds. *Karl Barth and American Evangelicalism*. Grand Rapids: Eerdmans, 2011.

Noll, Mark A. *The Rise of Evangelicalism: The Age of Edwards, Whitefield and the Wesleys*. Downers Grove, IL: InterVarsity, 2003.

Olson, Roger E. and Christian T. Collins Winn, *Reclaiming Pietism: Retrieving an Evangelical Tradition*. Grand Rapids, MI: William B. Eerdmans Pub. Co., 2015.

Ramm, Bernard. *After Fundamentalism: The Future of Evangelical Theology*. San Francisco: Harper & Row, 1983.

Runia, Klaas. *Karl Barth's Doctrine of Holy Scripture*. Grand Rapids: Eerdmans, 1962.

Spener, Philipp Jakob. *Pia Desideria*. Translated by Theodore G. Tappert. Philadelphia: Fortress, 1964.

Van Til, Cornelius. *Christianity and Barthianism*. Philadelphia: Presbyterian & Reformed, 1962.

Ward, W. R. *Early Evangelicalism: A Global Intellectual History, 1670–1789*. Cambridge: Cambridge University Press, 2006.

———. *The Protestant Evangelical Awakening*. Cambridge: Cambridge University Press, 1992.

Worthen, Molly. *Apostles of Reason: The Crisis of Authority in American Evangelicalism*. Oxford: Oxford University Press, 2014.

Abbreviations

CD Karl Barth, *Church Dogmatics*. Edited by by G. W. Bromiley and T. F. Torrance. Edinburgh: T. & T. Clark, 1956–75.

CL Karl Barth, *The Christian Life: Church Dogmatics IV/4: Lecture Fragments*. Grand Rapids: Eerdmans, 1981.

KD Karl Barth, *Die kirchliche Dogmatik*. Munich: C. Kaiser, 1932; Zürich: Theologischer Verlag Zürich, 1938–65.

Part I

Reframing the Conversation

1

Karl Barth and Evangelicalism
The Varieties of a Sibling Rivalry[1]
Donald W. Dayton

IN RECENT YEARS, WE have seen a flexing of the muscles of what both insiders and outsiders have come to call "Evangelicalism." This current of American religious life is no new phenomenon; what is new is that a culture that apparently thought it had moved beyond taking "Evangelicalism" seriously is being forced to reevaluate that easy dismissal. What is true on the cultural level is also reflected in intellectual circles—and in the discipline of theology.

This is perhaps especially true among students of the theology of Karl Barth, where a special affinity between "Evangelicals" and Barth has, for example, recently swelled the ranks of the Karl Barth Society with newcomers from a variety of "Evangelical" traditions. And the literature on this relationship has so grown that we now have a survey of the discussion, whose title I have appropriated for this article: *Karl Barth and Evangelicalism*, by Gregory C. Bolich.

But you will notice that I have quickly added to this title my own subtitle, "the varieties of sibling rivalry," to suggest that we are dealing with a matter of greater complexity than we (or Bolich) may at first imagine. Something of the difficulty of the path ahead of us in this essay may be suggested by the diversity of "evangelical" opinion about Barth. Reformed theologian Cornelius van Til, on the one hand, has consistently polemicized against Barth in such works as *Christianity and Barthianism*, with an emphasis on

---

1. Originally printed in *Theological Students Fellowship Bulletin* 8.5 (1985) 18–23. Reprinted with permission.

the implied dichotomy. In an essay titled "Has Karl Barth Become Orthodox?" he judged that of all the heresies that have evoked the great creeds as refutation, "no heresy that appeared at any of these was so deeply and ultimately destructive of the gospel as is the theology of Barth."[2] We could survey other such statements—like that of dispensationalist Charles Ryrie who finds "Barthianism" to be a "theological hoax"[3] because it attempts to be both critical and Orthodox. But on the other end of the spectrum we find other evaluations that could hardly be in starker contrast to the judgment of van Til. Donald Bloesch, for example, has insisted that "Karl Barth is himself an evangelical theologian"[4]—though with some qualifications. Between these two extremes may be ranged the variety of "evangelical" judgments on Barth.

But how do we get such diverse readings of Barth from "evangelicals"? From one angle this diversity should be no surprise. Barth has suffered much from his interpreters in all camps. He has often been interpreted from caricature or on the basis of fragmentary readings. Barth is, of course, not without fault in this process. The range of his writings makes the task of adequate interpretation a lifetime task. The dialectical and multifaceted character of his thought means that one is always in danger of reading and extrapolating from one of several facets. And the changes in Barth's thought—especially from the earlier dialectical period to the later Christocentric orientation in which his Christology and the doctrine of incarnation overcome earlier themes—have always provided problems for interpreters. "Evangelical" interpreters have, not surprisingly, shared all these problems.

But there are within the nature of what we call "Evangelicalism" itself issues and problems that complicate our discussion. The most profound of these is the "slipperiness" of the term *evangelical*. In the language of W.B. Gallie, it is an "essentially contested concept"[5]—one whose fundamental meaning is at debate. My own efforts to bring clarity to this issue have centered in the development of a typology of the meanings that the term *evangelical* may convey.[6] I would argue that there have been three primary periods in the history of Protestantism that have provided content to the word *evangelical*. Uses of the word may generally be shown to gravitate

---

2. Van Til, "Has Karl Barth Become Orthodox?" 181.
3. Ryrie, *Neo-Orthodoxy*, 62.
4. Bloesch, *Evangelical Renaissance*, 81.
5. Brown, "Concept of 'Evangelical,'" 104–9; Abraham, *The Coming Great Revival*.
6. This typology was first developed in Dayton, "Social and Political Conservatism," 72–74, but also in Dayton, "Whither Evangelicalism?"

toward one or another of these periods or modes of using the word. Let me indicate these meanings:

(1) Many users of the word *evangelical* have in mind primarily the Reformation and its themes, particularly the great *solas* (*sola fide, sola gratia, sola Christe, sola Scriptura*) that convey the Reformation call to grace and the centrality of "justification by faith." Usually correlated with these themes are an Augustinian/Reformed anthropology, a doctrine of election, and a predominantly forensic view of atonement and salvation. These themes are generally common to the figures of the magisterial Reformation, though we have articulated them in a pattern that may be tipped more toward Lutheranism than Calvinism. But this is in part to reflect the German usage where the word *evangelisch* roughly means "Protestant" but particularly Lutheran.

(2) In the Anglo-Saxon world, the word *evangelical* is more likely to gather its connotations from the "evangelical revival" and the "great awakenings." In this period, Protestant themes were pushed in new directions and into new configurations. There is an intensification of the soteriological orientation of the Reformation in the turn to a piety of "conversion" that involves a shift of emphasis from "justification" to "regeneration" and often indirectly to sanctification. This orientation flowered in missions, evangelism and the rise of benevolent societies to address every kind of human ill. Nineteenth-century revivalism emerged from these currents and accentuated the low-church, moralistic and ethical tendencies to be found in this form of Evangelicalism. It is important to notice that the preservation of "Orthodoxy" is not the major motif of this form of Evangelicalism. From the rise of Pietism on, it includes an element of protest against Orthodoxy in favor of spiritual vitality. The emphasis has been on conversion. The enemy is "nominal Christianity" on the right as much as rationalism and deism on the left. This form of Evangelicalism became the dominant form of religion in America for much of the nineteenth century. In Europe it was much more marginal and would have been known in German as *Pietismus* or in its more recent forms as *NeuPietismus*, or as the *Erweckungsbewegung*.

(3) Especially since the Civil War and particularly in the United States, there has been a growing split in American Protestantism that culminated in the twentieth-century fundamentalist/modernist controversy. Since World War II, a more intellectually articulate and socially and culturally engaged wing of the fundamentalist party has also appropriated the label "evangelical." It is this use of the word *evangelical* that has become the dominant one in our own time. The word in this context refers to a mixed coalition of a variety of theological and ecclesiastical traditions that have found common cause against the rise of "modernity" and the erosion of older forms of Orthodoxy

under the impact of biblical criticism, the rise of Darwinianism, and, perhaps even more fundamentally, the relativism occasioned by the impact of the social sciences and historical consciousness. In this use of the word, the primary thrust is "conservative" and is concerned with the preservation of "Orthodoxy"; the consistent "enemy" is "Liberalism" in a variety of forms. The German language was not well prepared to describe this current, but in the last decade or two it has taken over from the English a neologism, *evangelikal* with a *k*, to represent the post-World War II post-fundamentalist Evangelicalism that in the wake of the Laussanne Congress of early 1970s has also become a force in Europe.

This, then, is my typology of uses of the word *evangelical*. Like all typologies it has its problems. Many currents fall between my periods and types. Calvin's emphasis on regeneration, for example, puts him somewhat between types one and two. Some wings of type two were close to the classical Reformation. And type three includes groups shaped by the earlier currents. Even though one may discern certain continuities by emphasizing one strand or another, I find it both helpful and necessary to distinguish between these various connotations of the word *evangelical*—and to argue that they are finally irreducible. Strict advocates of type one will lump large segments of types two and three with Liberalism and Roman Catholicism as fundamentally in error in tending toward "Pelagianism." Similarly, strict adherents to type two will deny the label "evangelical" to many classical expressions of type one and some of the more confessional expressions of type three. Some of the ironies in the modern post-fundamentalist use of the word may be seen in the emerging neo-Catholic movement among evangelicals, whereby holding a commitment to "Orthodoxy" and "traditionalism" constant, an evolution into a new sacramentalism is possible. There is a tendency to use the label "evangelical" to describe all sorts of cultural and theological reasons, no matter what the fundamental issue at stake.

The value of this typology will be demonstrated as we turn more fully to examine Barth's relationship to Evangelicalism. We must distinguish these usages of the word, because in each case the shape of the discussion with Barth is quite different. But in each case, we will find the relationship ambiguous—sharing Barth's commitments to various degrees but also differing in the appropriation of themes. It is for this reason that we have subtitled this article "the varieties of a sibling rivalry"—to emphasize both the close relationships and the tensions present. With this background let us briefly examine Barth's relationship to each of these currents.

Evangelicalism as Fidelity to Reformation Themes

It is the first version of Evangelicalism that is most congruent with Barth's fundamental commitments. The movement of which he was a determinant force has been called "New Reformation Theology." An early British *Festschrift* for Barth was entitled *Reformation Old and New*. In his contribution to that volume, John McConnachie suggested that "no one has done more to reinterpret, transform, and illumine the issues of the Reformation for our day as Karl Barth."[7] It was in many ways the rediscovery of the Reformation that launched Barth on his new theological direction. Eberhard Busch traces this development at Göttingen largely in the words of Barth himself.

> In Göttingen things changed almost at a stroke. Barth now felt that his previous theological view was really a pre-Reformation position.... "Only now were my eyes properly open to the reformers and their message of the justification and the sanctification of the sinner, of faith, of repentance and works, of the nature and the limits of the church and so on. I had a great many new things to learn from them." At that time "I 'swung into line with the Reformation,' as they used to say," not uncritically, but certainly with special attention.[8]

These hints from early in the theological career of Barth were echoed at his retirement when in his final lectures, repeated on his American tour, he did not hesitate to use the word *evangelical* to describe his theology.

> The theology to be introduced here is *evangelical* theology. The qualifying attribute "evangelical" recalls both the New Testament and at the same time the reformation of the sixteenth century. Therefore it may be taken as a dual affirmation: the theology to be considered here is the one which, nourished by the hidden sources of the documents of Israel's history, first achieved unambiguous expression in the writings of the New Testament evangelists, apostles, and prophets; it is also, moreover, the theology newly discovered and accepted by the Reformation of the sixteenth century.[9]

This, at least, was the basic theological intention of Barth: to recover and restate the Reformation recovery of the New Testament gospel. In this Barth would be in accord with our first type of evangelical. But, of course,

---

7. McConnachie, "Reformation Issues Today," 103.
8. Busch, *Karl Barth*, 143.
9. Barth, *Evangelical Theology*, 5.

this congruence of intention does not answer all questions. There is much room for debate about precisely how to retrieve and articulate the Reformation message for our own times. Barth himself was clear about the need to revise Reformation theology at several points:

> Having in the 1920s swung in clearly behind the "Reformation line," "I soon saw that it was also necessary to continue it, to arrange the relationship between the law and gospel, nature and grace, election and christology and even between philosophy and theology more exactly and thus differently from the patterns which I found in the sixteenth century. Since I could not become an Orthodox 'Calvinist,' I had even less desire to support a Lutheran confessionalism."[10]

Barth also understood that in each case the basic reason for his reformulation was the same: the pressures of what he called his "Christological concentration." We cannot take time to work out the implications of this move for each of these themes. Let me merely indicate how this concern leads Barth to revise what is generally seen to be the center for Reformation faith (especially for Luther): justification by faith.

> The *articulus stantis et cadentis ecclesiae* is not the doctrine of justification as such, but its basis and culmination: the confession of Jesus Christ, in whom are hid all the treasures of wisdom and knowledge (Col 2:3); the knowledge of His being and activity for us and to us and with us. It could probably be shown that this also was the opinion of Luther. If here, as everywhere, we allow Christ to be the center, the starting point, we have no reason to fear that there will be any lack of unity and cohesion, and therefore of systematics in the best sense of the word.[11]

I find this move of Barth's not only appropriate, but a necessary revision of the patterns of thought in Reformation theology. I suppose other implications of Barth's Christological concentration might appear more problematic for some—especially in the doctrine of election, where the revisions seem much more radical. (I shall leave that debate to experts in the Reformed tradition.) I shall only note as an outsider that one sees, for example in the book by James Daane, *The Freedom of God*, the pressure, in what might be called evangelical circles, to move in a similar direction as Barth (though interestingly enough in this case without real acknowledgment of the apparent impact of Barth himself). From my vantage point,

---

10. Busch, *Karl Barth*, 210–11.
11. Barth, *CD* IV/1, 527–28.

these questions of Barth seem entirely appropriate and well within the range of the necessary for an "Orthodox" retrieval of the Reformation tradition for our own time. And I would concur with, for example, Colin Brown that

> The basic difference between Karl Barth and traditional Protestant theology lies, therefore, not only in his doctrine of the word of God. Barth has, in fact, more in common with traditional Protestantism on this score than is sometimes imagined. Whilst there are vital differences, there are things that evangelical theology could learn from Barth without any surrender of vital principle. The basic difference lies in Barth's understanding of the significance of Christ. It is summed up in the contrast between the older idea of the two covenants—the covenant of works and the covenant of grace—and Barth's idea of the single, all-embracing covenant of grace in Christ.[12]

It is in these areas that the discussion ought to be pursued.

If we were to look for a representative of Evangelicalism that has most pursued the dialogue with Karl Barth from a commitment to my first paradigm, it would have to be Donald Bloesch, who has found himself increasingly drawn toward Barth as a result of his commitment to the faith of the Reformation.[13] Perhaps we are now in a position to understand better his judgment that Barth is indeed an "evangelical theologian."

Evangelicalism as Expressed in the Pietist Traditions

Our second paradigm of Evangelicalism was that expressed most fully in the Pietist and Awakening traditions. When we turn to this paradigm we are immediately faced with an historical anomaly. Even though it could be argued that this paradigm has been the most influential in the Anglo-Saxon world, there has been almost no English literature of discussion with Barth from this perspective. (The major exception would be the work of Donald Bloesch, who, because he tends to see the rise of "evangelical Pietism" as the fulfillment of the Reformation, has engaged Barth from issues that arise from the Pietist vision. This can be seen particularly in his book *Jesus is Victor! Karl Barth's Doctrine of Salvation* with its concentration on Barth's soteriology.)

Ironically, we must turn to Germany for the major discussions with Barth from this second paradigm. This is in part because the German

---

12. Brown, *Karl Barth and the Christian Message*, 139.
13. This attitude is most fully evidenced in Donald Bloesch, *Jesus is Victor!*

counterpart of what we would call Evangelicalism in this country is less shaped by fundamentalist concerns and more by themes of nineteenth-century revivalism and which is called *NeuPietismus*. In part this is because of the dominance of what is called the *Gemeinschaftsbewegung*, a "fellowship" and "higher life" movement that has many affinities with what we call in the Anglo-Saxon world the "Keswick movement." As a result (as I discovered on a recent sabbatical term in Germany), Evangelicalism in that context has a distinctively different character than in America—though the scene is becoming increasingly muddied by recent American imports. Thus the German counterpart to the American InterVarsity Christian Fellowship, the *Studenten Mission Deutschland*, is less troubled by apologetics, the concern to preserve Orthodoxy, and the American "battle for the Bible," and more fully defined by its concern for the cultivation of the devotional life and its commitment to evangelism and mission. There is a growing interest in Barth in these circles, often mediated by Otto Weber, whose dogmatic work has served as a bridge from the concerns of Pietism into contemporary theology.

Slightly before the publication of Bolich's volume in America, there was a counterpart in the German discussion, *Karl Barth und die Pietisten*, by Eberhard Busch, the biographer of Barth and one of his last *Assistenten*. Busch has deep family roots in the leadership of the *Gemeinschaftsbewegung*. His book is concerned primarily with the early Barth, the critique of Pietism in the early editions of Barth's commentary on Romans, and the responses to it by writers in the various journals of the *Gemeinschaftsbewegung*. (This discussion has been extended in a series of articles by Busch on "Karl Barth und der Pietismus" and a response by editor Ulrich Parzany titled "Die Pietisten und Karl Barth" that appeared in *Schritte* [July-September 1980], a magazine representing roughly a cross between *His* and *Eternity* in this country.)

This dialogue immediately takes a different character because of a special burden not present in other forms of evangelical dialogue with Barth—Barth's own intense polemic against Pietism as merely another form of the anthropocentric orientation that manifested itself in liberal neo-Protestantism. In entering this discussion we are immediately drawn into the question of Barth's ambivalent relationships with Schleiermacher and Kierkegaard, both of whom, it has been argued, may have some claim to being a theological articulation of Pietist themes. What is primarily at stake in these discussions is Barth's so-called objectivism, with its concern to ground salvation in a cosmic, external event that is prior to and the ground of any experiential appropriation of it. As he put it in the first edition of the commentary on Romans:

> The Holy Spirit in us is no subjective experience concealed in mystic darkness but is the objective truth that has disclosed itself to us. . . . It is our life-basis, not our experience.[14]

Two themes regularly occur in Barth's critique of Pietism. One of these is related to one of the structural features of the fourth volume of the *Church Dogmatics* where ecclesiology takes precedence over the treatment of the response of the individual Christian. Barth attacks what he sees as the individualistic tendency of Pietism in which the experience of God's grace *pro me* obscures the priority of the *pro nobis*. Thus in IV/1, after almost six hundred pages of theological foundations—primarily Christological—Barth devotes only forty pages to the act of faith. In doing this Barth is self-consciously setting himself against both the *Glaubenslehre* tradition and Pietism.

> In the last centuries (on the broad way which leads from the older Pietism to the present-day theological existentialism inspired by Kierkegaard) the Christian has begun to take himself seriously in a way which is not at all commensurate with the seriousness of Christianity. . . . From the bottom up we can neither approve nor make common course with this procedure of modern doctrines of faith. We shall give to the individual Christian and his faith the attention which he demands, but it must be at this point—not at the beginning of our way, but very briefly at the end.[15]

The other side of Barth's critique of Pietism we have already indicated is grounded in his so-called objectivism. Barth is concerned to maintain the priority of the salvation wrought for us *extra nos* in the work of Christ. He fears that the *pro me* and *in me* of Pietism may obscure the *extra nos* as well as the *pro nobis* and *in nobis*. As Barth put it in his dialogue with Methodist pastors, "I do not deny the experience of salvation. . . . But the experience of salvation is what happened on Golgotha. In contrast to that, my experience is only a vessel."[16] We know this to be a fundamental theme in Barth, one that stretches minds shaped by more traditional theologies most with the difficult claim that all are not only *de jure* justified but also sanctified in Christ prior to and *de facto* appropriation or acknowledgment of that fact.

Here we are very close to the disputed question of how best to understand the universalistic themes in Barth. This issue arises in any "evangelical" discussion with Barth, though with different concerns in each of the

14. *Der Römerbrief*, 114, as translated by Smart in *Divided Mind of Modern Theology*, 85.
15. Barth, *CD* IV/1, 741.
16. Busch, *Karl Barth*, 447.

three paradigms. From the Pietist or second paradigm, the focus is less on election or eternal destiny and more on the efficacy of grace and Barth's relativizing of the boundary between believers and unbelievers. Busch reports that this has been the major unresolved issue in Barth's dialogue with representatives of Pietism.[17] Far be it from me to attempt to resolve these issues here. I am convinced, however, that Barth is often caricatured on this issue and that his denials that he is a universalist need to be taken more seriously than they often are. And several readings of IV/2 have convinced me that Barth posits more difference between believers and unbelievers than the awareness of the former of the salvation wrought for all. But the very difficulty of establishing that and the "slipperiness" of Barth's language in dealing with these themes indicate that there is a real issue here between Barth and the Pietists.

On the other issues—the priority of the *extra nos* and the *pro nobis* over the *pro me*—I have more difficulty seeing that the issue is one of genuine substance. It seems to me that Barth reads Pietism through its most decadent forms. I do not think that classical Pietists, at least, really understood themselves to actualize salvation so much as to fully appropriate it. And even if we grant a tendency toward individualism in this evangelical vision, we should also note that this vision has been exceedingly creative of communal forms of Christian life and piety—from the *collegia pietatis* of Pietism to the bands and societies of Methodism. At this point, there is clearly a difference of emphasis between Barth and representatives of this evangelical vision.

Barth's relationship to Pietism is not fully grasped by noting only his correctives to it. Busch points out the Pietist influences in Barth's own background. One cannot help but notice Barth's appropriation of and praise for Pietist exegesis (cf., for example, his use of Bengel on 1 Cor 13 at the end of IV/2). Nor are we prepared for Barth's growing appreciation for Zinzendorf and his piety. Barth discovered several of his basic themes in Zinzendorf, and came to see him as "perhaps the only genuine Christocentric of the modern age (fools would say Christomonist)."[18] In dialogue with modern Moravians, Barth shared increasing fascination with Zinzendorf's linking of Christ as Savior and Creator, his tending to speak of our sanctification as fulfilled in Christ, and his tendency to polemicize against less Christocentrically oriented representatives of Pietism.

Nor may we forget the impact of the Blumhardts on Barth and the significance of the slogan *Jesus ist Sieger!* that emerged in the much discussed

---

17. Ibid., 445–46.
18. Barth, *CD* IV/1, 683.

"exorcism" in Möttlingen. Barth is inclined to appreciate themes from this event as mediated by the younger Blumhardt and Leonard Ragaz in the religious socialist movement, with the implication that this movement toward a world-transforming understanding of grace is a decidedly "unPietistic" emergence from Pietistic roots. I am coming to the position that it is of the essence of Pietism's shattering of the Lutheran *simul Justus et peccator* with a strong doctrine of regeneration that soon overflows into culture and society. A similar movement has taken place in Methodism and elsewhere. And even though Barth's appropriation of "Jesus as Conqueror" and "Overcomer" may be given a new content by his "objectivism," it may well be that in this—one of his most central themes—Barth is more dependent on Pietist currents than he realizes. If so, Barth's relationship to this form of Evangelicalism is more dialectical than his polemics would at first suggest.

Evangelicalism as the Defense of Orthodoxy

Finally, we turn to the last paradigm, the one that is probably the most common use of the word *evangelical* in our own time. As we have already suggested, here we have less a movement that can be defined in terms of its positive commitments and more of a complex coalition in opposition to a common enemy—Liberalism or perhaps modernity in general. It is a much disputed question whether Fundamentalism, or Evangelicalism in this sense, can be more precisely defined theologically. Ernest Sandeen, for example, has argued in his *Roots of Fundamentalism*, that the movement must be seen theologically as the rise of premillenialism in the nineteenth century and its coalescence with the so-called Princeton theology of the same period—the bridge being the doctrine of Scripture, specifically the doctrine of inerrancy. Thus we see the effort of the Evangelical Theological Society, for example, to build its coalition since World War II on a single platform—the doctrine of the inerrancy of Scripture.

Any means of describing the character of Fundamentalism will inherently be reductionist and one-sided. To focus our discussion, however, we need to pick out one discernible tradition for analysis. Probably the most useful for our purposes is the "Princeton theology," already mentioned. This theological tradition, especially its doctrine of Scripture, has become influential beyond its normal confessional boundaries. The struggles at Princeton that led to the founding of Westminster Seminary in Philadelphia are in many ways the classical illustration of the fundamentalist/modernist controversy. The shape of this theology could be described in several ways, but for our purposes we may note that it attempted to preserve the theological formulations of Protestant scholastic Orthodoxy—particularly at the point of the doctrine of Scripture. The importance of Orthodoxy in this sense for modern Evangelicalism is confirmed by Bernard Ramm in *The Evangelical Heritage*, where he defines "evangelical" in terms of this movement and recognizes the influence of Princeton even upon his own Baptist tradition. I find this way of describing Evangelicalism highly inadequate, but do agree that this is the dominant theological construct in the post-fundamentalist evangelical experience that is epitomized in Westminster and Fuller seminaries, for example, or in the pages of *Christianity Today*. And most of the modern "evangelical" dialogue with Barth in this country has been out of this theological tradition.

We can also see in this paradigm the basis for both attention and revulsion between Barth and this variation of Evangelicalism. Barth emerged in the twentieth century as the most powerful critic of "Liberalism," the *bête noir* of modern Evangelicalism. Yet his standpoint was one of a "neo-Orthodoxy" that broke the categories of the older Orthodoxy. Barth attempted to articulate a biblical starting point, but his appropriation of Scripture was "post-critical" while most modern evangelicals were still committed to a largely "pre-critical" position that could only see such an agenda as a "theological hoax" (again to use the words of Charles Ryrie).

Barth even re-appropriated the traditions of Protestant Orthodoxy, while at the same time recasting them in new forms and conceptualities. This last point is worth further elaboration. Protestant Orthodoxy has by and large had bad press in modern theology. Yet it was the rediscovery of this Orthodoxy that played a crucial role in the emergence of Barth's own *Church Dogmatics*. Barth describes this and his relations to Orthodoxy in a preface to Heppe's *Reformed Dogmatics*:

> I shall never forget the spring vacation of 1924. I sat in my study at Göttingen, faced with the task of giving lectures on dogmatics for the first time. No one can ever have been more plagued than I then was with the problem, could I do it? And how? . . . Then it was that, along with the parallel Lutheran work of H. Schmid, Heppe's volume just recently published fell into my hands; out of date, dusty, unattractive, almost like a table of logarithms, dreary to read, stiff and eccentric on almost every page I opened. . . . I read, I studied, I reflected; and found that I was rewarded with the discovery, that here at last I was in the atmosphere in which the road by way of the Reformers to Holy Scripture was a more sensible and natural one to read, than the atmosphere, now only too familiar to me, of the theological literature determined by

Schleiermacher and Ritschl.... At the same time I was also aware that a return to this Orthodoxy... could not be contemplated.[19]

We may see in this quotation epitomized the frustration that Barth evokes among evangelicals. He seems to veer toward them and to share fundamental commitments, but at the last moment he moves off in a new direction that is beyond their comprehension. We could pursue this discussion from many angles. (Fortunately, much of the evangelical dialogue with Barth is summarized in Bolich.) Let me turn to only two of the most basic issues—Barth's doctrine of Scripture and whether his view of history allows the resurrection to occur in time and space.

The evangelical debate about Barth's view of Scripture has produced numerous articles and at least one full monograph, *Karl Barth's Doctrine of Holy Scripture* by Klaas Runia. On the most fundamental level, as we have already indicated, the clash is between pre-critical and post-critical use of Scripture. As Barth comments in the first preface to his commentary on Romans, if forced to choose between the older doctrine of verbal inspiration with accompanying modes of interpretation and the products of modern critical interpretation, he would go with the former. But Barth, of course, refuses to be captured by that way of putting the question and frustrates observers on both sides by using Scripture in a manner continuous with the classical theological traditions of the church while reflecting a critical consciousness. We cannot hope to resolve an issue that the church has struggled with for at least a couple of centuries. I will only comment from my own perspective that the pre-critical option still maintained by many, if not most, modern evangelicals is, at least for me, impossible. The significance of Barth for this issue is primarily that he transcends the evangelical way of putting the question.

Another point at issue in the evangelical dialogue with Barth is expressed in the accusation that for Barth, the Bible is not the word of God written and therefore objectively authoritative but only *becomes* the word of God in the moment of reading under the inspiration of the Holy Spirit or according to the subjective whims and predilections of the reader. My own reading of Barth finds this to be a caricatured and one-sided understanding of Barth, though it may point to a tendency of Barth's "actualism" and his unwillingness to permit a totally objective, absolute authority in the Bible as such. Perhaps I am too shaped by Pietist and Wesleyan exegesis—which, for example, in the interpretation of 1 Tim 2:16, has also, over against the Orthodox concern for the once-for-all process of inscripturation in the past, emphasized the present "inspiring" work of the Holy Spirit. But I must

---

19. Barth, "Foreword," v–vi.

confess that I find it almost ludicrous to accuse Barth of rampant "subjectivism"—especially in view of our earlier discussion of the Pietist concern with Barth's rigorous "objectivism."

More to the point are the implications of Barth's Christological concentration. For Barth, Christ is the epistemological hinge; for the evangelicals, it is the Bible. Most evangelical formulations answer the question of our knowledge about God by some version of "God wrote a book" that makes Christ epistemologically irrelevant. For Barth this generates the "irremediable danger of consulting Holy Scripture apart from the center, and in such a way that the question of Jesus Christ ceases to be the controlling and comprehensive question."[20] From the evangelical side, Barth's position reduces the Scripture to the role of a mere witness to the revelation of God and not the revelation itself. The level of absoluteness that the evangelicals invest in the text itself is obviously another reason for their reluctance to have that text open to critical analysis. Barth's shift of the fundamental hinge is one reason he can be more open to criticism. Those questions cannot be resolved here, and I would only reveal my own prejudices in indicating any further that I find Barth's formulations to be vastly superior. Suffice it to say that the evangelical grasp of Barth's doctrine of Scripture is becoming more subtle and appropriate,[21] and that Bolich argues that it is at the point of Scripture that Barth has the most to contribute to modern Evangelicalism.

A second major point of evangelical discussion with Barth has revolved around his views of history. Several evangelicals, including Cornelius van Til, John Warwick Montgomery, and Fred Klooster, have accused Barth of splitting history into two realms, *Historie* (the realm of actual, factual history) and *Geschichte* (the realm of meaningful history and God's transcendent action) so that, for example, the crucifixion happens in *Historie* but the resurrection only in *Geschichte*.[22] The range of questions involved here is very complex and the issues much debated, within and without evangelical circles. Evangelicals have not been the only ones to accuse Barth of splitting history in this way. Whether or not one accepts this particular criticism of Barth, it is clear that this aspect of Barth's thought—his views of history, historical method, their relation to revelation, etc.—is at least problematic and perhaps the Achilles heel of his theological program. It is clear that the theological programs of both Wolfhart Pannenberg and Jürgen Moltmann,

---

20. Barth, *CD* IV/1, 368.

21. Cf. for example the work of Loewen, "Karl Barth's Doctrine of Scripture," 33–49.

22. Cf. Klooster, "Karl Barth's Doctrine of Jesus Christ,"; Montgomery, "Karl Barth and Contemporary Theology of History,"; and the various writings of Cornelius van Til, especially those mentioned.

as different as they may now seem to be, were launched to some extent against Barth at some of these points.

It has become increasingly clear that the earlier evangelical critique of Barth (that his view does not allow the resurrection to be an "historical" event in the normal sense) cannot be sustained. In volume IV of the *Church Dogmatics* Barth became increasingly clear about his affirmation that "the event of God's loving" described in John 3:16 "did not take place in heaven but on earth. It did not take place in secret, but it can be known (i.e., not as a purely spiritual process, but as something which, according to 1 John 1:1, can be heard and seen with our eyes and touched, yes, handled with our hands)."[23] And of the resurrection, Barth has insisted that "it happened in the same sense as his crucifixion and death, in the human sphere and the human time."[24]

What is really at stake in the discussion with Barth at this point is an issue of historiography and historical method—whether there can be an "historical" or "apologetic" *proof* of the historicity of the resurrection. Barth is quite clear in his denial of this:

> There is no proof, and there obviously cannot and ought not to be any proof, for the fact that this history did take place (proof, that is, according to the terminology of modern historical scholarship).[25]

There is a genuine issue here—one described well by evangelical New Testament scholar George Eldon Ladd:

> The basic problem for the modern theologian is this: Shall we insist upon a definition of history broad enough to include such supra-historical events as the resurrection; or shall we accept the modern view of history as a working method but insist that there is a dimension within history which transcends historical control? The latter is the method of Karl Barth, and even though it calls down the wrath of Rudolf Bultmann . . . it appears to be the only adequate explanation.[26]

Since Ladd wrote these lines, the debate has proceeded along different lines and the first option has been powerfully defended by Pannenberg. The point to be made here is that the genuine debate that Barth raises is not one between Orthodoxy and heterodoxy or between Evangelicalism in

23. Barth, *CD* IV/1, 70.
24. Ibid., 333.
25. Ibid., 335.
26. Ladd, "Resurrection and History," 56.

this sense and a position that is not "evangelical," but an issue that faces all modern theology and one that has thus necessarily become also an "intra-evangelical" debate.

The evaluation of the evangelical debates about Barth's views of history and the resurrection perhaps illustrates how Barth has become the bridge for many evangelicals into contemporary theological discussion. The fact that Barth is in many ways no longer at the center of contemporary theological struggles which have often moved on in different directions may limit the significance of this "bridge." But in the present historical situation, with its inherited chasms between the grandchildren of both fundamentalists and modernists, we may need to value any bridges that are available. It may well be that the ecumenical significance of Barth's thought has as yet unexplored aspects. Barth's dialectical and ambivalent relationship to the varieties of currents that claim the label "evangelical" may be a means of drawing them all into closer theological dialogue not only among themselves but also into the broader theological world, hopefully for the mutual edification of all concerned. There is certainly extensive evidence that this has already taken place and that it is, among "evangelicals," gaining force. I would not wish to attempt to predict the future, but we should not ignore the significance of the continuing discussion between "Karl Barth and Evangelicalism" even amidst the confusing but sometimes illuminating complexities occasioned by the "varieties of a sibling rivalry."

Bibliography

Abraham, William J. *The Coming Great Revival.* San Fransisco: Harper & Row, 1984.
Barth, Karl. *Der Römerbrief.* Bern: G. A. Bäschlin, 1919.
———. *Evangelical Theology: An Introduction.* Translated by Grover Foley. New York: Holt, Rinehart and Winston, 1963.
———. "Foreword." In Heinrich Heppe, *Reformed Dogmatics*, revised and edited by Ernst Bizer, translated by G. T. Thomson, v–vii. London: Allen and Unwin, 1950.
Bloesch, Donald. *The Evangelical Renaissance.* Grand Rapids: Eerdmans, 1973.
———. *Jesus Is Victor! Karl Barth's Doctrine of Salvation.* Nashville: Abingdon, 1976.
Bolich, Gregory C. *Karl Barth and Evangelicalism.* Downers Grove, IL: InterVarsity, 1980.
Brown, Colin. "The Concept of 'Evangelical.'" *The Churchman* 95 (1981) 104–9.
———. *Karl Barth and the Christian Message.* London: Tyndale, 1967.
Busch, Eberhard. *Karl Barth: His Life from Letters and Autobiographical Texts.* Translated by John Bowden. Philadelphia: Fortress, 1976.
———. *Karl Barth und die Pietisten: Die Pietismuskritik die jungen Karl Barth und ihre Erwiderung.* Munich: Kaiser, 1978.
Daane, James. *The Freedom of God: A Study of Election and Pulpit.* Grand Rapids: Eerdmans, 1973.
Dayton, Donald W. "The Social and Political Conservatism of Modern American Evangelicalism." *Union Seminary Quarterly Review* 32 (1977) 71–80.
———. "Whither Evangelicalism?" In *Sanctification and Liberation*, edited by Theodore Runyon, 142–63. Nashville: Abingdon, 1981.
Klooster, Fred H. "Karl Barth's Doctrine of Jesus Christ." *Westminster Theological Journal* 24 (1962) 137–72.
Ladd, George Eldon. "The Resurrection and History." *Dialog* 1 (1962) 55–56.
Lowen, Howard. "Karl Barth's Doctrine of Scripture." *Studia Biblica et Theologica* 1 (1971) 33–49.
McConnachie, John. "Reformation Issues Today." In *Reformation Old and New: A Tribute to Karl Barth*, edited by F. W. Camfield, 103–20. London: Lutterworth, 1947.
Montgomery, John Warwick. "Karl Barth and Contemporary Theology of History." *Bulletin of the Evangelical Theological Society* 8 (1963) 39–49.
Ramm, Bernard. *The Evangelical Heritage.* Waco, TX: Word, 1973.
Runia, Klaas. *Karl Barth's Doctrine of Holy Scripture.* Grand Rapids: Eerdmans, 1962.
Ryrie, Charles C. *Neo-Orthodoxy: What It Is and What It Does.* Chicago: Moody, 1956.
Smart, James D. *The Divided Mind of Modern Theology: Karl Barth and Rudolph Bultmann, 1908–1933.* Philadelphia: Westminster, 1967.
Van Til, Cornelius. *Christianity and Barthianism.* Philadelphia: Presbyterian and Reformed, 1962.
———. "Has Karl Barth Become Orthodox?" *Westminster Theological Journal* 16 (1954) 135–81.

2

Karl Barth and Pietism
Eberhard Busch

THE WORD *PIETISM* AS it was used by Karl Barth referred to that movement in Europe which, since the eighteenth century, has existed in different forms, but with clear historical connections. For Barth, *Pietism* also meant the Awakening movement (*Erweckungsbewegung*) of the nineteenth century and the movement of community or confession (*Gemeinschaftsbewegung*) in the twentieth.

Introductory Remarks

Heinrich Gelzer was a friend of Barth for nearly fifty years. When he died, Barth called him a "remarkable representative of a great tradition in its own way to which I am also deeply indebted from the point of view of some of my ancestors, and then on the basis of my studies as well, in spite of any reservations I may have."[1] It might be that this remark surprises those who have seen Barth as an adversary of Pietism. But in fact he had an open door to Pietism during his whole life, only with one small exception. However, he was not an adherent of Pietism; rather, he was "an inconvenient friend" of it, as was said by a member of a Pietistic association in the nineteen-twenties.[2] He was *inconvenient*, because he put some serious questions to this movement, the aim of which was theological self-correction. But because he asked them in a kind and helpful way, Barth's theology is especially suitable for a dialogue with Pietists. Indeed, such a dialogue is not possible

---

1. Barth, *Briefe 1961–1968*, 205. Translation mine.
2. Thimme, *Im Kampf und die Kirche*, 33. Translation mine.

without hearing the very poignant questions that Pietism puts to other parts of Christianity. Conversely, Pietists need not fear a negation of Pietism from Barth, they have only to be open for some important theological questions. This all should happen under the assumption that in the end the really decisive issue is not that either side should win, but that God will be allowed to speak.

In the light of this assumption Christians are able to speak with one another. And if this dialogue is a struggle between different opinions, nonetheless, the discussion happens within that light. It makes dealing with one another an earnest matter, but also marks the clear boundaries of the argument. According to Barth, the person whom we are allowed to drop "could only be the arch-heretic, who is fully lost to the invisible church as well." But, as Barth adds: "We are not able to discern such arch-heresy, even not in a case which urgently arouses suspicions."[3] Such an opinion has consequences: A Christian is allowed to criticize other Christians only when he or she is in solidarity with them. He or she has not to separate from others with the sound of indignation, but only in the form of a sad dismay at a threat, which has turned into a temptation for me as well. But in the faith that the Shepherd of Israel is also not sleeping in the Church, I have to be open for the experience that the truth does not speak only in my favorite voices, but that we need also other voices that may not be welcome to us.[4]

Another assumption for our discussions with one another: I can stand up for my knowledge of the truth only with recognition that God's truth and my knowledge of it are always two different matters. If I forget this, in the very same moment that difference changes into an absolute frontier between *my* thoughts and *other* Christian ideas. In the very same moment we and those with whom we differ are no longer responsible before the same Judge, rather we become the judges of one another. Let us remember what Karl Barth learned from his Reformed ancestors: I have to assert my opinions always "provided I am open to being taught better by the Scriptures in the future." This insight so determined the theology of Barth that it cannot be described as a system, but a way along which he always journeyed. As a warning against mistaking my understanding of God's truth with God's actual truth, it is salutary to remember the words of Jesus about the judgment, according to which I place myself in grave danger in my criticism of others if I only consider the speck in my brother's eye, but not the beam in my own (Matt 7:3). This insight so influenced the theology of Barth that even in relation to "modern" theology, against which the Pietistic confessing movement

---

3. Barth, *Die protestantische Theologie*, 3. Translation mine.
4. Ibid.

entered its own protest, he could say: "I don't like to make the assumption of a nearly general stubbornness, but prefer to ask myself, what we might not have not done so well."[5] This kind of thinking is not skepticism, but the expression of a humble theology which knows that while we have nothing to say against our Lord, we have quite a lot to say against the way we speak about and relate to Him. A conversation between Pietistic and more or less non-Pietistic Christians will be fruitful only if these two assumptions are approved on both sides.

Stages on Barth's "Way" in Relation to Pietism

To reiterate, the theology of Barth did not want to establish a system, but it wanted to walk on a way. This kind of thinking is orientated by the pilgrimage of Israel to the Land of Promise, and by the holy shrine, which was housed in a travel tent and which was taken down and set up in new locations repeatedly. With this metaphor, Barth meant to exclude the idea that we can only speak again and again the *same* thing on the one hand, or that we must never repeat ourselves on the other. Rather, Barth thought that we have to say always the *same* thing in a *different* way. Therefore, he had at the different stages of his journey a different relationship to Pietism. Nonetheless, he took Pietism so seriously that this topic accompanied him at all stages of his way. On the other side, when we speak about Barth, we have to take into account at which stage of his journey he made this or that statement. At the same time, there are links between his earlier and later remarks. The remarks of the young Barth over-against Pietism are neither simply outdated, but nor do they exclude new emphases at other times in his life.

Certainly, there exists a picture of Barth's change in his relation to Pietism. It could be described as follows: first he fought very sharply against Pietism, especially in the second edition of *Romans* (1922). Because he overemphasized there the distance between the God of the other world and the humanity of this world, he found the work of God in our life deeply problematic, and therefore he did not have in mind the importance of our sanctification, rebirth, and conversion. In the 1930s the battle lines shifted: during this phase, Barth did discuss the work of God in this world, but he emphasized the objective dimension of salvation in such a way that the subjective—the acceptance of salvation—was forgotten or not emphasized enough. Only in the 1950s did he come closer to Pietism. Indeed, in *CD* IV/2 he declared that he wanted to do justice to the concerns of the Pietists,

---

5. Barth, *Briefe 1961–1968*, 55. Translation mine.

though he could not associate himself with them. This picture of Barth's relationship to Pietism, developed and propagated by Barth himself,[6] is still not the whole story. Therefore, here we will try to paint a more accurate portrait.

First: After his education in the moderate Pietism of his parents' home, Barth became a decidedly Liberal theologian. His fundamental concept was now "the individualistic religious experience."[7] Therefore his opponent was every form of Orthodox Christianity, in which we have to believe in certain historical or distant "facts" or in the declarations of an external authority. The divine truth, as he said in those days, can express itself strictly and purely only in the fact of a personal experience, conveyed through other spiritually alive persons, first of all through that which he called the "inner life of Jesus": through the vivid impression personally made on us by His person. Barth summed up his theology with the aphorisms of Angelus Silesius, which he called later "pious impudences,"[8] though at that time he thought that they were "fully right".[9] "If Christ would be born a thousand times in Bethlehem / but not in your heart: then you would be lost in eternity." It is noteworthy that he referred directly to Pietism at that time—especially to Tersteegen[10]—and he even thought that he could connect Pietistic concerns with his Liberal interests. When in the 1930s Barth argued for a connection between Pietism and Liberalism, and by extension the Enlightenment, this was under the shadow of his Liberal period in which he thought himself to be in the same boat with the Pietists. He saw the connection between the two movements in their conviction that that which can be proven and understood to be true in the court of the individual self and his experience is the only thing that can be recognized as divinely true.

The *second* stage was Barth's first commentary on Romans (1919). His interpretation of Paul is driven by the central notion of the kingdom of God, which is already growing among us, binding humanity together into an "organic" whole. This notion is set over-against the concept of individual experience which marked the beginning of Barth's theological work. Indeed, this book is a vehement attack on his former Liberal theology. But it is at the same time a strong attack on Pietism as well—and this is the one exception where Barth spoke directly against Pietism. Much like his former

---

6. Cf. Barth, "Gespräch mit Vertretern der Gemeinschaften 1959," 15ff. Already twenty years before Barth had declared that "the front against Pietism has become outdated" (*Freie reformierte Synode*, 3/4, 27). Translation mine.

7. Busch, *Karl Barth und die Pietisten*, 21ff. Translation mine.

8. Barth, *KD* II/1, 316. All translations from *KD* are my own unless otherwise noted.

9. Barth, "Der christliche Glaube und die Geschichte," 57. Translation mine.

10. See Barth, "Gerhard Tersteegen," 1–3.

emphasis on individual religious feeling(!), he now describes Pietism in the same terms: Pietism means individualism, individual conversion, individual sanctification, individual salvation.[11] But now Barth explains that exactly by this, Pietism takes part in the unredeemed essence of the "world," which consists in its constant focus on the "I." Even when the Pietist separates from worldly life, so long as he or she is interested in the (maybe even religious) satisfaction of the wishes of his "I," his pious "I" or alleged new life is still only a special case of a more deeply worldly thinking. Therefore: "How could it be possible that the Pietist knows to say or to do something against Mammon, war, illness . . . since his deepest nature consists in the same falling away from God as in the nature of those powers?"[12]

This critical question shows the juncture at which Pietism's interest in the private salvation of the soul often comes to an arrangement with the unholy powers, ruling in the "world." This explains the great interest in private sins, and the penchant for turning a blind eye to social sins—it is, as if Jesus had said: "You can serve God *and* mammon." We can illustrate it with the Pietism of Halle in the eighteenth century. Here, sanctification was counted as a reality which is visible in abstinence from alcohol, from excesses, etc., but with the result that this person became in the social sphere a subservient human, a greedy trader, a blind soldier, etc. This example shows that in its result "the new reality," which in Pietism is concentrated only on the private sphere, is merely instrumental because it only helps the "old," baneful world function in a "better" way. Barth put the question to Pietism of whether its claim of a "new reality" in the private sphere is only an illusion, only a refinement of the "*old*" life, because it has the effect of only strengthening the circumstances in the "old *world*." When Pietists in that time criticized the absence of a doctrine of sanctification in Barth's theology, they missed that his theology was not interested in "sanctification" in their sense, but rather was a protest against it. The protest was meant to expose that the assumption of the "otherness" of pious people is really only a guarantee of the continuance of the old, godless world.

Barth criticized Pietism's conception of "new life" from a position that argued that new life is really given when a person lets himself or herself be taken into the already growing powers of the kingdom of God. With this idea he was appealing to the tradition of Swabian Pietism, for instance that of Christoph Friedrich Oetinger. This means that in the very book in which Barth spoke most vehemently against Pietism, he was opposing only one aspect of it, while at the same time he was dependent on another Pietistic

---

11. Barth, *Der Römerbrief*, 205. Translation mine.
12. Ibid., 214. Translation mine.

tradition. This was especially seen in the concept that the new reality is growing so much within us that our sinfulness is more and more temporally behind us. By appealing to this concept, Barth was separated from the Reformation. Soon, however, Barth would discover that this was wrong, becoming aware of the truth that the justified remains always a sinner in relation to God.

This happened in the new, second edition of *Romans*, which was published shortly after the first edition in 1922. This marks the *third* stage in Barth's relation to the Pietism. Now his criticism was directed against a very subtle point.[13] Certainly, Pietism understood correctly that a self-righteous "Pharisaism" has no value in the presence of God. But Pietism makes from this correct idea a safe method by which the human person thinks they are able, once again, to earn God's grace. Barth would later call this the "Pharisaism of the publican."[14] The critique is directed at the opinion that we have a right to the grace of God certainly not by our good works, but by our repentance and the consciousness of our sins.

Barth's second *Romans* was filled with a prophetic protest against the slogan with which the Germans went into the First World War: "With God for nation and Fatherland." Barth's protest was directed against the use of the word "God" for the purpose of gaining a good conscience for a godless enterprise. Over-against such an alleged god it is necessary to become an atheist and this for the honor of the true God![15] The task of the second *Romans* was therefore the endeavor to wrest God from the hands of humanity, who uses Him to sanction their godless works. God is otherworldly precisely over-against such misuse of His name. With this critique Barth fought against the attempt of humanity to come to God by its own possibilities, but he did not fight against the belief that God is able to come to humanity by His own possibility. The book speaks clearly about God's living presence on earth, but with the view that God takes humanity in His hand, such that humanity is not enabled to take God in their hands.

Barth's critique was especially directed against Liberal theology. He reproaches it for its misuse of God, for its attempt to adapt Him to the rules of the present "world." And what about the Pietists? There is a big surprise! All in all Barth speaks very kindly about them in the second edition of *Romans*. He was lead to do this by Franz Overbeck, who was one of the obstetricians of his new theology, and who was a perspicacious mocker of modern liberal Christianity which had adjusted itself to modern cultural life. He gave Barth

13. Barth, *Der Römerbrief*, 2nd ed., 84. Translation mine.
14. Barth, *KD* IV/1, 688.
15. Barth, *Das Wort Gottes und die Theologie*, 14.

a new, positive understanding of Pietism. For Overbeck saw in Pietism a critical power by which Christianity could be freed from the grip of secularization.[16] We find in the second edition of *Romans* a similar view of Pietism, and an interpretation of "conversion" and "renewal" along these lines.

Perhaps no other text of Barth found such a hearing within German Pietism as the second *Romans*. It was a dramatic and complicated reaction. On the one hand, it was explained, Barth is "a prophet in the wilderness. God has sent him, when the tower of Babel nearly was finished." "The divine imperative in this theology" has to be heard by us Pietists. "We will be sorry, if we are not ready to hear it."[17] On the other hand, this "sarcastic" theology is "a full-scale illegitimate assault on our most sacred goods. Here are threatening dangers for the faithful congregation, which require a most earnest contradiction and most decisive defense."[18] Not least because of these strong reactions Barth was led to attempt to further clarify his thoughts.

This led to the *fourth* stage of Barth's relation to the Pietism. It is seen in his lectures on the history of Protestant theology (1932–33). Here he explains that God becomes part of the world as He reveals Himself to humanity. In this, God turns to confront us in His free and faithful grace, not abandoning us, but also not surrendering Himself to us. From this vantage point Barth understands Pietism in two ways. On the one hand, Pietism is the attempt to fight against the existence of the Lord in His freedom in relation to humanity. The Pietist wants to make the reality of God into a possession of his or her heart.[19] According to Barth, this is the movement of modern humanity, which wants to transform the vis-à-vis of God into an element of its own inner life. Examples of this include: the idea that the true birth of Christ happens in our heart; or in the use of the Bible as an instrument that merely tells us what we want to hear; or the replacement of God's authoritative voice by our own inner voice; or by the discovery of ourselves as the great mystery, instead of God.[20] Later Barth raised the same objections against the existentialism of Rudolf Bultmann—and indeed, he called him a secret Pietist.[21]

But on the other hand, according to Barth, one can also say something else about Pietism. "It is impossible to read its documents without having

---

16. Cf. Overbeck, *Christentum und Kultur*, 179, 286; quoted by Barth, *Die Theologie und die Kirche*, 7.

17. Busch, *Karl Barth und die Pietisten*, 259. Translation mine.

18. Ibid.

19. Barth, *Die protestantische Theologie*, 95.

20. Ibid., 94–103.

21. Barth, "Nachwort," 298f.

to say that Christianity as it was really lived always went beyond the sphere marked out by all these categories. All this, therefore, means that the attempt depicted was only a partial success; it remained an *attempt*."[22] This other side of Pietism is visible in its remembrance of the justification of the sinner by God, in spite of its inclination to understand it as a transitional stage on the way to gradually making believers truly good. And here the remembrance of Jesus Christ, the crucified, remained alive as the spring of all necessary strength, help, and renewal by undeserved grace, in spite of all Pietism's tendency to give a new interpretation of the blood and wounds of Jesus as a substance for diverse experiences. And here also was rediscovered the hope for the renewal of all things with the coming of God, despite the clouding of this hope with rash and presumptuous anticipations. At that time, Barth saw both light and shadow in Pietism. He certainly saw some good in this movement, but only in the *failure* of its problematic intentions. Therefore, he could not come to a standstill with this explanation

The view changed when he gave way to the knowledge that the "good" in Pietism was not only to be found negatively in the failure of its intentions, but that the intentions themselves were also justified. Now he acknowledged what the Pietists were seeking to underline with the concepts of sanctification, awakening, conversion, rebirth, and following Christ. The attempt to deal with those important themes of Holy Scripture happened in the *fifth* stage in Barth's relation to the Pietism. He deals with these in volume IV/2 of the *Church Dogmatics* in his discussion of the sanctifying work of Christ in the doctrine of reconciliation. He found access to this new view because his theology became ever more strongly oriented and concentrated on Jesus Christ. Through this he became favorably disposed toward the theology of Nikolaus von Zinzendorf, whom he called the greatest and perhaps the only true Christocentric theologian.[23] For his time Zinzendorf was indeed a Christocentric theologian, though because of this he was disapproved of by the Pietists in Halle, in Swabia, and in the Lower Rhine. Barth emphasized even more than Zinzendorf, that if I say Jesus Christ, then I say: true God *and* true human. In Jesus Christ both are true: God exists for the human, but so also the human exists for God. In Christ not only does God come to us, but in Him we become free, so that we come to God. In Christ God does not only justify us, but in Him he sanctifies us too, and awakens us so that we turn back, follow Jesus, do good works, and carry our cross.

---

22. Barth, *Die protestantische Theologie*, 103. Translation mine.
23. *KD* IV/1, 763.

Barth develops these themes in *Church Dogmatics* IV/2,[24] in explicit agreement with the Pietists.[25] How much he agrees with them is made clear by the following statement: "Whoever believes in God, believes also in the awakening of the human to conversion. He reckons that there is such a thing. No, that God gives, creates, and makes this thing real." We are not talking about "a question of improvement but alteration. It is not a question of a reformed or ennobled life, but a new one. And the alteration and renewal mean *conversion*—a term which we cannot avoid for all its doubtful associations."[26] Because they are sanctified in and by Christ, the sanctification of Christians is a "real change of their existence,"[27] so that they "*are* really different from the world."[28] Here the Pietists would have to correct their judgment that Barth was only espousing a one-sided objectivism, which, in their view, produces a sleepy conscience.[29]

But even with this agreement, Barth said that he did not become a Pietist himself.[30] He was indeed *also* critical over-against Pietistic notions. By this, he claims that one can speak in a biblical manner about conversion, sanctification, awakening like the Pietists, but without becoming a Pietist. In this way he brought the discussion with the Pietists to a higher level. It is no longer enough for the Pietists to say: "You only speak biblically, if you speak like us about conversion." Now, however, one has to explain *how* what one is saying is in fact biblical. Barth had taken up the central ideas of Pietism but he had spoken about them differently, and in doing this he implicitly asked his fellow Christians whether it might not be better (i.e., more faithful to the biblical witness) to speak and think about their cherished themes in a way that was different from how they had usually done so.

I name two points in particular: *First*, our sanctification is decisively not something that is done by us, but is given to us in Christ, in His work which he has done "in place of us, for us."[31] With Paul we must say, "Christ Jesus is made unto us . . . sanctification" (1 Cor 1:30 KJV), and we are saints in Christ Jesus (1 Cor 1:2; Phil 1:1). And with Jesus in John: "For their sakes I sanctify myself" (John 17:19 KJV). And, again, in Hebrews: "We are sanc-

---

24. *KD* IV/2, 578–694.
25. Ibid., vii.
26. *CD* IV/2, 560.
27. *KD* IV/2, 598.
28. Ibid., 593.
29. Rienecker, "Biblische Kritik," 15f.
30. Cf. *KD* IV/2, vii.

31. Ibid., 583f. Nicolas von Zinzendorf emphasized the same in a memorable argument with John Wesley. See Lindström, *Wesley und die Heiligung*, 93f.

tified through the offering of the body of Jesus Christ once for all" (10:10 KJV). This does not exclude our participation. Rather, our sanctification *consists* precisely in our faith in the reality of our sanctification in Christ. As the reflectors on a road shine during the night when light falls on them, so we also are new human beings when we are directed in faith to Christ. The reality of our sanctification is outside of us; and yet, we participate in it, if we are concentrated upon Christ. On the other hand, in our active participation in the sanctification that is in Christ, we acknowledge that which is already valid for all humanity in advance.

Second: The holiness of God is characterized by His covenant will: "I will be your God, and you shall be my people."[32] Holiness is therefore not merely separation. Holiness is first of all a communal holiness, the holy people of God, the holy Church. But there is more, for God's holiness encloses a freedom by which God can go beyond His own holiness to connect Himself with a reality that is totally different from Himself and with people who are unholy. For Barth, God's holiness consists in the fact that though He is "different from the world, he is devoted to it."[33] Therefore, our participation in the holiness of God which is revealed in Christ, will not only be a separation from others, but will also be a participation in and devotion to others, including the unholy.

The *sixth* stage: At the end of the sixties Barth made a further step towards Pietism. He did it in the hope that a "Theology of the Holy Spirit" would emerge in the Christian world. He was thereby willing to call his own Christocentric theology into question, at least as far as it was *his* starting point. The sense was not to replace Christ by something else. Rather, the hope was that this theology might provide a quite different way than was possible for Barth for speaking about Christ's presence and work among us in the creative power of the Holy Spirit. Barth expressly cultivated this hope "in favor of the Pietists," so that their old concerns would shine anew in the church, not as the truths of the individual who circles around himself but as truths of the Holy Spirit, who seizes the human heart.[34] In this sense Barth said in 1967, "What we need today is a kind of new Pietism"—not simply a repetition of the old Pietism, but its emergence in a renewed form so that it brings with it a new Pentecost.[35]

Barth had this expectation like the old Moses during his look over into the promised land. But he did not see it fulfilled in the appearance of

---

32. *KD* IV/2, 565; quoted from Jer 7:23; 31:33; Ezek 36:8.
33. Ibid., 579.
34. See Barth, "Nachwort," 310ff.
35. Barth, *Briefe 1961–1968*, 488. Translation mine.

the German Confessing Movement's "No other gospel." He saw this not as a step forward, but as a reactionary relapse in the nineteenth century.[36] Why? Because in his view this movement was ensnared by the same major mistake of which it accused its "enemies." Whether one fears that the truth of the gospel can be destroyed by humanity or one thinks that this truth depends on our defense of its validity, in both cases we make the dubious assumption that the truth of the gospel depends on human efforts. This further clarified the wrong-headedness of the old Pietistic emphasis on our appropriation of the reality of Jesus Christ. Rather, this relationship must be understood the other way round. Whenever this relationship is reversed, as in the old Pietism, then it becomes possible to think that the reality and truth of Christ depends on our efforts. Because it embodied this mistaken reversal, Barth therefore thought that the Confessing Movement was really a child of that spirit against which it wanted to fight.

But notice the nearly Pietistic language with which Barth formulated his objection against this: "We do not have to take care of our dear God, but he takes care for us. In every respect we must take this into account and live free of anxiety in response to this truth: He ensures that his truth does not fall by the wayside, but rather remains present." We do better to

> put our confidence in the Holy Spirit who always ensures that the truth remains the truth. There is no stopping the Holy Spirit. . . . What I have to say against the Confessing Movement, I want to paraphrase with the sentence: "A servant does not make noise." The Confessing Movement is a noisy movement. . . . With noise, with mass demonstrations, nothing is accomplished. . . . This is not the delicate, quiet walk of the Spirit. The Holy Spirit does not blow in mass assemblies, but goes a quiet, I would like to say, a modest, but a confident way. Whoever knows a little bit about the new birth and about the new life . . . is confident about what He is doing.[37]

One does not have to keep opposing others constantly, nor stress that *he or she* has the right confession, but the Spirit furnishes proof that the confession has him or her. One notices that Barth does not speak here against Pietism, but rather he thinks on its ground, and in the trajectory of the new life, given by the Holy Spirit. And therefore he thinks that Pietism could be able to live far more convincingly in faith than was the case in the Confessing Movement. But this would be already "a new kind of Pietism." If

---

36. See Barth, "Interview von M. Linz," 212–15.
37. Barth, "Gespräch mit Mennoniten," 423–26. Translation mine.

the Confessing Movement was a disappointment, it was not an impossible obstacle for his hope for a "theology of the Holy Spirit."

Barth's Questions to Pietism

On the Understanding of the Objective and the Subjective Reality of Salvation

Barth said sometimes that the problem of Pietism is that the work of God for us in Jesus Christ, which is unshakably certain quite apart from our faith, is made unimportant in favor of the "subjective" event of our own grasping of salvation. For Barth, this meant that Pietism had distorted the Christian faith. Over against this, Barth was concerned to emphasize from the 1920's onward the connection of the objective and the subjective reality of God's revelation and salvation.[38] Since the objective has to be seen absolutely together with the subjective reality, he thought he might have an open door from here to the motivations of the Pietists. Barth saw their concern summarized in the personal experience of salvation. When held in *isolation*, this idea is dangerous. But when *connected* with the objective reality of revelation it is legitimate.

But now the discussion with the Pietists becomes more complicated because, conversely, the Pietists accused Barth of his *own* one-sidedness, though it was a one-sided "objectivism." In addition, they argued that Pietism was also interested in "the creative unity of subjectivism and objectivism."[39] Unfortunately we cannot conclude that this was a simple misunderstanding. On the one hand, Barth did not dispute that Pietism also knows "something objective." But he called their form of the unity of subjectivism and objectivism "subjectivistic." On the other hand, the Pietists rightly noticed that Barth's own form of unity was "objectivist."

If we understand the subjective realization of salvation in the narrow sense of a human decision to live with God and Christ, then Barth can be seen as arguing that this question is of secondary importance. This is because, from Barth's view, the question of whether we say yes to God pales in comparison to the startling and miraculous fact of God's own emphatic Yes to sinful humanity. The worst statement found in the Pietist analysis of Barth is the claim that the grace of God so emphasized by Barth is treated as a foregone conclusion.[40] If there is anything that is not and never will be a

---

38. Cf. Barth, *Die christliche Dogmatik im Entwurf*, 380.
39. Rienecker, "Biblische Kritik," 16. Translation mine.
40. See Jochums, *Die große Enttäuschung*, 39.

foregone conclusion for Barth, it is the truth which was already unshakably true, valid even "when we were enemies" (Rom 5:10). This is the melody that we hear in his theology. Our decision for Christ is therefore not superfluous. Rather, the miracle of God's own Yes to us makes it possible all the more that we would turn to Him. But this is not to be expressed as "If you will not do this, then you are lost," but as "Because it is real for you also, therefore accept it!"

This leads to the other, the charge of subjectivism against Pietism. Once more, for Barth, this does not mean that Pietism knows nothing of the objective, but that it understands the reality of divine revelation like a thing which is lying on a table. As long as it lies there, it has nothing to do with me. Only by my grasping it does it take on real meaning for me. I would stand before the object therefore in free sovereignty to choose, and would have the "fateful future" of the object in my hand: if I do not take it, it is entirely useless to me. In fact, in this the objectivity of salvation is only a possibility. It becomes true salvation when I "translate this reality" by my acceptance. I make it real. Exactly this kind of connection of objective and subjective Barth calls "subjectivistic." For Barth the crucial question is, "whether there is an encounter between God and humanity, an encounter which could never conceivably be interrupted except by God; *or* whether man is conceived as possessing by nature or by acquisition the power himself to end this encounter."[41] Barth thought that the first approach was right. When God's reality is considered in such a way that it only receives reality through some human behavior, we go off the straight and narrow so that God's reality in the end is created by humanity and therefore has to be understood as illusory. According to Barth, the reality of God is fundamentally "other," withdrawn from every human attempt to grasp at it. It opposes its transformation into such a manipulable object, with which the human knower might attempt to "do" something, or not do something, as the case may be. That the objectively real revelation becomes also subjectively real for us, therefore, is "the breakthrough of the objective revelation into our affairs."[42] In that the objectivity of salvation makes it possible and works on its own so that we become grasped by it, and as a result of this we also perceive it, provision is made that we are not dealing with an illusion. This is the meaning of Barth's doctrine of the Holy Spirit. Those who criticize Barth because of an alleged defect in his doctrine of the Holy Spirit find themselves questioned as to whether they are seeking to assert for humanity that which only the Spirit can do, namely create an openness to God. And so

---

41. Barth, *Die Theologie und die Kirche*, 192. Translation mine.
42. *KD* I/2, 274.

this is Barth's first question to the Pietists: Are we in agreement that only the *reality* of God's prior decision to be with us makes possible our subsequent decision to be with Him?

On the Understanding of Grace and Sin

The second question is formulated with regard to the accusation of Pietists that Barth supported a doctrine of the *apokatastasis ton panton*. Therefore he knows "no longer sin, no longer hell, no longer a devil."[43] Indeed, he did want to show that the eternal mercy of God is far more essential than the reality of sin, but he did not teach the doctrine of the reconciliation of all things, because of its assumption of an automatic or guaranteed mercy. He was, however, particularly fond of certain verses in the Bible like "God . . . was reconciling the world unto himself" (2 Cor 5:19 KJV); or: "He is the propitiation for our sins, and not for ours only but also for the sins of the whole world" (1 John 2:2 ESV); or: ". . . and through him to reconcile to himself all things . . . by making peace through his blood, shed on the cross" (Col 1:20 NIV). It is also true that Barth, in reference to these Scriptures, emphasized that their truth was unconditionally valid, and not dependent on certain preconditions on our side.

According to Barth, however, this truth does not at all mean that sin is minimized. He would say with Ps 130:4: "But with you there is forgiveness, therefore you are *feared*."[44] Only when you know the one who is merciful, can you become aware of the great measure of your own sin and come to know rightly who it is that you have sinned against.[45] Before this one very likely understood sin as something like a deviation from a general code of decency. Here, sin is hardly seen as something substantial such that it can be easily excused or cast onto someone else; or, in the worst scenario as it was expressly said after 1945 by the Germans: "We got away with it once more!"[46] But when we know that Christ carried all sins, we are shocked and confronted by the truth that our sins are too big to be carried by ourselves. Therefore we know that the same Jesus Christ is also the judge, and that we have to pray to him: "God, be merciful to *me* a sinner" (Luke 18:13).[47] There is only the one comfort that this judge "has presented himself beforehand

---

43. Jochums, *Die große Enttäuschung*, 55. Translation mine.
44. Translation mine.
45. Barth, "Gespräch mit Strafanstaltsseelsorgern," 71f.
46. Cf. Barth, *Die christliche Lehre nach dem Heidelberger Katechismus*, 38f.
47. See Barth, *Die christliche Leben* 37, 113.

to the judgment of God for me."[48] As my sin is too great so that I am unable to save myself from it, so also is the devil so mighty that only the mercy of God in Christ is strong enough against him. But "if man thinks that he can and should fight by himself against the devil," then the devil has already overcome him, and "by this humanity has already become a great fighter at the side of the evil."[49]

Barth concludes that Christians do not have to demonstrate to others that they are sinners in order for non-Christians to become receptive to the gospel. They have, *first*, to witness to them the gospel and then those to whom they speak will, like Peter, say: "Lord, I am a sinful man!" (Luke 5:8)[50] We also do not have to put before them the alternative: Do you want to be saved or lost? Here again, the notion of neutrality appears, as if humanity is not already lost and as if to remain in sin is freedom. "Whoever commits sin is the servant of sin" (John 8:34 KJV). The "humanism" of which Pietists often accuse others is in fact a danger that they themselves face if they think that this "servant of sin" really has the ability to care about his or her salvation or disaster. Yes, as long as humans claim such freedom to decide, they remain trapped in their own un-free wills.[51] In this, Barth appeals to Jesus' own address to sinners as portrayed in the gospels. Where does he tell them abstractly, "You could be lost?" Where did he speak about the real threat of being lost, other than in the context that he had, "come to save that which was lost" (Matt 18:11)?[52] The second question to the Pietists is therefore: can Pietists really speak seriously of sin without giving divine mercy and its power over evil, predominance and priority?

The Meaning of the Human Decision of Faith

The *third* question concerns our personal relationship with Christ. Here also, it seemed that Barth had an alarming gap. According to the Pietists Barth wanted to inform people about something that they really don't need to know since it is already valid for them anyway. Certainly, Barth had questions about the concentration of the gospel upon the single individual. There is the danger that we will forget the "for *us*," and we will see only the "for *me*." Here again is the danger that God will be made to serve my own personal interests and matters, rather than my personal interests being put

---

48. Also, Heidelberg Catechism, Question 52, taken on by Barth in *KD* IV/1, 231.
49. *KD* IV/I, 500.
50. Cf. Barth, *Predigten, 1921–1935*, 330–32.
51. See Krötke, *Sünde und Nichtiges bei Karl Barth*, 69f.
52. Cf. with Barth, "Gespräch mit Vertretern de Gemeinschaften," 22–27.

in service to God. Nevertheless, even in the face of those dangers, Barth was not hindered from saying, "in earnest agreement with the Pietists," that the gospel is indeed addressed personally to the individual, so that "Jesus Christ in person encounters each individual in person on their journey, and becomes a conscious element of the story of their life."[53]

Here are two notable examples that highlight this:

> The gospel in its [Christian] retelling can be transformed into a lifeless, empty communication that does not really, but only apparently, proclaim the message of salvation. A biblical foundation [and] . . . continuity with the traditions of the church's past . . . do not have to be absent from such a retelling. But one thing that will be absent in this distorted form is that this retelling will not be thought of as an invitation and an exhortation to a concrete decision of faith and obedience.[54]

Then not only is something lacking, but everything is distorted. In a second text Barth asks, very pointedly and personally,

> Are we in fact born again, converted, renewed? . . . This question digs deeper and is actually more threatening than the one by which the Christian has been or could be . . . disturbed because of a philosophy or ideology. This question concerns him personally, which is in distinction from all of those other questions.[55]

This means that the decision of God for us calls for an answer from us, in which we renounce from our side our old life and begin to obey God as our Lord. Because of this, Barth wanted to recover what he saw as the New Testament meaning of baptism—an individual's public answer to God's decision. Therefore, no more infant baptism!

Barth speaks of this as a cheerful response to the gospel's claim on the person. It is not done out of fear or worry, i.e., that "I" have to do something now in order to be saved from damnation, but in great thankfulness that Jesus Christ saved me from sin and damnation. Therefore, it is not that I *must* convert, but that I *may* convert. And I do not have to force others to do it, but I may instill the *joyful desire* to do so. "It is clearly and solely the gospel, which is the revealed grace of God, through which conversion . . . is offered." "It has to be understood that the implied *must* is a vile and demonic thing from its base. The *must*, which man follows in conversion . . . is the

---

53. *KD* IV/3, 584.
54. Ibid., 931.
55. Ibid., 777.

free gift of *may*."⁵⁶ This permission happens in the freedom into which we are liberated by God's grace. It neither negates our own personal agreement, nor does it open an arbitrary choice of another "possibility." This, then, is Barth's third question to the Pietists: Are we in agreement that all talk about our personal decision, our conversion, must not be according to the legalistic "you must" but in agreement with the gospel should be declared in a free "you may"?

The Conversion of the Converted

The *fourth* question concerns the problem of whether the converted person has truly become new or if, and in which way, he or she is still a sinner who has constantly to repent and turn around. The Pietists missed in Barth's theology the statement that there was a clear and permanent difference between the former existence in sin and the new time of being saved.⁵⁷ But Barth also said that those who believe in Christ really differ from the world. In so far as we are speaking about the Christian life, we have to speak about a "past" and "present," a "then" and a "now." But we need to reflect on two additional points here.

First, because we see the reality of our sin all the more in the light of the gospel it is clear that we cannot leave behind us the need to repent in our life as Christians. The genuineness of the Christian life is shown in that we become all the more repentant. Barth pointed out that the radical criticism of the prophets in the Old Testament was especially directed against the people of God. Correspondingly, Jesus reserved his harshest words not for the publicans and sinners, but for the pious Pharisees.

Second, even the believing and converted Christian has reason enough to pray earnestly, "Forgive us our debts" (Matt 6:12). Barth stresses that the person of faith is always at the same time entirely a justified saint *and* entirely an evil sinner.

> The whole person is still the old and again the whole person is already the new human, and both in conflict with one another. How neatly arranged everything would be if we could say instead of this: man is *partially* the old person, and *partially* the new person! But we would be missing the point! . . . How powerful is the sin which played such a dominant role in the past, and how much more powerful is the grace by which he

---

56. *KD* IV/2, 654.

57. Barth, "Gespräch mit Vertretern der Gemeinschaften," 14–33.

is directed forward. The person who is really in the process of being converted knows himself in these terms.[58]

Therefore Barth does not like to speak about converted individuals—those who have it behind them—but about those who are in the process of being converted[59]—those who, after their first conversion, are converted again and again to the Lord. This, then, is the fourth question for the Pietists: Does the idea of a single conversion mean then that in the future real repentance is excluded?

For the Pietists, there is reason enough to pray also with regard to themselves, "Lord, be gracious with *us* Pietists!" I call attention here to only one example from the German context which illustrates that many from this group of Christians were adjusted to the spirit of the "Third Reich":[60] they glorified the greatness of the German *Volk*; they systematically disdained the democracy of the Weimar state; they dismissed the workers' hope for bread as ridiculous; they celebrated Hitler and Ludendorff as "the anointed of the people"; and they constantly slandered the Jews as national parasites. All of this was written in uppercase letters between articles about rebirth and new life in their leading magazine, *Light and Life*! Then, in 1933, one of the Pietistic leaders wrote the following poem: "Forward, brothers, fall in step! / we will walk side by side / with Adolf Hitler, Germany's most faithful son."[61] Later, in 1936, another head of German Pietism defended the importance of Pietism, but making the point that the life of the reborn has to prove itself today, knowing that the life of God is given "in the German heart"—by responding with a strong yes to "blood and race . . . and placing ourselves with both feet and a burning heart into the Volk of the Third Reich, in a real grateful love to the Führer (Adolf Hitler) . . . !"[62] This example is cited only to make it clear that the Pietistic call to repentance which is always addressed to *others* will begin to become plausible when it is heard first within its *own* house. Or, could it be that the idea of a single conversion hinders the possibility of further repentance?

---

58. *KD* IV/2, 647.

59. Ibid., 634.

60. For more specific documentation on this, see Busch, *Karl Barth und die Pietisten*.

61. Prolingheuer, *Kleine politische Kirchengeschichte*, 55f. It considers Paul Humburg. Translation mine.

62. Mund, *Pietismus*, 14f. Translation mine.

The Relationship to the Existing Church

Like many Pietists, Barth was also critical of the existing church. In response to the question about the condition of the church in eternity, he sighed in 1957: "Not eternally this church, which already bores people on earth so terribly!"[63] And in 1946: you could "often be nauseated by the whole system of the church. Within the church you are just like a bird in a cage, which repeatedly flies against the barriers of the cage. There is something greater to be considered than our ineffective 'sermon,' namely the Kingdom of God."[64] But, understood correctly, this addresses every form of church fellowship. Barth presented concrete questions, especially in regards to the *volkskirchliche* form of the church, arguing that it is finally time to cancel the traditional alliance between the church and the world, where the church seeks protection from the world and the state. He demanded that the church rise to its own feet in regards to the state and society.[65] It has to learn that to be a Christian means to be a mature and responsible Christian.

It may be that Barth's criticisms and concerns were close to those of the Pietists own church-criticism. This criticism may share in some ways Pietistic criticisms of the Pietists. But Barth also expressed objections to the Pietistic desire to forge a new and special way in relation to other churches. He thought that their conception of the congregation was problematically built on the pious individual. In Pietism, "the neighbor, the brother in Christ . . . basically shall no longer be considered as other . . . it shall not concern me that he is different . . . if possible, it should be that I find myself in him." I want him to be as I am myself. "The fellowship should not disturb me, but should affirm me . . . Then and under these conditions the individualist can and wants to love, to have brothers and be in the church." This is the reason for the dislike of the *Volk* Church and especially "against its form of Eucharist, in which it is expected of me, to be brother and sister together with every Tom, Dick and Harry."[66] Barth's dissatisfaction with the church does not mean that he is dissatisfied with the disturbing fact that in the real church of Christ I will always be together with people who are different from me, very different. The question which Barth raises here is: Does not your inclination to go a separate way from the church indicate a

---

63. From a conversation Barth had on 6/1/1957 in Rummelsberg with the Bavarian Pastors Brotherhood, according to the notes of Charlottle von Kirschbaum, in Karl Barth-Archiv, Basel. Translation mine.

64. Barth, *Dogmatik im Grundriß*, 172. Translation mine.

65. Barth, "Das Evangelium in der Gegenwart," 33f. Translation mine.

66. Barth, *Die protestantische Theologie*, 95. Translation mine.

running away from the togetherness with a truly different Other, preferring to be undisturbed "together with those who are like-minded"?

When Barth speaks about the unsatisfied yearning to rise above the church "as it is," he continues this way: "But also then . . . you do not run away. By cherishing the hope of the Kingdom [of God], we do not allow them to deny us the privilege of serving in the company of God as a simple soldier. Then we will not be ashamed of the church."[67] This does not mean that we have to resign ourselves to the church "as it is." But, even if we have to criticize it, serious criticism does not come from the secure distance of the spectator. Earnest "objections against it . . . can only be made in *solidarity*, in which you scrutinize yourself in this critique first and only then it [the church], who is subject to her living Lord. The legitimate assault on the church can be done only on its own ground, in the name of Jesus Christ, with the aim to establish it anew and more firmly on the ground, which it perhaps is about to deny."[68] This constitutes a second question: Are you making your critique of the church not merely because one or the other of your needs have not been met, but truly in the name of Jesus Christ and therefore not from a safe distance, but in solidarity with the church?

Service for the "World"

The *sixth* question concerns the relation to the world. According to Barth, the true addressee of God's saving will is the *world*: "God so loved the world" (John 3:16); "God was reconciling the world to himself in Christ" (2 Cor 5:19); and God "desires all people to be saved" (1 Tim 2:4 ESV). Barth emphasized this in such a way that it was almost an embarrassment to him to realize what the church should be doing according to God's will, but was not doing. The church only has meaning when it does not seek to be an end in itself, but understands itself to be sent forth in the service of witness to Jesus Christ and His reconciliation throughout the whole world.[69] This is why, for Barth, conversions in the Bible are not ends in themselves, but are stories in which people are called into service.[70]

This service will have different forms, and one cannot be evaluated against another, nor can one be elevated over others, as for instance, the elevation of the type of modern evangelism in which those who are committed

---

67. Barth, *Dogmatik im Grundriß*, 173. Translation mine.
68. *KD* IV/1, 773.
69. *KD* IV/3.2, 872f.
70. Ibid., 662–78.

Christians share the gospel with those who are nominal Christians![71] But Barth emphasizes that

> What is vital is that it should really say this, i.e., the gospel, and not something else!—What is vital is that concern for spurious results should not cause it to make the proclamation of freedom into propagation of a law, the promise of life (ostensibly on pedagogic grounds) into threatening with the terrors of hell, the declaration of what is eternally undeserved into an incitement to a praiseworthy Moral Rearmament, the artless indication of the truth into some clever or attractive apologetic![72]

Rather, the church must proclaim the gospel! If it truly is the gospel then it will be obvious in evangelism that God has loved them already, a fact that is much more important and takes precedence over the unbelief of the audience. Therefore, I have to speak to them not in a tone of indignation or accusation, but in the good spirit of the love of Jesus Christ—in the hope that they will come to the knowledge of the truth, that they will awaken from sleep, that they who are blind, will open their eyes to that which is prepared for them.[73] For Barth, the service of witness takes form also in foreign mission. He praises Pietism as having an advantage over the Reformation, since it discovered anew the missionary task of Christianity. He also thinks that this mission, even from its Pietistic beginnings, was overshadowed for a long time, being less a witness of the love of God than an act of Christian self-recommendation,[74] especially since that mission was so closely allied to the economic conquest of the world by the European trading powers.

But it is important to notice that what Barth called the social work (*diakonia*) of the church of Jesus Christ was one form of Christian witness, equal in value to the others. In it, the Christian community acts practically. Following Matt 25:31ff., the community "confesses Jesus Christ Himself as finally the hungry, thirsty, homeless, naked, ill, imprisoned human, and the royal man as such. In the diaconate the community makes plain its witness to Him as the Samaritan service to the man who has fallen among thieves— a service fulfilled in company with Him as the true Neighbor of this lost man. In the diaconate it goes and does likewise (Luke 10:29f.)."[75] And the congregation has to raise its own voice and "with its proclamation of the gospel call the world to awareness of social injustice and its consequences,

---

71. Ibid., 999–1002.
72. Ibid., 1002.
73. Ibid., 584–91. This refers, for example, to Eph 5:8.
74. *KD* I/2, 368.
75. *CD* IV/3.2, 891.

in order to change the circumstances and conditions."[76] Through *diakonia* a sign is erected for the cosmic character of reconciliation through Jesus Christ and his kingdom. This is what Barth would call the political worship of the Christian, and what we could also call the social *diakonia* of the church. It does not mean that the church takes on some party program or political catch-phrase in connection with the Christian faith. But it does mean that to serve God is not just to serve Him within the church, but is also to serve Him in the political and social sphere as well, because He is the Lord of all realms.

The Christian community will, as a rule, swim against the current because Christians are not to side with the ruling powers of this world, but with that which is bent by the ruling powers. They have to speak for suppressed truths, and for oppressed human beings. This is not an optional luxury. Christians would deny Christ if they will not give such a courageous witness. And this is the *sixth* question of Barth to the Pietists of today: Why do you often times denigrate such a social witness when compared to evangelism and mission and so often dismiss it as mere "humanism"?[77] Does this really come from the Spirit of the gospel? Or could it be a sign that despite your words, you are secretly connected with the ruling powers of the present world? Or why does one sense in your lives so little of the contagious spirit of Jesus' compassion for a humanity afflicted by disease, marked by hardship, and threatened by destruction? Why you are only interested in repentance in terms of private matters, but not with the turning away from the social sins? Are you not partly responsible for those sins through your participation in the friend-foe thinking, in regard to those who think differently, are of a different faith, or different character; or in the involvement in the exploitation of the poor in the North-South-relation?

Conclusion

The aim of Barth's criticism was not the removal of Pietists from the Pietistic movement. He was, rather, an uncomfortable *friend* of its members. He hoped for a "new kind of Pietism." But whether this will appear depends to a large extent on whether Pietists are open enough to being exposed to

---

76. KD IV/3.2, 1023.

77. Jochums, *Die große Enttäuschung*, 70, 74, and more carefully, Gassmann, *Karl Barth*, 80, accused Barth of having opened the door to the "humanistic spirit of the time." To him, the otherworldly God "disappears" and due to his dialectic gives credit to relativism and skepticism, therefore the atheistic "humanism" can or must spread over the earth. According to Jochums, the result of this is that God dissolves into the love of the neighbor, and therefore things like pornography or dictatorship take over.

the *uncomfortableness* of his friendship. He did not think that they had to adhere to "his" theological opinions, but that they, the "converted," needed to allow themselves to be challenged by his questions, to make themselves ready to be again and again in the process of conversion.

Bibliography

Barth, Karl. *Briefe 1961-1968*. Edited by Jürgen Fangmeier and Hinrich Stoevesandt. Zürich: Theologischer Verlag Zürich, 1979.

———. *Die Christliche Dogmatik im Emtwurf Erster Band: Die Lehre vom Worte Gottes: Prolegomena zur Christlichen Dogmatik 1927*. Edited by Gerhard Sauter. Zürich: Theologischer Verlag Zurich, 1982.

———. "Der christliche Glaube und die Geschichte." *Schweizer Theologische Zeitschrift* 29 (1912).

———. *Die christliche Leben: Die Kirchliche Dogmatic IV/4, gradmente aus dem Nachlaß*. Zürich: Theologischer Verlag Zürich, 1976.

———. *Die christliche Lehre nach dem Heidelberger Katechismus*. Zollikon: Evangelischer Verlag, 1948.

———. *Dogmatik im Grundriß*. Zürich: Evangelischer Verlag Zürich, 1947.

———. "Das Evangelium in der Gegenwart." *Theologische Existenz Heute* 25 (1935).

———. "Gerhard Tersteegen." *Gemeinde-Blatt für die Deutsche reformierte Gemeinde Genf* 7 (1910) 1-3.

———. "Gespräch mit Strafanstaltsseelsorgern." In *Gespräche 1959-1962*, edited by Eberhard Busch, 53-90. Zürich: Theologischer Verlag Zürich, 1995.

———. "Gespräch mit Vertretern der Gemeinschaften 1959." In *Gespräche 1959-1962*, edited by Eberhard Busch, 13-41. Zürich: Theologischer Verlag Zürich, 1995.

———. "Gespräch mit mennoniten (13.12.1967)." In *Gespräche 1964-1968*, edited by Eberhard Busch, 418-34. Zürich: Theologischer Verlag Zürich, 1996.

———. "Interview von M. Linz, Norddeutscher Rundfunk (23.3.1966)." In *Gespräche 1964-1968*, edited by Eberhard Busch, 210-21. Zürich: Theologischer Verlag Zürich, 1996.

———. "Nachwort." In *Schleiermacher-Auswahl*, edited by Heinz Bolli, 290-312. München: Siebenstern Taschenbuch Verlag, 1968.

———. *Die protestantische Theologie im 19 Jahrhundert: Ihre Vorgeschichte und ihre Geschichte*. Zürich: Theologischer Verlag Zürich, 1960.

———. *Predigten, 1921-1935*. Edited by Holger Finze-Michaelsen. Zürich: Theologischer Verlag Zürich, 1998.

———. *Der Römerbrief*. Bern: G. A. Bäschlin, 1919.

———. *Der Römerbrief*. 2nd ed. Munich: Kaiser, 1922.

———. *Die Theologie und die Kirche*. Munich: Kaiser, 1928.

———. *Das Wort Gottes und die Theologie*. Munich: Kaiser, 1924.

Busch, Eberhard. *Karl Barth and the Pietists: The Young Karl Barth's Critique of Pietism and Its Response*. Translated by Daniel W. Bloesch. Downers Grove, IL: InterVarsity, 2004.

———. *Karl Barth und die Pietisten: Die Pietismuskritik die jungen Karl Barth und ihre Erwiderung*. Munich: Kaiser, 1978.

Gassman, Lothar. *Karl Barth: Das Verhängnis der Dialektik*. Berneck: Schwengeler, 1995.

Jochums, Heinrich. *Die große Enttäuschung: Karl Barth und die Theologien, Philosophien, Antropologien und Ideologien der Gegenwart, sonderlich im deutschen Sprachraum*. Wuppertal: Verlag und Schriftenmission de Evangelische Ges. Fur Deutschland, 1986.

Krötke, Wolf. *Sünde und Nichtiges bei Karl Barth*. Berlin: Evangelische Verlagsantalt, 1971.

Lindström, Harald Gustac Aake. *Wesley und die Heiligung*. Frankfurt am Main: Anker, 1961.

Mund, Fritz. *Pietismus–Eine Schicksalsfrage an die Kirche heute*. 2nd ed. Marburg: Spener, 1938.

Overbeck, Franz. *Christentum und Kultur: Gedanken und Anmerkungen zur modernen Theologie*. Edited by Carl Albrecht Bernoulli. Darmstadt: Wissenschaftliche Buchgesellschaft, 1919.

Prolingheuer, Hans. *Kleine politische Kirchengeschichte: 50 Jahre evangelischer Kirchenkampf von 1919 bis 1969*. Cologne: Pahl-Rugenstein, 1984.

Rienecker, Fritz. "Biblische Kritik am Pietismus alter und neuer Zeit." In *Badener Konferenz, zweiundneunzigste Versammlung, Mittwoch, den 25. April 1951*. Basel: Heinrich Maier, 1952.

Thimme, Ludwig. *Im Kampf um die Kirche: Versuch einer Lösung der Spannungen zwischen Kirche, Theologie, und Gemeinschaft*. Gotha: P. Ott, 1930.

3

Bringing an Elephant and a Whale into Conversation

Karl Barth and Pietism

Kimlyn J. Bender

Introduction

IN A LETTER TO Rudolf Bultmann in 1952, Karl Barth compared Bultmann and himself to a whale and an elephant, two great beasts that are so different that communication is difficult, if not impossible.[1] In Barth's assessment, Bultmann's emphasis upon the subjectivity of faith and his own emphasis upon the objectivity of God's revelation made any real understanding or affinity between them difficult if not impossible. Barth could not help but see Bultmann's theology as a continuation of the Protestant liberal tradition that Barth had resoundingly rejected, and if in Barth's estimation Bultmann was the end product of the liberal tradition, Pietism was its forerunner. Barth understood Pietism in the history of Christian thought as a turn toward subjectivity that grounded faith in inner experience, and little could be more problematic for Barth than this emphasis upon inner religious subjectivity. Yet, as far removed as Pietism may appear to be from Barth at first blush, in this chapter I am going to try to bring the whale and the elephant into conversation.

---

1. *Karl Barth and Rudolf Bultmann Letters*, 105. Barth could use the same image for his relation to Emil Brunner elsewhere.

It may seem strange to attempt a positive examination of Pietism in relation to Karl Barth, for Barth's open antipathy towards this movement is well known, and Barth could speak disparagingly of Pietism in both his early and later works.[2] Barth's relationship with Pietism was a complex and troubled one. While Barth grew within a familial and ecclesial climate amenable to Pietism, he himself could not be classified as belonging to this movement. His own very early sympathies with Pietism were in fact not due to an identification with Pietism itself, but to the affinities he believed existed between the liberal theology he embraced as a student and the concerns of Pietism. In Barth's mind, both were marked by a religious individualism and the autonomy of religion, two elements fundamental for modern theology that Barth esteemed to be united in that Pietist of a higher order, Friedrich Schleiermacher. Barth could thus see the merger of the concerns of Pietism and of Protestant Liberalism expressed in the thought of his early teacher, Wilhelm Herrmann.[3]

When, however, Barth rejected the liberal theology of his youth he turned on Pietism with a vengeance. The earlier coupling of Pietism and Liberalism remained valid for Barth, but this relation was no longer seen in a positive fashion, for a break with Liberalism now meant a rejection of Pietism itself. After his break from the theology of his former teachers, Barth came to hold that Pietism turned from the revelation of God *extra nos* to an internal experiential religion, from a focus on the revealing God to the Christian subject, and thus stood as one source, along with medieval mysticism and Enlightenment rationalism, behind nineteenth-century Neo-Protestantism and its anthropological orientation.[4] Moreover, Barth could also link Pietism with the romanticism of Schelling and Herder, Pietism and romanticism being sibling sources behind the subjectivity and

---

2. The classic study of Barth's early relationship to Pietism remains that of Eberhard Busch, *Karl Barth and the Pietists*. For Barth's early negative assessment of Pietism's place in the history of theology and the church, see Barth, *Protestant Theology*, 113–23. Barth's critical references to Pietism extend from the early to the late volumes of the *CD*; see, for example, his discussion of the devolution of hymnody through the influence of Pietism (*CD* I/2, 250–57) and his late reference to Pietism in a similar vein with regard to hymnody as a companion to Mysticism and Romanticism and these as the precursors of Neo-Protestantism (*CD* IV/2, 795–98).

3. Busch, *Karl Barth*, 12; 14–17.

4. Barth, *Protestant Theology*, 97–99; see also Barth's comments on "Pietistic and Rationalistic Modernism" in *CD* I/1, 35–36, 251; cf. *CD* III/1, 17; *CD* IV/1, 757. For Barth, the subjectivism of Pietism was quintessentially evident in its hymnody (*CD* I/2, 250–57). Barth could, however, classify Paul Gerhardt's hymns differently, placing him on the side of Luther, though he was an influence upon the later hymnody of Pietism (*CD* I/2, 255); cf., however, *CD* III/3, 32.

individualism of the Protestant Liberalism he came to reject.[5] Pietism's turn to the subjectivity of faith and away from the objectivity of revelation was seen by Barth as its greatest failure.

Whether or not Barth's assessment of Pietism was fair will not be definitively adjudicated here, though it can be said that Barth treated Pietism more as a type of theological failure than as a true historical movement in all of its complexity. Indeed, Barth's early criticisms of Pietism in the first and second editions of the *Romans* commentary (and interestingly Barth's criticisms seemed to differ between the first and the second editions) were made by defining the essence of Pietism as a focus upon the inner religious subjectivity of the individual. While this may have been a generally fitting description of certain branches of Pietism, it did not adequately capture the complexity of other branches and their concerns.[6] Barth's early criticisms thus focused more upon the radical spiritualistic Pietists than church Pietists such as Philip Jacob Spener and August Hermann Francke.[7] Furthermore, Barth's criticism of Pietism on this score was itself ironically based upon discoveries for which he was indebted to other branches of Pietism which he appreciated, most notably, to figures such as J. A. Bengel and C. H. Rieger, as well as to those who had come out of the Pietist tradition even if not remaining comfortably within it, most notably Christoph Blumhardt.[8] Barth thus saw classic church Pietism, with its retention of external means of revelation and grace in Scripture, sacrament, and doctrine, as "inconsistent" Pietism, but this was so only because Barth defined the essence of Pietism as reli-

---

5. See *CD* III/3, 137.

6. It should come as little surprise that Pietism is to this day a contested concept with disagreement as to its definition, with those who see it strictly as a historical movement of the seventeenth and eighteenth centuries begun by Philip Jacob Spener, and those who see it as extending beyond that period to all groups with similar tendencies to those of Spener and the early German Pietist movement. See Lindberg, "Introduction," 1–20; also Brecht and Lindberg, "Pietism," 218–24; Olson, "Pietism," 3–16.

7. Busch, *Karl Barth*, 24; also 61–62.

8. See Busch, 31, 36, 54, and esp. 62–64, for a discussion of Barth's dependence upon figures affiliated with Pietism in his criticism of Pietism itself in the first edition of the *Römerbrief*. While Barth's criticism of Pietism turned from focusing upon its individualism in the first *Romans* commentary to its religiosity in the second edition, Barth continued to quote certain Pietists such as Bengel approvingly, while still remaining critical of Pietism as a movement. For Barth's shift in his criticisms of Pietism between the first and second editions of the *Romans* commentary, see Busch, *Karl Barth*, 91–130. Busch summarizes Barth's criticism in the second edition this way: "In Barth's view Pietism knows man is dependent on God's grace but does not know that man *remains* dependent on it, or does not know that grace *remains* free; instead it finally reestablishes a pious 'possession' of grace in the sight of God" (*Karl Barth*, 97). Insofar as this is true, Barth's criticisms of Pietism foreshadow those he made of Protestant Liberalism and Roman Catholicism in the following years.

gious individualism expressed in inner subjectivity, this essential definition in turn becoming the criterion by which all forms of Pietism were evaluated. Pietism for Barth was thereby treated as a pure type in turn used to judge its various instantiations under a common name.[9] Regardless of the perceptiveness of Barth's critique of the dangers inherent within the religious subjectivity of Pietism, which is not in any way here called into doubt, such essentialism is nevertheless problematic and raises the question of Barth's fairness to the complexity of and diversity within Pietism as a whole.[10] So it should come as no surprise that Barth has been accused of reading all of Pietism through the eyes of its most spiritualistic figures.[11] Barth's criticisms of Pietism at times seem more akin to criticisms of Mysticism and Spiritualism, and while not entirely immune from Barth's criticisms of religious subjectivity, classical Pietism cannot be equated with Spiritualism, for its emphasis upon inner regeneration was always set against an emphasis upon Christ and the Bible as external means of revelation and grace, a fact that must in fairness be noted regardless of one's estimation of Barth's critique as a whole.[12] Even Barth would concede late in life that he had not given Pietism its fair due.[13]

Barth was aware of the ambiguity of Pietism, and gave his own initial assessment of it, much earlier. In Barth's early student years, his liberal

---

9. This was certainly true for the early Barth of the first *Römerbrief* (see Busch, *Karl Barth*, 62), but I would add that this never really changes even in the later *CD*.

10. See Busch, *Karl Barth*, 24–25.

11. F. Ernest Stoeffler thus states that Barth, with the exception of his appreciation for Zinzendorf, "consistently chose to subjectivize Pietism by making the spiritualistic element within the movement, typified by Tersteegen, the Pietistic norm. . . . This understanding of Pietism fitted in with Barth's thesis, of course, but it tends to do violence to the historian's sense of *was wirklich geschehen ist*" (*German Pietism*, 166 n. 1). Stoeffler has questions even with regard to Barth's appreciation and treatment of Zinzendorf. He also emphasizes that Pietists like Spener himself warned their followers against the dangers of subjectivism (see Stoeffler, *Rise of Evangelical Pietism*, 10).

12. This is not to say that Pietism and Spiritualism were entirely unrelated. One sees a movement into Spiritualism with some of the persons usually identified with Pietism, such as an early forerunner of Pietism, Johann Arndt, and some of his followers. As Johannes Wallmann states, "One may speak of a left wing of the Arndt school when Arndt's intention for Orthodoxy is ignored and his intent to give the mystical and spiritualist traditions a proper home on the ground of Orthodox Lutheran ecclesiology is no longer maintained. The left wing of Arndt's followers inclined toward a church-critical Spiritualism that at times crossed into the camp of extra-ecclesial Spiritualism" ("Johann Arndt," 34). Nevertheless, to emphasize inner piety and godliness at the expense of the central place given to the Bible would be to misunderstand Pietism (see Lindberg, "Introduction," 4). For this reason, Barth's criticisms of Pietism seem more fitting for Spiritualists such as Jacob Boehme than for Spener.

13. Barth, *Theology of Schleiermacher*, 262.

convictions led him to appreciate the religious subjectivity and interiorization of faith in Pietism as he understood it and to criticize its inconsistency in maintaining external objective elements such as the Bible and Orthodox doctrine as norms for faith and belief. Yet it was precisely after his break with Liberalism that such inconsistency was understood in Barth's estimation as that which saved Pietism from total rejection.[14] There was always an external objectivity to faith in Pietism's emphasis upon Christ, the Bible, and the church (and indeed in the confessionalism of many early Pietists, even though downplayed in relation to the Orthodox scholastics). And when the actual elements of Pietism related to this external objectivity of revelation and faith are taken into consideration, there appear to be areas of overlap, like those in a Venn diagram, with Barth's own theological concerns and even convictions. For while Barth's rejection of religious subjectivity was consistently maintained after his turn from the Liberalism of his teachers, his appreciation for Pietism could grow in time as he examined its understanding of the objective elements of faith.

In drawing attention to these similarities, I am not making a claim for a direct genetic relationship between the theological themes within Pietism and those found in Barth, though some may exist. While genetic studies of the influences upon Barth's early and mature thought have significant value, they also have some real limitations.[15] There is no claim (nor denial) here for a direct influence of classical Pietist sources on Barth's own theology, for while Barth was certainly influenced by the Pietist heritage of his family and his early engagement with Pietist figures and their works, any evidence for his direct reliance upon classical Pietism for the development of his mature theology is spotty at best. While a direct influence of Barth's reading of classic sources of his Reformed heritage, e.g., Calvin and the Reformed confessions, upon his early and later thought is quite readily confirmed in light of his early extent lectures upon these topics and their direct or indirect incorporation into his mature works,[16] his actual references to Pietist figures in *CD* are sporadic and do not display an extensive reading or sustained interaction with their writings.[17] Even where a substantial interaction is

---

14. Busch, *Karl Barth*, 18, n. 73.

15. For the limitations of genetic studies with relation to the search for sources in Barth's thought, see Webster, *Barth's Early Theology*, 7–8.

16. For these examples, see Barth, *The Theology of John Calvin* and *The Theology of the Reformed Confessions*.

17. Barth's actual references to Continental Pietists are quite sparse within the *CD*. He rarely references Francke or the oft-considered founder of Pietism itself, Spener, and does not discuss their writings in any engaged way. He can refer positively to and quote from the hymnody of Paul Gerhardt, who, though not technically a Pietist, displayed

more readily discerned, Barth took his own questions to the texts as much as he took things away from them. This problem of determining the nature of influence does not mean of course that there were no Pietist influences upon Barth's early or later development. One must immediately remember the important role played by Johann Christoph Blumhardt and his son Christoph Friedrich of the Württemberg Pietist tradition in Barth's development and even later work, though this admittance must itself be qualified by noting that Barth seemed to appreciate in the Blumhardts what he esteemed was most un-Pietistic about them, namely, their turn from inner subjectivity to history as the plane of spiritual conflict and God's in-breaking activity predicated upon an eschatological hope for the coming kingdom of God not only for the individual but for all.[18] Nor does a recognition of the sparseness of references to Pietists in *CD* deny Barth's own later openness to concerns of Pietism and even an affinity for some of its classic fathers, most significantly, Nicholas Ludwig von Zinzendorf, though as with the Blumhardts, Barth was drawn to what he thought was most un-Pietistic in Zinzendorf's thought, namely, his emphasis upon the objectivity of Christ rather than the subjectivity of inner conversion and renewal of the individual.[19] Barth could in his later years soften toward Zinzendorf, yet do so by identifying Zinzendorf not as a Pietist but as an opponent of the Pietism of his own day.[20] This was precisely because Barth worked with a definition of Pietism

---

Pietistic themes (see *CD* IV/2, 273, 613, 729, et al.—and in spite of his criticisms of Pietist hymnody), yet these references are brief and almost always made in passing. There is little or no mention of such Pietists and Pietist forerunners as Johann Arndt, Gottfried Arnold, Gerhard Tersteegen, or Friedrich Christoph Oetinger. The two most important Pietists for Barth's own thinking, excluding the later Blumhardts, seem to be the biblical scholar Johann Albrecht Bengel, whom Barth can often cite with approval, and Nicholas Ludwig von Zinzendorf, who did not escape Barth's criticisms but with whom Barth later expressed an affinity for his Christological concentration (see *CD* IV/1, 683; cf. *CD* II/2, 568). This assessment does not, however, overlook the notable collection of Pietist works discovered in Barth's own personal library.

18. For the deep and abiding impact of the Blumhardts upon Barth, see Collins Winn, *"Jesus Is Victor!"* That Barth was attracted to what he esteemed were the Blumhardt's departures from, rather than faithfulness to, Pietism, see Barth, *Protestant Theology*, 643–53. Barth writes of J. C. Blumhardt's discovery of Jesus as victorious redeemer: "For Blumhardt in the midst of Pietism this breakthrough represented a quite unPietistic discovery and recognition" (644). In *"Jesus is Victor!"* Collins Winn himself shows the movement away from classical Pietism from father to son (xv–xvi); he also notes the disagreement among those who debate whether the Blumhardts are within or without the bounds of Württemberg Pietism (68–76). Nevertheless, the elements that Barth thought most unPietistic in the Blumhardts themselves may have had precedents within Württemberg Pietism (72, 74).

19. *CD* IV/1, 756.

20. See Barth, "Gespräch mit Vertretern der Gemeinschaften," 27. For later cordial

as a pure type of religious subjectivity, and those persons and movements within Pietism that did not neatly fit within this definition but also focused upon external objectivity in revelation, such as Zinzendorf, were thus extolled not because of but in spite of their identification with Pietism. Hence Barth's late comment that Zinzendorf was not a Pietist but an opponent of Pietism (i.e., of Pietism as pure inner subjectivity).[21]

However strong or tenuous the historical influence of Pietism upon Barth's own writings may be, this study will now turn from historical questions to take a different path of exploration. Instead of attempting to draw a line from Pietism to Barth in some kind of genetic fashion, I will instead take up the easier task of drawing attention to "family resemblances" (in the broadly Wittgenstinian sense) or common themes between Pietism and Barth with regard to their respective theological programs with a particular look at the early Pietists Spener and Zinzendorf. These similar themes need not be directly traced from Pietism to Barth, for they are more like overlapping areas of theological affinity than identical themes traced through a direct line of descent or essentially defined.[22] I hope that this examination of similarities between the concerns of Pietism and the theology of Barth might shed light on how a further discussion between studies in Pietism and Barth studies might be conducted, and show that these similar concerns in Pietism and Barth might allow for a broader discussion in Evangelicalism today pertaining to its own identity.

Family Resemblances between Pietism and Barth

When one looks at the external objectivity of Christian revelation in Pietism and the theology of Barth with regard to Christ, Scripture, and church, one can discern among all the significant and very real differences a number of shared convictions and concerns. Such can be described as family resemblances rather than shared concepts essentially, analytically, and systematically defined or traced through history in a direct line from Pietism to Barth. The first family resemblance between the theology of Pietism and that of Barth is a singular emphasis upon Jesus Christ as the

---

discussions of Barth with Pietists, see ibid., 13–41, and Barth, "Gespräch mit Vertretern der Herrnhuter Brüdergemeinde," 124–57.

21. Barth, "Gespräch mit Vertretern der Gemeinschaften," 27. See also *CD* IV/3.2, 568–69.

22. Wittgenstein can say in the *Philosophical Investigations* in reference to family resemblances: "we see a complicated network of similarities overlapping and crisscrossing" (§66).

center of theology and Christian life witnessed in Barth's growing appreciation for Zinzendorf in particular. Such an emphasis upon the centrality of Christ took a different form for Barth than Zinzendorf, of course, for Barth emphasized the centrality of Christ not so much for a life of personal piety, as did Zinzendorf, but for the church's proclamation and confession and theology's center. Barth certainly had dogmatic theological interests and questions that Zinzendorf did not, most notably evident in a complex web of dialectical relationships between questions of election and Christology, and certainly it would be remiss to treat Zinzendorf or his thought in systematic categories that misconstrued his own intentions and work.[23] Yet Barth could, nonetheless, see in Zinzendorf a kindred spirit. Hence Barth's ability and willingness, in light of what he understood as a Christocentric concentration in Zinzendorf, to say in a letter to Bultmann in 1952 that "I have become increasingly a Zinzendorfian to the extent that in the NT only the one central figure as such has begun to occupy me."[24] By this, Barth did not mean that he had become a Pietist. But remember, he did not really consider Zinzendorf one either, at least according to his essentialist definition. Barth's numerous positive references to Zinzendorf later in life illustrate his own estimation of a common central concern between himself and this particular figure of Herrnhut Pietism.[25]

A second family resemblance between Pietism and Barth is found in their pneumatological emphasis upon Scripture as the Word of God that through the work of the Spirit speaks into the life of the church and the believer today. Barth, like the Pietists before him, places a more sustained emphasis in his theology upon the role of the Holy Spirit in the reading of Scripture in the present than upon the writing of Scripture in the past, especially if such writing is understood in light of elaborate theories of the inspiration and inerrancy of the text.[26] Barth shared with Pietism, against the progeny of the Orthodox scholastics of his time and theirs, an indifference to such theories. And while some may believe that the Pietists of the seventeenth century and even later *did* hold to a doctrine of the inerrancy of the text, there is no question that the focus of Pietism was not upon the

---

23. Indeed, Zinzendorf, of all the Pietists, was perhaps the one most opposed to systematic thinking, saying that "as soon as truth becomes a system, one does not possess it" (Stoeffler, *German Pietism*, 143). Certainly Zinzendorf and Barth differ here, though Barth also did not think of the theological task as constructing a static and finished "system" that could capture the truth of revelation.

24. *Karl Barth-Rudolf Bultmann Letters*, 107.

25. See note 17 above.

26. For Barth's understanding of Scripture, see esp. *CD* I/1, 99–111, and *CD* I/2, 457–538; also McCormack, "Being of Holy Scripture," 55–75.

text as a repository of inerrant information and even less upon formulating theories of inspiration or inerrancy, but upon seeing Scripture as the medium of God's self-revelation and communication to the believer through the work of the Spirit.[27] For both Barth and the earlier Pietists, the Bible was not seen as a collection of inerrant propositions but as the locus of the active revelation of God through the Spirit.[28] Both thus emphasized the illumination of Scripture in the present through the work of the Spirit with equal if not greater intensity than the inspiration of Scripture in its composition.[29] Barth, like the classical Pietists, understood the Bible as a book through which God spoke in a living and powerful way into the present life of the church and the believer, though again we should not flatten the differences between Barth and the Pietists, for Barth was more inclined to emphasize *God's action* in speaking to the believer in Scripture, whereas the Pietists could emphasize *the experience* in the life of the believer of God's action in Scripture.[30] Nevertheless, what we see in both Barth and Pietism (and here Spener specifically) is an emphasis upon the superiority and authority of Scripture in dynamic terms that relativizes creeds and confessions even as it recognizes their secondary and relative authority.[31]

There is a further similarity here with regard to the Bible, if of lesser import. Barth's own relation to the Bible expressed in his language for it

---

27. Whether Pietists did or did not adhere to a doctrine of inerrancy is a disputed question in contemporary Evangelicalism. See Dayton, "Pietist Theological Critique," 76–89. For an attempt to argue that Bengel in particular held to the inerrancy of the biblical text, see Thompson, "Pietist Critique of Inerrancy?" 71–88. Spener, however, does not seem to have held such a view; see Stein, "Philipp Jakob Spener," 87–89; also Stein, *Philip Jakob Spener*, 151ff.; Stoeffler, *Rise of Evangelical Pietism*, 239–40.

28. So Spener could say that true faith is that which is "awakened through the Word of God, by the illumination, witness, and sealing of the Holy Spirit" (*Pia Desideria*, 46). For Barth on this point, see McCormack, "Being of Holy Scripture," 62.

29. Stein, "Philipp Jakob Spener," 88. What is said of Spener by Tappert in his introduction to Spener's *Pia Desideria* with regard to the Scriptures could also be said of Barth with little qualification, namely, he was "more interested in their content than in their form and in their effect than in their origin" (25).

30. Notice, for instance, Barth's reticence to speak of the experience of the Word of God. See *CD* I/1, 110.

31. Barth's understanding of creeds and confessions in this way is already evident in his early lectures of *The Theology of the Reformed Confessions*, 1–64. Spener himself could say with regard to creeds and confessions, "I do not oppose them, but hold fast to them with mouth and heart. However, my faith is not grounded upon the Nicene Creed or the Augsburg Confession but on the divine Word itself, from which all creeds have their authority" (quoted in Stein, "Philip Jakob Spener," 89). What Barth and Spener hold in common is a firm conviction of the Word's superiority over the relative authority of creeds and confessions, a conviction they both emphasize against the Orthodoxies of their own respective periods, and Lutheran Orthodoxy in particular.

displays affinities with Pietism's own devotional reading of and love for the Bible. Late in life, Barth could speak of the importance of daily Bible reading and meditation upon passages of Scripture not only for clergy and professional theologians, but as a source of joy for all believers (he did not like the word "laity"), and he could say, "One must get used to living with the Bible" (*Man muß sich daran gewöhnen, mit der Bible zu leben*).[32] In this, we see that while the primary locus for the revelation of God in the present was for Barth the church gathered in community, he retained an important place for the reading of Scripture in the life of the believer. While Barth may have rejected religious individualism, he did not reject the reading of Scripture by the individual believer. Both Barth and the Pietists had a deep desire to see Scripture read and reflected upon not only by professional clergy, but by all members of the church. This leads to a third theme worthy of exploration.

It is this third family resemblance between the theology of Pietism and Barth that I will explore in the most detail by examining the chief work of Spener, i.e., the *Pia Desideria*, and the theology of Barth. This resemblance is the dedication of both Spener and Barth to an intentional church composed of serious members expressed in a strong commitment to the priesthood of all believers. Now it must be said that the personal moral concerns with regard to the church evinced in early Pietism, and in Spener in particular, would have had little or no appeal for Barth. Yet if one can look below the surface of Spener's worries over drunkenness and personal greed,[33] one can discern a deep conviction, shared by Barth, that the reformation of the church is an ongoing task not only in its doctrine but in its life, and that one sign of such ongoing reformation is that the church as a gathered body of believers take its task of being the church seriously.

This seriousness is evident in Spener's concern for the church's renewal. In the *Pia Desideria*, Spener outlined a number of proposals for improving the condition of the churches. Spener's writing demonstrates a spirit of ecclesial dissatisfaction that calls for church reform yet also eschews separation from the church itself. Spener and the Pietists thus attempted to carry on the tradition of protest in Protestantism, and protest that was directed especially against "ecclesiasticism, theologism, and sacerdotalism," as well as against moral compromise and failure, or any easy accommodation of church and world.[34]

---

32. Barth, "Interview von Fr. Klopfenstein," 243. Barth could go on in this interview to speak of prayer in a way that also is reminiscent of Pietism (244).

33. Spener, *Pia Desideria*, 58ff.

34. See Stoeffler, *Rise of Evangelical Pietism*, 2.

In the *Pia Desideria*, Spener begins his proposal to correct diagnosed problems with an appeal to the Word of God and a call for a renewed focus upon Scripture.[35] He writes that the Word of God, i.e., Holy Scripture, is "the powerful means [to this end of reform], since faith must be enkindled through the gospel, and the law provides the rules for good works and many wonderful impulses to attain them. The more at home the Word of God is among us, the more we shall bring about faith and its fruits."[36] Spener may see Scripture more as a treasury of practical and personal moral instruction than Barth would, but both hold firm to the centrality of Scripture for the revelation of God to the church and for the renewal of its life in and for the world.

Part of the problem, Spener maintained, is that corporate worship did not expose Christian congregational members to enough of the Bible, but his answer was not simply more solitary home devotional reading. Rather, Spener espoused reading in community, first in the family (and for Spener, as a product of his time, this meant readings by the father of the house as the one responsible for its practice); second, in public readings of large portions of Scripture (without homiletical comment); and third, and most famously, in home meetings for the reading and discussion of Scripture, which Spener believed returned to a Corinthian pattern of worship.[37] These home meetings became the famous (or infamous) *collegia pietatis*, or *ecclesiolae in ecclesia*, church groups within the state churches.

While Spener did see the ordained clergy as having an authority over such groups and in no way sought to undermine this authority, such reading was predicated upon a radical commitment to the common priesthood (today referred to most commonly as "the priesthood of all believers"). For Spener, it was the responsibility of all Christians to reflect upon Scripture and provide biblical instruction to others.[38] Appealing once again to Luther, Spener emphasized that not only ordained ministers but all members of churches are priests, and that they are responsible not only to study the Word of God but to "instruct, admonish, chastise, and comfort their neighbors."[39] He continued: "Every Christian is bound not only to offer himself and what he has, his prayer, thanksgiving, good works, alms, etc., but also industriously to study in the Word of the Lord, with the grace that is given him

---

35. Spener, *Pia Desideria*, 87ff.

36. Ibid., 87. Spener's words of Scripture being "at home" with the members of the church sound akin to Barth's words to "live with the Bible." See note 32 above.

37. Ibid., 88–90.

38. Ibid., 89–92. See also Spener's treatise on the spiritual priesthood in Erb, *Pietists*, 50–64; see also Stoeffler, *Rise of Evangelical Pietism*, 5, and the important discussion of Strom, "The Common Priesthood."

39. Spener, *Pia Desideria*, 93.

to teach others, especially those under his own roof."[40] What one sees in Spener is a serious attempt to address sacerdotalism, to break down absolute clergy and lay divisions while preserving their differentiation, and to deny any form of neo-clericalism that would limit the study, instruction, and theological reflection of Scripture only to a professional class of theologians and ministers.[41] For this reason, Stein can conclude that Spener was marked by a democratic principle and a desire to empower the laity to be the church, and he deems Spener "an unintentional democrat with a concern that the laity (including those of the peasant and laboring classes) be empowered and involved in the Church's mission."[42]

When one looks at Barth's understanding of the church, it is impossible not to see significant differences between his and Spener's theological and ecclesial positions, differences that cannot simply be dismissed by appeal to differing centuries and contexts. Yet while these cannot be minimized or dismissed, there are also noteworthy similarities as well, for while Barth did not advocate *ecclesiolae* in *ecclesia*, one would not be remiss to say that he advocated that the church itself be, from top to bottom, an intentional community of reform gathered around Scripture that embraced the seriousness of Spener's call for mission. What Spener hopes for the *ecclesiolae* Barth hopes for the *ecclesia* itself.[43]

This is seen in a number of areas. First, like Spener and some later Pietists, Barth has no place for strong clergy and laity distinctions. This rejection is evident already in his first cycle of dogmatics lectures, the *Göttingen Dogmatics*, where Barth readily rejects strong hierarchical distinctions

---

40. Ibid., 94.

41. As Strom writes, "So while Spener preserves the clear distinction of laity and ministry and grants the ministry a certain priority, he nevertheless makes clergy and laity fundamentally interdependent" ("Common Priesthood," 49).

42. Stein, *Philipp Jakob Spener*, 5. This emphasis upon the spiritual priesthood recedes in later Pietism, even by the time of Franke, according to Strom ("Common Priesthood," 51–54). For this reason, Strom argues that Spener is closer to Luther than Franke (or his Lutheran Orthodox detractors). Spener thus stands against both a spiritual elitism of the clergy in later Pietism, and against the Orthodox conception of the authority of the clergy based purely on office (*Amtsgnade*).

43. Barth does not outline a program for *ecclesiolae in ecclesia* (a solution he would have rejected), but instead describes the church itself as a *Gemeinde*, a community. Barth is looking past not only the establishment of the church, but its strong lines of institutionalization and the *corpus Christianum* itself. If this entails that the church be smaller, so be it. He is thus indifferent and even opposed to polity that is universally ordained, to strong notions of office, and to views that see theology as pertaining only to professionals. He wants the common priesthood of all believers to be the norm, and in this sense we can say that he embraces the spirit of Luther that survived in Pietism. For Barth's ecclesiology in this regard, see Bender, *Karl Barth's Christological Ecclesiology*.

between clergy and laity and displays ambivalence for strong conceptions of ecclesial office (one would be hard-pressed to find any appreciation for the term *laity* in all of Barth's corpus).[44] Later, Barth reiterated that such strong distinctions are mistaken, and that all members of the church, and not only professional clergy, are to live out a life and law of service. This service includes the interpretation of Scripture and the task of theology itself, which Barth states is not the precinct of a few, but of all members of the church.[45] Like Spener's picture of the conventicles, and perhaps even more radical than they, Barth conceives of the church not in institutional or sacerdotal terms but as a *Gemeinde* (i.e., community or fellowship) of persons who take responsibility for the study and teaching of Scripture and live this out in a life of obedience and service. Barth's picture of the priesthood of all believers translates the intentional nature of the conventicle into the law of service of the church itself which pertains to all of its members.[46] There can be no hard demarcation beyond that of function between pastors and "ordinary" church members, for "the community is not divided by this ordering into an active part and a passive, a teaching Church and a listening, Christians who have office and those who have not."[47] Barth can thereby write with Pietistic moral chastisement: "The statement: 'I am a mere layman and not a theologian,' is evidence not of humility but of indolence."[48] The church is a place for instruction in which every individual member need participate as a theologian among theologians, a member among members.[49] Indeed, Barth can have his own place for catechetical instruction which is intended for the purposes of asking questions, providing answers, and the receiving of biblical and theological training that cannot be accommodated in formal worship. Barth's description of this instruction is similar if not identical to Spener's description of his purposes for the small meetings and thus displays Barth's own unique description of a *collegia pietatis*.[50] In sum, both Spener and Barth take the Reformation principle of the priesthood of all believers with radical seriousness and provide guidelines for an informed and intentional church gathered around Scripture in which all are responsible for its interpretation and teaching. Spener and Barth share this central

---

44. Barth, *Unterricht in der christlichen Religion*, vol. 3: *Die Lehre von der Versöhnung/Die Lehre von der Erlösung, 1925/1926*, 372–75. Hereafter cited as *GD*, vol. 3.
45. *CD* IV/3.2, 870–71, 882.
46. See *CD* IV/2, 692–95; also *CD* III/4, 489–90.
47. *CD* III/4, 490.
48. *CD* IV/3.2, 871.
49. *CD* III/4, 497–99.
50. *CD* IV/3.2, 870–72; cf. Spener, *Pia Desideria*, 89–92.

and unwavering commitment to the priesthood of all believers that denies absolute distinctions between pastors and laity.[51]

This family resemblance between Spener's and Barth's ecclesial vision is not meant to deny very real differences between their ecclesiologies. Barth infamously divided Pietism from the church, stating that he would rather be with the church in hell than with the Pietists in heaven.[52] Yet this statement should not be given more weight than it merits. Barth certainly opposed any Pietistic calls for separatism or perfectionism. But Spener opposed such separatism as well, and he was not deluded into expecting or believing that a personal or corporate perfectionism was possible.[53] Spener shared with Barth an abhorrence of separatism and could say: "I confess honestly that with all my heart I have a horror of separation and even consider it better to be in a corrupted church than in none at all."[54] In the end, is this exclamation really so different than Barth's earlier sentiment of wanting to be at home with the church in hell than in a heaven of the Pietists' own making? Here too, Spener does not seem to fit Barth's Pietistic norm. Instead of a pure type in opposition to Barth, we have a family resemblance yet again. Moreover, even where the Pietists and Barth seem most divided, on the question of holiness and perfection, there are areas of overlap. For whereas Barth consistently rejected any hint of perfectionism which Spener may have denied but to which he believed all should aspire,[55] he nonetheless could speak in his first cycle of dogmatic lectures of the need for church discipline, so that while those in the church remain sinners, there is a need that justification be accompanied by sanctification and obedience.[56]

---

51. Spener, *Pia Desideria*, 92–95.

52. Barth, *Epistle to the Romans*, 337.

53. Spener, *Pia Desideria*, 80. Nevertheless, Spener did maintain that a type of perfection was to be striven for, and for those who failed to address sin, church discipline was an imperative (ibid., 81; see also 95). Yet here too, while Barth seems ambivalent and even acrimonious toward a personal drive to perfection, he could be just as hard on the complacency and cultural accommodation of the church in his own day, though for him, such failures were more theological and social than personal and moral.

54. Quoted in Stein, "Philipp Jakob Spener," 87. That Barth rejected separatism is evident in the *Romans* commentary (see 371). Barth could write in a letter of 1925: "Naturally it dare not be a *new* church that we want but rather the *church* in distinction to sects or even to our own personal prophesying. Also our *protest* against the church, so far as it was valid, was intended as specifically *by the church*" (*Revolutionary Theology*, 216).

55. For one example of Barth's rejection of any attempt to purge the church of hypocrites, see *GD* vol. 3, 366–67.

56. Ibid., 369–72.

Where Barth's conception of the church is closest to that of Pietism is in the centrality of mission for its identity. The rediscovery of the church's mission mandate in the modern era was in no small part due to Pietism, and its theological rediscovery by Barth was in no small way due to his discovery of its advocacy in Pietism. It was precisely on this question that Barth was the most openly appreciative of Pietism, for it was among Pietists and other "sects," Barth states, and not among the state churches of the magisterial Reformers, that the great truth of the indivisibility of church and mission, mission and church, was discovered and practiced.[57] Here Barth has his most positive if nonetheless qualified appraisal of Pietism, with Francke and the Pietism of Halle singled out for commendation, but none so praised as Zinzendorf and the Moravian community.[58] This last family resemblance in ecclesiology is therefore most noticeable in the centrality of mission for both Pietism and Barth with regard to understanding the church's calling, life, and very existence, a theme put into practice by Pietism throughout the world and thoroughly explored in the fourth volume of Barth's *CD*. So, in bringing full circle Barth's emphasis on mission with the commitment to an intentional community grounded upon the priesthood of all believers in a way that Pietists early and late could affirm, and thus bringing this section to a close, we end with Barth's own words: "We have to remember that every Christian is to be a missionary, a recruiting officer for new witnesses. If our congregations do not recognize this and act accordingly, they cannot be missionary congregations, and therefore they cannot be truly Christian."[59]

Pietism and Barth in Retrospect and Prospect

The preceding investigation of family resemblances between the convictions of Pietism and those of Barth should moderate the stark antithesis that is often placed between them, in no small part due to Barth's own expressed antipathy to Pietism, an antipathy in turn adopted by many. Pietism has been both lauded and chastised, identified as both "a narrow-minded moralistic, biblicistic flight from the world or as the most significant Christian movement in modern times."[60] It has in fact become the victim of a carica-

---

57. For Pietism's emphasis upon mission as central to the church's calling and existence, see Stoeffler, *Rise of Evangelical Pietism*, 2, and Pierard, "German Pietism," 285–95. For Barth's discovery of the central place of Pietism and the left wing of the Reformation for the rediscovery of the church's missionary duty, see *CD* IV/3.1, 25–38.

58. *CD* IV/3.1, 25.

59. *CD* III/4, 505.

60. Brecht and Lindberg, "Pietism," 219.

ture of itself, portrayed as ascetic, world-denying, and purely introspective. In reality, Pietism could produce a tradition that, while often moralistic and subjective in the worst senses of those terms, could also turn from inner experience to a public communal life that channeled its moral intensity into programs that impacted culture, addressed social problems, and effected missions in unparalleled ways.[61]

If this study has demonstrated points of overlap between the concerns of Pietism and those of Barth, it has done so with modest intent. As stated, there is no attempt here to produce a strong relationship of influence between classical Pietists and Barth. Certainly the subjective emphasis in Pietism had little or no appeal for Barth, and he had no sympathy for an unmediated religiosity at all, whether of the spiritualist or radical Pietist variety. He would reject all anti-ecclesial forms of Spiritualism, seeing the movements of Spiritualism, Mysticism, and Pietism as problematic siblings of one family. He would do the same for social movements that abandoned the church as well, such as any form of socialism which grew out of an identification of the kingdom of God with the present age and sacrificed the eschatological character of Christian faith.[62] Nor would Barth have any time for the emphasis for "life" over "doctrine"—a view that he saw as fundamentally mistaken.[63]

Yet in spite of such significant differences, there are resemblances between ecclesial Pietism and Barth in the areas of Christ, Scripture, and church that mark out places of real if qualified agreement, for between Barth and Spener in particular there is a happy convergence of a commitment to a church centered on Christ, grounded upon Scripture, indebted to but not imprisoned by its confessions, intentional in its existence towards the world, and not tied or captive to cultural or civil respectability. Where Pietism displayed affinities to Spiritualism and to introspective religious subjectivity, Barth opposed it. But it was also the case that where Pietism remained grounded in objectivity—with regard to the external Word of Scripture, the eschatological nature of God's relation to history, and the church and its practices—Barth had overlapping concerns with those of Pietism.

Most surprising of all, Barth himself could against all expectations even make a place for the introspection and self-examination so derided in Pietism. In the final volumes of *CD*, Barth could quote August Tholuck,

---

61. See Crowner and Christianson, "Introduction," 7–10.

62. See Barth's discussion of this and his own complicated history with the Blumhardts and the socialist movement in *CD* II/1, 633–38.

63. See *CD* I/2, 254.

the nineteenth-century Pietist of the German Awakening, in a way that no doubt must have surprised many a reader:

> At every moment and in every situation we have to ask soberly and honestly: Who am I, and where do I stand, and what am I doing, and by what am I compelled? How is it with me? "Brother, how is it with thine heart?" as the ageing Tholuck privately used to ask his students, rather penetratingly, but, rightly understood, very relevantly. And again: At any given moment and in any given situation in my life, how is it with my response to the grace and commandment of God?[64]

Barth could not have said this directly after his break with Liberalism. But he could here. Just as Barth at the end of life could charitably look to the concerns of Schleiermacher, if not his solutions, so Barth could take up the concerns of Pietism, even if they themselves were taken up in a new key. Truly, they were in a new key, for Barth was ever careful that the subjective concerns of self-examination could never be divorced from and could only follow the larger context of Christology and the centrality of Christ as the sanctified one, and in quoting Tholuck's question again in a different context later in *CD*, this is quite clear.[65] Nevertheless, there is without question a concern and commitment to address these Pietist themes in the later Barth, such that their questions are honored and respected, even if placed in a larger dogmatic framework. Whether or not all Pietists, historic or contemporary, would agree with Barth's own answers to their questions is of course another matter. Barth both embraced and qualified his self-chosen moniker as a Zinzendorfian. But in light of Barth's mature attempt to respect and answer these questions, perhaps Barth himself might be deemed to be a "Pietist of a higher order."

Final Reflections

A nuanced evaluation of Barth's relation to Pietism might lead us to consider anew Barth's relation to Evangelicalism as well. There are two ramifications that we might discern in light of the conclusions made above.

First, any discussion of Evangelicalism and Barth need not and should not restrict itself to areas of Evangelicalism that are usually identified with its strictly confessional and more scholastic traditions. Barth's relationship to Evangelicalism of this type could be rocky (e.g., the Westminster theology

---

64. *CD* IV/1, 497.
65. *CD* IV/3.2, 677–80.

of Cornelius van Til). Yet, with regard to understandings of Scripture and confessions in particular, Barth may be more amenable to Evangelicalism if seen in the light of its Pietistic traditions and not solely in terms of those that espouse a more rigid subscriptionism as heirs of Protestant Orthodoxy, whether of the Lutheran or Reformed variety. The future of Evangelicalism may thus find in Barth an ally, but not an ally that some might expect or even desire. Moreover, if such a nuanced estimation of Barth's relation to Pietism has validity, then comparisons between Barth and Pietism conducted by evangelicals need to be based upon an informed evaluation of the relation between a complex and subtle thinker and a complex and diverse tradition, not between a theologian dismissed through tired clichés and a concept essentially defined such that it is ruled dubious by its very definition, a tradition portrayed as a caricature of itself. Such things will not do. Perhaps the simplistic caricatures (but not informed criticisms) of Pietism should now be laid to rest for good, and this should be done for Barth, too.[66]

The second ramification pertains not strictly to a comparison between Barth and Evangelicalism, but to an understanding of Evangelicalism itself. For Evangelicalism, like Pietism, is also a contested concept, in no small way due to the confluence of various traditions that have formed it (English Puritanism and Continental Pietism being two of the most important, and these themselves distinct but with their own areas of overlap).[67] If so, then the attempt to give essentialist definitions here, too, falls short. What we have in Evangelicalism are various traditions not always directly related or derived from one another, but traditions able to recognize shared convictions and concerns between them. Such different traditions, both those primarily confessional and those primarily Pietistic, bear family resemblances to one another. These traditions cannot be subsumed into one another but neither can they be entirely separated. Barth's essentialist understanding of Pietism could not do justice to its complexity and diversity, but neither can

---

66. Estimations of Barth's criticisms of Pietism may thus not only reflect how one views Pietism but how one views Barth's own concerns. Some might laud Barth as perceiving the deficiencies of anthropomorphic religion, seeing Pietism as the true forerunner of the turn from God to the human subject celebrated in Romanticism. Others might criticize Barth for a pneumatological deficiency or an underdeveloped theology of the third article for which Pietism is an answer. Whether this is really fair to either Pietism or Barth is itself a question of importance, but not one that can be taken up here.

67. That Puritanism and Pietism can no longer be seen as isolated traditions even if they can be distinguished is made evident not only in the scholarship of Stoeffler but also that of Ward—see his *Early Evangelicalism*. This conclusion is now generally accepted in historical scholarship—for example, see Noll, *Rise of Evangelicalism*, esp. 50–75. For Stoeffler's own comment on the pluriform influences behind American Christianity and both the virtues and vices of Pietism, see *Continental Pietism*, 266–71.

an essentialist definition of Evangelicalism that sees it solely as the product of Protestant Orthodoxy or Reformed confessionalism truly capture Evangelicalism's diverse pedigree and character.

American Evangelicalism is the product of a cross-fertilization of confessional and Pietistic traditions. The cross-fertilization of English Puritanism (with its Reformed roots and doctrinal proclivities) and Continental Pietism (with is Lutheran roots and experiential proclivities) produced seeds that blew across the Atlantic to germinate in the soil of America, producing the mixed harvest of New England Puritan Orthodoxy but also the Great Awakening and later revivalism. This was a world of Whitefield and Wesley, Zinzendorf and Edwards, a world where the Puritan Cotton Mather could write and communicate appreciably with the Pietist Francke.[68] No longer can these traditions be seen as strictly isolated and neatly contained and circumscribed ones; they are not parallel lines that never touch, but strands crisscrossing in a tightly-braided rope connecting the Old World and the New. A rope tightly woven cannot be neatly undone, nor can its identity, or even strength, be isolated to one strand, for as Wittgenstein relates, "the strength of the thread does not reside in the fact that some one fibre runs through its whole length, but in the overlapping of many fibres."[69]

Modern Evangelicalism is indeed a multi-braided rope of many strands, its unity found not in a single narrative but in a weaving of various narratives recognized as similar through resemblances and common themes.[70] No wonder that some both on the Reformed and Wesleyan wings of this movement have thought that perhaps it best to abandon the term Evangelicalism altogether. But that is only to move the question back a step, for "Reformed" is also a contested concept. Is Barth a Reformed theologian? Van Til might give one answer; G. C. Berkouwer may give another.

The future of a theological conversation is thus informed by historical narratives we tell ourselves—but it is and need not be defined by them. This is as true for conversations pertaining to Evangelicalism's evaluation and appropriation of Barth's theology as it is for conversations of the future (and meaningfulness) of Evangelicalism's own identity. Typologies order

---

68. For the interconnections of all of these figures within the New World, see Ward, *The Protestant Evangelical Awakening*.

69. *Philosophical Investigations*, §67. One is also reminded of Eccl 4:12. Wittgenstein himself intertwines the illustrations of family resemblances and those of a rope here in the *Investigations*, and so we may as well: while some may try to write the history of Evangelicalism by excising Pietistic influences, this is like someone cutting embarrassing cousins out of family photos. They remain part of the family. One can try to form a new family, and one need not invite the cousins to future family gatherings, but one cannot change the past—only try to rewrite it.

70. Collins, *Evangelical Moment*, 19–22.

experience, and thus they may be necessary, but neat and tidy typologies imposed upon history can classify traditions and schools and movements in ways that often distort as much as illumine the past. As with so many areas of historical investigation, in Evangelicalism we are not left with clean lines of genetic descent, but crisscrossing and overlapping patterns of similarities. Perhaps the future of theology thus belongs more to Wittgenstein than to Plato. And in the face of increasing secularization, perhaps some pause to evangelical infighting is opportune and need not betray doctrinal indifference. We should at least take time to ponder Ward's conclusion: "Whether either tradition [Pietist or Orthodox] can excogitate an effective approach to populations with no smoldering embers of faith to revive is doubtful . . ."[71] The reason that we need not in the end despair over this prognosis is due to a promise that God himself upholds and both Spener and Barth could claim, for both knew that it is no human hand that fans the flame.

---

71. Ward, *Protestant Evangelical Awakening*, 355.

Bibliography

Barth, Karl. *The Epistle to the Romans*. Translated by Edwyn C. Hoskyns. New York: Oxford University Press, 1977.
———. "Gespräch mit Vertretern der Gemeinschaften 1959." In *Gespräche 1959-1962*, edited by Eberhard Busch, 13-41. Zürich: Theologischer Verlag Zürich, 1995.
———. "Gespräch mit Vertretern der Herrnhuter Brüdergemeine 1960." In *Gespräche 1959-1962*, edited by Eberhard Busch, 124-157. Zürich: Theologischer Verlag Zürich, 1995.
———. "Interview von Fr. Klopfenstein (30.4.1966)." In *Gespräche 1964-1968*, edited by Eberhard Busch, 242-47. Zürich: Theologischer Verlag Zürich, 1996.
———. *Protestant Theology in the Nineteenth Century: Its Background and History*. Translated by Brian Cozens and John Bowden. Valley Forge, PA: Judson, 1973.
———. *Revolutionary Theology in the Making: Barth-Thurneysen Correspondence, 1914-1925*. Translated and edited by James D. Smart. Richmond: John Knox, 1964.
———. *The Theology of John Calvin*. Translated by Geoffrey W. Bromiley. Grand Rapids: Eerdmans, 1995.
———. *The Theology of the Reformed Confessions, 1923*. Translated by Darrell L. Guder and Judith J. Guder. Louisville: Westminster John Knox, 2002.
———. *The Theology of Schleiermacher: Lectures at Göttingen, Winter Semester of 1923-24*. Edited by Dietrich Ritschl. Translated by Geoffrey W. Bromiley. Grand Rapids: Eerdmans, 1982.
———. *Unterricht in der christlichen Religion*. Vol. 3, *Die Lehre von der Versöhnung/Die Lehre von der Erlösung, 1925/1926*. Edited by Hinrich Stoevesandt. Zürich: Theologischer Verlag Zürich, 2003.
Barth, Karl, and Rudolf Bultmann. *Karl Barth-Rudolf Bultmann Letters*. Edited by Bernd Jaspert. Translated by Geoffrey W. Bromiley. Edinburgh: T. & T. Clark, 1982.
Bender, Kimlyn J. *Karl Barth's Christological Ecclesiology*. Burlington, VT: Ashgate, 2005.
Brecht, Martin, and Carter Lindberg. "Pietism." In *The Encyclopedia of Christianity*, edited by Erwin Fahlbusch et al., translated by Geoffrey W. Bromiley, 4:218-24. Grand Rapids: Eerdmans, 2005.
Busch, Eberhard. *Karl Barth and the Pietists: The Young Karl Barth's Critique of Pietism and Its Response*. Translated by Daniel W. Bloesch. Downers Grove, IL: InterVarsity, 2004.
Collins, Kenneth J. *The Evangelical Moment: The Promise of an American Religion*. Grand Rapids: Baker Academic, 2005.
Collins Winn, Christian T. *"Jesus is Victor!": The Significance of the Blumhardts for the Theology of Karl Barth*. Eugene, OR: Pickwick, 2009.
Crowner, David, and Gerald Christianson. "Introduction." In *The Spirituality of the German Awakening*, edited and translated by David Crowner and Gerald Christianson, 5-41. New York: Paulist, 2003.
Dayton, Donald W. "The Pietist Theological Critique of Biblical Inerrancy." In *Evangelicals and Scripture: Tradition, Authority, and Hermeneutics*, edited by Vincent Bacote et al., 76-89. Downers Grove, IL: InterVarsity, 2004.
Erb, Peter, ed. *The Pietists: Selected Writings*. New York: Paulist, 1983.

Lindberg, Carter. "Introduction." In *The Pietist Theologians: An Introduction to Theology in the Seventeenth and Eighteenth Centuries*, edited by Carter Lindberg, 1–20. Oxford: Blackwell, 2005.

———, ed. *The Pietist Theologians: An Introduction to Theology in the Seventeenth and Eighteenth Centuries*. Oxford: Blackwell, 2005.

McCormack, Bruce. "The Being of Holy Scripture Is in Becoming: Karl Barth in Conversation with American Evangelical Criticism." In *Evangelicals and Scripture: Tradition, Authority, and Hermeneutics*, edited by Vincent Bacote et al., 55–75. Downers Grove, IL: InterVarsity, 2004.

Noll, Mark. *The Rise of Evangelicalism: The Age of Edwards, Whitefield and the Wesleys*. Downers Grove, IL: InterVarsity, 2003.

Olson, Roger. "Pietism: Myths and Realities." In *The Pietist Impulse in Christianity*, edited by Christian T. Collins Winn et al., 269–84. Eugene, OR: Pickwick, 2011.

Pierard, Richard V. "German Pietism as a Major Factor in the Beginnings of Modern Protestant Missions." In *The Pietist Impulse in Christianity*, edited by Christian T. Collins Winn et al., 285–95. Eugene, OR: Pickwick, 2011.

Spener, Phillipp Jakob. *Pia Desideria*. Translated and edited by Theodore G. Tappert. Philadelphia: Fortress, 1964.

Stein, K. James. "Phillipp Jakob Spener: 1635–1705." In *The Pietist Theologians: An Introduction to Theology in the Seventeenth and Eighteenth Centuries*, edited by Carter Lindberg, 84–99. Oxford: Blackwell, 2005.

———. *Phillipp Jakob Spener: Pietist Patriarch*. Chicago: Covenant, 1986.

Stoeffler, F. Ernest, ed. *Continental Pietism and Early American Christianity*. Grand Rapids: Eerdmans, 1976.

———. *German Pietism during the Eighteenth Century*. Leiden: Brill, 1973.

———. *The Rise of Evangelical Pietism*. Leiden: Brill, 1965.

Strom, Jonathan. "The Common Priesthood and the Pietist Challenge for Ministry and Laity." In *The Pietist Impulse in Christianity*, edited by Christian T. Collins Winn et al., 42–58. Eugene, OR: Pickwick, 2011.

Thompson, Alan J. "A Pietist Critique of Inerrancy? J. A. Bengel's Gnomon as a Test Case." *Journal of the Evangelical Theological Society* 47 (2004) 71–88.

Wallman, Johannes. "Johann Arndt (1555–1621)." In *The Pietist Theologians: An Introduction to Theology in the Seventeenth and Eighteenth Centuries*, 21–37. Oxford: Blackwell, 2005.

Ward, W R. *Early Evangelicalism: A Global Intellectual History, 1670–1789*. Cambridge: Cambridge University Press, 2006.

———. *The Protestant Evangelical Awakening*. Cambridge: Cambridge University Press, 1992.

Webster, John. *Barth's Early Theology*. New York: T. & T. Clark, 2005.

Wittgenstein, Ludwig. *Philosophical Investigations*. 3rd. Ed. trans. G. E. M. Anscombe. Englewood Cliffs, NJ: Prentice Hall, 1958.

Part II

Reconceiving Christian Experience and Practice

4

Christ in Us

The Hope of Glory or the Sentimentality of a "Bohemian Private Enterprise"?[1]

Barth, Pietists, and Pentecostals

Terry L. Cross

Introduction: *Pectus facit theologum—* The Heart Makes the Theologian

"How about your heart—is it right with God?"[2] One might expect a Pentecostal or evangelical origin to these words, and this is the case. Pentecostal songwriter and minister Bennie Triplett penned this famous gospel song in the 1950s. At about the same time yet quite unexpectedly, words similar to

---

1. This phrase, "the sentimentality of a Bohemian private enterprise" (*oder auch sentimentalen oder auch zigeunerhaften Privatunternehmen zu werden*), comes from Barth's words in *CD* IV/1, 756; cf. *KD*, 845. In a discussion of Pietism and the appropriate way to understand justification by faith as *pro me* within the context of *pro nobis*, Barth says, "It [such faith] will therefore be prevented from becoming a morose or humdrum or sentimental or Bohemian private enterprise." Some aspects of this chapter were presented at the English-German Colloquium in New Testament/Das English-Deutsche Kolloquium für Neues Testament, Tübingen Universität, under the title, "CHRISTUS PRAESENS or CHRISTUS OTIOSUS? The Role of *extra nos* and *in nobis* in Relation to the *unio cum Christo* in the Theology of John Calvin, Wilhelm Herrmann, and Karl Barth," June 2, 2008.

2. Words and music by a Church of God minister, Bennie S. Triplett (1954).

these came from the pen of Swiss theologian Karl Barth. "How are things with your heart?" Barth asked people to consider.³ Citing a "virtuoso of the heart,"⁴ Pietistic theologian August Tholuck, Barth described this nineteenth-century Halle professor going about "most privately" from student to student in their rooms, asking, "*Bruder, wie steht es mit deinem Herzen?*" (Brother, how is it with your heart?).⁵ One could almost hear Billy Graham asking the same question to crowds throughout Europe in the 1950s. Such a question is a centerpiece of evangelical and Pentecostal mission today. Is Barth the 1950s theological counterpart to Billy Graham? Is Barth really concerned about the inner workings of the heart?

While he met with Billy Graham twice and heard him speak at a stadium in Basel once, Barth did not want to become such an evangelist—namely, one that offers the gospel at gunpoint.⁶ As a theologian known for his emphasis in the 1920s–1940s on the *objective* work of Christ *outside of us*, how does Barth arrive in the 1950s at this *subjective* "heart theology" that points to the work of Christ *inside of us*? It is this apparent shift in thought toward a more Pietistic—perhaps even evangelical/Pentecostal—view of the subjective reception and work of Christ *in us* that we will examine in this chapter, attempting to show some reasons for Barth's movement towards these Pietistic "concerns" in his later years.⁷ Twice in his writings, Barth cited a

---

3. Barth, *KD* IV/1, 554; *CD* IV/1, 497. Barth also refers to this question and to Tholuck's question in *KD* IV/3.2, 777; *CD* IV/3.2, 677; and in Barth, *Evangelical Theology*, 83.

4. Barth, "Die dogmatische Prinzipienlehre bei Wilhelm Herrmann, 1925," 589. Barth mentions that Herrmann worked as a secretary to Tholuck, "*dem großen Herzenvirtuosen.*"

5. *KD* IV/1, 554.

6. Barth had a very favorable impression of Graham when he met with him personally on two occasions in August 1960, but he felt very different about his influence on the crowds when he heard him preach in St. Jacob stadium in Basel. "I was quite horrified. He acted like a madman and what he presented was certainly not the gospel. . . . It was the gospel at gun-point." See Busch, *Karl Barth*, 446. In conversations with evangelical groups, Barth rehearsed a similar reflection. "As I heard him [Graham] I said, 'That was not a happy message; that was a pistol shot in the air [*ein Pistolenschießen*]. It appealed to the people in a forcible manner—you must, you should! It was a legalistic beating whereby I could not grant that it was essentially 'evangelization.' It was preaching of the law, it was not a message that brought joy. It had people frightened. Threats—this always makes an impression. People much rather want to be frightened than to be delighted. The more one makes hell hot for them, the more they run [to the altar]." See Barth, "Gespräche mit Methodistenpredigern, 16 May 1961," 180–81. Translation mine.

7. *KD* IV/2, vii. Cf. *CD* IV/2, x. Barth notes that he has tried in this volume to deal with the "concerns" of the Pietists and "Evangelical groups" (*dem Anliegen unserer Pietisten und Gemeinschaftsleute*). I have formulated that concern in a more focused manner—what is it that happens inside of us as believers in this time and place?

slogan from Pietism of the nineteenth century: *pectus facit theologum*—the heart makes the theologian.[8] Was he approving this slogan—recommending it for himself and others? Was this Swiss Reformed theologian actually an "evangelical" in the North American sense of the word?[9]

Church Dogmatics IV/4 and Gespräche (Conversations)

Over the years, Barth has been characterized as emphasizing the transcendence of God to such a degree that the human being was considered unduly insignificant in actions related to salvation, conversion, or sanctification.[10] As he ramped his way up to the fourth volume on the doctrine of reconciliation, Barth signaled some definitive yet subtle changes in his view of what happens *within* the human being in the salvation event. He saw this development as a progression of the inner logic of his Christological thinking.[11]

A. "Touched" by God: The Real Change in Us

In *CD* IV/4, readers notice a distinct difference from what has been written in the previous volumes of the *CD* IV/1–3. Barth notices this also. In the preface, he comments that he will turn to an entirely other line in this fragment: "And so along the whole way, [this volume] was to handle Christian (human!) work in its corresponding and therefore autonomous character in comparison to the divine work of reconciliation outlined in IV/1–3."[12] Previously, Barth had accented the divine side—the initiative of reconciliation

---

8. Barth, *Die christliche Dogmatik im Emtwurf,* 116; Barth, *Die protestantische Theologie,* 466.

9. The word *evangelisch* is a Reformation term to describe groups or churches stemming from the magisterial reformers—Lutheran or Reformed churches, in other words. It is possible, however, to translate this German word as "Evangelical" in English. Barth was *evangelisch,* but not *evangelical* (i.e., evangelical in the North American sense of the term). See Dayton, "Foreword," x.

10. For a discussion of several of these, see Klooster, "Aspects," 6–14.

11. It should be noted that Barth felt he had not changed in the fundamentals of his theology, but only in organizing its presentation and relationship. See *KD* IV/2, vii; *CD* IV/2, x. "Insightful companions of my journey up to now will surely make note that there is precisely now not a break with my basic viewpoint that I held since my departure from Liberalism, but rather a logically consistent change in its blossoming." Translation mine. Space does not allow us to consider the relation of Barth to Pietism, but our comments throughout arise from the excellent study by Eberhard Busch, *Karl Barth and the Pietists.*

12. Barth, *KD* IV/4, ix. Translation mine. For some reason, Bromiley's translation leaves out the exclamation point after the word "human"!

belongs to God alone. Yet there seems to be something different intimated with Barth's insertion of "human!" at this point.[13] Barth seems intent on having the reader *hear* his emphatic shift in tone to the human side of redemption—to what happens in the human heart.

Upon reading the first segment of *CD* IV/4, one is struck by how much Barth explains the work of God *in* us. It is clear that the 'warning' he offered in the preface was justified. As an illustration of this turn towards the human, the phrase *in nobis* is used eleven times in this brief fragment (alongside the contrasting *extra nos* and *pro nobis*). Previous uses of this phrase in the *CD* occur in explanations of Roman Catholic dogma (e.g., *KD* IV/1, 90: *in nobis sine nobis; in nobis cum nobis*) or Calvin's view of the Spirit dwelling in us (e.g., *KD* IV/2, 573: *in nobis habitat*). In no other previous writing by Barth can I find such an extensive use for *in nobis*, especially if one narrows the focus to what happens *in us* by the power of the Spirit. My point is that some of Barth's turn towards Zinzendorf and finally his conversations with the Pietists assisted in his development of language to speak decisively about *Christus in nobis* in *CD* IV/4. Rather than being a curious oddity at the end of Barth's life, *CD* IV/4 suggests a turn that started in the mid-1940s when he reconsidered Zinzendorf and Pietism.[14] It was complemented by his turn

---

13. *CD* IV/4 contains several articles that Barth wrote for Festschriften as well as material sketched for his *Dogmatics*. The "fragment" with which we are most concerned will be the one to honor Ernst Wolf. See Barth, "Extra Nos—Pro Nobis—In Nobis," 15–27. This is transferred over to *CD* IV/4 with transitional material before it and behind it. According to Busch, it was probably written between 1959 and 1961, and offered during his winter lectures. It is very difficult to piece together the precise timing of this document since Barth also rewrote some of the lectures. See the editors' discussion in their preface to Barth, *Christian Life*, x–xi. It appears he lectured on the *KD* IV/4 material in the winter semester of 1959–60 (especially on §74, which contains "Ethics as a Task of the Doctrine of Reconciliation"). He met with the Pietists for conversation *before* delivering these lectures (October 6, 1959), but probably *after* they had been written during the summer break. He rewrote the substance of many of these lectures later on before publication (1967). However, the section with which we are most concerned (§75, "Baptism as the Foundation of the Christian Life" in which is contained the Festschrift chapter and the section on baptism with the Spirit) he seems to have offered as lectures in the summer semester 1960. The point is that while he engages in these dialogues with Pietists (between 1959 and 1961) he is writing, lecturing, and rewriting his *CD* IV/4 lectures. It seems a reasonable conjecture to posit some relation between the conversations and the final outcome of the *CD* IV/4 material. See also Busch, *Karl Barth*, 443–45.

14. In 1946 and 1947, Barth prepared for publication his history of Protestant theology. In it he surveyed Pietism and also reconsidered the Christocentrism of Zinzendorf with much praise. See Barth, *Protestant Theology in the Nineteenth Century*; cf. Barth, *Die protestantische Theologie*. A Pietist pastor, Friedrich Gärtner, also noticed this change. See Gärtner, "Karl Barth und Zinzendorf," 3–51. In 1947, Barth worked through the Heidelberg Catechism and published form *Learning Jesus Christ through*

away from baptism as a sacrament and *means* of grace and towards the idea of baptism—only fully developed in his *Church Dogmatics IV/4*—as a *human response* to God's grace. This coincides precisely with his more fully developed conceptuality for the work of Christ *in us* by the Spirit.

In the first section of this volume, titled "Baptism with the Holy Spirit," Barth clarifies any confusion readers may have held concerning the role of the human being in responding to God's gracious act:

> It is not enough, then, to describe this possibility [of becoming a friend of God instead of an enemy] as one whose actualisation, while it affects man supremely [*zwar aufs höchste anginge*] by setting him in the light of a new, gracious, and consequently positive divine judgment, does not do more than affect him, simply touching him from without [*ihn selbst aber nur von außen*], or strictly speaking not touching him at all [*ja genau genommen gar nicht berührte*], since he is as it were sealed off [*eine Glasglocke abgesichert bliebe*] against it, and is not touched and altered by it in his inner being [*von ihr nicht erreicht, in seinem Sein durch sie nicht verändert würde*]. On this view, how can one claim man seriously—and this is our theme—as one who for his part is a faithful partner in the covenant of grace?[15]

Surely the power of the resurrection from the eternal realm must "touch" and "alter" humans in this realm of history! Yet Barth inserts the claim that we cannot view God as offering humans some "magical infusion of supernatural powers [*als eine Art Magie zu beschreibenden—Einflösßung übernatürlicher Kräfte*] by whose proper use man can do what he cannot do in his own strength, namely, be faithful again to the faithful God."[16] So, on the one hand, Barth speaks in a very Pentecostal manner of God truly "touching" believers and changing their lives; on the other hand, he clarifies that this touch from God cannot be viewed as some "thing" that humans can manipulate in order to live righteously before God.

---

the *Heidelberg Catechism*. In it are the first hints that I can find in his writing that he has opened himself up to begin speaking of Christ *in us*.

15. CD IV/4, 4; KD IV/4, 4. In a related matter, Barth uses the phrase *"in uns"* some ninety-seven times in *Die kirchliche Dogmatik* (KD), vol. IV (on reconciliation). It is used thirty-one times in KD IV/1 (1953) and thirty-three times in KD IV/2 (1955). Further, it is used twenty-four times in KD IV/3, part 1 (1959) and seven times in KD IV/3, part 2 (1959). In none of these instances *before* KD IV/4 is there a *concrete* expression of what is actually occurring within human beings at regeneration or sanctification. The phrase is used only two times in KD IV/4.

16. CD IV/4, 4; KD IV/4, 5.

Order here is crucial for Barth's understanding of this event within humans. Before humans turn towards God, there must be an antecedent "divine turning" towards them. God of his own free will has chosen to turn towards humanity and therefore the basis of the Christian life always must have its accent on the divine initiative.[17] It is a "divine change" (*göttlichen Wendung*) in which God moves humans from the impossible to the possible, from faith to faith.[18] If unfaithful humans are to become faithful to God, "a change must come over humans themselves."[19] It must be "such an inner change [*innere Veränderung*] by virtue of which one becomes a different person so that as this different person in freedom, from within and by his/her own resolve, thinks, acts, and behaves differently from before."[20] Evangelicals and Pentecostals revel in the use of such language that depicts inner transformation!

It is precisely here that Pentecostals and evangelicals today could learn something from Barth's stalwart stance on the importance of emphasizing the objective act of Christ in the cross-resurrection event. All too frequently, salvation is considered something that we possess—a gift from God's grace, to be sure, but a gift that *we now own*! It's mine! Barth chides a group of Moravian Pietists precisely against this point: "However, it would be incorrect now to sink into arrogance and say, 'I have it!'"[21] Neither God nor God's gift to humans through Jesus Christ becomes our "possession"—a "direct given" (to cite the 1922 *Römerbrief*).[22] Barth's words remind us that we do not possess God or God's gifts in our paltry human hands to shape as we will.

B. The Ground of Our Reconciliation

With a flurry of Latin terms describing the Christian life and Christ's work that establishes it, Barth moves forward to speak boldly of Christ *in us*— with the proviso that the *Christus in nobis* is grounded on the *Christ extra*

---

17. *CD* IV/4, 6.
18. *KD* IV/4, 18; *CD* IV/4, 17.
19. *KD* IV/4, 19. Translation mine.
20. Ibid. Translation mine.
21. Barth, "Gespräche mit der Herrnhuter," 144. Translation mine.
22. Barth says clearly in 1922, "There is and remains the determination of the new subject, the predication 'we are—new humans!' This predication is always grounded dialectically, indirectly, and through faith alone: '*through his blood*' we have been declared righteous, '*as enemies*' we are 'reconciled with God through the death of his Son,' and at no moment may this dialectical presupposition harden and petrify into a direct given." See Barth, *Der Römerbrief* (1922), 141. Translation mine.

nos. As it had since 1922, the *Christus extra nos* continues to lead the way through the discussion. There is nothing new with this phrase or idea in Barth's theology. However, what is unique for *CD* (as far as I have been able to discern to this point) is the juxtaposing of *in nobis* alongside of the *extra nos*.[23] The only place where Barth had come close to juxtaposing *in nobis* and *extra nos* was in an address to a pastors' conference in Neuchâtel on October 5, 1910.[24] In describing the relation between faith and history—subjective and objective aspects of belief—Barth says,

> The method of Christian faith knows only a Christ outside of us [*Christus außer uns*]. It does not know any Christ in himself. It knows only a Christ in us [*Christus in uns*]. One cannot be astonished by the contradictory proposition between the first and third sentence. It is no unscientific evasion [*Ausflucht*] into some edifying, but factually necessary justification.[25]

How does one overcome the apparent individualism and subjectivity of this "method of faith"? Barth suggests that the personality of Christ has an "affect" upon the inner life of believers in such a way that it produces its own "objectivity." He proposes that faith connects believers to revelation and produces the object to our consciousness.

> For the truth of the feeling [*die Wahrheit des Gefühls*], everything—*justificatio* and the life derived from it—depends on the

---

23. The only other place that I have found this juxtaposition with *precisely these terms* is in a *Gespräch* in November 1962—after this segment of the fragment had been composed. Barth responded to several Zürich doctoral students who questioned him regarding Ebeling and Bultmann in November 1962. He noted that Bultmann seems to work without a concept of "encounter" (*Begegnung*) and Ebeling seems to miss having a "concrete object" (*einen Gegenstand konkret*). Encounter requires an "object" (*Gegenstand*). For Ebeling, everything that is "object" is "already contained in faith." Barth insists that encounter requires two—God and humans. He concludes, "At any rate, I lay great emphasis on the '*extra nos*' because from there the '*pro nobis*' and the '*in nobis*' first obtain their importance." See Barth, "Gespräche mit Züricher Promovenden, 19 November 1962," 399–404, 401–2. Translation mine. Cf. also Barth's comments on Bultmann's method of demythologization. Barth claims that there must be an objective side in the history of Jesus Christ in which he is different and distant from all humans. Yet Jesus' death and resurrection occur as events within time and space. If it is only some subjective determination of human existence, then what assurance do we have that this is not all in our heads? Barth concludes, "Then there is no Christ *for* us and *over* us to substantiate the existence of Christ *in* us" (*Learning Jesus Christ*, 75).

24. Barth, "Der christliche Glaube und die Geschichte, 1910," 149–211. This lecture also appeared originally in print in 1912 in *Schweizerische Theologische Zeitschrift*. Hereafter, I shall cite the page number of the Gesamtausgabe edition first, followed by the page number of the journal article from 1912.

25. Ibid., 188 (56). Translation mine.

fact that Christ is outside of us, and for the truth of the perspective [*die Wahrheit der Anschauung*], everything—*fides* and the experience derived from it—depends on the fact that Christ is in us. The Christ outside of us is the Christ in us. The effectual [*wirksame*] history is the effected [*gewirkte*] faith.[26]

Here is a clear depiction of the experiential role that Christ in us plays in the faith process for the "liberal" Barth. "The Christ outside us is the Christ in us!"

With Barth's break from Liberal Protestantism in the next decade, the *extra nos* becomes accented and the *in nobis* almost disappears![27] Is its reappearance here in *CD* IV/4 a sign of Barth's return to Protestant Liberal thinking? Of course not. It is rather a logical progression of his Christological thinking. Having laid stress in *CD* IV/1–3 on the external, objective, and forensic act of God in the history of Jesus Christ (*Christus extra nos*), Barth believes he can now turn to the internal, subjective, and transformative act of God in the life-history of human beings (*Christus in nobis*) without fear of readers confusing the two or laying too much stress on the subjective element. The ground of our reconciliation can never be based on our inner psychical movements—as if a microscope were attached to them and Christian belief were merely a description of their fluctuations. However, once the reality of Jesus' history has been applied to our hearts by the Spirit, we can expect a change to occur in the human heart.

George Hunsinger has said with regard to Barth's doctrine of reconciliation and more specifically "justification" in *CD* IV/1, "The Spirit does not signify, as in so many Spirit-oriented Christologies, that salvation consists exclusively or chiefly in effecting something *in nobis*, whether religious experiences, renewed dispositions, or a new mode of being in the world. On the contrary, the presence and power of the Spirit are understood to attest what the incarnate Word of God has done for our salvation apart from us (*extra nos*) and to mediate our participation in it by faith (*participatio Christi*)."[28] While this is true as far as it goes, it seems that the description of

---

26. Ibid., 193 (58). Translation mine.

27. The use of "Christ in us" or "*Christus in nobis*" is almost nonexistent before the late 1940s in Barth's writings. Emphasis is on God's objective work in Christ that takes place *outside us* and on our behalf (*pro nobis*). When "in us" or "*in nobis*" is used, it commonly has connections to quotes from Luther, Calvin, or Protestant Orthodoxy. When reflecting on these ideas in 1956, Barth suggested that he had turned the rudder of the ship too hard, too fast: "redemption was viewed as consisting in the abolition of the creatureliness of the creature, the swallowing of immanence by transcendence" (Barth, "Humanity of God," 43).

28. Hunsinger, *Disruptive Grace*, 157–58.

Barth's understanding of the Spirit and the work of Christ *in us* is a rather lopsided account with all of the focus landing on the objective reality of Christ *extra nos*. With the discussion in *CD* IV/4, we have the balancing side of *Christus in nobis*, whereby the Spirit applies the change in a human's status wrought by the history of Jesus Christ not only to the eternal realm (where we are considered "a new being"), but also to the physical, temporal realm (where *Christus in nobis* transforms us so that we are freed to be faithful to God).

But how does that history *then and there* become relevant and life-changing for us *here and now*? Returning to *CD* IV/4, we read a surprisingly frank statement that opens our understanding of this event: "If something took place *extra nos*, it is an event which is not merely distant in time and space, but also completely different from all our own possibilities and actualities.... How can that which [Jesus Christ] was and did *extra nos* become an event *in nobis*?"[29] In order to answer this critical question and move forward his argument, Barth begins by explaining we cannot view *in nobis* here as an "appendage [*ein unselbständiger Annex*], a mere reflection [*als bloße Spiegelung*] of the act of liberation accomplished by Jesus Christ in His history, and hence *extra nos*. Jesus Christ, then, is fundamentally alone as the only subject truly at work."[30] We also cannot view *in nobis* as if this means the human being *alone* is the subject of the action in "his transformation into a Christian."[31] Jesus' history is only useful as an example. These attempted "solutions" to the question of how Jesus' history then can be effective *in nobis* now both possess the problem of coming at the issue "from outside and with the aid of an alien concept of unity. They do not allow the matter to be its own interpreter."[32]

So how are we to understand this act of God in us? Here the ordering of the Latin phrases shows the way. Jesus' history is a unique history; it has power over humanity. "Having taken place *extra nos*, it also works *in nobis*, introducing a new being of every man. It certainly took place *extra nos*. Yet it took place, not for its own sake, but *pro nobis*."[33] Jesus Christ was there in our place—in the place of those who had been unfaithful to God—being faithful to fulfill the covenant for us. "But if he acts *extra nos pro nobis*,

---

29. *CD* IV/4, 18; *KD* IV/4, 19–20.

30. *CD* IV/4, 19; *KD* IV/4, 20.

31. *CD* IV/4, 19; *KD* IV/4, 20.

32. *CD* IV/4, 19; *KD* IV/4, 20. Cf. Barth's comments in the various drafts of his preface to the first edition of the *Römerbrief* (1919) where he stated that the difference that his commentary held was in its desire to be "more in accordance with its subject matter." See Burnett, *Karl Barth's Theological Exegesis*, 277.

33. *CD* IV/4, 21. Cf. *KD* IV/4, 23.

and to that extent also *in nobis*, this necessarily implies that in spite of the unfaithfulness of every man He creates in the history of every man the beginning of his new history, the history of a man who has become faithful to God."[34] Here we see all three of these phrases tied together in one sentence!

To illustrate this point for a group of Moravians, Barth rehearsed the story of the nineteenth-century Pietistic theologian H. Friedrich Kohlbrügge, who was once asked, "'When did you convert?' to which he replied, 'On Golgotha!'"[35] The important event is not what *we* experience in our hearts at conversion (if anything at all), but rather what *he* experienced on the cross. Our history becomes intertwined with his history; the *then and there* is the basis for any conversion *here and now*. The *extra nos* is the ground of the change that occurs *in nobis*.

C. Christus in nobis!

As the discussion continues for several pages with these three Latin phrases continuing to organize Barth's "ethics of reconciliation," readers see the clearest and most poignant explanation of God's work *in us* in the *CD*. Barth provides several themes to support his understanding of *Christus in nobis*, each building upon the other until a crescendo is reached.[36]

Divine Initiative

First, only God could have performed this task faithfully on behalf of humans. "Human beings do not make this new beginning for themselves. They do not of themselves make themselves into another. They do not transform themselves as unfaithful people into people faithful to God."[37] In addition to repeating a lifelong understanding on Barth's part, stressing the divine initiative has been the task of *CD* IV/1–3 up to this point. The accomplishment of any aspect of our salvation always has the accent on God.

---

34. *CD* IV/4, 21. Cf. *KD* IV/4, 23.

35. Barth, "Gespräche mit der Vertretern Herrnhuter Brüdergemeine, 1960," 134.

36. While this is in the midst of a larger chapter in KD IV/4, it is also the concluding paragraphs of the Festschrift chapter for E. Wolf. See *KD* IV/4, 23–25, and Barth, "*extra nos—pro nobis—in nobis*," 25–27.

37. *KD* IV/4, 23. Translation from Hunsinger, *Thomist*, 509.

Divine Change in Our Hearts—but Not "in Our Pockets"

Second, the new life of the Christian corresponds to the history of Jesus Christ because it is based on the divine change *in our hearts*. Barth says it precisely with these words: "And even from this beginning in the history of Jesus Christ, they [believers] may and can live here and now a new Christian life corresponding to the divine change of their hearts, which happened there and then."[38] There is a transformation *in our hearts* that causes a corresponding faithfulness of life in our own history and lives—here and now under the conditions of existence. This is what *in nobis* implies. And again here evangelicals and Pentecostals would offer hearty agreement although perhaps with a caveat: what about *our experience of salvation* in our hearts? Does not this inner alteration spark something experientially in me, providing a joyous certainty? How might Barth respond to this query?

To a group of Methodist preachers who wanted to know his opinion with regard to the "psychological experience of salvation," Barth responded clearly and firmly. It is the Holy Spirit who is at work in our lives, creating the change in us and the assurance of our salvation. It is not anything that abides in us doing these things. Indeed, the Spirit's work "pertains to something lying entirely outside of me, not in me."[39] Any of us who look inside can feel something—*our* experience, *our* theology. It is something we "have," yet our experience of it is not the thing of which we are certain. Barth states,

> I am not sure of my certainty; I do not believe in my faith, rather I believe in that which God has done in Christ. That is the great miracle that I am allowed to believe—something that stands high over me, which has come down from God to me here, and at no time something that I have in my pocket. I must always only refer myself to the cross on Golgotha.[40]

To be sure, salvation is experiential (*erfahrbar*) because humans are made as psychological beings (*psychologisch konstruiertes Wesen*).[41] But the experience must never be the central point for Christians. Utilizing Paul's words in 2 Cor 4:7, Barth reminds the hearers that "we have such treasure in earthen vessels." We cannot switch the treasure and the vessel. Barth continues: "So I do not want to say that in my little soul or little head the Holy

---

38. *KD* IV/4, 23. Translation mine.
39. Barth, "Gespräche mit Methodistenpredigern, 1961," 175.
40. Ibid.
41. Ibid.

Spirit is present" but rather I must look towards that which comes "from above" (*anōthen*) and not from below.[42]

And then Barth states something personal—a rather rare thing for him: "I do not deny the experience of salvation; nevertheless for all that, it is not breaking in on me [*Ich leugne das Heilserlebnis nicht, fällt mir doch nicht ein*]! The experience of salvation is that which has happened at Golgotha. Over against this, my own experience is only a vessel."[43] While Barth may have not felt such an experience of salvation as the Methodists support, it does not matter. The basis of one's faith cannot be the inner movements of the soul or the feeling of the heart. Surely, this is not what is important with *Christus in nobis* since the basis of our faith is not the vessel that carries the treasure, but the treasure itself! Here in one stroke is the balance that Barth is trying to achieve theologically. Certainly there is experience within humans at salvation—we are, after all, psychological creatures. But if we focus on these movements of the psyche, we will lose the objective reality of the transcendent nature of our salvation in Jesus Christ. The result makes faith into a subjective experience that becomes some reality "for me" but not worth much beyond that.[44] For Barth, this pulls the "guts" out of faith and reduces it to subjective experience. Christian faith must rest on the fact that God became an enfleshed human in our time and space. Without this objective side of salvation, there can only be various individual descriptions of psychological movements and encounters. If our salvation's certainty rests on our experience of it, then the basis for our faith lays on the chimera of our emotions instead of the historical datum that God became flesh, died, and was raised for us. As he warned a group of Methodist preachers on the subject of experience, "Pay attention! Place the weight more on Christ and less on the experience of salvation!"[45] It is a lesson still fruitful for Pentecostals and evangelicals who place such stress on experience and feeling in salvation.

---

42. Ibid.

43. Ibid., 176.

44. It is, indeed, precisely the problem that Barth sees with Rudolf Bultmann and the existentialist theologians: they have sidestepped history for the sake of overcoming the problems in it created by modernity and have instead focused on inner experiences as the pole of certitude for individuals. See Barth, "Gespräche mit evanglischen Buchhändlern, 1962," especially 362–72, for his discussion on Bultmann and existential theology.

45. Barth, "Gespräche mit Methodistenpredigern," 202.

Deliverance of Humans for Relationship with God

Third, the history of Jesus Christ *liberates* humans—or, to use more Pentecostal jargon, it *delivers* humans so that they can become faithful to God.[46] "This is our liberation through the divine change effected in the history of Jesus Christ."[47] But what does this mean for us who are not Jesus Christ? How is it that Christ's history, "which took place *extra nos*, took place *pro nobis*, that this *pro nobis* is efficacious, and that it thus includes the fact that, as it took place then and there, as the history of that One, it also takes place here and now, *in nobis*, in the life of the many?"[48]

It is here in the development of his argument that Barth becomes most clear. How does the history of Jesus Christ connect with our own history? God does not discover and confirm "an immediate (or direct) relation [*eine unmittelbare Beziehung*] between Godself and us, but without a doubt creates and enters into a relation—one which we could not create and enter into for ourselves, one which God does for us—from which we cannot withdraw."[49] As with the *Römerbrief* period, there is no "direct given"—no immediate relation—from God's side into our side. However, what has changed is that in the sovereign freedom that belongs to God, there is created *for us* a relationship that God himself enters and thereby elicits our obedient, faithful response. "Interceding for us in Jesus Christ, [God] is now present to us, not at a distance, but in the closest proximity [*in größter Nähe gegenwärtig*], confronting us in our own being, thought and reflection."[50] In what way is Christ present to us—in us? What difference can this make?[51]

And here is another aspect in Barth's theology regarding our relationship with Jesus that evangelicals and Pentecostals will understand—fellowship or

---

46. KD IV/4, 23. Barth uses the noun *Befreiung*, which can mean liberation or deliverance.

47. CD IV/4, 22; KD IV/4, 24.

48. CD IV/4, 22; KD IV/4, 24.

49. KD IV/4, 24. Translation mine.

50. CD IV/4, 22; KD IV/4, 24.

51. Barth uses Calvin's imagery of being "inserted" into Christ as well as the image of the "distant Christ" versus the "near Christ" to underscore his own point of *unio cum Christo*. See CD IV/2, 522. Cf. CD IV/3.2, 539. Barth also speaks of this *otiosus Christus* ("distant Christ") in other places. Cf. CD IV/1, 287. The citation is from Calvin, *Institutes of the Christian Religion*, III.1.1, and 3. This is my translation from the Latin. Barth also used this section from Calvin's *Institutes* in his Göttingen dogmatics. See Barth, *Unterricht in der christlichen Religion*, 3:246–48. See also his 1928–29 lectures on ethics at Münster: Barth, *Ethics*, 289–90. These ideas were originally stated by Barth in a discussion of Osiander in his 1910 lecture, "Der christliche Glaube und die Geschichte, 1912," 189 and 192.

union with Christ. Barth remains nervous of a mysticism that sinks into an ontological sharing of properties. It is for this reason that he cannot allow for any deification or divinization. But what does it mean to be united with Christ—to have "fellowship" (*Umgang*) with him?[52] What arises from this fellowship, this connection? Barth urges that it cannot be the arrogant response of possession of salvation. Instead, if it is understood correctly, "The connection with [Christ] also establishes a recognition of 'What should we do?' But this will always be something momentary. It is all about the Christian *decision*, about the *life*, about the *way*, which must be lived out. It is not an ethical principle that we possess. What matters is that I remain in the 'connection'—when I 'feel' it *and* when I don't—and then it will lead more and more to this recognition."[53]

Feelings in Us—A "Sentimental Journey"?

While discussing Nikolaus von Zinzendorf's concept of the "personal connection with the Savior," Barth explains to the Moravians that Zinzendorf's thoughts in this regard do not spill over into a dangerous mysticism, but rather reflect a "genuine mysticism" as found in Gal 2:20.[54] Quoting a hymn written by Zinzendorf, Barth makes a strong point about "feeling" as it relates to one's connection with Christ. The hymn "*Herz und Herz vereint zusammen*" ("Heart and Heart Together United")[55] expresses the real dimension of mysticism in the lines of its first verse:

---

52. In the conversations from 1959–1962 as well as in the fourth volume of the *CD*, Barth uses the term *Umgang* to describe the social exchange, association, or society of God with Godself or God with humans. While the term *der Umgang* could be translated variously, I have chosen to use "fellowship" because in the conversations the term is closely related to the relational connection of the believer with Christ. I think that the Pietists might be using this term in the way a number of evangelicals or Pentecostals in the U.S. use "fellowship" to describe this social interaction between God and humans as well as between believers and other believers.

53. Barth, "Gespräche mit Vertretern der Herrnhuter Brüdergemeine, 1960," 145. Translation mine. I have translated rather conceptually the line, "What matters is that I remain in the connection—when I feel it and when I don't—and then it will lead more and more to this recognition." The German reads, "*Es kommt darauf an, daß ich in der 'Konnexion' bleibe—im 'Gefühl' und im Dunkel—und dann wird sie je und je zu dieser Erkenntnis führen.*" The phrase "in the feeling and in the dark" seems to refer back in the dialogue to the third verse of a hymn that Barth had just cited by Julie Hausmann, "*So nimm den meine Händ.*" It reads, "If I also similarly feel nothing of your power, you lead me still to the goal, even through the night."

54. Ibid., 143.

55. This hymn was written in 1725. It was translated into English by Frederick William Foster in 1789 and is known as "Christian Hearts, in Love United." However, the

Heart to heart together united
seek your rest in the heart of God.
Let your flame of love
burn from the Savior.
He the Head, we the limbs,
He the Light and we the glow,
He the Master, we the brothers,
He is ours and we are his.

In this hymn Barth sees unity with distinction—a genuine mysticism where "the two remain in the connection."[56] Then he brings a line from the fourth verse forward: "*Daß du, unsichtbarer Meister, uns so fühlbar nahe bist*" (that you, invisible Master, are so near us we feel you). Some have asked him whether this last line could not be stated better if one were to say "*uns im Glauben nahe bist*" (you are so near us *in faith*).[57] Barth responds

---

English version usually does not show all seven verses from the German; in addition, the translation is a very free one so as to make the rhymes work in English. Barth's precise points lie in the German text itself. Here is the first verse in German on which my conceptual translation in the text above is based:

Herz und Herz vereint zusammen
sucht in Gottes Herzen Ruh.
Lasset eure Liebesflammen
lodern auf den Heiland zu.
Er das Haupt, wir seine Glieder,
er das Licht und wir der Schein,
er der Meister, wir die Brüder,
er ist unser, wir sind sein.

56. Barth, "Gespräche mit Vertretern der Herrnhuter Brüdergemeine, 1960," 143. It is important for Barth to maintain this distinction between God and humans while at the same time maintaining this union/fellowship. Using the same word for this communion (*Verkehr*) as did his teacher, Wilhelm Herrmann, Barth insists that genuine mysticism requires the two to remain distinct. "Communion [*Der Verkehr*] between God and humans does not cease therefore in the work of the Holy Spirit, rather it begins to be a genuine communion [*echter Verkehr*] in which the human partner, far away from the divine [partner], exchanges with or wants to take the place of the divine, takes up the approaching place directly opposite him/her" (*KD* IV/4, 30). Translation mine.

57. Barth, "Gespräche mit Vertretern der Herrnhuter Brüdergemeine, 1960." Here is the text of the fourth verse and my conceptual translation:

Halleluja, welche Höhen,
welche Tiefen reicher Gnad,
daß wir dem ins Herze sehen,
der uns so geliebet hat;
daß der Vater aller Geister,
der der Wunder Abgrund ist,

84 Part II—Reconceiving Christian Experience and Practice

that thirty years ago, he also would have said that, but now he views things differently.

> "To feel" [*Fühlbar*] is thought of here not as something sentimental, but rather emphasizes that one is close to something. I would not place the emphasis on that aspect, but some feeling has already been in the process; indeed, faith cannot be a callous affair [*kaltschnäuzige Angelegenheit*]! It is about a feeling that you have in faith. You can become a little warm in the process! [*Man darf ruhig ein bißschen warm Werden dabei!*][58]

Perhaps it is my Pentecostal proclivities, but this sounds so much like the solid evangelical, Pentecostal teaching that I heard in my youth! Faith has something of experience in it, but this should not be the focus of the believer's attention. Surely one can get "a little warm" or excited by experiencing the closeness of Christ, but such feeling cannot be the primary basis for faith. Barth adds,

> Feelings are secondary and can cease. One can turn feelings off and on. Feelings are the relative part of faith, not the absolute. But in this relation [*Relation*], the relatedness [*Bezogenheit*] shows itself exactly. It is *only* relatedness [*Bezogenheit*], but even so it is *our* relatedness [*Bezogenheit*].[59]

---

daß du, unsichtbarer Meister, uns so fühlbar nahe bist.
Hallelujah, what heights,
what depths of rich grace,
that we see him in the heart,
the One who has loved us so;
that the Father of all spirits,
the One who is the great depth of miracles,
that you, invisible Master,
are so near us we feel you.

58. Ibid., 144. Translation mine.

59. Ibid. Of related interest is Barth's allowance of talk about *Christus pro me*—the individual. However, this is always in the context of *Christus pro nobis* and *Christus in nobis* (not *in me*). Reducing the "in us" of salvation to some individualistic "in me" is *the* problem of Pietism for Barth. He believed Zinzendorf sidestepped this problem in his day. Justification and sanctification are not personal belongings or private enterprises in some secret relationship between God and the individual. No. They are part of the relation Jesus Christ established *with the community of faith* and therefore "prevented from becoming a morose or humdrum or sentimental or Bohemian private enterprise." See *CD* IV/1, 736.

Christ or Contradiction "Lodged" in Our Hearts

So is the *Christus in nobis* in reality some type of mysticism? What is interesting in Barth's development of his argument in *CD* IV/4 is that there is not a substance or divine aspect of God lodged in our hearts by Christ, but rather once again something that we cannot control—a "contradiction" (*Widerspruch*)! What happens is simply this: "*in nobis*, in our heart, in the very center of our existence, a contradiction is lodged against our unfaithfulness. It is a contradiction that we cannot dodge, but have to validate.... Because Jesus Christ intervenes *pro nobis* and thus *in nobis*, unfaithfulness to God has been rendered a basically impossible possibility."[60] Notice that this contradiction occurs because Christ is *in nobis*—in our hearts! There is a "divine change" that occurs in our participation in the history of Christ, by which humans obtain deliverance and freedom to be faithful to God (corresponding thereby to their Lord's own faithfulness). Barth brings this final point to a deafening crescendo:

> This change [the human becoming faithful to God] is our deliverance through the divine change that happens in the history [*Geschichte*] of Jesus Christ. This change carried out by God is really the deliverance of humans. It happens to them entirely from the outside, entirely from God—but as their own deliverance. As it is conceived in general so here in particular, the omnicausality [*Allwirksamkeit*] of God should not be interpreted as the sole-causality [*Alleinwirksamkeit*] of God. The divine change—which by virtue of being carried out a person becomes a Christian—is an event of genuine communion [*echten Verkehrs*][61] between God and humans. And if surely this change has its source in God's initiative, then just as surely humans are not ignored and passed over in it, but on the contrary, are taken seriously as independent creatures of God. They are not overrun and overpowered [*nicht überrant und überwältigt*], but set on their own two feet. They are not infants—declared legally incapable of making decisions [*entmündigt*], but rather are spoke to and handled as adults—legally capable of making decisions [*mündig*]. Thus, the history of Jesus Christ does not blot out the history of our human lives but instead by that history, their own life-history becomes new—but truly their own new life-history. The faithfulness to God to which we are called is not something like an emanation of the faithfulness of God, but rather is

---

60. *KD* IV/4, 24. Translation from Hunsinger, *Thomist*, 510.

61. Cf. Herrmann, *The Communion of the Christian with God, Described on the Basis of Luther's Statements.*

really our own faithfulness, our own decision and act. Humans could not act on this, were they not delivered for it [*dazu befreit würde*]. But in the process, humans are delivered for it; they perform it as their own deed—as their response to the Word of God addressed to them in the history of Jesus Christ.[62]

So here is Barth's final point on this matter *in nuce*: the history of Jesus Christ *extra nos et pro nobis* contains the power to posit a new beginning as well as a true 'communion' *in nobis*—to deliver humans from the bondage of sin and disobedience to God and to transform their behavior by freeing them to walk in righteousness and obedience *on their own feet*! While most evangelicals and Pentecostals would not have phrased it in this manner (especially with respect to the *history* of Jesus), they would recognize the deliverance from disobedience so that humans can be free to obey. This is the *effect* of Christ *in nobis*—in our hearts. On the one hand, Barth is careful not to fall into the ditch of Protestant Liberalism with its focus on the human being's inner spiritual movements; on the other hand, he is just as careful not to fall into the ditch on the other side of the road—Pietistic religious emotionalism with its focus on the human being's inner spiritual movements, but for entirely different reasons from the Protestant Liberals. This is a warning for all evangelicals and Pentecostals today. If we lessen the importance of the historicity of the life, death, and resurrection of Jesus Christ for our salvation (its "objective" side, so to speak), we run the risk of crafting a salvation from human hands rather than from the transforming, powerful hands of God. This human crafting of salvation cannot "save" or "deliver" us from our own evil. It mystifies us with its magical potion of inner feelings and experiences, but in the end only seals our fate to ourselves. If God does not deliver us and set us free, we will remain in our sins regardless of how many feelings to the contrary we may possess.

This is a lesson that Barth offers us in this final volume of his *Church Dogmatics*. The fact that it comes under the heading "Baptism with the Holy Spirit" should help us understand its importance—even if Barth's understanding of this baptism is completely different (for the most part) from Pentecostal understandings. This is the lesson of *Christus extra nos, pro nobis, in nobis*!

---

62. *KD* IV/4, 25. Translation mine.

Conclusion

Navigating the theological waters of evangelical and Pentecostal soteriology is a painstaking task due to the shallow shoals and barely hidden rocks that threaten any ship in the stream. The same was true of Barth's soteriological journey—there were treacherous dangers just under the surface. Barth's navigation between the shoals of Protestant Liberalism's experiential faith and the rocks of Pietism's experiential salvation offers any theological pilot today a path to follow. Pentecostal soteriology in particular can learn from Barth's stress upon the *Christus extra nos* in Jesus' history as the foundation for the subjective appropriation of that distant Christ into our hearts by the Spirit. To keep Christ only at a distance is to have an alien Christ—not a Christ of the Scriptures. To keep Christ only in closest nearness to one's inner life is to have an illusory god of one's own making—not the Lord who fulfilled all righteousness on our behalf and delivers us from sin. Barth shows us that the navigation necessary to get us to a truly Christian shore requires a dialectical asymmetry. By keeping the accent on the *Christus extra nos* yet without ignoring the *Christus in nobis*, Barth is able to hold both truths in dialectical tension without collapsing them into one (as in 1910) or sublating (*aufheben*) their tension into a higher "third" or synthesis. This is a delicate tension to maintain because the accent must always begin with and remain on the first pole—the objective aspect of the history of Jesus Christ outside of us; yet the reciprocating movement must also remain on the second pole—the subjective aspect of human reception of and response to the work of Christ applied to our hearts by the Spirit.

Pentecostals tend to stress the subjective side of atonement and its reception in human hearts to such a degree that the objective side remains aloof and distant. We tend to focus on the emotional and experiential events in our inner lives—in our hearts. Barth has taught us that to see only *Christus in nobis* is to engage in some religious subterfuge of our own psyche. The *Christus in nobis* has no meaning for the Christian *without* the *Christus extra nos, pro nobis*.

While Barth did not engage in any direct dialogue with Pentecostals in his lifetime, he did answer a question about the Pentecostal movement from a group of Mennonites in December 1967. While he admits that he is not that familiar with Pentecostalism, he conjectures that movements of the Spirit—if they are truly that—are not to be feared but embraced by the church. Barth says, "Indeed, the Holy Spirit is the one of whom we have need."[63] Then, as if prescient, Barth says, "And if they [Pentecostals] do this [seek the Spirit], and if something of Pentecost becomes visible there now again, who can say something against it? Against this, nothing is to be said and for it everything is to be said. If it happens the right way, then we should praise and thank God that there is a Pentecostal movement. But one would have to see up close how things turn out with them."[64] And these words may still be said of us—especially those of us who work in theology. Perhaps it will begin to "happen the right way" when we are able to ask and answer, "How are things with your heart?"

---

63. Barth, "Gespräche mit Mennoniten, 13 Dezember 1967," 431. Translation mine. I should note that he did have a dialogue with a Pentecostal "statesman," David du Plessis (1905–87).

64. Ibid., 431. Translation mine.

Bibliography

Barth, Karl. *Die Christliche Dogmatik im Emtwurf Erster Band: Die Lehre vom Worte Gottes: Prolegomena zur Christlichen Dogmatik 1927.* Edited by Gerhard Sauter. Zürich: Theologischer Verlag Zürich, 1982.

———. "Der christliche Glaube und die Geschichte." *Schweizerische Theologische Zeitschrift* 29 (1912) 1–18, 49–72.

———. "Die dogmatische Prinzipienlehre bei Wilhelm Herman, 1925." In *Vorträge und kleinere Arbeiten, 1922-1925*, edited by Holger Finze, 545–603. Zürich: Theologischer Verlag Zürich, 1990.

———. *Ethics.* Edited by Dietrich Braun. Translated by Geoffrey W. Bromiley. New York: Seabury, 1981.

———. *Evangelical Theology: An Introduction.* Translated by Grover Foley. Grand Rapids: Eerdmans, 1963.

———. "Extra Nos—Pro Nobis—In Nobis." In *Hören und Handeln: Festschirift für Ernst Wolf zum 60*, edited by Helmut Gollwitzer and Hellmut Traub, 15–27. Munich: Kaiser, 1962.

———. "Extra Nos—Pro Nobis—In Nobis." Translated by George Hunsinger. *The Thomist* 50 (1986) 497–511.

———. "Gespräch mit Vertretern der Herrnhuter Brüdergemeinde (12.10.1960)." In *Gespräche 1959-1962*, edited by Eberhard Busch, 124–57. Zürich: Theologischer Verlag Zürich, 1995.

———. "Gespräch mit Methodistenpredigern (16.5.1961)." In *Gespräche 1959-1962*, edited by Eberhard Busch, 169–205. Zürich: Theologischer Verlag Zürich, 1995.

———. "Gespräch mit evangelischen Buchhändlern (24.6.1962)." In *Gespräche 1959-1962*, edited by Eberhard Busch, 335–80. Zürich: Theologischer Verlag Zürich, 1995.

———. "Gespräche mit Züricher Promovenden, 19 November 1962." In *Gespräche 1959-1962*, edited by Eberhard Busch, 399–404. Zürich: Theologischer Verlag Zürich, 1995.

———. "The Humanity of God." In *The Humanity of God*, translated by John Newton Thomas and Thomas Webster, 37–68. Richmond: John Knox, 1960.

———. *Learning Jesus Christ through the Heidelberg Catechism.* Translated by Shirley C. Guthrie Jr. Grand Rapids: Eerdmans, 1964.

———. *Protestant Theology in the Nineteenth Century: Its Background and History.* Translated by Brian Cozens and John Bowden. Grand Rapids: Eerdmans, 2002.

———. *Die protestantische Theologie im 19 Jarhundert: Ihre Vorgeschichte und ihre Geschichte.* Zürich: Evangelischer Verlag, 1947.

———. *Der Römerbrief (1922).* Zürich: Theologischer Verlag Zurich, 1940.

———. *Unterricht in der christlichen Religion.* 3 vols. Zürich: Theologischer Verlag Zürich, 1985–2003.

———. *Vorträge und kleinere Arbeiten, 1909-1914.* Edited by Hans-Anton Drewes and Hinrich Stoevesandt. Zürich: Thologischer Verlag Zürich, 1993.

Burnett, Richard. *Karl Barth's Theological Exegesis: The Hermeneutical Principles of the Römerbrief Period.* Grand Rapids: Eerdmans, 2004.

Busch, Eberhard. *Karl Barth: His Life from Letters and Autobiographical Texts.* Translated by John Bowden. Philadelphia: Fortress, 1976.

Dayton, Donald W. "Foreword." In Eberhard Busch, *Karl Barth and the Pietists: The Young Karl Barth's Critique of Pietism and Its Response*, translated by Daniel W. Bloesch, ix–xii. Downers Grove, IL: InterVarsity, 2004.

Gärtner, Friedrich. "Karl Barth und Zinzendorf: Die bleibende Bedeutung Zinzendorfs auf Grund der Beuteiling des Pietismus durch Karl Barth." *Theologische Existenz Heute* 40 (1953) 3–51.

Hermann, Wilhelm. *The Communion of the Christian with God: Described on the Basis of Luther's Statements*. Edited by Robert T. Voelkel. Translated by J. Sanduys Stanyon and R. W. Steward. Philadelphia: Fortress, 1971.

Hunsinger, George. *Disruptive Grace: Studies in the Theology of Karl Barth*. Grand Rapids: Eerdmans, 2000.

Klooster, Fred H. "Aspects of the Soteriology of Karl Barth." *Bulletin of the Evangelical Theological Society* 2 (1959) 6–14.

5

Karl Barth on Fellowship with Jesus Christ

The Calling of the Christian

James Nelson

Karl Barth's *Church Dogmatics* comprises a vast array of Christian theological themes and constructs, illuminating the mystery of God's relations with humanity and the cosmos. The range of his discussions and insights, rich in comprehensive elaboration, beauty, and style is breathtaking. To say that his theology is systematic is to underestimate his accomplishment. What we have in Barth's approach is a many-sided discussion centered in Jesus Christ as the revelation of God, as the reconciling of God and humanity within a cosmic context issuing in the redemption of all things. The theme of this discussion is concerned with what Barth calls the calling of the human, or the goal of the process of reconciliation as actualized in the appropriation of Christian existence in the Christian believer. This discussion will seek to understand what Karl Barth says regarding how a person becomes a Christian and what that means for the transformation that takes place in the existence and life of the human who receives by faith the new life in Christ.

From all eternity, according to Barth, God has established by election of Jesus Christ a covenant with all humanity as the basis of human salvation. This covenant is universal in dimension, encompassing all creation and the entire human race, or all humans who have existed and shall exist. The center of this covenant is the reconciliation accomplished in Jesus Christ as effective for all and having transformative power in redemptive significance for the entirety of humanity, especially for believers who receive by faith this reconciliation with God. While this theological vision is understood by Barth as an objective reality of reconciliation for all humanity and a redemptive power affecting all humans, it has a subjective, experimental side of appropriation that initiates for the believer the transformation envisioned in the redemptive covenant established in the death and resurrection of Jesus Christ.

It is by the power and work of the Holy Spirit, sent by Jesus Christ, that humans are made contemporary with the reconciling work of Christ. It is through the form of the Spirit's action in which "it is made present to the man to whom He gives Himself and who receives Him as the action which in its singularity takes place today . . . as he participates in it, it makes him its contemporary."[1] It is by this present power of the Holy Spirit that God calls humans to their goal of fellowship with Jesus Christ as their personal salvation. Christ lives in the Christian and the Christian is "in Christ." "'In Christ' means that Christ lives where this man, the Christian, is, . . . in the sphere of his free thinking, volition, resolution and action, in such a way that He takes up His abode . . . in his innermost being or heart, being present there as the Lord of the house."[2] For Barth this being in Christ is for the Christian the equivalent of the kingdom of God as the ruling principle of being of the Christian. Though the Christian is given the benefits of Christ's life in righteousness and goodness, which is described by Barth as the classical view, it is not this that Barth finds as the center of the being of the Christian. Barth can even talk of the believer as a "co-operating subject" of what is received in Christ. However, the being in Christ of the believer is related to the action of Jesus Christ in the obedience or correspondence of the Christian to the reconciliation wrought in Christ as the basis of the Christian life. "The man in whom Christ lives, and who lives in Christ, has no option but to confirm in his action the living relationship in which God and the world are held together in the work of Christ, the self-determination of all men for God."[3] What Barth understands as the Christian living in Christ and Christ in the believer is related to action in obedience in working out the kingdom of God in community and for the world. It is in this that there is knowledge and unity with Jesus Christ. This is what Barth means by fellowship with Christ and the knowing of God.

---

1. *CD* IV/1, 648.
2. *CD* IV/3, 594.
3. Ibid., 598.

1

The calling of the Christian is to fellowship with Jesus Christ. This calling is the goal of the Christian, which finds its basis in the justification and sanctification of the human in Jesus Christ's reconciliation of the world to God. As persons are called and awakened to conversion by the Holy Spirit, direction is given to them so that they can live in holiness in correspondence to Jesus Christ. It is then that the Holy Spirit dwells in the believer as the power of Jesus Christ. As the Spirit dwells in the believer by faith and gives freedom, "it takes place that Jesus Christ Himself 'dwells in your hearts by faith' (Eph 3:17). Apprehended by the grace of our Lord Jesus Christ and therefore by the love of God ('shed abroad in our hearts by the Holy Ghost which is given to us,' Rom 3:5), man is placed in the most direct fellowship with this Lord of His, and as a Christian he becomes a man who may exist in this fellowship with Him. That this should be achieved is the goal of his vocation, illumination and awakening."[4]

Barth asks what the nature of this fellowship of Christians with Jesus Christ is. Barth denies that there is an identification of the Christian with Christ. For Barth "Christ does not merge into the Christian nor the Christian into Christ."[5] For all the directness and intimacy of the Christian's union with Christ there is a distinction between Christ and the Christian, and a freedom in response that the Christian has in the empowerment by the Spirit. For Barth this is not described by the term mysticism, even though Calvin in his *Institutes* refers to "*a unio mystica*."[6] For Barth mysticism is the psychological concentration of the spirit of the human to induce a union with God, an elevation of the human self-consciousness to the experience of God. In Barth's view, the calling of the Christian is by grace as an encounter with the sovereign freedom of God, calling for a response of faith and adoration. Therefore, to call this "Christ-mysticism" would not be appropriate.

Barth states that the end of the calling of the Christian is "the fellowship of Christians with Christ, which is the goal of vocation, is a perfect fellowship inasmuch as what takes place in it is no less than their union with Christ."[7] This union with Christ is what makes a person a Christian. This takes place as a "self-giving" on both sides, God to the person and the person to God. This union is hidden and not directly visible, only being revealed at the end. Barth says that this union in Christ "is what the whole

---

4. Ibid., 538.
5. Ibid., 539.
6. Calvin, Institutes, III, 736–38.
7. CD IV/3, 540.

of creation, with all men and Christians too, is waiting and groaning for. The purpose for which Christians are already called here and now in their life-histories within universal history is that in the self-giving of Jesus Christ to them, and theirs to Him, they should enter into their union with Him, their '*unio cum Christo*.'"[8] This union is founded upon the self-giving of Christ to Christians whereby they are made His own. This union is what is celebrated in the Lord's Supper, which is "instituted to represent the perfect fellowship between Him and them which He has established."[9]

This union with Christ is what Barth means by being born again from above, where Christ gives his life to the Christian and dwells within the believer, causing his life to be that of the Christian. From this relationship of union with Christ there is a continual nourishing of the Christian. However, for Barth this is not a one-way relationship, for there is not only a union of Christ with the Christian, but a union of the Christian with Christ. Christ is not outside the Christian in reconciliation but within the Christian. "Their fellowship would not be complete if their relationship were actualized only from above downwards and not also from below upwards, if it were not reciprocal."[10] By the power of the Spirit, the Christian is made free to make a response to correspond in his or her own action to the reconciling act of God in Christ. This action is the believers' own by the Spirit. By his act of faith, the Christian finds his true existence "as a member of the world reconciled to God in Him."[11] The response of the Christian to the calling given in the self-giving of Christ is to continually actualize what he or she may become in union with Christ, that is, a knowing fellowship and union with Christ and the atoning power of God in Christ.

Now Barth asks the question what is meant by the word "in" when speaking of Christ in the Christian and the Christian in Christ. Barth's answer to the question of Christ being in the Christian is "that Christ speaks, acts and rules—and this is the grace of His calling of this man—as the Lord of his thinking, speech and action. He takes possession of his free human heart. He rules and controls in the obedience of his free reason (2 Cor 10:5)."[12] That the Christian is in Christ means that by the freedom given in Christ by the power of the Spirit, the believer, while making a free decision, experiences in his or her life the "ruling and determinative principle" of corresponding to the action and rule of Christ. The Christian is orientated to

---

8. Ibid.
9. Ibid., 542.
10. Ibid., 543
11. Ibid., 544–45.
12. Ibid., 547.

Christ in the power of the Word of God by the power of the Holy Spirit. The Christian does not exist for himself or herself, but is called to be "awakened rather to genuine humanity."[13] This is what makes a person a Christian and is true of all Christians generally, and not just of a higher kind of Christian existence. This is the Christian's divine "sonship" as a person's attachment to Christ whereby there is realized a new life by the power of the Holy Spirit.

In an excursus on Luther and Calvin, Barth shows that they both gave emphasis to the faith of the believer issuing in and arising out of union with Christ.[14] It is Calvin that gave faith and union with Christ greater emphasis and development in his *Institutes* and commentaries, especially that on the Gospel of John. By faith there is a mysterious exchange of life with the Christian, with Christ "invested with our unrighteousness and we with His righteousness."[15] This is what makes a person a Christian and makes us new creatures in Christ. Barth is careful to follow Calvin in rejecting this union as understood by Osiander, as deifying the Christian as sharing in the being of Christ.

However, there is a real, active sharing of the life and action of Jesus Christ in the believer, issuing in obedience and witness of the Christian in fellowship with Christ as the goal of the Christian in the event of calling. Barth will not go beyond this in describing the inner transformation of the Christian in union with Christ, however intimate and direct it is claimed to be. In an aside, Barth states that for Calvin, and the Reformed theology that follows, the mystic union of the soul with Christ had already within it the concerns of Pietism, with its emphasis on the "I in Thee, Thou in me" of the Gospel of John. In this Barth is not advocating Pietism, but only asserting that Pietism's concerns were there in Calvin and Reformed theology in the sixteenth and seventeenth centuries. Barth can say that "all the works of God can take place, however, only in the fellowship in which God always and in every respect intervenes for man. : . . Recognising it, he can and should wholly count upon it, and live unconditionally in the confidence that it is his true being. This truth of his being in this fellowship, however, is the declaration of his union with Christ. And this is what makes this declaration materially necessary."[16]

---

13. Ibid., 548.
14. Ibid., 549–54.
15. Ibid., 551 with reference of Calvin's *Institutes*, IV, 1361–62.
16. Ibid., 554.

2

As the believer is in union with Christ, it means that a person is living under the lordship and power of the Son of God, and therefore is under the direction of the Holy Spirit. The Holy Spirit is sent by Jesus Christ and is the power of Christ in the Christian. Barth asks how the Holy Spirit acts: what does it mean to receive the Spirit and walk in the Spirit? To live by the Spirit is not to have some romanticized emotional experience. The power and lordship of the Son of God is the reality of the Spirit, and the aim of the Spirit is that direction is given to the Christian in wisdom and life. The Holy Spirit encounters Christians in this way and has the reality of a continually renewed action and power. Such is the transition from Jesus Christ to us. "The Holy Spirit does not create the ghost of a man standing in decision, but the reality of the man concerning whom decision has already been made in the existence of the man Jesus Christ."[17] The person called by God in Christ to be a Christian is already determined by the reality of the decision of God to reconcile the world in Christ and is given a freedom by the Spirit to accept this reconciliation to God. "In Him we have both our justification and sanctification, both our regeneration and conversion. All this has been done and is in force. It does not need to be repeated or augmented. It is true and actual. What is at issue in the fellowship and operation and direction of the Holy Spirit is that we should accept this, so that it is just as true and actual in our lives as it is in itself."[18] That the Spirit's power in Christians is true and actual does not leave us passive but active in pressing on to the call of God to obedience and action in realizing the new life in Christ. The victory of Christ in the new life of transformation in obedience, founded on the reconciliation of the world, "has nothing whatever to do with deification, but everything with humble subjection to God," so that "since the instruction of the Holy Spirit is His and not ours . . . it is powerful, effective, fruitful and victorious. Yes, even here and now it is fruitful and victorious. No one ever attends the school of this Teacher in vain."[19]

In *CD* IV/4, the fragment volume, Barth discusses the "Baptism with the Holy Spirit" as the foundation of the Christian life. The coming of the Holy Spirit to a person is grounded in the reconciliation of the world in Christ to God. The history of salvation "comprehends the world around, i.e., the whole world of mankind. Indeed, it comes with revolutionary force into the life of each and every man. Having taken place *extra nos*, it also works

---

17. *CD* IV/2, 363.
18. Ibid., 369–70.
19. Ibid., 377.

in nobis, introducing a new being of every man."[20] As the center of existence of every person there is the reconciling reality of God in Christ. It is on this foundation that a person begins to live the Christian life which follows from the divine transformation which has taken place through Jesus Christ in the event of death and resurrection. In this event, Jesus Christ takes the place of persons and gives freedom to them to become Christians. Barth is careful to say that as a person becomes a Christian, God is not the only cause. Humans are independent creatures of God and are not overpowered in the event of becoming Christians, but given the freedom to act in faith in response to God. "But being thus liberated, he does it as his own act, as his answer to the Word of God spoken to him in the history of Jesus Christ."[21] This means there is no Christomonism.

For Barth, the baptism with the Holy Spirit, which is the foundation of the Christian life, is not an event separate from the death and resurrection of Jesus Christ. Barth speaks of two factors, the first being reconciliation, the second of which is the impartation of Jesus Christ to a specific human being as the action of the Holy Spirit, which is the foundation of the Christian life. "When Jesus Christ does this to a man, when He enters his life as this Guarantor, He baptizes him, as only He can, but as He can and does, with the Holy Spirit. He brings about the change which as a divine change only He can bring about—the change in which a man, in virtue of God's faithfulness to him, becomes faithful to God in return and thus becomes a Christian."[22] Barth describes this as being "beset" by God as an event of grace that calls for the decision of obedience that corresponds to the faithfulness of God to the Christian. In this divine change by the Holy Spirit, a person is granted the freedom to respond. This is not a mechanical operation or an overpowering of a person. As Barth expresses it, "It can only be his very own free decision for this way. It can only be his own walking according to the Spirit with whom he is baptized—a walking genuinely on his own feet as he is thus beset by God."[23]

As this is the beginning of the Christian life, a person becomes a part of the Christian community as a fellowship in the Holy Spirit in love, bonded together in the body of Christ and given the fruits of the Spirit. As such, the Christian can move forward and experience a growth in the Christian life, living the fruits of the Spirit. However, this growth, according to Barth, is not a continuation of the beginning of the Christian life. "In all

20. *CD* IV/4, 21.
21. Ibid., 23.
22. Ibid., 33.
23. Ibid., 36.

its actions the work of the Holy Spirit is always and everywhere a wholly new thing. At each moment of its occurrence it is itself another change, a conversion, which calls for an even more radical conversion. As the change to the Christian life was radical in its inception, so it must and will always be in its continuation."[24] For Barth a person is not a Christian if he or she does not "move forward," not by the force of his own power but by the "impulsion and direction of the Holy Spirit." This means that there must be "a daily penitence," an active effort for new possibilities that are given the Christian on the basis of the grace of the Holy Spirit which is given ever afresh.

The Christian lives his or her daily life in striving for the perfection which he or she has in Christ, but without attaining such perfection. This life is given signs and pledges of the new life in Christ, which point to what shall take place when Jesus Christ is manifested in the "absolute future" when Jesus Christ shall come in final manifestation and we see "face to face." The Christian is given the grace to seek the holiness, the perfection to be revealed at the last time, but without attaining it or possessing it in his or her own life. However, the Christian does experience signs and pointers in the fruits of the Spirit that give eschatological evidence of the foundation of reconciliation in Christ. Barth closes the discussion of the baptism with the Holy Spirit by saying that the Christian "lives in a daily renewal to which he can never grow tired of subjecting himself. The rest which is available for him, too, as a member of God's people is the meaning of his existence in the movement in which he finds himself provisionally but ineluctably caught up here and now. This power of the life to come is the power of his life in this world."[25]

3

When Barth speaks of the liberation of the Christian and the experience of that liberation subjectively in the person called by God, he is careful not to turn to the believer in that experience so as to center the basis of salvation in the Christian and the act of faith. The Word of God in reconciliation by Christ comes to the person called as an objective power bringing newness of life. The calling of the Christian is a call to discipleship and direct fellowship with Jesus Christ. The act of calling has in view the removing of the distance that separates God and the person to actualize in the Christian the full communion between Christ and the believer. In the event of calling, the benefits that Christ has won for the whole world in his death and resurrection are

24. Ibid., 39.
25. Ibid., 40.

received by the Christian and now apply to the believer. Barth calls the liberation of the Christian a freedom that takes place in a 'twofold sense' in which the benefits of Christ are appropriated by the Christian. Barth describes this as "the personal knowledge, reception, possession and enjoyment of the '*benefica Christi*,' personal participation in the marriage-feast of the Lamb, appears and is, as we may well say, self-evidently assured to the one who, like the Christian as His witness, is with Christ in this way."[26]

For Barth, the experience of the Christian is not in looking to his or her own fulfillment, but in bearing witness to Jesus Christ and the reconciliation of the world, even the cosmos, to God. It is to work for God and in love to the neighbor. In this is the Christian's liberation. However, there is more to be said. And that is "he [the Christian] certainly cannot and will not fail also to have a place for himself personally in his psycho-physical existence which is his and his alone, in his life-history . . ."[27] In striving for the Christian life, the Christian, though fail as he or she might, "will continually come to taste and feel again that God has not lost sight of him," that "he himself may rise afresh each morning after every troubled night to take a few steps forward on the path of his little life-history."[28] Barth can say of the Christian "that he may again and again summon all his feeble resources to do either well or badly the most immediate of the many things laid upon him by way of witness."[29]

Basic to the personal experience of the Christian is to love God. For Barth to love God is not the same thing as loving the neighbor and ethical action. Loving God is the foundation for loving others. Barth defines loving God as giving oneself to God.[30] The danger of not having a response of love for God is to move into a rationalistic moralism, reducing Christianity to ethics, and in not having "a true and direct love for God and Jesus there is no place for prayer."[31] Barth compares the experience of loving God to the source of a river, and without a source the river dries up. This has often been the experience of the church and Christians where the life of Christian experience is withered and becomes dry. "It was because they were once confronted by dried-up river beds of this kind . . . that the older Mystics, Pietists and Romantics revolted, defying the instruction giving by domesticated Christianity, raising again the question of the source, finding it again . . . and

26. *CD* IV/3, 652.
27. Ibid., 653.
28. Ibid.
29. Ibid., 653–54.
30. *CD* IV/2, 798.
31. Ibid., 795.

raising their corresponding hymns of devotion."[32] For Barth without the passion of love for God and Jesus Christ, our hymns and preaching would be arid and dry. However, we must uphold "that which takes place at the center where Christian love is originally direct love for God and for Jesus. Here, then, we must think and speak with the measure of sober passion or passionate soberness which corresponds on the one hand to the fire which burns at this center and on the other to its holiness and purity."[33]

The love of God in Jesus Christ is "His coming together with all men" and the fulfilling of the covenant for the world in the reconciliation wrought in the death and resurrection of Jesus Christ. It is Christians who know this by faith, and this is what makes them Christians. Persons are called to be active in response to God as God exists in their activity as this is worked out as an "active being of man in God." "And this active being consists in the fact that man for his part in answer to that divine activity not merely knows himself to be brought together but does actively come together with God in thought and word and work . . . humbly seeking the One who has already found him in His free grace."[34] Barth can say a person's active response in love to God is a mirror of the election in Jesus Christ of all humanity, where from all eternity God willed not to be without the human, so that now persons can now will not to be without God. Thus, in recognizing the election of humanity to God in Christ, a person's activity can be characterized "by the will to seek God and to find Him."[35] For the Christian, existence in the love of God is the primary reality. What is left behind is the self-sufficiency of a life without God, of being our own masters, which is based on a lie and delusion. As the old life, this is still there, but it has no more power over the Christian. The goal of the calling of persons to Christ is "that man for his part will seek the God who in Jesus Christ has already sought and found him that was lost . . . realizing on his side the fellowship which has been set up by God. And above all we will be careful not to separate the concept of this love for God and therefore of this seeking of God from the human activity conditioned by it. We need not be fanatically anti-mystical. As one element in the activity which puts the love of God into effect, there may be a place for a feeling of enjoyable contemplation of God."[36] The reality of a Christian being reconciled with God, as the experience of conversion to God, is sanctification, as characterized by an active response of love to God.

32. Ibid., 797–98.
33. Ibid., 798.
34. *CD* IV/1, 103.
35. Ibid., 104.
36. Ibid.

In the reality of this being a person is able to give himself to God, experiencing the love of God and loving God.

Here we can see that the evangelical experience of the gospel of Christ and his kingdom in reconciliation to God is anchored in the election of humanity in Christ, and is worked out in an active response to the calling of the Christian to know Christ and be in union with Christ. The goal of this calling is fellowship with Jesus Christ and is experienced by faith, in the power and direction of the Holy Spirit, binding the Christian to Christ in experienced participation and love toward God.

Bibliography

Calvin, John. *Institutes of the Christian Religion*. Edited by John T. McNeill. Translated and Indexed by Ford Lewis Battles. Philadelphia, PA: The Westminster Press, 1960.

6

Barth and Testimony

John L. Drury

THE PURPOSE OF THIS essay is to draw on the practice and concept of testimony for rethinking the function of Scripture. My thesis is that testimony, when critically reconstructed as participation in Jesus Christ's living self-witness, adequately describes the role of Scripture in God's life with us. The argument in support of this thesis consists of three parts.

The first part makes the case that the practice of personal testimony matters to evangelicals in general and Wesleyans in particular. Although valued and practiced in other traditions, the Wesleyan/Holiness tradition contributes a unique formation of and theological justification for personal testimony. However, testimony is not without its problems. In order to take seriously these problems, the second part critically reconstructs the concept of testimony by means of a conversation with the later theology of Karl Barth. After developing this critical reconstruction of the concept of testimony, I will turn to the reality of Scripture to rethink its function in terms of testimony, i.e., Scripture participates in Jesus Christ's living self-attestation by testifying to him.

I.

Why testimony? What is it about the practice of personal testimony that makes it fruitful for evangelical theology in general and Wesleyans in particular? My claim in this first section is a simple one: testimony matters to Wesleyans. This claim has both an historical and a normative side. Historically, the practice of personal testimony has taken on a unique form and function in the Wesleyan/Holiness tradition, and as such has emerged as one of the tradition's signature practices. Normatively, the distinctive theological commitments of the Wesleyan/Holiness tradition are embedded socially in the practice of personal testimony, and as such warrant the preservation of the practice despite its problems. Because the historical and the normative are truly two sides of the same coin in theological reasoning (as I understand it), I will substantiate both sides simultaneously by means of a series of theses.

Thesis 1: The practice of testimony is the concrete form of the Wesleyan/Holiness order of salvation.

The practice of personal testimony is not unique to the Wesleyan/Holiness tradition. Furthermore, the Wesleyan/Holiness tradition is not unique in emphasizing the practice of personal testimony. Rather, an emphasis on personal testimony is a mark of the wider phenomena of modern religious awakening in and through which Methodism emerged. One of the marks of the Pietist impulse in Protestant Christianity is the correlation of one's personal testimony with the *ordo salutis*, or order of salvation. Whereas Protestant Orthodoxy distinguished between the logical and the chronological senses of the order of salvation, Pietism regarded the order of salvation as descriptive of (and normative for) personal religious experience. The movement from awakening to regeneration could be narrated in terms of one's actual life history. The same goes for the movement from the initial sanctification accompanying regeneration to total consecration and entire sanctification, accented by the Wesleyan/Holiness tradition. Accordingly, doctrinal formulations regarding the *ordo* were not only to be believed, but also to function as a sort of itinerary for one's personal testimony. In fact, the correlation also runs in the other direction, so that the *ordo salutis* is the conceptual redescription of the plot of one's personal testimony.[1]

Within this context, doctrinal differences over the order of salvation became central in polemical theology. It is fitting, then, that Wesley consistently expressed his disagreements with others in the form of a dispute over the *ordo*. The *ordo* is not just one doctrine among others, but a supremely practical matter. For example: if adoption coincides with justification, then the experience of freedom from fear is an essential mark of the event of justification.[2] For another example: if regeneration immediately follows jus-

---

1. This bidirectional correlation is a fundamental warrant for consulting experience in theological work.

2. Cf. Wesley, "Spirit of Bondage and of Adoption," 248–66. See also the discussion

tification, then sin in believers is not to be tolerated.³ For a third example: if entire sanctification follows justification as a distinct event, then testimony to entire sanctification ought to have two distinct plot points. Of course, this third example does not find so succinct expression in John Wesley. For that we will have to turn to a later period, and with it to our second thesis. But at this point, it is evident that the practice of personal testimony is the concretization of Wesleyan doctrinal distinctives.

Thesis 2: The practice of testimony is itself internal to the Wesleyan/Holiness order of salvation.

The story of the transformation of Wesleyan theology on American soil is well known. What interests me is the transformation of the practice of testimony within this story. It is during the nineteenth century that the twofold testimony clearly emerges. Conversion and entire sanctification are two distinct events in one's life, and therefore one testifies to them by means of two distinct testimonial acts. Although there are reasons for challenging this schema, it is an important development within the Wesleyan/Holiness tradition inasmuch as it follows through on the logic of an *ordo* with two crucial plot points.⁴

Within this development, we see the shift from testimony as a practice merely correlated with the order of salvation to testimony as an event internal to the order of salvation itself. This shift emerges distinctively though not exclusively in the work of Phoebe Palmer. For Palmer, the narrative of one's testimony continues to be structured by the *ordo*, but for her the act of testifying is also the final step in the experience of sanctification. After consecrating one's self wholly to God, one claims in faith that one is sanctified, and then seals that sanctification by means of a personal testimony. Without this seal, entire sanctification is lost.⁵

After Palmer, testimony is no longer just a practice to which doctrines are applied, but itself a concept in its own right worthy of explicit doctrinal

---

of assurance in Collins, *The Theology of John Wesley*, ch. 4, and Maddox, *Responsible Grace*, ch. 5. Their differences of interpretation notwithstanding, Maddox and Collins concur on the important connection between assurance and regeneration in Wesley.

3. Cf. Wesley, "On Sin in Believers," 314–34.

4. For more on the twin-foci *ordo* of the American Holiness movement, see Dayton, *The Theological Roots of Pentecostalism*, and Dieter, *The Holiness Revival of the Nineteenth Century*.

5. For Palmer's soteriology and the role of testimony therein, see Palmer, *The Way of Holiness* and *Pioneer Experiences*. Cf. also Dieter, *Holiness Revival*, 36, and Heath, *Naked Faith*.

reflection. Despite the objections one must raise against her scheme,[6] Palmer is significant for my case because she explicitly renders the practice of personal testimony internal to the experience of entire sanctification, and so offers a unique theological justification for the necessity of the practice of personal testimony. Even though her formulations are inadequate, her commitment to the necessity of testimony is a genuine expression of the Wesleyan spirit.

Thesis 3: The practice of testimony is pivotal for the inclusion of unauthorized voices within Wesleyan/Holiness churches.

During the nineteenth-century revivals many unordained persons, including women, publicly testified. Recent research has shown the extent to which the line between testifying and preaching was blurred by this practice, at least by the hearers.[7] Accordingly, the practice of testimony has functioned historically as a pivot towards the ordination of women. Testimony is a liminal concept, operating between everyday religious discourse and authorized proclamation. This pivotal function is not a mere historical accident. Once the practice of testimony is emphasized to the point of being rendered necessary, then one is theologically driven to include the voices of those who would otherwise remain voiceless. The revolutionary potential of Wesleyan/Holiness theology—often highlighted by those of us in the tradition, despite its foibles—is socially embedded in the practice of testimony. One wonders whether our churches, having now authorized certain voices, will be blinded to future inclusions on account of the decline in the practice of testimony.

---

6. For instance, the notion of "sealing" a prelinguistic religious experience presupposes an unnecessary metaphysics of the subject. However, it is precisely this notion of "sealing" that has so much potential, for testimony is a speech-act that creates the sort of public recognition and accountability that the experience of sanctification requires for its confirmation and further development. A private experience of sanctification is practically speaking impossible.

7. Hardesty, *Women Called to Witness*, and Florence, *Preaching as Testimony*. Cf. also Hatch, *The Democratization of American Christianity*. Phoebe Palmer's own thinking on women preachers can be found in her 1859 classic, *The Promise of the Father*.

Thesis 4: The practice of testimony is formative for Wesleyan/Holiness congregations.

Public testimonies benefit not only the testifier (by confirming his or her sanctification) but also the community that recognizes and receives the testimony (by holding out the hope and means of entire sanctification). At the heart of the Wesleyan/Holiness tradition is the commitment to concrete holiness as a real possibility for all in this life. Public testimony attests this possibility. Without the accompaniment of public testimony, the call to holiness is empty, functionally performing the same task as non-Wesleyan/Holiness doctrines of sanctification: holding out an impossible ideal as a judgment and/or inspiration. So it is fitting that the decline in the practice of testimony can be closely correlated with the decline in interest in entire sanctification. The practice of testimony is formative for communities by keeping the possibility of entire sanctification alive.

Thesis 5: The practice of testimony is the site par excellence where the personal and the public aspects of the gospel are explicitly united.

As we have already stated, testimony concerns both the testifier and the hearers. Testimony is thus both intensely personal and inherently public. The intensely personal aspect of testimony is obvious, inasmuch as the content of a personal testimony is one's own personal story. However, one's personal spiritual narrative is not yet a testimony until it is uttered publicly. The public utterance of a testimony transforms a personal spiritual narrative into a liturgical act of the community, and thus brings it under public accountability. The personal testimony is not, therefore, a merely subjectivist practice protected from public scrutiny behind a wall of indefeasible prelinguistic religious experience.

The concept of testimony, originally rooted in a juridical context, entails its public function as a defeasible line of evidence in a dispute between parties. Its religious use significantly alters but does not destroy this juridical meaning. As Paul Ricouer observes, in the New Testament the concept of testimony inextricably unites both the confessional and narrational pole of the gospel, i.e., both its meaning and its facticity.[8] Since holding together the intensively personal and the inherently public aspects of the gospel is

---

8. Here I summarize the second and third sections of Paul Riceour's essay "The Hermeneutics of Testimony," in *Essays on Biblical Interpretation*.

one of the hallmarks of the Wesleyan/Holiness tradition, it is fitting that testimony is one of its signature practices.

These five theses conspire to substantiate the rather straightforward claim that testimony matters to Wesleyans. The practice and concept of testimony is near the heart of the Wesleyan/Holiness tradition, both historically and normatively. On this basis, we have good reason to think it fruitful for Wesleyan reflection on the function of Scripture. But—and here's the rub—the practice and concept of testimony have been in sharp decline for some time now. And not without reason, for testimony has its problems, which brings us to the second step of my argument: critical reconstruction.

II.

Testimony is in decline. Theological and sociological developments, as well as reaction to abuse, have contributed to a decline in the value and use of testimony as both a practice and a concept. The list of problems is long: the accusation of subjectivism, the problem of false testimony, the control of the testimonial practice by older generations, the formulaic character of many testimonies, the difficulty of fitting testimony within current worship renewal movements, etc. Although many of these problems can be addressed, the intensity and extent of contemporary critique must be taken seriously before drawing positively on the concept of testimony. In order to do so, I will critically reconstruct the concept of testimony in conversation with the mature theology of Karl Barth.

Why Barth? On the one hand, he unrelentingly criticized the practice of personal testimony. His entire project is directed against the move to make one's own personal spiritual narrative the proper object of theological reflection. He is the apotheosis of the Reformed instinct to turn away from one's self and turn toward God and his glory. He carries this instinct to its logical conclusion by critiquing even his own tradition for making too much of self-abnegation, which functions as a twisted sort of negative natural theology. So Barth's critical potential with regard to personal testimony is indisputable.

On the other hand, Barth reconstructed the entire theological enterprise in terms of *Zeugnis* (testimony, witness). Theology itself participates in the Christian community's service of witness by testing its contemporary proclamation against its own norms.[9] Even in this critical function,

---

9. This definition of dogmatics is asserted on the first page of his *Church Dogmatics*, i.e., §1.

Part II—Reconceiving Christian Experience and Practice

theology is itself testimony in a unique mode of discourse.[10] So, although he is a great critic of personal testimony, Karl Barth is *the* theologian of Christian witness.[11]

In order to critically reconstruct the concept of testimony, I will draw on the final complete volume of the *Church Dogmatics*, IV/3, in which Barth argues that the Christian's personal liberation is incidental yet indispensable to her vocation as witness with and to Jesus Christ. Let me first put this argument in context.

In the prior part-volumes of *CD* IV, Barth treats the humiliation of God and the exaltation of humanity in Jesus Christ's life of obedience unto death. The justification and sanctification of humanity has taken place *de jure* in this one representative human being. Barth thus relocates the order of salvation in the life history of Jesus Christ. This Christological relocation fundamentally relativizes the soteriological significance of communal and personal realization of the reconciliation actualized in Jesus Christ.[12]

Does this mean that our realization of reconciliation has no significance whatsoever? By no means! The Christian life is fundamentally a life of witness, a life that testifies to the conversion of the world that took place in Jesus Christ. This claim too is Christologically grounded: Jesus Christ is risen from the dead and as such attests himself, calling his own to join him in his self-attestation. Barth develops this claim throughout volume IV[13] but takes it up as his theme in the third part-volume, in which he redefines the prophetic office of Jesus Christ as his own living self-declaration of the work of reconciliation accomplished in his life. The life of God and humanity actualized in him is also light. His existence has a name. His reality is also truth. His work is also word.[14]

In contrast to the previous two forms of reconciliation, human beings cooperate in this prophetic work of Jesus Christ. As he is on his way of self-witness, the risen Christ is present with his community in the promise of the Spirit, who empowers them to share in the harvest.[15] The essence of the Christian life is thus to be a witness—to testify—before the world on Christ's behalf.[16] The primary subject of this witness is the risen Christ him-

---

10. Barth makes this clear in his discussion of theology as a form of the Christian community's service of witness in *CD* IV/3, 879–82.

11. Hence Joseph Mangina's aptly titled introduction to Barth's theology: *Karl Barth: Theologian of Christian Witness*.

12. Cf. esp. *CD* IV/1, §61, and *CD* IV/2, §66.

13. Cf. esp. the "transitional discussions": *CD* IV/1, §59.3, and *CD* IV/2, §64.4.

14. *CD* IV/3, §69.2.

15. Ibid., §69.4.

16. Ibid., §71.3.

self. But we too as his disciples bear witness to him, and thereby participate in him. Our service of witness is thus the form of our fellowship with the risen Christ.[17]

In the context of this larger argument, Barth includes a brief sub-section on the personal liberation of the Christian.[18] The location of this discussion is in itself significant. The "purely personal"[19] aspect of the Christian life is located not within the doctrine of justification and/or sanctification, but rather within the doctrine of vocation.[20] Barth's central claim in this sub-section is that the Christian's personal liberation is incidental yet indispensable to his or her vocation to testify: "for all its incidental and relative character the personal liberation of the Christian is an indispensable presupposition, a *conditio sine qua non*, of his existence as a witness of Jesus Christ and therefore of his Christian status."[21] Both sides of this claim are essential to a critical reconstruction of the concept of testimony.

On the one hand, the Christian's personal liberation is *incidental* to her testimony. This much should be obvious from the whole weight of Barth's doctrine of reconciliation. But it comes out especially clearly in his exegesis of the call narratives in the Bible. Barth goes through all the major call stories

17. Ibid., §71.2. Cf. also *CD* IV/2, §64.4.

18. *CD* IV/3, §71.6.

19. Ibid., 647.

20. I think this relocation is crucial for a critical reconstruction of the concept of testimony. I do not explicitly develop this claim here, but it is implicit throughout the remainder of what I have to say.

21. *CD* IV/3, 662. The incidental-yet-indispensable pairing and its equivalents recur throughout §71.6: "The personal significance of vocation for the Christian is a phenomenon which only accompanies the ministry [*Dienst*] of witness [*Zeugnis*] which properly makes him a Christian. . . . Nevertheless, this personal aspect must not be ignored nor dismissed too summarily. The Christian does have his own existence in relation to what he has to attest as such" (648); "Incidentally perhaps, but unavoidably, all these things are also to their own judgment and salvation" (650); "as he can be concerned only with the ministry [*Dienst*] required of him, he will incidentally, without any desire, longing or effort, yet quite infallibly, have a care for his own best interests" (653); "all this, even the very best of it, is only incidental. . . . But . . . it is inevitable" (654); "We have defined and understood this as something incidental and additional, as a by-product of the real thing which makes him a Christian, of his appointment as a witness. But this cannot mean that it is an unimportant and even dispensable determination of Christian existence" (655); "the incidental but necessary question of the existential determination of the Christian by the content of his witness" (655); "its relative necessity" (656); "his little personal liberation, his own faith, knowledge and experience, are an indispensable prerequisite, a *conditio sine qua non*" (657); "I myself as a Christian . . . am an indispensable instrument to myself as a theologian, as a preacher and pastor, as the witness which I am to be like others. But I am not a theme or object" (677).

and argues that, despite the deep alteration of one's personal existence that takes place in it, the focus of the event of calling is on the task of testifying to God's being and activity.[22] This God is for the world and its liberation, and so God's testifying community is also for the world and its liberation. The Christian's witness is at its heart not about her and her experience of salvation, but about God and God's reconciliation of the world to himself in Jesus Christ. Therefore, one's own personal liberation is incidental to the task of testifying to this reality.

On the other hand, the Christian's liberation is *indispensable* to her testimony. This side is not so obvious given Barth's emphasis on the actuality and objectivity of the gospel. However, against Protestant Orthodoxy he explicitly and repeatedly asserts the indispensability of one's personal experience of the gospel to which one testifies.[23] On what grounds does he make this assertion? Generally speaking, the authority and credibility of our testimony depends on our being personally affected by that to which we attest.[24] Specifically, three characteristics of the content of the Christian's testimony entail the indispensability of the Christian's personal liberation. First, the Christian is called to attest to the world that Jesus Christ is not a dream, illusion or mere theory, but a supremely relevant fact. Therefore, she must be personally affected by it for her testimony to be credible.[25] Second, the Christian is called to attest to the world the radical demand of the gospel. Therefore, the Christian must personally contend and struggle with the living God for her testimony to ring true.[26] Third, the Christian is called to attest to the world the good news of great joy that in Jesus Christ the vicious circle of sin has been broken and humanity has been sent forth to serve the Lord. Therefore, the Christian must be personally joyful for her testimony to have any authority.[27] In brief, the credibility (though not the truth) of the Christian's testimony depends on the correspondence between her personal existence and the reality to which she attests.

---

22. *CD* IV/3, 577–92. Barth revisits this exegetical point at the beginning of §71.6 (648–49).

23. Barth explicitly sets his sights against Protestant Orthodoxy on 655–56.

24. Ibid., 657–58.

25. Ibid., 658: "He has to attest to the world that the light of the act and revelation of God in Jesus Christ is not a dream, nor an illusion, nor a subject of mere theory, but a fact, and indeed a fact which is relevant and significant for each and every man." The Christian must follow Jesus Christ in his self-witness "in such a way that in his action, his human words and attitudes and conduct, he brings before the world a phenomenon which corresponds and therefore points to the self-witness of Jesus Christ."

26. Ibid., 659–70.

27. Ibid., 660–62.

Barth goes on to identify seven marks of this personal liberation. Although they need not be rehearsed, Barth's decision to identify concrete markers underscores that he is speaking in this context of the concrete, human phenomenon of personal liberation. Although these marks are decisively not set forth as a sequence, they do each point to the history, the event, of the Christian's liberation. Therefore, one finds in Barth a version of the Pietist correlation between doctrinal formulation and one's personal narrative. What Barth takes away with one hand, he gives back with the other, albeit in a radically altered form.

However, before getting too excited about Barth's case for the indispensability of personal liberation for the Christian's witness, we must acknowledge the final turn of his dialectic. In the final pages of §71.6, Barth makes four points of clarification: i.e., the Christian's personal liberation is fragmentary, exemplary, indirect, and subordinate. Although he does not rescind the claim of its indispensability, Barth reasserts the incidental character of personal liberation. Under his third point, Barth explicitly rejects the practice of personal testimony. "The personal liberation of the Christian can and should fit him for this ministry of witness. But it can and should not become the content of his witness."[28] So the Christian "must spare his fellows any direct information concerning himself and the way in which the Word of God has become significant and effective in his own life in some such application."[29]

Although I would concur with Barth that one's personal liberation is only fragmentary in form, exemplary in function, and subservient to the task of witness, I do not find Barth's absolute rejection of personal testimony compelling.[30] Instead, I would take the remainder of his delimitations as cri-

---

28. Ibid., 676.

29. Ibid., 677. The general target of this criticism is explicit. Just prior to this delimitation Barth criticizes the proposition of nineteenth-century Protestant theology that "I myself as a Christian am the most proper object of knowledge to myself as a theologian." Barth admits that "I myself as a Christian . . . am an indispensable instrument to myself as a theologian." But he goes on to say that "I am not a theme or object. I am not the object of my knowledge and proclamation, nor of my witness, in any conceivable form." However, there may be a more specific target in mind. Immediately following this delimitation, Barth goes on to say, "It need hardly be indicated against what kind of proclamation this delimitation is directed." Although this also could be taken as a general statement against Barth's historic and contemporary opponents, I cannot help wondering if he had some specific, perhaps local, person(s) in mind.

30. It seems to me that this delimitation is the result of prior prejudice rather than the consequence of the present argument. Surely much of what passes for testimony falls rightly under Barth's censure. But is a gag rule warranted by such widespread abuse? I think not. Perhaps a moratorium could be recommended, but an absolute gag rule goes too far.

teria for evaluating the adequacy of a given testimony. A personal testimony that would satisfy these delimitations might be rare, but it is not absolutely inconceivable, and so Barth's absolute gag rule is unjustifiable. Better to root out abuse than to bar use. It seems to me one's indispensable personal liberation, however incidental it may be, would at least occasionally make its way into public proclamation.

What have we learned from Barth in this section? In Barth we find both an unrelenting critic of the subjectivist impulse in theology and a thoroughgoing advocate of theology as witness/testimony. Barth has undercut the typical justification for and function of personal testimony by relocating the *ordo salutis* in the life history of Jesus. The Christian's testimony is thus always referred to that which is prior to and outside of herself. However, the Christian's personal liberation, though incidental, is indispensable to this testimony. Thus Barth's theology provides a critical reconstruction of the concept of testimony as participation in the risen Christ's self-attestation. This critical reconstruction can be used (against his own judgments) to warrant a rightly ordered practice of personal testimony.

III.

What does this have to do with the function of Holy Scripture? This critical reconstruction of the concept of testimony is wide enough to include the function of Scripture in God's life with us. Testimony is participation in the risen Christ's self-attestation. There are many forms of this participation. The primary form of participation in the living Jesus Christ's self-attestation is the prophetic and apostolic testimony—first spoken, and then written, and now handed down. The secondary form of participation in the risen Christ's self-witness is church proclamation. So the testimony is threefold: Jesus Christ, Holy Scripture, and Church Proclamation. At this point I have said nothing new, inasmuch as I have simply restated Barth's doctrine of the threefold Word of God.[31] Drawing on impulses from the Wesleyan/Holiness tradition, what I want to add to Barth's schema is the *corroborating witness of personal testimony*.

Christian testimony is thoroughly *kergymatic*, proclaiming the liberation of the world for the sake of the world. The Christian's testimony to her own personal liberation is only incidental to this *kerygmatic* testimony, but as such it is indispensable for her credibility. And so for every *kerygmatic* testimony there is an accompanying personal testimony. To use the language of the courtroom: personal testimony only *corroborates kerygmatic*

---

31. *CD* I/1, §4, and *CD* I/2, §§19–24.

testimony. But even as a corroborating witness, it nevertheless participates in Jesus Christ's living self-attestation.

What would this addition mean for the doctrine threefold Word of God? It does not alter the threefold structure; rather, it further elucidates the nature of Barth's concept of witness, enfolding the voice of the here and now in God's economy of revelation, while also offering a needed Christological corrective to Wesleyan/Holiness practice. Personal testimony may not be regarded as an independent source of revelation, but rather as a participant in the risen Christ's own ongoing self-witness. Only on such terms can Barth's thought be stretched to include personal testimony. And it is precisely on these terms that the abuses of Wesleyan/Holiness practice may be curtailed.

In regard to Barth's conception, the first form of the Word of God is Jesus Christ. Jesus Christ in his resurrection testifies to the liberation of the world accomplished in his life of obedience unto death. Since for Christ there is no gap between personal and global liberation, *kerygmatic* and personal testimony are identical in him. However, this gap does apply to the prophets and apostles. So Holy Scripture, as the second form of the Word of God, is incidentally but indispensably accompanied by the corroborating witness of the personal testimony of the prophets and the apostles. Such testimonies to personal liberation can be found throughout Scripture. Barth is right to say that they are not the main theme. But they are nevertheless there. Finally, Church Proclamation, as the third form of the Word of God, is incidentally but indispensably accompanied by the corroborating witness of the Christian's personal testimony. Such testimonies must always serve the primary purpose of the service of witness to the world. But inasmuch as they do, they also in their own way participate in Jesus Christ's living self-attestation.

Bibliography

Collins, Kenneth J. *The Theology of John Wesley: Holy Love and the Shape of Grace.* Nashville: Abingdon, 2007.

Dayton, Donald W. *Theological Roots of Pentecostalism.* Grand Rapids: Francis Asbury, 1987.

Dieter, Melvin E. *The Holiness Revival of the Nineteenth Century.* Lanham, MD: Scarecrow, 1996.

Florence, Anna Carter. *Preaching as Testimony.* Louisville: Westminster John Knox, 2007.

Hardesty, Nancy. *Women Called to Witness: Evangelical Feminism in the Nineteenth Century.* Nashville: Abingdon, 1984.

Hatch, Nathan O. *The Democratization of American Christianity.* New Haven: Yale University Press, 1989.

Heath, Elaine A. *Naked Faith: The Mystical Theology of Phoebe Palmer.* Eugene, OR: Pickwick, 2009.

Maddox, Randy L. *Responsible Grace: John Wesley's Practical Theology.* Nashville: Kingswood, 1994.

Mangina, Joseph. *Karl Barth: Theologian of Christian Witness.* Louisville: Westminster John Knox, 2004.

Palmer, Phoebe. *Pioneer Experiences.* 1868. Reprint, New York: Garland, 1984.

———. *The Promise of the Father.* 1859. Reprint, New York: Garland, 1985.

———. *The Way of Holiness.* 1867. Reprint, Kansas City: Beacon Hill, 1981.

Riceour, Paul. *Essays on Biblical Interpretation.* Philadelphia: Fortress, 1980.

Wesley, John. "The Spirit of Bondage and of Adoption." In *The Works of John Wesley*, vol. 1, *Sermons*, edited by Albert C. Outler, 248–66. Nashville: Abingdon, 1984.

———. "On Sin in Believers." In *The Works of John Wesley*, vol. 1, *Sermons*, edited by Albert C. Outler, 314–34. Nashville: Abingdon, 1984.

7

Jesus's Earthly Father as Protector and Example for the Church

How Karl Barth's Theology Challenges the Contemporary Evangelical Masculinist Movement

Stina Busman Jost

Introduction: The Masculinist Movement in American Evangelicalism

In recent years within conservative American Evangelicalism there has been a move toward embracing and proclaiming a Christianity that is explicitly and enduringly masculine. In January 2012, for example, John Piper declared "that God has given Christianity a masculine feel."[1] Other leaders within Evangelicalism have embraced this same impulse, and hence

---

1. Piper, "'The Frank and Manly Mr. Ryle'—The Value of a Masculine Ministry." The full quote in which this statement is uttered is interesting and worth noting here. Piper's description, after citing a few biblical texts regarding the divinely ordained leadership of men, is as follows: "From all of this, I conclude that God has given Christianity a masculine feel. And, being a God of love, he has done it for the maximum flourishing of men *and women*. He did not create women to languish, or be frustrated, or in any way to suffer or fall short of full and lasting joy, in a masculine Christianity. She is a fellow heir of the grace of life (1 Peter 3:7). From which I infer that the fullest flourishing of women and men takes place in churches and families where Christianity has this God-ordained, masculine feel. For the sake of the glory of women, and for the sake of the security and joy of children, God has made Christianity to have a masculine feel. He has ordained for the church a masculine ministry."

a growing body of sermons, books, and blogs have understood and professed Christianity to be distinctly masculine. This movement both stems from and aligns with the complementarian position, and many within this movement's ranks see this current effort as one of recovery—that is, the reclaiming of the life and beliefs of the community of faith as God originally intended them.

This contemporary movement within Christianity has not only included the enforcing of limiting structures on communities of faith (e.g., in terms of who can and cannot serve in leadership positions), it also entails a distorted approach to Scripture. It espouses a method of interpretation that overemphasizes the masculinity of various characters of the Bible—both human and divine. Moreover, it often entails the pitting of masculine against feminine, and with such division, the resulting masculine accentuation leads to caricaturization as well as very limited descriptions of the roles of men and women.[2] In this re-visioning, men of the Bible are considered through a predetermined lens of masculinity. This then implies, for example, that Adam's significance does not foremost lie in his being the first human being; it lies in his being the first man. As Douglas Wilson describes,

> I used the phrase "provider and protector" a moment ago. ... When we look at the beginning of our race, looking carefully at our circumstances when God placed us in the world, we see these roles *assigned* to the man. Again, men were put into this world in order to work it and to keep it. They were placed here with this twofold mandate in mind. This is what men are *for*.
>
> All men are called, like Adam our first father, to provide for their families and to protect their families.[3]

Similarly, Job is described not just as an exemplar of godly character but as an exemplar of godly masculine character. Thus, in reference to Job 29, Randy Stinson and Dan Dumas assert,

> This is an astounding model of bold, masculine servant leadership. Job didn't see the blessings of his life as a reason to lord over those around him. ... Like Job, be diligent and masculine

---

2. See for example, John Eldredge's description of masculinity in his text *Fathered by God*). Eldredge summarizes, "If I were to sketch out for you the masculine journey in broad strokes, I believe this is how it unfolds, or better, how it was *meant* to unfold: Boyhood to Cowboy to Warrior to Lover to King to Sage. All in the course of about eighty years or so, give or take a decade or two" (13). Undeniably, there is not uniformity in this contemporary masculinist movement. Richard Phillips, for example, in a recent book disagrees with the approach of Eldredge and discusses what he terms the "Wild at Heart Fallacy." See: Phillips, *The Masculine Mandate*, 5f.

3. Wilson, *Father Hunger*, 9.

in your response to needs and in "breaking the fangs of the unrighteous" to free their prey.[4]

Even Jesus and his father, Joseph, are portrayed and described according to their manliness. Patrick Morley, in his book *Pastoring Men*, writes,

> Jesus wasn't just born to a virgin woman, he was born to a virgin couple. Joseph planned to divorce Mary quietly. Jesus was going to grow up without a dad. God thought it was important enough for Jesus to have a father in the home that he intervened supernaturally to change Joseph's mind (and so Mary would not be disgraced as an unwed mother). Mary may have had the baby, but Joseph taught Him how to be a man. Jesus was a man's man, and He didn't learn that from His mommy.[5]

For those who are writing in this contemporary masculinist movement, Adam, Job, and Joseph are indeed human beings who uniquely related to the Creator, but they are more fundamentally *men* who uniquely related to the Creator.

These masculinist readings, I submit, are most accurately understood not as recovery but revision, and such revisionist efforts profoundly undermine the commonality among the people of God. The men of faith depicted in Scripture must be understood as examples for all believers. So too, the women of faith depicted in Scripture must be understood as examples for all believers. Such emphasis on commonality in no way eliminates the situational distinctiveness of individuals—be that uniqueness in terms of class, gender, ethnicity, or some other dimension of identity. In fact, for the sake of both the community and the individual, this distinctiveness cannot be overlooked or discarded—especially where injustice persists. At the same time, the overemphasis of the masculinist features of biblical characters—and the concomitant roles prescribed to men—engenders divisions within Christian communities instead of fostering unity and reconciliation among the diverse parts that make up these communities.

In the remainder of this essay, with this contemporary evangelical movement of masculinist revision in mind, I will engage in a theological examination that underscores the importance of identifying the commonality among believers within Christian communities. Specifically, I will consider the example of one male character in Scripture—Joseph, earthly father of Jesus—and thereby demonstrate the significance in seeing Joseph not foremost as a father, although this is undeniably important, but foremost as a

---

4. Stinson and Dumas, *Guide to Biblical Manhood*, 20.
5. Morley, *Pastoring Men*, 187.

servant of God and thus a model for the entire faith community. To complete this task, my investigation will draw on the insights of Karl Barth and specifically his interest in Joseph as a protector and example for the church. In what follows, I will first highlight Barth's brief consideration of Joseph in the *CD* and then identify the development of Barth's interest in Joseph in Barth's later life. Next I will consider carefully the theological suggestions Barth makes regarding Joseph as a model for the entire church. I will conclude this essay by returning to the subject of the evangelical masculinist movement and considering how an understanding of Joseph as an example for the church as a whole assists in affirming the unity of the Christian community.

Karl Barth's Theological Reflections on Joseph

Discussion of Joseph in the *Church Dogmatics*

Joseph, who is undeniably an influential character in the early life of Jesus, has no recorded speaking lines in the gospel accounts. Similarly, little ink has been spilled over his significance in Protestant theology. Barth is not the exception here, and thus like many other Protestant theologians, he does not devote significant attention to the figure of Joseph. For example, within the *CD*, Barth spends only a brief amount of time considering the role of Joseph—specifically, in his discussions of both the genealogies in the gospels and the virgin birth.

In a section of writing that focuses on the Christmas Miracle, one gets the distinct sense that Barth understands Joseph primarily as a member of the Jewish community who is chosen to be intimately involved in this radically new beginning for humanity found in Jesus Christ. It is Joseph's Davidic lineage that Barth discusses as significant—especially the non-biological yet genealogical nexus between Joseph and Jesus.[6] Barth goes on to note the active role Joseph is called to play in the narratives. With reference to Joseph's dream recorded in Matthew 1, Barth indicates that "Joseph's conversation with the angel is directed toward helping Joseph over the stumbling-block which he must see to be involved in the pregnancy of Mary."[7] Such involvement is undertaken not because of a biological connection to the unborn child, as this does not exist; it is undertaken through faith.

Joseph's decision to be involved with Mary and the child parallels the decisions that all members of the community of Israel face. Election of the

---

6. Barth, *CD* I/2, 175.
7. Ibid., 187.

new community that the Messiah has come to establish is different than the election of the old community. As Barth describes in a later discussion of the communities of God,

> For what begins with the rise of the Christian community is not a natural people, a nexus of blood, a succession of generations, a complex of tribes and families and fathers and sons which are as such the bearers and recipients of the promise. Even the individual Israelite is now confronted with a question which is not answered by the mere fact that he is an Israelite, or is circumcised, or has the blessing of the high-priest.... Even within Israel there is a new election and decision, and the summons to a new calling and personal faith.[8]

The new community of both Jews and Gentiles is "constituted and gathered" by the Spirit of God not by blood.[9] So, too, Joseph is called to be involved with Mary and the unborn child not because of blood but because of the work of the Spirit in the body of Mary.

Discussion of Joseph in Barth's Later Life

Apart from these brief discussions noted above, Barth gives little attention to the figure of Joseph in the *CD*.[10] Interestingly, though, in his later life Barth voices a specific interest in this biblical figure. Instead of understanding Joseph solely through his Israelite lineage and identity, Barth suggests that Joseph, in relation to Jesus Christ, is both a protector of the church and an example for the church to follow. Two key factors seem to prompt this theological interest surrounding the figure of Joseph. First, Barth is deeply concerned with the theological foundation and development of Mariology within the Catholic Church.[11] Instead of understanding Mary as protector

---

8. Barth, *CD* III/2, 584.

9. Ibid., 585.

10. Discussions of Joseph are also quite sparse elsewhere in Barth's work. See, for example, *Göttingen Dogmatics*, 161f.; see also Barth, *The Great Promise*.

11. Barth's concerns stem from the very development of the theological lineage of the Mariological tradition in the Catholic Church. His position on this matter is succinctly articulated in a letter penned to a colleague in 1966 shortly after reading this colleague's lecture on Mariology. Barth notes, "You know as well as I do, and admit it at the start, that the '*theotokos*' of the Council of Ephesus (and also the normal sense of the term before that) was a formula to aid in expressing Christology, and not a mariological statement, nor the enunciation of an independent dogma besides the one which the Council stated as the doctrine of the 'two natures' of Christ. When this '*theotokos*' was used to build a Mariology—I must say here, misused—it became, however

of the church and considering her to be a figure that the church should emulate, Barth suggests the other parental figure of Jesus—namely Joseph—should be lifted up. This inclination to consider Joseph instead of Mary as protector and exemplar is evident in Barth's visit to the United States in 1962. While in Chicago, Barth encountered one of the foremost Catholic scholars on Joseph studies, the Jesuit theologian Francis Filas. A month after the two theologians met, Filas wrote these words about Barth's perspective on Joseph:

> My final experience of Karl Barth dealt with something related to my major life's work in theology—the nature, history and theology of the devotion to St. Joseph. Mindful of *Time* magazine's quotation from Barth's works to the effect that Roman Catholic Mariology is an "excrescence" of theology, I asked Professor Barth at a reception after his final lecture what he thought of the theology of St. Joseph. . . . With no warning beforehand that such would be my query and with probably no knowledge of Catholic Church documents on the subject, he answered at once, using substantially these words, "Ah, a Josephologist! If I were a Roman Catholic theologian, I would lift Joseph up; he took care of the Child; he takes care of the Church." One could not ask for a more piercing and succinct summary of the reasoning used in Catholic Josephology.[12]

This description by Filas reveals a nascent but clear interest of Barth in the figure of Joseph.

Such interest is fueled by another event that occurred later in 1962. Thus the second factor that prompts Barth's theological interest in Joseph is the decision made on November 13th at the Second Vatican Council to include Joseph in the canon of the Mass. In three letters written by Barth between November 1962 and March 1963, these two factors are mentioned together. To Oscar Cullmann, the famous Lutheran ecumenist who was an invited observer of the Second Vatican Council, Barth writes the following:

> You can imagine that it is with the closest attention and even with "burning concern" that I receive from the holy city the news filtering through from the fringe of the mystery council, and I anxiously await your direct reports. . . . What has been

---

unobjectionable it was and is in itself, the starting point of a development which I can only regard as grotesque." See Barth, *Ad Limina Apostolorum*, 60.

12. Filas, "Barth as Seeker of God's Truth." See also the excellent resources Filas has produced on Joseph: *Joseph: The Man Closest to Jesus* and *St. Joseph after Vatican II*. Perhaps the most compelling contemporary work on Joseph is by Leonardo Boff; see his *Saint Joseph*.

decided about St. Joseph greatly pleases me. Is not the relationship between [Joseph] and Jesus Christ ("foster-father") a much more exact model for the church than Mary's relationship is?[13]

A few weeks later Barth writes something very similar in correspondence with Hans Küng. In this letter Barth provisionally congratulates Küng on his role as *peritus* at the Second Vatican Council, and then goes on to write, "Do you know I am one of the few Protestants who is not annoyed but pleased that Joseph has been put in the canon of the mass? His function as foster-father of Christ makes him a much more appropriate patron of the church than the *theotokos*, who is usually mentioned in this connection."[14] So too, Barth decides to communicate this same conviction to another Catholic theologian. In March 1963, Barth pens a letter to Dominican B. A. Willems and enthusiastically shares,

> What will you say when I tell you I am one of the few Protestants who was not annoyed by the insertion of St. Joseph into the canon of the mass? I find this biblical figure, movingly obedient and ministering, much more suited to be the protector (and exemplar!) of the church than Mary, with whose function that of the church is not to be compared. I cannot assume John XXIII had this in mind with his move toward Joseph theology. But is it not permissible and perhaps even obligatory to think further in this direction and then perhaps to reach further clarifications in ecclesiology as well?[15]

It is this last question—and specifically the charge "to think further in this direction"—that I will address below.

Nascent Tenets of a Barthian Josephology

What is evident in these letters penned by Barth in 1962 and 1963 is a strong theological impulse—an impulse of an important yet undeveloped ecclesiological motif. Yet, before proceeding to winnow out a Barthian explication of Josephology, a couple observations concerning Barth's discussion of Joseph must be briefly considered here. Undeniably, the comments Barth makes in and after 1962 about Joseph as a model for the church are sparse; in no way does he develop a robust Josephology. Moreover Barth's comments about Joseph are made in the casual mediums of letters as well as

---

13. Barth, *Letters, 1961–68*, 75.
14. Ibid., 84.
15. Ibid., 94.

interviews conducted with him in the 1960s. These factors must engender caution in any attempt to sketch a theology of Joseph in the spirit of Barth's work.

At the same time, these factors do not wholly limit this endeavor. I submit that Barth's limited commentary in this era of his life does reveal a sense of where the development of this theology—and specifically, ecclesiology—may lead. His comments about Joseph, in both letters and interviews, are profoundly consistent. In fact, in a letter to Hans Küng dated March 10, 1967—over four years after the letters quoted above—Barth avers the same conviction about Joseph. He writes, "I remain obstinate in my view that St. Joseph—if only he were—is to be preferred to Our Lady with her crown of glory."[16] Additionally, even while the mediums in which he communicates his views on Joseph may be less formal than a traditional academic text, these alternative formats in no way suggest or imply Barth is speaking imprecisely about the theology he is suggesting.

With that said, in the remainder of this section, based on his letters and interviews I will delineate four tenets of a potential Barthian Josephology for the church that emerge from Barth's commentary on the biblical figure of Joseph. The first two tenets of this theological motif focus on the position of Joseph; the last two tenets focus on the nature of Joseph's service. In what follows I will consider each of these four components and specifically address their ecclesiological significance.

First, as it concerns the earthly position of Joseph, it is significant for Barth that Joseph is not genetically linked to Jesus. The lack of a biological nexus entails a lack of ontological dependency. In other words, the genesis and human existence of Jesus does not depend upon the actuality of Joseph. In the same way, the existence of Jesus—including his work and power as well as the continuing work and power of the Holy Spirit—does not depend upon the existence of the church. Rather, the church exists because of its head, Jesus Christ. In an interview in November 1962, just a day after he penned the previously quoted letter to Oscar Cullmann, Barth elaborates on the difference between Mary and Joseph in their relations to Jesus Christ. He states,

> [In] my eyes Joseph has played the role of the church to Christ. I know that the Roman Catholic Church prefers to compare their role with the more glorious Virgin Mary. They bring the world the message of the Gospel the same way Mary has given

---

16. Ibid., 245. It should be noted that Barth's comments are made in the wider context of his discussion of Küng's *Die Kirche*—a copy of which Barth had just received from Küng via mail.

us Christ. But the comparison is false. The Church cannot give birth to the Savior . . .[17]

In affirming Joseph as the appropriate model for the church, Barth is alluding to one of the deepest themes in his own work—namely, a Christocentric ecclesiology.

For Barth, no exemplar for the church can be affirmed that implies the church is before or above Jesus Christ. The church is witness to Jesus Christ, but unlike Mary the church is not the source of Jesus Christ. The church exists as a witness because it has a divine sending source; the church's task, then, is to witness to the source that sends it.[18] Barth is quite explicit on the parameters of the role of this witness. He states that the church "is no less, no more and no other than the ministry of witness required of it and constituting it."[19] Barth intensifies this statement by noting the following:

> [The church] is not commanded to represent, introduce, bring into play or even in a sense accomplish again in its being, speech and action either reconciliation, the covenant, the kingdom or the new world reality. It is not commanded even in the earthly-historical sphere to take the place of Jesus Christ. In so doing it would only arrogate to itself something which is absolutely beyond its capacity, in which it could achieve only spurious results, and which would finally involve it in failure. In so doing it would do despite to Jesus Christ Himself as the one Doer of the work of God and the primary and true Witness of this work, becoming a hindrance to what He Himself wills to do and accomplish. Its prophecy would *ipso facto* become false, unauthorised and misleading prophecy.[20]

This strong statement about the church in the *CD* parallels Barth's consistent and critical judgments against Mary as exemplar for the church. Any proposed model of the church cannot imply or suggest a distorted understanding of the church's ministry of witness. For Barth, affirming Joseph as a model does not beget such distortion; Joseph's position in relation to Jesus carries correspondence to that of the church in relation to Jesus.

The second tenant of a nascent Barthian Josephology is linked to divine intentionality in human history. Namely, Joseph's chosenness as the father

---

17. Barth, "Interview mit T. de Quénétain," 415–16. Translation mine.

18. For the best engagements of the themes of mission and sending in Barth's ecclesiology, see Guder, *The Continuing Conversion of the Church*. See also John Flett's excellent work: *The Witness of God*.

19. Barth, *CD* IV/3.2, 834.

20. Ibid., 836.

Part II—Reconceiving Christian Experience and Practice

of the Son of God by the divine Father is not accidental. As aforementioned, Barth dedicates time in the *CD* to the Davidic lineage of Jesus through Joseph. For example, Barth mentions the erroneous efforts made in the early church to rewrite the New Testament genealogies to excise the link between Joseph and Jesus. Barth states, "We will certainly do well to renounce the attempts of early Church commentators to convert genealogies of Joseph into those of Mary."[21] Such an act of rewriting, for obvious reasons, cannot be undertaken—nor does it need to be. Here Barth underscores a key semantic point. For the gospel writers, the notion of familial descent was not exclusively understood as biological.[22] Barth quotes the words of Matthean commentator Adolf Schlatter on the implications of this understanding. Schlatter writes,

> Neither the thought that connexion with David dispenses with miracle, nor the idea that miracle dissolves Jesus' connexion with David were possible for Matthew. What he expected of Christ lay beyond nature and history and was God's very own revelation which makes His almighty grace effective. Hence the genealogy by itself never proved the kingly rights of Jesus. But just as little did miracle invalidate Scripture or disrupt nature and history. It rather strengthens and completes them. So Matthew narrates that an express direction of God assigned Jesus to Joseph the Son of David. The link forged by nature could not from Matthew's standpoint have bound Jesus more firmly to the house of David than did the will of God made manifest.[23]

Joseph's chosenness as the father of Jesus was not a vicarious chosenness—as if whomever Mary was betrothed to marry would have sufficed as the earthly father of Jesus. In quoting Schlatter, Barth is affirming the particularity of Joseph's calling.

In addition to his chosenness, this second tenant also addresses the active nature of the role Joseph was given. Alongside Mary, Joseph was given his own responsibility in service to Jesus; Joseph is called to participate actively in the life and safety of this child. Making the connection to ecclesiology, Barth utters this simple yet compelling phrase: "[Joseph] took care of the Child; he takes care of the Church."[24] In a very real sense, the church

---

21. *CD* I/2, 175.
22. Ibid., 175–176.
23. *Der Evangelist Matthäus*, 5f., as quoted in Barth, *CD* I/2, 176.
24. Quoted in an editorial footnote in Barth, *Letters, 1961–68*, 75. See also Filas, "Barth as Seeker of God's Truth."

is indebted to Joseph's enactment of service. The church benefits from his obedience to take on the responsibility of protection set before him.

As it concerns this second tenant explicating Joseph's position, there exists a strong parallel to the role of the church. Like Joseph, the church is uniquely chosen. Its election is grounded in Jesus Christ, who is its head; its tasks are not ethereal but must be undertaken at the direction of the Spirit in the concrete moments of history. For Barth, "The Church *is* when it takes place, and it takes place in the form of a sequence and nexus of definite activities."[25] Like Joseph, the church must decide in the time and space it occupies if it will take on the tasks set before it. And most importantly, like Joseph's responsibility, the tasks of the church are undertaken in service to Jesus Christ.[26]

Exactly how Joseph enacted his service to Jesus Christ leads to the final two tenants of the Barthian Josephology to be articulated here and further grounds the biblical figure as an exemplar for the church in the world. Thus, the third tenant of this nascent theology is humility. In an interview, Barth discusses artistic depictions of Joseph that reveal something about the biblical figure's character, noting that in these pictures Joseph "is so humble, modest, receding in the background."[27] Yet for Barth, this is not a passive role; he notes that "[Joseph] plays . . . a very active role but a submissive role, not a ruling one."[28] In another interview, Barth makes the ecclesiological connection as it concerns this quality of Joseph. In reference to the orientation the church is to have to Christ, he avers, "[The church] can and must serve him with humble zeal, and critically. That was exactly the role that Joseph played, which was always in the background, giving all the glory to Jesus. This is exactly what the role of the church should be, if we want the world to rediscover the splendor of the Word of God."[29]

The church must undertake its calling in the world with humility. If the church chooses not to play this role but rather assumes a glorious one for itself, the church radically distorts its witness. If the church assumes a certain prideful security in its salvation in relation to the world, its witness is also distorted. For Barth, the church always needs to humbly ask the Holy Spirit to bring again the power and hope of the Gospel to it. Thus Barth asks

---

25. *CD* IV/1, 652.

26. Barth's discussion of the different tasks of service (*Dienst*) is an important elaboration of this point. See *CD* IV/3.2, 865–901. Darrell Guder also provides excellent reflection on this section of the *CD*. See, for example, Guder, "Practical Theology in Service," 13–22.

27. Barth, "Gespräch mit Tübinger," 102. Translation mine.

28. Ibid.

29. Barth, "Interview mit T. de Quénétain," 416. Translation mine.

in his discussion of evangelization, "Do not even [the assembly of serious Christians] continually find that they themselves are nominal Christians and urgently in need to receive the Gospel afresh?"[30] The church must humbly and joyfully recognize that its very livelihood is sustained by its head, Jesus Christ.

Such humility in service to Christ must be paired with faithfulness in service to Christ. Thus, the final tenant that is to be drawn out of Barth's commentary on Joseph is that of faithful obedience. Writing about Joseph to B. A. Willems, Barth declares, "I find this biblical figure, movingly obedient and ministering, much more suited to be the protector (and exemplar!) of the church than Mary."[31] In an interview, Barth again draws the ecclesiological connection: "Joseph is faithful and honest, a good servant. This is the Church."[32] Joseph's faithfulness is grounded in a messianic promise delivered to him by an angel of the Lord (Matt 1:20–21). So, too, the church's faithfulness is sustained in the promise of this Messiah. Barth eloquently elaborates on the depth of this reality:

> The community can live neither by what it achieves and produces in its service, nor by the fulfillments granted to it. It may live, however, and it can and should do so, by the promise of its ministry fulfilled in Jesus Christ. This cannot and will not fail as such. . . . The promise is unshakeable and infallible. It may also be clearly seen and firmly grasped. It exerts a superior counter-pressure against every pressure. It is its security in the insecurity, its strength in the weakness, its health in the latent or acute sickness, its wealth in the poverty, and its glory in the gloom of its service. It causes it to awaken out of every sleep, to take new courage in every hesitation, to venture new steps in every weariness. It thus enables it to endure and its history to go on from one day and generation to another.[33]

The faithfulness to which the church is called is not sustained by the church itself. Its source of faithfulness is its cornerstone, Jesus Christ.

---

30. *CD* IV/3.2, 873.
31. Barth, *Letters, 1961–68*, 94.
32. Barth, "Gespräch mit Tübinger," 102. Translation mine.
33. *CD* IV/3.2, 843.

Conclusion:
The Relevance of a Barthian Josephology for Today

These four tenants are theologically compelling and specifically highlight Barth's understanding of Joseph in the later years of his life—an understanding that has remained largely undeveloped in scholarship done in the wake of Barth's work. Yet for the purposes of this essay, an important question still remains: how do we relate Barth's theology of Joseph—and specifically his role as example for the church—to the contemporary realities articulated at the beginning of this essay? Certainly, Barth's commentary is not seamlessly applicable in light of the very different historical context in which his comments were made. Specifically, it is the Catholic context that is most pressing for Barth. Thus, he often qualifies his comments about Joseph by revealing his own Protestant identity. For example, in an interview in 1964, Barth declares, "If I were a Catholic theologian . . . then I would like to join the Josephological direction."[34] For Barth, as it concerns the Catholic tradition, Joseph is the sound theological alternative to Mary as an exemplar for the church. Thus he notes, "As much as I am averse to the development of 'Mariology,' so I'm inclined towards 'Josephology.'"[35] For Barth, emphatically drawing this contrast between these two biblical figures is not necessary in Protestant churches because no strong Mariological movement exists in the form it does in the Catholic tradition.

Yet today, I contend, lifting up Joseph as a model for the whole church is indeed important in the Protestant tradition—specifically in those communities that are being encouraged to embrace the masculinist revision of the Christian faith. Thus, Barth's encouraging challenge to the Catholic Church can be extended to the American Protestant evangelical church. Undeniably, the issues that these communal bodies face are quite different. As Barth saw it, the challenge in the Catholic communities of faith was a Mariology that problematically elevated both Mary as well as the role of the church in the world. Quite differently, the challenge in the American evangelical church is the problematic identification of male biblical figures with a particularly defined masculine identity. While these two communities are distinct and while Barth was primarily considering the context of the Catholic tradition, I contend that the Josephological impulses in Barth's comments bear relevance for the American Evangelical church today.

The figure of Joseph—as one who is humble, faithful, and obedient—is important for the entire church to draw upon as an example. Probably

---

34. Barth, "Gespräch mit Tübinger," 101. Translation mine.
35. Barth, "Interview mit T. de Quénétain," 415. Translation mine.

more than any other biblical figure, Joseph's function specifically as a father is unique; the role of earthly father of Jesus is *sui generis*. And yet, Joseph serves not foremost as an example only for fathers; he serves as an example for the entire church. With this understanding, the revisionist readings of Scripture must be addressed. If Joseph is principally identified by his masculinity, he ceases to be that example for the whole church; rather, he is relegated to being an example for only some.

These contemporary evangelical masculinist readings do damage to all members of the community of believers, and thus they must be challenged. It is not enough to simply ignore them—as if "boys will be boys" or, rather, "evangelical men will be evangelical men." Through the power of the Holy Spirit, the church is called to break down barriers of sexism—and other systemic sins—within the community of believers instead of disregarding or tolerating such sin in the body of Jesus Christ. In fact, if the church is to live in service to Jesus Christ and to remain faithful and obedient as Joseph did, challenging these masculinist readings is a part of the church's call. In speaking of the defeat of the powers of sin within the Christian community, Barth writes,

> Jesus is their Conqueror. If we are His disciples, we are necessarily witness of this fact. . . . It must be attested in the world as a declaration of the victory of Jesus. The world which sighs under these powers must hear and receive and rejoice that their lordship is broken. But this declaration cannot be made by the existence of those who are merely free inwardly. If this message is to be given, the world must see and hear at least an indication, or sign, of what has taken place. The break made by God in Jesus must become history. This is why Jesus calls His disciples.[36]

Contrary to John Piper's declaration, God has not given Christianity a masculine feel. Humanity has given Christianity a masculine feel. God in Jesus has given the community of believers freedom from such sinfulness and the destructive power this sin brings.

---

36. *CD* IV/2, 544.

Bibliography

Barth, Karl. *Ad Limina Apostolorum: An Appraisal of Vatican II.* Translated by Keith R. Crim. Richmond: John Knox, 1967.

———. "Interview mit T. de Quénétain, Réalités." In *Gespräche 1959–1962*, edited by Eberhard Busch, 405–16. Zürich: Theologischer Verlag Zürich, 1995.

———. "Gespräch mit Tübinger (2.3.1964)." In *Gespräche 1964–1968*, edited by Eberhard Busch, 31–129. Zürich: Theologischer Verlag Zürich, 1996.

———. *The Göttingen Dogmatics.* Translated by G. W. Bromiley. Grand Rapids: Eerdmans, 1991.

———. *The Great Promise: Luke 1.* Translated by Hans Freund. New York: Philosophical Library, 1963.

———. *Letters, 1961–1968.* Edited by Jürgen Fangmeier and Hinrich Stoevesandt. Translated and edited by G. W. Bromiley. Grand Rapids: Eerdmans, 1981.

Boff, Leonardo. *Saint Joseph: The Father of Jesus in a Fatherless Society.* Translated by Alexandre Guilherme. Eugene, OR: Cascade, 2009.

Eldredge, John. *Fathered by God: Learning What Your Father Could Never Teach You.* Nashville: Thomas Nelson, 2009.

Filas, Francis L. "Barth as Seeker of God's Truth: A Jesuit Theologian Responds to the Lectures by Karl Barth at Rockefeller Chapel, University of Chicago." *The Christian Century* 79 (1962) 685–86.

———. *Joseph: The Man Closest to Jesus; The Complete Life, Theology, and Devotional History of St. Joseph.* Boston: Daughters of St. Paul, 1962.

———. *St. Joseph after Vatican II: Conciliar Implications Regarding St. Joseph and His Inclusion in the Roman Canon.* Staten Island, NY: Alba House, 1965.

Flett, John. *The Witness of God: The Trinity, Missio Dei, Karl Barth, and the Nature of Christian Community.* Grand Rapids: Eerdmans, 2010.

Guder, Darrell. *The Continuing Conversion of the Church.* Grand Rapids: Eerdmans, 2010.

———. "Practical Theology in Service of the Missional Church." In *Theology in Service of the Church: Essays in Honor of Joseph D. Small*, edited by Charles A. Wiley et al., 13–22. Louisville: Geneva, 2008.

Morley, Patrick. *Pastoring Men: What Works, What Doesn't, and Why It Matters Now More than Ever.* Chicago: Moody, 2008.

Phillips, Richard. *The Masculine Mandate: God's Calling to Men.* Lake Mary, FL: Reformed Trust, 2010.

Piper, John. "'The Frank and Manly Mr. Ryle'—The Value of a Masculine Ministry." January 31, 2012. http://www.desiringgod.org/resource-library/conference-messages/the-frank-and-manly-mr-ryle-the-value-of-a-masculine-ministry.

Schlatter, Adolf. *Der Evangelist Matthäus.* Stuttgart: Calwer, 1929.

Stinson, Randy, and Dan Dumas. *A Guide to Biblical Manhood.* Louisville: Southern Baptist Theological Seminary Press, 2011.

Wilson, Douglas. *Father Hunger: Why God Calls Men to Love and Lead Their Families.* Nashville: Thomas Nelson, 2012.

8

"Thy Kingdom Come!"
Karl Barth and the Promise of a Prophetic Evangelical Church

Christian T. Collins Winn and **Peter Goodwin Heltzel**

Introduction

EVANGELICAL THEOLOGY IS A theology in search of the church. While evangelical thought has traditionally been grounded in a strong biblicism and Trinitarian Christocentrism, its low ecclesiology has often been a point of embarrassment, provoking younger evangelicals to join the historic, sacramental churches—Eastern Orthodox, Roman Catholic and Anglican Communions.[1] The low-church impulses that have animated much of evangelical ecclesiological practice, however, need not be seen as inadequate. Rather than abandoning these Pietist impulses, what is needed is a further deepening and development of the theological logic at work in them. This is a vital task for evangelical theology today and the great Swiss theologian Karl Barth (1886–1968) can be an important interlocutor in this work.

Though Barth's theology of the church has yet to receive the attention it deserves from evangelicals, the direction of his ecclesiology moves remarkably along lines that would be familiar to many evangelicals and is especially resonant with those communities that might be described as

---

1. Vanhoozer, "Evangelicalism and the Church," 40–45.

embodying congregational or low-church forms of polity and practice.² It should, therefore, be no surprise that in a recent collection on Barth's relationship to American Evangelicalism, the two essays on Barth's theology of the church were written by Baptist theologians, one of whom wrote one of the most significant monographs on Barth's ecclesiology to appear in some time.³

Though we share the concerns of these and other authors, our aim is to engage Barth's ecclesiology to see what it might have to offer to a constructive, socially engaged evangelical ecclesiology. In this vein, we are particularly concerned to explore the constitutive role that prayer or invocation plays in what we are calling Barth's *prophetic ecclesiology*. The Christian church receives its being and its calling from beyond itself. Prayer is the act wherein the church participates in the righteous invocation of the man Jesus, who is the Head of the body, and thereby places itself at the disposal of the living God to be and become a community of witness which lives beyond itself in acts of righteousness and in the proclamation of the Crucified. For Barth, the Lord's Prayer in particular, and especially the second petition, "Thy kingdom come," denotes a community shaped and concretized in and through invocation and transformation. The call for the kingdom is an invocation of the power and presence of the Living God embodied in Jesus of Nazareth, who in and through this act of invocation empowers the people of God to prophetically act in the world.⁴ The church is thus a community of worship and witness, always seeking to embody the dialectic of prayer and action. Barth's vision of the church as a community of invocation and transformation offers an important theological trajectory for the twenty-first century, and especially for the evangelical community.⁵

---

2. See Bender, *Karl Barth's Christological Ecclesiology*, 284–86.

3. See Bender, "Church in Karl Barth and Evangelicalism," 177–200, and Johnson "Being and Act of the Church," 201–26. See also Bender, *Karl Barth's Christological Ecclesiology*.

4. See Barth, *CL*, 102. See also *CD* IV/3.2, 890–98.

5. In an earlier work we re-positioned Barth's doctrine of God within his doctrine of reconciliation, bringing his theology proper into closer proximity with his missional ecclesiology. In that essay we gave special attention to the role that the Holy Spirit plays in the mission of the triune God and the church's witness. Through our investigation of Barth's doctrine of reconciliation, two themes emerged as immediately relevant for a missional ecclesiology: the prophetic office of Jesus and the energizing mission of the Holy Spirit. In the present essay, we begin to explore how Barth's prophetic and pneumatological insights provide important resources for a prophetic evangelical ecclesiology today. See Heltzel and Collins Winn, "Karl Barth, Reconciliation, and the Triune God," 173–91.

Part II—Reconceiving Christian Experience and Practice

Of course, our suggestion that Barth has something to offer to evangelical theology begs the question of exactly what we mean by "evangelical." Our working assumption is that in regard to ecclesiology, the denominator "evangelical" refers to congregational and low-church forms of polity and practice. Because of the limitations of an essay format, we will not seek to demonstrate the truth of this claim. Rather, we share the larger assumption that frames the current volume, which is that "evangelical" has more in common with Pietism, Wesleyan-Holiness, Pentecostalism, and baptistic forms of ecclesiology than with the high church traditions that animate Roman Catholic, Orthodox, and many of the churches which emerged from the sixteenth-century reformations which took place in Europe.

That Barth, the great modern interpreter of the Reformation traditions of Luther and Calvin, would have anything other than criticism to offer to these traditions would seem to be counterintuitive. However, Barth's relationship to Pietism was far more nuanced than has commonly been understood. In particular, the tradition of Württemberg Pietism as embodied in the life and thought of Johann Christoph Blumhardt (1805–80) and his son Christoph Friedrich Blumhardt (1842–1919) was seminal in forming Barth's interpretation of the second petition of the Lord's Prayer. Thus, Barth's ecclesiology and theology of prayer carries within it impulses that are remarkably consonant with evangelical sensibilities.

In what follows, we briefly note the connections between Barth and the Pietism of the Blumhardts. We then offer an outline of what we call Barth's prophetic ecclesiology. In this section, we are not attempting to offer a general outline of Barth's ecclesiology[6] or his theology of prayer,[7] but rather to highlight their intersection in the context of Barth's interpretation of the second petition of the Lord's Prayer, and to draw out the prophetic trajectory that Barth's conception implies. A dialectic of invocation and transformation is implied in the church's practice of prayer—in the petition "Thy kingdom come" the church calls out to God to establish God's own reign, but it is also empowered by the Spirit to live in the light of God's coming kingdom through acts of love and justice. Finally, we offer a constructive proposal for a socially engaged evangelical ecclesiology using elements from Barth's theology. We are particularly concerned to bring Barth's conception

---

6. For detailed discussion of Barth's ecclesiology, see O'Grady, *The Church in the Theology of Karl Barth*; Buckley, "Christian Community, Baptism, and Lord's Supper"; Yocum, *Ecclesial Mediation in Karl Barth*; Bender, *Karl Barth's Christological Ecclesiology*.

7. For a detailed discussion of Barth's theology of prayer, see Migliore, "Freedom to Pray"; Meyer-Blanck, "Gottesdienst und Gebet bei Karl Barth"; McDowell, "'Openness to the World.'"

of a church called both to pray and to act into dialogue with the struggle for racial justice in North America, especially as embodied in the life and thought of Martin Luther King, Jr., in an effort to indicate a useful trajectory for a prophetic evangelical ecclesiology after Barth.

Karl Barth and Pietism: Toward a New Reading of Barth

While some have interpreted Barth as categorically critical of Pietism, a growing number of theologians argue that Barth's relationship to Pietism was far more complicated, and that alongside of his criticism one can also find Barth appropriating and re-constructing central Pietist themes in his own theological work.[8] One area where this can be detected is in Barth's vision of the church as a worshiping community of social witness. Pietism began as a movement for spiritual renewal and church reform in the seventeenth and eighteenth century over against confessional Lutheranism.[9] Concerned that Lutheranism was too hierarchical, statist, and rigidly confessional, the Pietists sought to renew the church, society and the personal faith of Christians by cultivating a robustly Protestant theology of faith, hope and love in and through new forms of community. And though Harry Yeide's argument that ecclesiology was the primary focus of the early Pietists—especially Philip Jakob Spener (1635–1705)—is an overstatement, nevertheless, concern with the communal nature of the Christian life was certainly central.[10] The communities envisioned by Spener and others were meant to serve as a space through which the Living God could work in visceral, embodied, and transformational ways.

Barth shared some sympathies with Pietism's critique of the abstract character of scholastic theology, arguing instead for a "concrete truth that can only be heard, thought and told when one is existentially involved."[11] A theologian of the Word of God, Barth argued that the Word should be personally appropriated in the communal life of the church.[12] He was drawn to

---

8. See, for example, Busch, *Karl Barth and the Pietists*; Collins Winn, *"Jesus is Victor!"*; Hitchcock, *Karl Barth and the Resurrection of the Flesh*.

9. For a helpful introduction to the academic study of Pietism, see Strom, "Problems and Promises of Pietism Research"; Lindberg, *The Pietist Theologians*; Collins Winn et al., *The Pietist Impulse in Christianity*; Shantz, *An Introduction to German Pietism*.

10. See Yeide, *Studies in Classical Pietism*, 5–9.

11. Busch, *Karl Barth and the Pietists*, 192.

12. This argument was especially prominent in Barth's first cycle of dogmatics given at the University of Göttingen in 1924–25. See Barth, *Göttingen Dogmatics*, 1:23–41.

those forms of Pietism that understood that the Christian response to revelation must occur in *concrete* and embodied witness in and for the world in history.[13] A disciple, who has heard the call of Christ, must live into a faith that is existentially experienced and socially embodied.

The strongest stream of Pietism to shape Barth's theology comes from the Blumhardts—the elder Johann Christoph and his son Christoph Friedrich.[14] Even Barth's sometime antagonist Emil Brunner claimed that, "the real origin of the Dialectic Theology is to be traced, however, not to Kierkegaard, but to a more unexpected source, to a place still farther removed from the main theological thoroughfare—to the quiet Boll of the two Blumhardts."[15] The Blumhardts' prophetic theology and struggle to embody the faith in intentional community and political struggle is an important stream in the final volumes of the *Church Dogmatics*, as pointed out by Timothy Gorringe and Christian T. Collins Winn.[16]

The Blumhardts represented two generations of a school of German Pietism that was spiritually attuned, socially engaged, and cosmic in scope. The catchphrase of Blumhardt's theology was "Jesus is Victor," a theme that became a *theologumenon* in Barth's later theology of reconciliation.[17] By way of this Christological eschatology, Barth articulated a vision of the ongoing disruptive power of the resurrection of Christ, which eventuated in an ecclesiology of prophetic witness. In Barth's later thought, eschatology is not so much about "last things" (i.e., *eschata*), or even the "last time" (i.e., *eschaton*), rather it is about the "last One" (i.e., *eschatos*). Jesus is this "last One," the One in whom the kingdom is embodied. The resurrection of this One means that the *eschaton* is not locked in the past, but is now present to all of history pressing in upon humanity is various ways in and through the Spirit.

In addition to "Jesus is Victor," Barth appropriated another Blumhardtian motif: "Thy Kingdom Come!" While "Jesus is Victor" expresses the Christological eschatology—that Christ truly is the center—"Thy kingdom come" highlights the human task to hope and struggle for the final victory of Jesus in the hustle and bustle of everyday life. It stands as both a prayer and a promise for the church that seeks to embody Jesus' revolutionary teaching of the kingdom through its collective life in the world. The Lord's Prayer offers both a pattern for how to pray and is also a call to prophetic Christian

---

13. See Barth, *CD* IV/3.1, 18–38.
14. See Collins Winn, *"Jesus Is Victor!"*, 155–280.
15. Brunner, "Continental European Theology," 141.
16. See Gorringe, *Karl Barth*, 224, 238–43; Collins Winn, *"Jesus Is Victor!"*, 208–80.
17. Barth is quite clear that this phrase, and multiple dynamics it names, comes from the "underground stream of the insight" of the Blumhardts (*CD* IV/3.1, 169–71). See Collins Winn, *"Jesus Is Victor!"*, 246–73.

ethics, a fact that Barth sought to highlight in his ethics of reconciliation. Through the lens of the Blumhardts, Barth's treatment of the second petition in relation to ecclesiology foregrounds the importance of prayer as the church seeks to embody its social witness.

"Thy Kingdom Come":
An Outline of Barth's Prophetic Ecclesiology

For Barth, as praise is the most basic form of ecclesial speech, so prayer is the most basic form of ecclesial action.[18] This is because prayer is the acknowledgement that God's act and being are the source of the act and being of the church. The life of the Christian community, and therefore of Christian persons, is to be understood as an event of "invocation" or prayer.[19] In this context, the Lord's Prayer is not simply a prayer by which we remember Jesus or learn a potentially disembodied spiritual practice; rather it is the lifeblood of Christian existence.[20] When Jesus shared the Lord's Prayer with the disciples, it was a call to surrender to a new form of life; one marked not by death-dealing, but by the life-giving power of love and justice, which was meant to be socially embodied. The surrender called for was *total*—one was called to live out the ideals of the Gospel even unto death, a fate for which Jesus and most of his disciples were destined.

According to Barth, though much of modern German theology had domesticated the radicalism of the Lord's Prayer, the prophetic stream that included the Blumhardts, Hermann Kutter, and Leonhard Ragaz offered a different trajectory.[21] This *prophetic Pietism* challenged the status quo that prevailed in the church and in the broader external socio-economic order. These theologians were interested in the political implications of the second petition and were motivated to actively seek a more just world. They thought that the petition "Thy kingdom come" was more than a verbal prayer, it was a materialist manifesto—a call for Christian disciples as a collective to make a concrete difference in the world, seeking to embody a fundamentally new and better social order, as captured in the pithy remark of the elder Blumhardt: "To believe in God is easy; but to believe that the world will become

---

18. See *CD* IV/3.2, 882–84
19. See *CL*, 85–109.
20. "To be a Christian and to pray are one and the same thing; it is a matter that cannot be left to caprice. It is a need, a kind of breathing necessary to life" (Barth, *Prayer*, 15).
21. Barth, *CD* VI/3.1, 29.

different—for that one must be faithful unto death."[22] Faith in God should be reflected in hope that a better world is possible. Though Barth had some reservations about the political translation of this materialist vision, nevertheless his exposition of the second petition moves along the same track.[23]

It was particularly the two Blumhardts who drew Barth's attention in this regard. Their relationship to the church was complicated, in that they were as convinced of its apostasy as of its faithfulness.[24] Nevertheless, the Blumhardts affirmed that through the proclamation of Scripture and especially the practice of communal Christian disciplines—whether prayer, sacramental celebration, diaconal service, or the struggle for justice—the kingdom that Jesus announced and embodied was re-presented in the midst of the community of faith and the world. The final *telos* of the kingdom, however, was not just a transformed community, but a transformed world. The younger Blumhardt in particular believed that the end goal of the kingdom was the transformation of the cosmos. The task of the Christian community, which Blumhardt called the "little flock," was to discern the contours of the new reality—a new reality shaped by just social relations and genuine love—and to live in a way that prayerfully expected the new world to break forth like the glistening green blades of grass on a spring blue sky morning. He believed that all people of good conscience could actively participate in this vision. Thus, some of the best *prophetic* advocacy and public service often happened outside of the purview of the institutional church and of organized religion in general. The church's missional witness would be strongest when it was seeking to care for others in the places of the world's greatest need.[25] Wherever there were cries for help because of suffering and injustice, people of good conscience were called to respond with compassionate aid and a public advocacy strategy that could eradicate the concrete injustices that were plaguing the poor.

Barth's understanding of the nature and purpose of prayer is especially focused on the second petition of the Lord's Prayer—"Thy kingdom come"—and was shaped by the Blumhardts' interpretation, seeing it as both a call to deeper spirituality and prophetic activism.[26] Predictably for Barth, the basis of the kingdom is Christological. For the kingdom to be really

---

22. Eller, *Thy Kingdom Come*, 5.

23. Key in this was Barth's allergic reaction to all things "ideological." See *CD* IV/3.2, 890–93; *CL*, 213–33, 260–71. See also Gorringe, *Karl Barth*, 1–23.

24. See Collins Winn, *"Jesus Is Victor!"*, 129–36.

25. This is characteristically expressed in Christoph Blumhardt's well-known sermon "Jesus among the Wretched." See Lejeune, *Christoph Blumhardt and His Message*, 186–97.

26. See Barth, *CL*, 256–60.

and truly *God's* kingdom, it must be beyond our reach. Therefore, Barth understood the kingdom as the space and time—i.e., the realm—in which God has confronted the powers and principalities, reconciling the world. This space and time, however, is no abstract realm; rather, it is found under the life-history of Jesus of Nazareth: "What is meant in the New Testament by the presence of the kingdom of God, by its coming as already an event? What is meant is the center, the whence and whither, the basis, theme, and content of all the New Testament sayings, namely, the history of Jesus Christ, the words and deeds and suffering and death of the one Son of the one God as the Messiah of Israel and the savior of the Gentiles."[27] The kingdom, then, is the event of Jesus Christ; the event in space and time, in which God has acted, reconciling humanity to itself and to God. To call for this kingdom to come is to call upon God to definitively and universally unveil that which has been accomplished in Christ for the whole world.

In light of this divine action, however, it is important to stress that for Barth the petition "Thy kingdom come" also carries within it a deep affirmation of human action which is to be undertaken in the light of God's action. On the most basic level, the act of prayer itself is the human response to the God who has first addressed humanity. But prayer is also a call to arms, a prophetic challenge to Jesus' followers to embody justice in their life together. When the church prays, "Thy kingdom come," it is awakened to action, to "know this kingdom even in the midst of the kingdom of disorder, to look toward it and to call for it."[28] The call for the kingdom, then, awakens the church to inhabit God's redemptive order in its double placement; for the church simultaneously lives in the kingdom of lordless disorder, but also in the light of the coming kingdom of God. There is, however, a dissymmetry in the church's positionality in these two kingdoms, as the kingdom of God is "over against the disorder and demonization of human life."[29] The kingdom of God is humanizing while the kingdom of disorder is dehumanizing; the kingdom of God is creative, while the kingdom of disorder is destructive. In this double placement, the church is called to struggle against unrighteousness in society as an expression of the struggle against the lordless powers. What the church is, "commanded to do—and as in all simplicity they give thanks and hope and pray they cannot escape this command—is to work for human righteousness."[30] Barth does not imagine that this is easy, nor are Christians to be timid. Rather, "this is inevitable if

---

27. Ibid., 248–49.
28. Ibid., 233.
29. Ibid., 234.
30. Ibid., 264.

in their hearts and on their lips the petition 'Thy kingdom come' is not an indolent and despondent prayer but one that is zealous and brave."[31]

To be sure, human righteousness and divine righteousness are not the same thing, in that the former cannot overcome the lordless powers in a definitive way. Nevertheless, Christians are called to attend to the doing of human righteousness, which Barth describes as "kingdom-like."[32] The Lordship of God, identified directly with the presence of the Living God, is nonetheless indirectly identified with "parables of the kingdom." The revelation of God's Lordship, the kingdom of God, is manifest in the person of Jesus Christ which is expressed in the "time between the times" (*zwischen den Zeiten*) in his presence through "parables of the kingdom." "Parables of the kingdom" are limited human correspondences to God's justice and love, which point beyond themselves to the final coming of the kingdom. It is in these moments of faithful prayer and action that we see a provisional manifestation of the *totus Christus*,[33] Christ in his totality graciously embracing and reconciling the whole of creation, because the action of God does not exclude, but includes faithful human action.

In light of this, one could say that a prophetic ecclesiology is driven by the dialectic of invocation and transformation. The two go hand in hand. It is the Holy Spirit who mediates the dialectic of invocation and transformation. Barth writes, "If one prays for the coming of God's kingdom, one prays also that the Holy Spirit may come within us."[34] The Holy Spirit is the spiritual power of the Father and the Son in the world that empowers the church for its prophetic ministry, which is embodied primarily in the work of prayer[35] and acts of justice: "the Holy Spirit is the *forward* which majestically awakens, enlightens, leads, pushes, and impels, which God has spoken in the resurrection of Jesus from the dead, which he has spoken and still speaks to the world of humanity: *forward* to the New coming of Jesus and the Kingdom. . . . Endowed and equipped with freedom for this, Christians grasp this promise, look and move forward, and pray, 'Thy kingdom come,' 'Come, Lord Jesus.'"[36] The link between the coming of the kingdom and the coming of the Spirit further elucidates the transformative *telos* of the prayer. The cry for the coming kingdom is a cry for transformation in the one who prays, but also for the community and for the world as a whole. The Spirit

---

31. Ibid., 263.
32. Ibid., 266.
33. See Barth, *CD* IV/3.1, 216.
34. Barth, *Prayer*, 40.
35. See Barth, *CL*, 52, 90–91.
36. Ibid., 256.

bears the community along, drawing it into the struggle for God's righteousness to be manifested in "kingdom-like" parables which point beyond themselves, and yet also make a concrete difference in the here and now.

Thinking of the kingdom as a new order of political economy animated figures like the Blumhardts, Barth also wanted to affirm the political character of the kingdom, while arguing that human action is always a response to the lure of the gracious loving action of the Living God.[37] Because the kingdom of God is *God's* kingdom, all human attempts to achieve righteousness in the material circumstances of the world are always provisional and limited. The prayer for the kingdom is a prayer for the justice and righteousness of God. Barth argues that God "comes and creates righteousness, zealous for his honor as creator and burning with love for his creature. He creates the righteousness which is the right order of the world that belongs to him. He comes and in creating righteousness he abolishes the unrighteousness of the people both in their relationship to him and also in their relationship to one another."[38] Yet the prophetic church, energized by the Spirit in its work of prayer and its embodied life in, for, and with the world makes a difference, an important difference, a concrete difference in the world; especially in the lives of "the least of these."[39] Seeking to embody the righteousness of God entails the intentional work of community organizing with the end of abolishing unrighteousness within the relationships and social structures of society.

Toward a Prophetic, Intercultural Evangelical Church

The theological vision of the Blumhardts and Barth provoke challenging questions for evangelicals today: How do our lives relate to the kingdom of God? Do we believe that the world can become more just and equitable? What concrete things are we doing in our lives to show that a better world is possible? Just as the Blumhardts and Barth found avenues for contextually specific activism in Germany, iterations of a prophetic evangelical church in North America have also discerned places to join the movement for justice. The struggle for racial justice has been important in this respect. Building on the abolition movement's struggle to end slavery, the civil rights movement empowered African Americans and their allies to work together for voter's rights and inclusive democratic participation for all Americans. Bearing witness to God's love for the suffering and oppressed, the civil rights

37. Ibid., 95
38. Ibid., 237.
39. See *CD* IV/3.2, 891.

movement was a parable of the kingdom of God. Charles Marsh has described this struggle as part of the drama of redemption being played out in human history.[40] As a parable of the kingdom, the civil rights movement bore witness to God's gracious action in the world.

Martin Luther King, Jr. emerged as not only the activist leader of the civil rights movement but also its great theologian. Trained in liberal theology at Boston University, King tapped into his deepest prophetic evangelical impulses as he began his first pastorate at Dexter Avenue Baptist Church in Montgomery, Alabama. After successfully leading the Montgomery Bus Boycott, King sought to spread the movement around the state, region, and nation; however, he met stiff resistance from white Christian leaders. In response to some "white moderates" in Birmingham who told King to put on the brakes and slow down his activism, he penned "Letter from Birmingham Jail," calling on both black *and* white faith leaders to join the struggle for racial justice.

On the whole, King felt that the white moderates had abdicated their call to embody justice and was motivated to search for a faithful remnant within the church; he wrote, "Perhaps I must turn my faith to the inner church, the church within the church, as the true *ecclesia* and the hope of the world."[41] Like Pietist theologians Spener, Zinzendorf, and the Blumhardts, who argued for a more authentic Christianity, King longed for the embodiment of a church rooted in God's shalom and burning with an unconsuming flame of courage when it came to standing up with and for the suffering and oppressed.

In his invocation of the *ecclesiolae in ecclesia*, King offers a clear example of a prophetic black Christian reinterpretation and embodiment of a central trope in Lutheran Pietism. According to Pietist teaching, the *ecclesiolae in ecclesia* was a call for Christians to "truly" follow Christ into a deeper experience of community. Together radically obedient Christians embody a prophetic collective force for active neighbor love in the community. In King's context, the "true *ecclesia*" in the United States were those prophetic Christians who were joining together to fight against injustice. The social struggle crystallized around concrete political goals, including overcoming segregation and securing the right to vote for all American citizens. Because of their position on the underside of history, black Christians had both prophetic perception and a noble destiny. King wrote, "I am grateful to God that, through the Negro church, the dimension of nonviolence entered

---

40. See "The Civil Rights Movement as Theological Drama."

41. "Letter from Birmingham Jail," 300. For a longer discussion of the influence of Pietism on the theology of Martin Luther King, Jr., see Heltzel, "The Inner Church Is the Hope for the World."

our struggle."[42] Forged in the fires of resisting slavery and the ubiquitous presence of the ideology of white supremacy, prophetic black Christianity formed an "inner church," providing a fuller communal embodiment of the Gospel's call to neighbor love and social justice. Prophetic black Christianity was a vital embodiment of the inner church in the Americas, because it was here among a people whom Howard Thurman argued had their "backs up against the wall," that a form of community developed that worked through the suffering induced by oppression through creative, collective struggle. From their position on the underside of modernity, enslaved African Christians created the conditions through which prophetic Christianity in the Americas emerged so robustly in the civil rights movement.

While finding its heart in the prophetic black Christian tradition, King's vision of the "inner church" included antiracist whites. For King, the true church was a community of righteousness, whoever they may be. The true church included anyone, black, white or any shade in between who are willing to join the struggle for love and justice.

The prophetic evangelical church today needs to build an intercultural community through a common focus on the struggle for justice. The Lord's Prayer provides a template for our ethical action in the world. In praying this prayer with Jesus, we join with our great intercessor; however, this prayer is more than a channel for spiritual union with the Holy Trinity, it also offers marching orders for what we are to do with our bodies and our very lives. For, in the time between the resurrection and final appearing, Jesus is present in the power of the resurrection Spirit, working to create a provisional instantiation of the new humanity. Being an inclusive charismatic communion of worshipful witness, the church is called to invite people into the kingdom and gift them with the task of parabolic witness. Because Jesus is the kingdom, it is not the task of the Christian community to build the kingdom of God on earth. Rather, the calling is to become a witness to Jesus, to become like Jesus. Through our prophetic life together as a charismatic community for justice we can become provisional parables of the kingdom of God. Yet, given the contingencies and challenges of life, how do we embody prophetic parabolic witness through living the prayer, "Thy kingdom come"?

In the face of life's unpredictability, the moral and political imagination of Jesus, confirmed by the resurrection and the manifestation of the Spirit, inspires us to improvise. Because no human encounter is ever repeated exactly, living out the Gospel is always improvisational. It is an ongoing process of creating the conditions for God's righteous river to flow through

---

42. King, "Letter from Birmingham Jail," 297.

communities and creation. As a jazz ensemble improvises to make music together, the church is called to improvise for love and justice in creative ways. Every member of the church is a minister—women and men alike—who should use her or his gifts toward a Christ-centered, parabolic movement of the just and peaceable Kingdom.

Faithful improvisation requires that we be creative and willing to live out the most radical implications of the Gospel. How does the church live out the prayer "Thy kingdom come" in a nation that is still plagued by racism? Racism is one of the lordless powers that the church must confront today. With the genocide of native peoples, racism is one of the original sins of America. A prophetic evangelical vision of the church must be anti-racist and intercultural, truly open to all people regardless of their race or ethnicity. Naming the idol of racism is the beginning of transforming evangelical theology in the Americas today. Through the long hard work of dismantling lordless powers like racism, evangelical theology can begin the process of living into a new prophetic, intercultural future.

A new generation of evangelical theologians is seeking to articulate visions of the church that are energized by this dialectic of invocation and transformation, seeking to embody a new social reality, especially one that is serious about the struggle for racial justice.[43] The prophetic evangelical church needs to finds ways to embrace and include people of all races, creeds and color and live into a prophetic intercultural future. Confessing and collectively repenting of sins like racism play an important role in embodying the prophetic imperative in the church today. In this missional work of transformation we need to transform social structures as well as the lives of individuals. As the body of Christ, the church is energized by the Spirit to be a missional community of prayer and righteous action. When the church is energized by this dialectic of prayer and action, it becomes a provisional sign of the Coming God.

Conclusion

Informed by impulses from the Blumhardts, Barth's prophetic ecclesiology, especially the pneumatologically animated dialectic of invocation and transformation offers a promising trajectory for evangelical ecclesiology today. Evangelicals are known for a prayerful spiritual piety and an activist posture, thus, this Barthian dialectic is consonant with an evangelical sensibility. Barth emphasizes that it is the presence and power of the Living

---

43. Franke, "Church," 139–49; Heltzel, *Resurrection City*, 9–13, 122–44; Heltzel, "The Inner Church Is the Hope for the World"; Rah, *The Next Evangelicalism*.

God that is the sustaining source and ground of humanity's work of prayer and acts of justice. At the same time, the cry "Thy kingdom come!" is also a summons to the church to embody in a provisional way, through parabolic witness, the coming reign of God wherein the lowly are lifted up through acts of mercy and justice. As the evangelical justice movement continues to grow, Barth's theology of parabolic witness is a clear reminder to evangelicals to be humble in our ministries of peace and justice.

In our North American context, joining the struggle for racial justice is one concrete way we can embody the prayer "Thy kingdom come." Our work of racial reconciliation and justice should grow out of our response to the cries of the suffering and oppressed. In our North American context, these cries often come from communities of color. The cry "Thy kingdom come!" will become all the clearer when the church fulfills its destiny of being a truly intercultural charismatic community committed to the struggle for a just and peaceable world.

Bibliography

Barth, Karl. *The Göttingen Dogmatics: Instruction in the Christian Religion*. Edited by Hannelotte Reiffen. Translated by G. W. Bromiley. Vol. 1. Grand Rapids: Eerdmans, 1991.

———. *Prayer*. 50th anniv. ed. Louisville: Westminster John Knox, 2002.

Bender, Kimlyn. "The Church in Karl Barth and Evangelicalism: Conversations Across the Aisle." In *Karl Barth and American Evangelicalism*, edited by Bruce L. McCormack and Clifford B. Anderson, 177–200. Grand Rapids: Eerdmans, 2012.

———. *Karl Barth's Christological Ecclesiology*. Burlington, VT: Ashgate, 2005.

Blumhardt, Christoph Freidrich. "Jesus Among the Wretched." In *Christoph Blumhardt and His Message*, edited by Robert Lejeune, 186–97. Rifton, NY: Plough, 1963.

Brunner, Emil. "Continental European Theology." In *The Church through Half a Century*, edited by S. M. Cavert and H. P. Van Dusen, 133–44. New York: Scribner's, 1936.

Buckley, James J. "Christian Community, Baptism, and Lord's Supper." In *The Cambridge Companion to Karl Barth*, edited by John Webster, 195–211. Cambridge: Cambridge University Press, 2000.

Busch, Eberhard. *Karl Barth and the Pietists: The Young Karl Barth's Critique of Pietism and Its Response*. Translated by Daniel W. Bloesch. Downers Grove, IL: InterVarsity, 2004.

Collins Winn, Christian T. *"Jesus Is Victor!": The Significance of the Blumhardts for the Theology of Karl Barth*. Eugene, OR: Pickwick, 2009.

———, et al., eds. *The Pietist Impulse in Christianity*. Eugene, OR: Pickwick, 2011.

Eller, Vernard, ed. *Thy Kingdom Come: A Blumhardt Reader*. Grand Rapids: Eerdmans, 1980.

Franke, John R. "Church." In *Prophetic Evangelicals: Envisioning a Just and Peaceable Kingdom*, edited by Bruce Ellis Benson et al., 139–49. Grand Rapids: Eerdmans, 2012.

Heltzel, Peter Goodwin. "The Inner Church is the Hope for the World: The Pietist Impulse in the Theology of Martin Luther King Jr." In *The Pietist Impulse in Christianity*, edited by Christian T. Collins Winn et al., 269–84. Eugene, OR: Pickwick, 2011.

———. *Resurrection City: A Theology of Improvisation*. Grand Rapids: Eerdmans, 2012.

Heltzel, Peter Goodwin, and Christian T. Collins Winn. "Karl Barth, Reconciliation, and The Triune God." In *The Cambridge Companion to the Trinity*, edited by Peter C. Phan, 173–91. Cambridge: Cambridge University Press, 2011.

Gorringe, Timothy J. *Karl Barth: Against Hegemony*. Oxford: Oxford University Press, 1999.

Hitchcock, Nathan. *Karl Barth and the Resurrection of the Flesh: The Loss of the Body in Participatory Eschatology*. Eugene, OR: Pickwick, 2013.

Johnson, Keith L. "The Being and Act of the Church: Barth and the Future of Evangelical Ecclesiology." In *Karl Barth and American Evangelicalism*, edited by Bruce L. McCormack and Clifford B. Anderson, 201–26. Grand Rapids: Eerdmans, 2012.

King, Martin Luther, Jr. "Letter from Birmingham Jail." In *A Testament of Hope: The Essential Writings and Speeches of Martin Luther King Jr.*, edited by James Melvin Washington, 289–302. San Francisco: HarperCollins, 1986.

Lejeune, Robert. *Christoph Blumhardt and His Message*. Rifton, NY: Plough, 1963.

Lindberg, Carter, ed. *The Pietist Theologians: An Introduction to Theology in the Seventeenth and Eighteenth Centuries.* Oxford: Blackwell, 2005.

Marsh, Charles. "The Civil Rights Movement as Theological Drama—Interpretation and Application." *Modern Theology* 18 (2002) 231–50.

McDowell, John C. "'Openness to the World': Karl Barth's Evangelical Theology of Christ as the Pray-er." *Modern Theology* 25 (2009) 253–83.

Meyer-Blanck, Michael. "Gottesdienst und Gebet bei Karl Barth." *Zeitschrift für Dialektische Theologie* 24 (2008) 131–40.

Migliore, Daniel L. "Freedom to Pray: Karl Barth's Theology of Prayer." In *Karl Barth, Prayer*, 95–113. Louisville: Westminster John Knox, 2002.

O'Grady, Colm. *The Church in the Theology of Karl Barth.* Washington, DC: Corpus, 1968.

Rah, Soong-Chan. *The Next Evangelicalism: Freeing the Church from Western Cultural Captivity.* Downers Grove, IL: InterVarsity, 2009.

Shantz, Douglas H. *An Introduction to German Pietism: Protestant Renewal at the Dawn of Modern Europe.* Baltimore: Johns Hopkins University Press, 2013.

Strom, Johnathan. "Problems and Promises of Pietism Research." *Church History* 71 (2002) 536–54.

Vanhoozer, Kevin J. "Evangelicalism and the Church: The Company of the Gospel." In *The Future of Evangelicalism: Issues and Prospects*, edited by Craig Bartholomew et al., 40–45. Grand Rapids: Kregel, 2004.

Yeide, Harry, Jr. *Studies in Classical Pietism: The Flowering of the Ecclesiola.* New York: P. Lang, 1997.

Yocum, John. *Ecclesial Mediation in Karl Barth.* Burlington, VT: Ashgate, 2004.

Part III

Renewing Christian Doctrine

9

"Speak, for Your Servant Is Listening"
Barth, Prayer, and Theological Method

Joel D. Lawrence

Introduction: Speak, Lord . . .

FOR COUNTLESS YEARS, THE woman prayed. She prayed out of the depths of her pain, she prayed out of the depths of her hope, and she prayed out of the depths of her soul. If only God, the LORD, would give her a child. Up until now, her prayers have been unanswered, her longings unfulfilled, her desires unmet. One day, she goes to the Tabernacle at Shiloh, where Eli the priest is serving the LORD. There, after eating a sacrificial meal, the woman prays that God would take notice of her, a lowly, shamed woman. Eli takes notice of the woman, whose lips are moving as she is lost in her prayer; to him, she appears drunk. He rebukes her, but she defends herself, pouring out her heart to the priest, telling him of her request, seeking his blessing. Hearing her faith, the priest blesses: "Go in peace, and may the God of Israel grant you what you have asked of him."[1] What she asked was that God would bless her with a son, and if He did, Hannah would dedicate her son to God, to His service, to a life of prayer and prophecy, to be the possession of the LORD.

God heard her prayer and answered. The son was born. Hannah raised the boy until he was weaned, and then brought him to Eli to present Him to the LORD. It was a time when there were few visions, when the voice of the

---

1. 1 Sam 1:17

Lord was muted. One night, the young Samuel hears a voice calling to him, and, having mistaken the voice for Eli's, runs to his master. However, the voice was not Eli's. He goes back to his bed, but once again he hears the voice that calls to Samuel, but once again the voice is not Eli's. And again a third time: The calling voice, the misidentification of Eli. At this point, Eli realizes whose the voice is, and instructs Samuel to respond to the LORD, for it is He who is calling. This time, when the voice cries out, Samuel responds as Eli has instructed him: "Speak, for your servant is listening."

The story of the young Samuel is an apt image for the theological method of Karl Barth. And, it is a story that I propose can help Evangelicalism in its continuing dialogue with the legacy of Karl Barth. Over the past few years, numerous volumes have appeared exploring the connection between Barth and evangelical theology. And while these various explorations have yielded much fruit, the majority of these conversations have taken place at the level of theological *loci*: what does Barth say about Scripture, about the Church, about Salvation, etc.? But there is an area of Barth's theology that has gone largely unnoticed by evangelical theological commentators, but one that I believe has much to say to evangelical theology moving forward. It is this aspect of Barth's theology that is illustrated by the story of Samuel.

In this passage we see Samuel, the future prophet, when he hears the voice of the living God, do what is the only responsible thing to do when God speaks: *Samuel prays*. His prayer takes the form of an offer to be a humble hearer and receiver of God's Word. In this, Samuel demonstrates that the life of the servant of God is the life of humble, receptive prayer. For Barth, theology follows the way of Samuel, and the theologian is one who would have Samuel's words constantly on her or his lips. This understanding of theology as listening prayer is at the heart of the "Barthian revolt,"[2] a revolution driven by Barth's renewed vision of the theological life as a life of receiving the Word of God, and thus a revolution in which prayer is placed at the very core of theological method. Listening prayer *must* be prior to any attempt of the theologian to speak the Word of God. As this essay will establish, what we find in Barth's theology is a thoroughgoing demonstration that the theological task is foundationally a task of prayer. And, I will propose through this exploration that evangelical theology has much to learn from Barth's emphasis on listening prayer in our approach to theological method.

In this essay, we will explore Barth's notion of theology *as* prayer through numerous steps. First, we will look more broadly at Barth's conception of theology as prayer. Having engaged with this overview, we will then

---

2. This is borrowed from the title of Gary Dorrien's book *The Barthian Revolt in Modern Theology*.

look more closely at the convictions that underpin this stress on prayer as theological method in Barth, looking at Barth's understanding of theology as a science and the way that this influences his stress on prayer, and then exploring Barth's epistemology and the connection between this and prayer. Following these investigations, I will conclude the essay with some comments on how Evangelicalism can appropriate insights from Barth's union of prayer and theological method.

Theology as Prayer in Barth

That the theological life is a life of prayer is not a discovery first made by Barth. Many theologians have described this dynamic, and many have offered important treatises on the nature of theology as a prayerful task.[3] But none grounded the life of prayer as the basis of the theological task more consistently than has Barth.

There are two ways to look at the place of prayer in Barth's theology. The first is the emphasis in Barth on a theology *of* prayer. On this, Don E. Saliers writes, "Whatever else is said of the monumental legacy bequeathed to the world by Barth's life and work, this must be emphasized: his theology and his life manifest what it means to 'begin and end in prayer.'"[4] In the same vein, Daniel Migliore writes, "No other theologian of the twentieth century took prayer more seriously or developed a more extensive theology of prayer than did Karl Barth."[5] There is no question that these thinkers point us to an important emphasis in Barth. He did view the life of prayer as essential to the work of ministry and preaching for which he was writing the *Church Dogmatics*, and he gave a great deal of attention to the place of prayer in the life of the theologian and preacher.

While both of these thinkers point us to the importance of Barth's theology of prayer, there is another way of seeing the function of prayer in Barth's theology, which is the emphasis that we will give our attention to in this essay: theology *as* prayer. John Hesselink helps us see this function of prayer in Barth when he writes, "Some, but by no means all, theologians have devoted a chapter in their dogmatics or systematic theologies to prayer, but no one to my knowledge relates prayer so intimately *to the*

---

3. Barth himself learned to approach theology in this manner through his reading of Anselm's *Proslogion*, in which he discovered a theological treatise that was, in fact, a prayer. See Barth, *Anselm: Fides Quaerens Intellectum*.

4. Saliers, "Prayer and Theology in Karl Barth," ix.

5. Migliore, "Freedom to Pray," 95.

doing of the theology."⁶ This quote demonstrates most clearly that we have in Barth is something more than a theology *of* prayer. What we find in Barth is a presentation of theology *as* prayer, in which Barth's theological method is best understood *as prayer*. For Barth, prayer and theology are unified at the deepest levels; in fact, as we will see, they are one and the same thing, and Barth's conviction regarding this unity is grounded in his conviction concerning the task of theology.

Perhaps the classic expression of Barth's view of the unity of theology and prayer can be found in his later work *Evangelical Theology*. In this book, Barth summarizes his experience of nearly fifty years of preaching, teaching, and writing. Concerning prayer and its place in the theological task, Barth writes,

> The first and most basic act of theological work is prayer. . . . Undoubtedly, from the very beginning and without intermission, theological work is also *study*; in every respect it is also *service*; and finally it would certainly be in vain were it not also an act of love. But theological work does not merely begin with prayer and is not merely accompanied by it; in its totality it is peculiar and characteristic of theology that *it can be performed only in the act of prayer*.⁷

This last phrase is the center of my claim in this essay: that theology can only be performed in the act of prayer means that theology can only be understood *as prayer*. Barth's claim here is that the relationship between prayer and theology is not that one prays *before* one does it or even that one prays *while* one does it, for this understanding would view prayer and theology as *two separate tasks*, the one accompanying the other. Instead, for Barth, prayer is theology and theology is prayer.

We are now in a position to turn to the questions that this essay seeks to answer: What is it that leads Barth to see theology as prayer? Why is it that for Barth any dogmatics that divorces itself from prayer has lost its vital function? And how can this understanding help Evangelical theology to reinvigorate its own theological task? How can the prayerful Barth inform Evangelicalism in its approach to theology?

---

6. Hesselink, "Karl Barth on Prayer," 75, emphasis mine. Later in the essay cited in note 5 above, Migliore speaks more specifically on the relationship between theological method and prayer when he writes, "Although Barth considers prayer to be indispensible to every aspect of Christian life, he is especially attentive to its essential role in the work of theology" ("Freedom to Pray," 102).

7. Barth, *Evangelical Theology*, 160, emphasis mine.

To answer these questions, we turn now to a more detailed analysis of Barth's theological method. It is one thing to say that Barth's theology can only be understood as prayer, but it is quite another to understand *why* this is the case. In exploring this question, we will be driven to Barth's underlying presuppositions for the doing of theology. In doing this, I believe that Evangelicalism can be challenged to grapple with Barth at a more fundamental level than doctrines, and so come into a more fruitful dialogue with him centered on the praxis of prayer in the doing of theology.

Barth's Theological Method

As is well known, Barth is most often described as a theologian of *revelation*. His theological task from beginning to end is a disciplined engagement with listening to the voice of the living God as He speaks to us in and through the text of Scripture by the Spirit. The foundational conviction of Barth's theology is *Deus dixit*, God speaks. In his own context, Barth is rebelling against two hundred years of theological endeavor that muzzled God, denying revelation by making human being and human thinking the object of theology. Barth's analysis was that theology was in desperate need of reorienting itself to its proper object, the God who reveals Himself through His Word.

Barth's theological method, then, demands that the Christian task of theology be oriented to listening to the God who speaks. He puts this plainly in *Evangelical Theology* when he writes, "The task of theological work consists in listening to Him, this One who speaks through His work, and of rendering account of His Word to oneself, the Church, and the world."[8] This is a summary of Barth's conviction that dogmatics exists, not to state once and for all propositional truths about God that can take their place in a system, but rather to test the Church's proclamation of the Gospel by reflecting on her speech in light of the speech of God given in Christ, Scripture, and preaching. Theology, then, is a function of the Church as she tests her speech against God's speech. Consequently, this means that the Church's speech must recognize that it doesn't have freedom to go its own way, but rather must go about "thinking after" God's own speech. As Barth says, "Within the framework of the Church which thus teaches, and in complete solidarity with it, [theology] reminds the Church . . . that there exists a prior to and above and after every *ego dico* and *ecclesia dicit* a *haec dixit Dominus*; and the aim of Church proclamation is that this *haec dixit Dominus* should prevail and triumph not only before, above and after, but *in* every *ego dicit*

---

8. Ibid.

and *ecclesia dicit*."[9] Thus, the first movement of theology is not a movement of speaking, but a recognition that God *has spoken* and *will speak*.

This conviction of the Church's theological task creates a new disposition of the theologian: the disposition of listening prayer. Barth writes, "If the teaching of the Church is an uncertain action from the human standpoint, the teaching Church will not only have to have heard . . . but it will constantly have to hear again—not to hear any kind of voice, but to hear specifically the voice which has called the Church into being and to which all Church proclamation must give some sort of answer. . . . The only resource is to seize the weapon of continually listening."[10] This listening is the way of the Church. And it is the way of prayer. Barth writes, "To put it in the strictest terms, we must say that dogmatics must go with the teaching Church in the fellowship of prayer, out of the past, through the present and into the future."[11]

At the heart of Barth's understanding of the Church and her task of theology is the action of seizing the weapon of continually listening, an action that is an action of continually saying to God, "Speak, for your servant is listening." This listening is a recognition, an acknowledgement, that God's Word is always prior, and that the Church lives from this prior Word which becomes present as God continues to speak. Theology must to be attentive to this voice, this living voice, and to allow God's Word, and no other, to determine the content of her theological reasoning.

But how is it that theology goes about its way of listening to the speaking God and so function as true theology, theology as prayer? To answer this, we must understand Barth's conception of theology as a science as seen in the opening pages of the *Church Dogmatics*. Understanding what Barth means when he says that theology is a science will enable us to see more clearly the epistemology of prayer espoused by Barth and so gain a clearer understanding of the place of prayer at the center of Barth's theological task.

The Science of Theology

According to Barth, theology is a science. It employs a scientific method. And, as any science, the method is determined by the object that is studied. God, as the One who speaks, is the object of theology's scientific investigation. Theology thus receives its method for grasping God from Him, from

---

9. Barth, *CD* I/2, 801.
10. Ibid., 804.
11. Ibid., 840.

the nature of his self-revelation.[12] For Barth, this means careful attention to Jesus Christ, the one about whom Scripture states, "For God was pleased to have all his fullness dwell in him,"[13] and that he is "the radiance of divine glory and the exact representation of [God's] being."[14] If we are to see who God is, we look to Jesus Christ, for, as Jesus tells us, "If you had really known me, you would know who my Father is. From now on, you do know him and have seen him."[15]

The danger for the theologian comes when he or she is tempted to import the methods and questions from other sciences and allow those to determine the scientific task of theology. Barth's engagement with the theology of the eighteenth and nineteenth centuries, illustrated particularly by his continued dialogue with Friedrich Schleiermacher, demonstrates the danger of theology giving over its task to methods derived from other sciences. Barth accuses German liberal theology of having allowed its attention to the object of theology to be drawn away, and its theology became what Barth labels "theosophy," a pseudo-theology that is no longer driven by the concerns of its primary object, the revelation of the speaking God in Scripture, but instead is driven by the philosophical and anthropological concerns of the day.[16]

While theology must, of course, be attentive to the concerns of the day because it must be open to the insights it can receive from philosophy, anthropology, and all the fields of science, Barth is insistent that theology must not give its task over to these. If it does this, it allows the other disciplines to provide theology with its method, which will then ultimately mean that theology is no longer theology. To do so is to import methods and questions from a different field of science, and allow those methods and questions to overtake the proper method and questions of theology. Other sciences do not do this: physics does not allow biology to drive its concerns. You will find very few cadavers in a physics lab, and if you do, something may not be quite right. The object of physics creates a method *for physics*. The object requires a disciplined engagement through a focused method. One can later correlate the findings of differing scientific fields, but the methods of each must be disciplined in their attention to their own object, or else the object sought will not be found.[17]

12. See Barth, *CD* I/1, 5–11.
13. Col 1:19 NIV.
14. Heb 1:3.
15. John 14:7.
16. Barth, *CD* I/1, 6.
17. Ibid., 7–10.

Barth argues that this means we cannot import criteria from other sciences and expect them to achieve the goal of hearing God speak. In his commentary on *Galatians*, J. Louis Martyn, though not directly commenting on Barth, writes a sentence that captures well this emphasis of Barth's theological method: "Since the gospel is God's own utterance, it is not and can never be subject to ratiocinative criteria developed apart from it."[18] Or, as Barth himself puts it, "If theology allows itself to be called, or calls itself, a science, it cannot in so doing accept the obligation of submission to standards valid for other sciences."[19] The Gospel, the Word of God's revelation, creates its own criteria and because of this it cannot be judged by criteria from outside. It must be accountable to the criteria of its own scientific discipline, but must not give its task away by trying to be that which it is not, and seeking to answer questions that are outside of the purview of its task.

Barth's understanding of theology as a science comes into clearer focus when we see why he resists understanding theology as the systematization of theological thinking frozen in time,[20] but instead depicts it as a discipline that is ever-attentive to its Object, the Living Subject who speaks. This notion that the Object of the science of theology is a Subject is critical to Barth's outlining of the task of theology. Theology is a unique discipline because the Object of its inquiry is the Living Lord, the Free, Sovereign, Creating, Speaking God, before whom we could not stand if not for His grace. Theology is not a task of systematization because God is not an Object that we can analyze and systematize; He is the Living, Speaking God, whom we approach rightly only as we fear Him and realize His right over us in all of our thinking about Him. He is God. He does not stand before us so that we might scrutinize Him and make judgments concerning His goodness or existence. We stand before Him to be scrutinized and judged in all our ways, and to hear the Word of grace and forgiveness that He speaks to us in Jesus Christ.

By focusing on Barth's notion that the Object of theology is a Living Subject, we see yet more clearly why it is that prayer *is* theological method for Barth. The reason that Barth writes that "the first and basic act of theological work is prayer," is because Barth has recognized, perhaps more clearly than any other, that the Christian doctrine of revelation demands prayer as the responsive attitude of the theologian who would hear, and then speak, the Word of God. Because the object of Christian theology is a Subject, is *The Subject*, the theologian recognizes that this Subject must be listened to in

18. Martyn, *Galatians*, 22.
19. *CD* I/1, 10.
20. *CD* I/2, 841.

prayer, and if we fail to do this, our theology loses its way. Theology, then, can only be performed as an act of prayer because theology is the practice of faithfully listening to God.[21] It is in this life of faithful listening to God that the theologian's mantra is continually in her or his heart: "Speak, Lord, your servant is listening."

Barth's Epistemology of Prayer

This understanding of Barth's methodological commitments inherent in his understanding of theology as science leads us next to a closer inspection of Barth's epistemology. God's speech creates its own epistemology, an epistemology that is grounded *in faith*.[22] The ability to hear God speak is not available to unaided human senses. We gain knowledge of the speech of God not through general epistemological categories available to humanity in general, which are then applied to hearing God, but through the epistemology that comes with faith, which is a gift of God.

We see this emphasis on faith its connection to prayer in *CD* I/1, paragraph 6, "The Knowability of the Word of God." In subsection 4, "The Word of God and Faith," Barth explores in depth the reality of faith as a way of knowing, an epistemology that is created by God's Word and so is a unique way of knowing that cannot be compared with epistemologies that are based on human capacities or potentialities. There is no potential in humanity for coming to know God's Word; there is nothing inherent in humans that make humans able to know God. This is, or course, at the heart of Barth's theology: there is no *schwerpunkt*, no "point of contact," no possibilities for humans to know God's Word. The only way that humanity can know God's Word, and thus God Himself in His Word, is by the free grace of God to make Himself known. The question of the knowability of God's Word is not a question that has its determination on the human side but rather on the Divine. God makes God's Word knowable by the free decision of grace.

Faith, then, is that which God's Word produces in the human as a possibility for knowing God. But what of the human side of this knowing? As I said above, the question of the knowability of God's Word can be answered decisively only from the divine side, but does this mean that there is no human side to knowing God? Clearly for Barth this is not the case. He goes to great pains to state that humanity can truly know God's Word as humans in their humanity. The very core of Barth's understanding of theology, the reflection of the Church on her proclamation of the Gospel, assumes that

21. Ibid., 23.
22. Ibid., 229–37.

God can be truly known. On this we read, "In the concept of Church proclamation and hence also in that of dogmatics it is obviously taken for granted that it is possible for man to hear and even speak, and hence also to know, the Word of God."[23] So there is a very real *knowledge* of God that humans are capable of, and this knowledge is the knowledge of faith. Barth's emphasis on the priority of God does not erase the human knower, but does deny that the ability to know God lies intrinsically in the human knower.

It is in this context that we speak of an epistemology of prayer in Barth. We know God, and thus the Gospel that the Church is called to proclaim, through faith, which is the way of knowing created by God's free act to make Himself known through His Word. Since theology is a disciplined engagement with the voice of the living God, done in faith, Barth's conviction of the prayerful theological life now becomes clear. In the early pages of the *CD*, as Barth is outlining the task of theology, he describes the unity between the work of theology and prayer. He writes, "We . . . repeat the statement that dogmatics is possible only as an act of faith . . . when we point to prayer as the attitude without which there can be no dogmatic work."[24] As we have seen, for Barth, to do theology is to grasp the weapon of listening to God. As such, we only understand theological epistemology in its relationship to the way of knowing created by God, a way of knowing that is, at its heart, listening prayer. Barth states, "Dogmatics must always be undertaken as an act of penitence and obedience. But this is possible only as it trusts in the uncontrollable presence of its ontic and noetic basis, in the revelation of God promised to the Church, and in the power of faith apprehending the promise."[25] This work of penitence is the work of humble, listening prayer, allowing the Object of theology, the speaking God, to guide our theological work as we receive His Word and correct our ecclesial thinking and practices in light of His Word.

Conclusion: Evangelicalism and Barthian Method

In this essay, I have presented an understanding of the theological method of Karl Barth that demonstrates that, for Barth, to do theology is to pray, and to pray is to do theology. Barth's convictions concerning the task of theology are built on his understanding that the Church stands, or should I say kneels, always in the position of a hearer of God's Word. When this basic understanding of the Church's work of theology is missed, she can all too

---

23. Ibid., 187.
24. Ibid., 23.
25. Ibid., 22.

easily lapse into a theological task that is divorced from its true object, the Living God who speaks His Word to His servants.

The import of this for evangelical theology is critical. All too often, evangelical theologies have wandered away from the Object of our theology, and have instead attempted to prove the truth of our theology by appealing to standards and criteria apart from the disciplined listening of the Church to the voice of the living God. Ironically, in appealing to the standards of other sciences, Evangelicalism has all too often gone the way of the German Liberal tradition that Barth stridently opposes. Other disciplines (philosophy, psychology, the social sciences, etc.) have been allowed to set the rules of the game by which we appeal to the truth of the Gospel. Evangelicalism all too often operates as if we could prove the Gospel based on the rules of the other disciplines, and that if we do this, those disciplines would have to acknowledge the truth of the Gospel. One of the main motivations for doing this is the desire of evangelicals to carve out a place for themselves in larger academic conversations in order to shape those conversations. This apologetic and evangelistic desire is a constant temptation for Evangelicalism, with our good and right emphasis on proclaiming the truth of Jesus Christ. But the danger in this is that in giving away the rules of the game to other disciplines, evangelical theology loses its own unique task, as task that can be shared only by those of faith.

So what does Evangelicalism need to learn from Barth? What are the implications of Barth's theological method of prayer *as* theology that we must adopt? Let me suggest two things. First, we must understand that Barth's theology is *confessional*. While evangelical theology all too often has engaged in the apologetic task of theology, it has run the risk of giving away the task of theology in order to convince the academy, and the larger world of thought, that we are worthy of having access to the table. In doing this, evangelical theology has not placed prayer at the heart of its theological method. While there has been plenty of engagement with a theology *of* prayer, and while evangelicals have engaged much with the *discipline* of prayer, the integration of theology and prayer into an understanding of theology *as* prayer has been lacking. The presuppositions of evangelical methodology have been those of the larger academy rather those of a confessional theology. A theological method built to satisfy the "ratiocinative criteria" of the larger academy will struggle to define itself as theology *as* prayer. But a theology that is built on the Object of the speaking God whose speech that theology is called to *confess* rather than defend can go along its way without embarrassment or the need to justify itself to those who view the task of theology in the larger academy quite differently.

Second, and following from this: Evangelicalism would do well to remind itself regularly of Barth's words in *CD* I/2: "The Word of God did not found an academy but the Church. If, therefore, an academy is required to serve the Word of God, it can only be the academy of the Church, founded and maintained at a definite time and place by the existence of the Word of God." Barth consistently maintains throughout his theology that theology is the task of the Church. Only those who confess Christ are equipped to do theology because, as we have seen, God can only be known in His revelation and heard in His speech by those of faith. Only those who believe can take up the weapon of listening to God. As such, theology belongs not in the academy, but in the Church, and if, as Barth says, the academy is needed, it must understand itself as a gathering *of the Church*. It is unfortunate that Evangelicalism has succumbed to the bifurcation between academy and Church. But Barth enables us to see more clearly that the task of theology only *is* because God is at work to reveal His glory by building His Church. Theology exists for that sake and for no other.

We have seen in this essay that Karl Barth's conception of theology *as* prayer is not simply a matter of developing a better theology *of* prayer. Instead, it is rooted deeply in core convictions about the task of theology, the communication of the Living Word, an understanding of epistemology that is deeply rooted in faith, and so a vision of theological method that is proper to the conviction that theology is a task of the confessing Church, rather than the academy. I believe that Evangelicalism, in its continuing engagement with Barth's theology, has much to learn from the union of theology and prayer, and from the theological methodology that gives rise to that union. In taking on these lessons, evangelical theologians can be encouraged to continually pray the words of Samuel as we take up the weapon of listening prayer: "Speak, for your servant is listening."

Bibliography

Barth, Karl. *Anselm: Fides Quaerens Intellectum: Anselm's Proof of the Existence of God in the Context of His Theological Scheme.* London: SCM, 1975.

———. *Evangelical Theology: An Introduction.* Translated by Grover Foley. Grand Rapids: Eerdmans, 1992.

Dorrien, Gary. *The Barthian Revolt in Modern Theology: Theology without Weapons.* Louisville: Westminster John Knox, 1999.

Hesselink, I. John. "Karl Barth on Prayer." In Karl Barth, *Prayer,* 74–94. Louisville: Westminster John Knox, 2002.

Martyn, J. Louis. *Galatians: A New Translation with Introduction and Commentary.* Anchor Bible 33A. New York: Doubleday, 1997.

Migliore, Daniel L. "Freedom to Pray: Karl Barth's Theology of Prayer." In Karl Barth, *Prayer,* 95–113. Louisville: Westminster John Knox, 2002.

Saliers, Don E. "Prayer and Theology in Karl Barth." In Karl Barth, *Prayer,* ix–xx. Louisville: Westminster John Knox, 2002.

10

Better News Hath No Evangelical than This

Barth, Election, and the Recovery of the Gospel from Evangelicalism's Territorial Disputes

Chris Boesel

Framing the Question: Four Coordinates

I WOULD LIKE TO SET the context for my engagement with Barth by identifying four framing coordinates through which I understand and from which I approach the thesis of this collection.

A Personal Confession

The thesis of this book asks us to challenge the conventional "reception narrative" of much scholarship on Barth and Evangelicalism, asserting that it wrongly assumes Evangelicalism—as a modern historical phenomenon, forged in the polemical fires of resistance to the rising cultural authority of science and secularism—to be largely an expression of Reformed Orthodoxy to the exclusion of Pietist and Arminian traditions (conversionist, revivalist, perfectionist, emphasis on personal experience and agency).[1]

---

1. For what I have in mind by what I call the differing "strands" of Evangelicalism, and their respective histories of Barth reception, see Thorne, *Evangelicalism and Karl Barth*; Bolich, *Karl Barth and Evangelicalism*; and most recently, Gibson and Strange, *Engaging with Barth*. The latter two volumes—especially *Engaging with Barth*—focus on the Reformed Orthodox strand of Evangelicalism to the extent that one might

What if the central characteristics of evangelical identity were broadened across what has been a long standing, conflictual divide, from the limited sphere of the philosophical and doctrinal positions of Reformed Orthodoxy to include more Arminian-Pietist regions privileging the personal experience of conversion, regeneration and holiness? Would the relation to Barth be cast in different light? And would this be a more positive light—a light of common commitments, fruitful mutual engagement and a shared future?

I have no doubt that Barth's relation to Evangelicalism will be seen in a different light. But I have my suspicions as to how much more promising this light will prove to be with regard to commonality and mutuality, at least in relation to the corner of Barth's theological corpus that I will reflect upon in light of the above question: Barth's doctrine of election. My fundamental suspicion is that no matter who wins the fight for legitimate evangelical identity the winner will have plenty to dislike about Barth, and to that extent will, to my mind, leave much to be desired with regard to the Gospel of Jesus Christ.

No, I am not saying that Barth's theology has a corner on the Gospel. Barth would of course balk at the suggestion that the Gospel could be possessed with proprietary rights by which a theologian or a theology could fix and secure pride of place over against others. In matter of fact, his driving conviction that faithfulness to the Gospel forbids any such identification with human theological effort is central to my reading of Barth, both generally and in specific relation to the contest between Reformed Orthodoxy and Arminian-Pietist strands of Evangelicalism. This, then, is what I *am* saying:

a. The traditional and ongoing internal territorial disputes and proprietary squabbles over authentic evangelical identity and theology are a distraction from the Gospel, such that securing one's authentic evangelical identity on this terrain does not secure one's relation to it.

b. This, because current foundations and contours of evangelical identity and theology, no matter who is laying claim to them, are not sufficient to the goodness of the news about Jesus that the Gospel proclaims.

And I am saying *this* because I was raised a believer in the belly of a trans-denominational born-again Evangelicalism wherein Billy Graham, Francis Schaeffer, Josh McDowell, Charles Swindoll, Dallas Theological Seminary, Multnomah School of the Bible, and Moody Bible Institute were all taken as reliably authoritative theological voices. And it came to pass

---

conclude that Reformed Orthodoxy itself constitutes Evangelicalism as such, thereby demonstrating the thesis of this book.

that I heard, believed, and was converted by the Gospel anew—though what felt like for the first time—upon encountering Barth's theology in my early twenties. I was, so to speak, born again, again. The news of the Gospel as rooted in the disputed landscape of the Evangelicalism that raised me was simply not very good. It was certainly no match for the goodness of the news heard by Barth in the witness of Scripture to the God who is for us—each and every one—from all eternity in Jesus Christ in the power of the Spirit.

My *confession*, then, is that despite all my arduously acquired, so-called scholarly acumen, with its commitment to rigorous objectivity and practices of careful, unbiased analysis, I am one of those recovering evangelicals who is simply incapable of approaching the relation of Barth to Evangelicalism—and its current territorial disputes—free of the fundamental conviction that Evangelicalism of whatever stripe needs Barth significantly more than Barth needs Evangelicalism. Reader be warned; buyer beware.

Barth as Ecumenical Theologian

> Of course there is within the Church an evangelical theology which is to be affirmed and a heretical non-theology which is to be resolutely denied. But I rejoice that *in concrete* I neither know nor have to know who stands where, so that I can serve a cause and not a party, and mark off myself from a cause and not a party, not working either for or against persons. Thus I can be free in relation to both ostensible and true neighbours.[2]

Barth did not presume to locate theological proprietary rights to the Gospel of Jesus Christ within any particular tradition or denomination—not even the Reformed tradition.[3] Nor did Barth understand the establishment of proprietary rights to the Gospel to be the task of theology, e.g., mounting an apologetic for the truth, authenticity and authority of one tradition or denomination over against others. For Barth, the heretical "other" (which is always *within* and so *belongs to* the Church) of genuine evangelical theology

---

2. Barth, *CD* I/1, xv. Note that he places heretical non-theology *within* the Church, as a possibility of faith (ibid., 33–34). This highlights an inclusive and ecumenical dynamic to Barth's theology that is often easy to miss.

3. Though he clearly presumed the Protestant Reformation constituted a real recovery—a genuinely new hearing—of the Gospel of Jesus Christ, such that the voices of the reformers entailed a relative authority as theological corrective to the Roman Catholic and Eastern traditions for the doing of theology in contemporary contexts; though even here, this did not mean exclusive authority—Roman Catholic voices would still inform Barth, and Reformation voices were not immune to withering critique.

over against which he attempted to articulate the way and content of the Church's faithful speech about God was not the Roman Catholic tradition or the Lutheran tradition or Reformed Orthodoxy or Pietism or Pentecostalism or either European or American Fundamentalism or even modern liberal Protestantism. It was the theological project that he called "natural theology," which, according to Barth, could and in fact did take the form of any and all of these various concrete traditions of the Church, including the various forms of Protestant "Evangelicalism."[4]

The broadest strokes of Barth's theology can be said to "cut both ways," against the grain of modern Liberal Protestant theology on the "left" and the Roman Catholic tradition on the "right." But also falling under the critical blade of this cut to the right, though more parenthetically, are, among other things, the specific and contesting strands of Evangelicalism that we are dealing with here: what Barth sees as

a. the scholastic tendencies of Protestant Orthodoxy;
b. both the mystical and Pelagian desires of Pietism; and
c. the biblicist dogmatism of Fundamentalism.[5]

And for Barth, all of these various traditions on the left and the right fall under the scythe of critique only to the extent that they, in various ways at various times and places and for various reasons, constitute or capitulate to

---

4. What Barth means by the term *evangelical*—as with most European theologians generally—is not necessarily synonymous with what the term indicates in American usage. For Barth, as with European theologians generally, the term is synonymous with Reformation or Protestant theology as distinct from the Roman Catholic tradition. The specific historical phenomenon that came to be known as Evangelicalism in the United States, emerging out of the Fundamentalism of the late nineteenth and early twentieth centuries, required a name that would distinguish it from Protestant theology generally conceived. The term *Evangelikale* was invented in German theology to mark this distinction.

5. In this sense, Barth's theology does not simply cut *both* ways, in terms of a binary logic of opposition, but *multiple* ways, in relation to what are always multiple and complex alternatives. Indeed, as Barth was launching his *Church Dogmatics*, he was cognizant of the fact that the Church for which he was writing those dogmatics did not seem to be much in evidence: "For where is today the Evangelical Church which desires to be taken seriously and to confess itself in the sense of the present book?" (*CD* I/1, xv). In this sense, Barth's theology was calling the Church universal to a faithfulness and obedience, not to partisan loyalty to the fixed propositions of its various competing historical traditions, but to that living Other who is its true source and goal—calling the Church to a concrete life corresponding to its very "being," which is not reducible to its empirical history and historical existence, but is the living, personal, Trinitarian divine-human reality that is Jesus Christ, who freely and scandalously gives himself to and in that empirical history and existence.

an instance of natural theology. And what Barth calls natural theology itself only presents a danger requiring vigilant critique to the extent that, in transforming the Gospel into a "constantly available" human possession—always for very compelling reasons and always in response to what are perceived to be very real dangers—it inevitably compromises the goodness of its news about Jesus.[6]

In focusing on Barth's relation to the Reformed Orthodox and Arminian-Pietist strands of modern Evangelicalism, then, the subject matter of this book represents only a narrow corner of Barth's engagement with the wide spectrum of the Church's theology both ancient and modern; a rather small intramural skirmish on the margins of a vast, rich and complex theological vision and contest. With these broad and complex dimensions of Barth's work in mind, I will attempt to demonstrate a kind of double movement:

a. Barth's doctrine of election not only cuts against the grain of these particular strands of Evangelicalism as "conservative" forms of natural theology—on the "right" in relation to the Church's whole theological spectrum.

b. It also cuts both ways—*between* these strands—in terms of their relation to each other. It cuts against Reformed Orthodoxy, on the one hand, and against the Arminian-Pietist traditions, on the other hand, and in each case precisely by resonating with the other at classic points of their mutual disagreement.

Because neither constitutes the focus of Barth's theological vision, inasmuch as Barth attempts to focus that vision solely upon the free, living personal reality of Jesus Christ in the power of the Spirit, his critical relation to both of these strands of Evangelicalism can be seen as a consequence of an ecumenical freedom to both critique and resonate with each of them in different ways, on and at different points.

The Reception Narrative[7]

The history of the evangelical reception of Barth can be read as a reflection of the evolution of evangelical identity in the twentieth century, at least

---

6. Consequently, Barth's theology never comes to rest, there is never a neutral place of rest and security that constitutes a theological tradition, ecclesial or denominational identity, as a place to finally and securely stand. And especially not in terms of a "Barthianism," whatever that might be.

7. I am relying on Thorne, Bolich, and the volume edited by Gibson and Strange for

in the Anglo-American context. And it does so fairly consistently whether one looks at the Reformed Orthodox or Arminian-Pietist strands of Evangelicalism. This shared trajectory of Barth reception moves from an early twentieth-century general consensus of polemical rejection among the Reformed Orthodox and virtually no engagement at all among the Arminian-Pietist traditions to an ever-widening consensus of positive constructive engagement and assessment qualified by continued critical reservations on a few key issues (though the level of engagement remains significantly limited with the Arminian-Pietist camps).

Throughout this shared trajectory of increasingly—yet not wholly—positive engagement, a central point of critique has endured. Reformed Orthodox and Arminian-Pietist strands of Evangelicalism both target Barth's Christocentric approach in both theological method and content, a Christocentrisim so radical as to constitute a "Christomonism."[8] The critique charges that the multidimensional richness of the biblical narrative and the resulting breadth, diversity and interrelationship of traditional doctrinal themes expressing the Church's understanding of and proclaiming of the Gospel, get collapsed into one, albeit central, part of the story: God's redemptive decision, will and action in Jesus Christ. As a consequence, other seemingly essential parts of God's nature and God's history of active commerce with creation, together with the creature's critical response to and participation in that commerce, appear to lose their distinctive integrity or are lost from view.

For the Reformed Orthodox, given their emphasis on inerrancy, apologetics and sovereignty, the Christoentric distortion tends to be "front loaded," centered on methodological issues encountered early in the doctrinal system: revelation, Scripture, human epistemology (anthropology), and the doctrines of God and providence. The Christocentric mischief worked here is judged as too personalist and subjectivist, the result of Barth's Christological doctrine of revelation wherein the whole of theology receives its content in Jesus Christ as the living, personal Word of God addressing us in a free, contingent event of personal encounter. It is not irrelevant to our concerns here that personalism and subjectivism are the central characteristics of Reformed Orthodoxy's critique of Pietist and Arminian traditions.

The Christocentric distortion decried by the Arminian-Pietist traditions, by contrast, tends to be "back-loaded," centered on the issues of human believing response to divine activity: human experience and agency

---

much of what follows regarding the differences and similarities between the strands of Evangelicalism with regard to Barth reception.

8. Gibson and Strange, *Engaging with Barth*, 26–27, 272, 339.

in salvation and sanctification; the status and work of the Holy Spirit in the life of the believer. Here Barth's Christocentrism has the effect of being too objectivist, and this—again, pertinent to our concerns—not least because, from the Arminian and Pietist perspectives, it is too Reformed. The entire drama of the God-human relation appears to be accomplished by divine decree and divine action taken in Jesus Christ as an objective fact over against and regardless of human subjective response, participation and commitment.

This charge of Christomonist Christocentrism and its variously perceived distortions deserves serious consideration that cannot be given here. I will only suggest that a sound response will no doubt interrogate the extent to which the charge may not do full justice to the extent to which Barth understands Jesus Christ to be the Word of God and so the content of revelation—and consequently of Christian doctrine—as a radically Trinitarian reality, event and action.[9] What I will focus on in this essay is the twofold effect that Barth's undeniably Christological concentration has upon his doctrine of election, and the impact that this has upon his reception by Evangelicalism, of both Reformed Orthodox and Arminian-Pietist strands.

First, Barth's Christological concentration allows a reading of Barth's doctrine of election wherein he can be seen to be, simultaneously, both robustly Reformed and surprisingly Arminian-Pietist. And this, precisely on the issues that most starkly divide these strands of Evangelicalism from each other on the biblical theme of election. Again, Barth's theological and doctrinal decisions in relation to the goodness of the news about Jesus Christ allows him to resource and resonate with both traditions in precisely the way and at the very points at which they disagree with and reject each other. As such, Barth's doctrine of election highlights the partisan—and ultimately distracting, irrelevant and futile—conflict between them while finding in Jesus Christ an "indisputable bow of peace which overarches them," stretching across the conflict and embracing all involved.[10] In cutting both ways, Barth resources them both ecumenically beyond the conflictual limits they impose on each other in the territorial disputes and identity politics of Evangelicalism

---

9. Note that the central content of Barth's Doctrine of the Word of God in the first volume of the *Church Dogmatics* is his doctrine of the Trinity. The Word of God, then, does not only mean Jesus Christ as the *second* Person of the Trinity's hypostatic union with the human from Nazareth. Rather, the Word of God—and so, the name Jesus Christ—entails the interrelated activity and identity of the *entire* Trinity.

10. Barth, CD I/1, 33. This phrase occurs as part of his treatment of heresy as belonging to and within the Church as an essential possibility of Christian faith.

Second, Barth's Christological approach to the doctrine of election brings to light the theological issue on which both the Reformed Orthodox and Arminian-Piestist charges of Christomonism in Barth sing with one accord, even in the voices of their more generous interpreters of Barth. The element of Barth's theology that remains a bridge too far for Evangelicalism across the board, of yesterday and today, is his vision of the universal and eternal consequences of God's reconciling decision, Word and action in Jesus Christ and the resulting eschatological status of judgment and damnation. For both the Reformed Orthodox and Arminian-Pietist strands, the shared and equally intractable objection to Barth's doctrine of election boils down to its soteriological and eschatological consequences. Barth seems to suggest that there may not be anyone in hell at the end of the story; that God may have decided, from before the foundations of the world, to enter the regions of hell Herself in Jesus Christ and blow through the bottom of it, as it were, obliterating it from the inside out—destroying its possibility and possessive power as a final, binding and irrevocable determination of the human being.

Perhaps the most fundamental disagreement between Reformed Orthodoxy and the Arminian-Piestist strands of Evangelicalism is whether God condemns unrepentant sinners to hell based on an eternal divine decree in the wake of which said sinners are predestined to unrepentance and so eternal damnation; or based on the fact that, while fully able to repent, believe and be saved, the sinner exercises God-given creaturely freedom and responsibility to refuse repentance and choose a God-less life of unbelief and rebellion, thus deserving said condemnation to eternal damnation. However, the fundamental thing they *share* amidst this dispute, thrown into stark relief in the light of their respective engagements with and assessments of Barth, is that *someone* is getting condemned to hell. Regardless of whether atonement is limited or universal there is still plenty of eternal hell fire to go around. For both, the good news of the Gospel can only be—and it seems *must* be, given the strenuous tone of the objections to Barth—good news for some and bad news for everyone else. What Barth calls a "mixed message of joy and terror."[11]

And Barth's judgment upon this mixed message stands as judgment upon any Evangelicalism—or any form of natural theology—that compromises the goodness of the news about Jesus Christ and thereby falls short of the Church's responsibility as witnessing community to that news. As Barth rather pointedly states, "if it is the shadow which really predominates, if we must still fear, or *if we can only half rejoice and half fear . . .* then it is

---

11. Barth, *CD* II/2, 13.

quite certain that we can never again receive or proclaim as such the Gospel previously declared."[12]

Good News for Whom? An Unasked Question

If this book succeeds in recasting Barth's relation to Evangelicalism, and in so doing, the question of what that might mean for the future of both Evangelicalism and Barth scholarship, it will still remain to be asked whether the resulting status of Barth and Evangelicalism is a good or bad thing for the future of the Church and of the world. Whatever the status of their relationship, both Barth and modern Evangelicalism stand beyond the pale of viable Christian faith and practice for many, many sincere and passionate Christians—theologians, ministers and laypeople. This is largely due to the extent to which they both depart from and critically resist fundamental assumptions of modern liberal, progressive and liberation theologies—and most particularly, the ethical instincts and commitments that drive those assumptions—at decisive points.[13] To that extent they represent for many Christians the continuation of a literalist distortion of the Christian message that has resulted in an ugly history of imperialistic, patriarchal exclusivity in relation to the religious neighbors of the Church as well as many if not most of its own members. That is, they represent a long history of certain historically privileged voices in the Church turning what is believed to be genuinely benevolent resources entailed in the message of Jesus as expressed in certain Christian symbols into some very bad news indeed.

While this critical view of both Barth and Evangelicalism within the wider Church—and the very legitimate theological and ethical concerns and commitments that it entails—can and should be addressed (though whether it can ever be sufficiently addressed for those who hold these critical objections must necessarily remain an open question), that work clearly falls outside the stated questions of this volume. While the ways in which

---

12. Ibid., 14.

13. This, because they both assume that Scripture is the unrivaled authority for the Church, that the God known fully in Jesus Christ in the power of the Spirit is the one true God, and that said God has acted salvifically, for all the world, once for all, in Jesus Christ and the Holy Spirit, in history for all of history. So, for example, they both believe the Gospel is a piece of news about God's particular, concrete saving action in history—in Jesus Christ in the power of the Spirit—and as such is not reducible to one of many religious symbol systems giving expression to a particular experience of universal, universally accessible, and salvifically efficacious divine presence. This leaves other religious traditions and their practitioners unfairly outside the loop of the salvific history between God and the human creature.

Barth works against the grain of the Reformed Orthodox and Arminian-Pietist strands of Evangelicalism that I will attempt to demonstrate here do indeed touch upon certain dimensions of these critical concerns and commitments (e.g., the universal embrace of God's albeit radically particular electing decision in Jesus Christ), a full engagement with this important critique must wait for another time and place.[14]

Election as Good News: Between and Beyond the Reformed Orthodox/Arminian-Pietist Divide

> The doctrine of election is the sum of the Gospel because of all the words that can be said or heard it is the best: that God elects man; that God is for man too the One who loves in freedom.[15]

The fact that Barth can hear the best word ever to be personally addressed to the human creature in the most dreaded doctrine within the Christian doctrinal arsenal signals from the very first sentence that Barth is up to something quite unheard of in the history of the doctrine of election. The conviction that election is the best news possible for the human creature is foreign to both the Reformed Orthodox and Arminian-Pietist traditions. This can only mean critique of Barth from an understanding of Evangelicalism understood as fidelity to these traditional positions. But as I mentioned above, Barth reaches this universally unheard of conclusion by a path that resonates with both traditions precisely at the points of their disagreement.[16]

This path begins and ends with Barth's doctrine of revelation, which presents the content and sets the parameters of all the doctrinal work to

---

14. I have addressed two key dimensions of this critique—the imperialism and exclusivism of Barth's theology, particularly but not exclusively in relation to the Jewish neighbor—in my *Risking Proclamation, Respecting Difference*. Much could also be said about the inherently social and material dimensions of Barth's understanding of the reconciliation between God and creatures accomplished in Jesus Christ as strongly resonant with the concerns and commitments of liberation theologies. This theological understanding is no doubt a primary reason for Barth's lifelong partiality toward—at times expressed in active participation in—the socialist movement and corresponding hostility to capitalism. See Hunsinger, *Karl Barth and Radical Politics*.

15. Barth, *CD* II/2, 3.

16. The universal strangeness of Barth's move here includes modern theologies on the left. For while various notions of universal salvation may be a staple of modern liberal or progressive theology, it is certainly not so through an unqualified commitment to and celebration of a doctrine of election. Rather, such theologies see the doctrine as a major obstacle to universally good news, and its surgical removal from the doctrinal lexicon as one of modern theology's necessary transformative procedures to purify the ancient tradition of its rational and ethical toxins for the modern mind and heart.

follow. Barth asserts that all the Church's knowledge of and speech about God—and God's commerce with creation—is only made possible by God's self-disclosure to us in God's Word. That Word is identical with the living personal reality of Jesus Christ. For Barth, then, "theology must begin with Jesus Christ," such that what is revealed to the Church in the name of Jesus Christ is "the beginning and end of all our thoughts."[17] Barth's conviction that the doctrine of election is wholly good news and not a mixed message of joy and terror is only possible—and understandable—in this context.

In what follows I will focus on how this methodological commitment to God's decision, Word and action in Jesus Christ determines Barth's doctrine of election, pausing along the way to trace its consequences for Barth's slippery relationship to both Reformed Orthodox and Arminian-Pietist strands of Evangelicalism, diverging from one in resonance with the other, and vice versa. In short:

a. Despite Barth's Reformed privileging of the doctrine of election as determinative of all God's works and ways, both the innovative placement and content of Barth's doctrine of election result in an unqualified assertion of universal atonement that skews Arminian-Pietist.

b. Similarly, this good news of God's irrevocable electing decision to will the salvation of each and every human creature in Jesus Christ confronts the creature in an event of personal address calling for a genuinely creaturely response—it is news proclaiming a divine Yes that desires a human yes in return.

c. Continuing on Arminian-Pietist side of the ledger, said creaturely response, whether yes or no, is able to determine in a real way the human creature's status in relation to divine decision, so far as a certain theological employment of the doctrinal categories of elected and rejected are concerned.

d. However, swinging back the other way, because of Barth's commitment to the sovereignty and freedom of God's decision, Word and action in Jesus Christ, this creaturely response, while a *genuine* creaturely decision, word and action, is genuinely *creaturely*. As such it cannot finally change or determine the eternal divine decision to be for the creature, and so cannot finally and eternally determine the ultimate reality or eschatological future of creaturely existence.

17. Barth, *CD* II/2, 4.

The Electing God in Jesus Christ

Barth's doctrine of revelation—wherein the content of all Christian doctrine is determined by God's Word to us in the Trinitarian event that is Jesus Christ—has radically innovative consequences for both the doctrine of God and the doctrine of election, including their systematic relation to one another in Barth's *Dogmatics*. All that can be said of God in the doctrine of God "is disclosed only in the name of Jesus Christ"—"wholly and entirely enclosed in Him."[18] Consequently, "we know and have God only in Jesus Christ."[19] But this is not merely an epistemological limit for us, the creature, such that God is only *known* in God's self-communication to the creature in Jesus Christ. Barth goes further, asserting that God *is only God*—in God's very self; God this way and no other—in God's self-communication to the creature in Jesus Christ. This allows Barth to say that there is no God behind, before, beyond or apart from the God who *decides* in and from the heart of God's eternal triune life to be for, with, and as—and so in radical relation to—the creature in Jesus Christ.[20]

It is this eternal divine decision to be God only in and for this particular relationship that Barth identifies as the primary content of the doctrine of election. Consequently, because he sees it as first and foremost a decision of divine self-determination—with God's very self as its primary object; God in this way and no other—Barth is convinced (in departure from virtually the entire doctrinal tradition) that its treatment in the doctrine of election belongs properly within the doctrine of God.

This innovative placement of the doctrine of election within the doctrine of God has radically narrowing consequences for the doctrine of God (a narrowing already anticipated in Barth's Christo-Trinitarian doctrine of revelation): God only *is* God in and through the decision to be for the creature in Jesus Christ. Put differently, Jesus Christ *is* the electing God. Alternatively, this placement unleashes a revolutionary widening of the soteriological consequences of the doctrine of election. It does so in the following way. Its placement in the doctrine of God significantly reorients the focus of the doctrine of election from its traditional pre-occupation with the creature as the primary object of the divine electing decision. Everything that is to be said about the creature in relation to God's eternal electing decision can here only have its meaning in light of and as a consequence of what

---

18. Ibid., 5.

19. Ibid., 7.

20. Ibid., 95. He continues: ". . . before Him and above Him and behind Him and apart from Him there is no election, no beginning, no decree, no Word of God."

God decides about Herself in that decision—to be "God only in this way and not in any other."[21] And the eternal divine decision to be God "only in this way"—that is, only with, for and as the creature in Jesus Christ—leaves no God, nor any divine decision, that could be in any way eternally *against* the creature.

Here, in the very orientation and placement of the doctrine we can see Barth at once affirming and departing from both the Reformed Orthodox and Arminian-Pietist traditions on election. On the one hand, Barth is very much in line with the Reformed tradition in giving the doctrine of election a privileged place within the doctrinal system, whereby it exerts a decisive determining influence over all the ways and works of God, and so over the whole of Christian confession, thought and teaching. Indeed, Barth could be said to out-reform Reformed Orthodoxy in this respect, in that he gives it an even higher "pride of place." Reformed Orthodoxy places the doctrine of election immediately after the doctrine of God, and before the doctrine of creation, from whence it governs all of God's works and ways with creation. Barth goes one better by placing it within the doctrine of God itself. And here is the "other hand." Within this *uber*-Reformed privileging of election emerges an Arminian-Pietist result: universal atonement. For the consequence of what is decided about Godself in the eternal electing decision is that there is simply no God to make an eternal decision determining any creature as reprobate, rejected, judged, or damned. As the "Word of God . . . in whose Truth everything is disclosed," Jesus Christ "is the decree of God behind or above [or beside] which there can be no earlier or higher [or other] decree. . . . He is the election of God before which and without which and beside which God cannot make any other choices."[22] In eternally electing Godself to relationship with the creature in Jesus Christ, then, "God elects man"—an election that is not balanced by an eternally willed rejection of a certain group of human beings, who would then fall outside the reconciled relationship that is willed and accomplished by God in Jesus Christ.

The Elected Creature in Jesus Christ

While primarily about God's *self*-determining decision (as signified by its placement in the doctrine of God), Barth's doctrine of election does *include* the election of the creature in this divine decision. Yet here again, his radically Christocentric commitment to Jesus Christ as the content of all Christian theology results in doctrinal innovation. When attention is

---

21. Ibid., 6.
22. Ibid., 94.

finally turned to the creature as the secondary object of election, Barth defies the doctrinal tradition's common-sense tendency to identify a certain group of human individuals, variously conceived, as the creaturely object of God's electing decision. In Barth's formulation, Jesus Christ—fully divine and fully human—is not only the electing God. Jesus Christ is also the one true elected human creature. All other human beings—and as we shall see, Barth does indeed mean *all*—are the object of election only as represented in and by Jesus Christ, the one true human being. In Barth's formulation, then, the election of the creature in the eternal divine decision is, in the first instance, radically narrowed, taking as its object the one human person, Jesus of Nazareth. Its consequences for all other human beings, however, are radically expanded. For *in and with* Jesus Christ, "the eternal divine decree has as its object and content the execution of the divine covenant with man, the salvation of all men."[23]

Just as the category of rejection cannot be employed theologically to express a second, different eternal divine will and decision concerning the creature balanced alongside election, the category of the rejected cannot be properly employed to describe and define a second, different group of human beings—alongside the elect—as the proper and final objects of this second, different will and decision. Similarly, just as there is no God outside the decision to be God in relation to the creature in and through Jesus Christ, so there is no creature that falls outside this relation or outside the one divine will expressed in the decision establishing this relation. In Barth's own words, "That which has been eternally determined in Jesus Christ is concretely determined for every individual man to the extent that in the form of the witness of Israel and of the Church it is also addressed to him and applies to him and comes to him."[24] For Barth, then, "in light of this election the whole of the Gospel is light."[25]

In as much as human beings receive their status as the elect by virtue of what is decided in God's sovereign eternal decision, Word, and action rather than by the creaturely response of faith, Barth is clearly working from the playbook of classic Reformed doctrine. However, the fact that what is eternally decided is the expression of one divine will whose sole desire is the reconciliation of all in and through Jesus Christ aligns with Arminian-Pietist traditions in contradiction to Reformed Orthodoxy. What continues

---

23. Ibid., 116. See also 117: "The election which is absolutely unique, but which in this very uniqueness is universally meaningful and efficacious."

24. Ibid., 309. He continues: "... by His Word [God] makes him an elected man ... It is for him that this self-giving is effective. . . . He is the object of the divine election of grace."

25. Ibid., 14.

to run against the grain of Arminian-Pietist affirmation of unlimited atonement, however, stands in contradiction to the former is Barth's conclusion that God's one eternal will for atonement is *effective* and *actual*, with the result—an offense to *both* parties—that all actually *are* reconciled in and through Jesus Christ as the content of God's one eternal decision, Word, will, and action.

Elected as Rejected

But are things as sunny as they appear? Not a shadow of rejection or judgment in sight?

Not quite.

Barth is perfectly clear about the fact the creature elected in the election of Jesus Christ is "*forgiven* man"—that is, a sinner who in Jesus Christ is, from all eternity, forgiven.[26] The creature elected in the election of Jesus Christ, then, is always the elected *rejected*. It is for the sake of sinners—for the human being who is alienated and makes themselves an enemy of God, i.e., those who reject their election in Jesus Christ and thereby live as the rejected—that Jesus Christ is elected, is The Elect, from all eternity.

This is a complex business, requiring an effort of analysis that far exceeds what can be done in this already over-long essay. Here I will attempt to briefly identify, if not unpack, the counter-intuitive complexity entailed in what is, in a many ways, Barth's a-logical theological logic.

First, the timing is ass-backwards. If the creature elected from all eternity in Jesus Christ is the sinner, then sin—and the fall—somehow appear to precede creation. If this is the case, then how to make sense of the status of the goodness of creation and the human being prior to the fall? And furthermore, according to this line of thinking the human creature appears to be elected—predestined—to sin. And this would seem to make God responsible for sin and all its destructive consequences.

Barth is aware of these problems, and addresses them.[27] Giving an account of his treatment of these issues would take us too far afield here.

---

26. Ibid., 315.

27. The central issues are treated in Barth's long parenthetical assessment of the Infralapsarian-Supralapsarian debate that occurred in the belly of Reformed Orthodoxy during the seventeenth century. While Barth both affirms the strengths and critiques the weaknesses of both sides of the debate, he ultimately comes out in favor of the losing side—the Supralapsarians—not for their final position but for the way in which they seemed to glimpse and fight to preserve—to a point ultimately intolerable—what Barth feels to be the true heart of the issues at stake: that God is only for and never against the rejected sinner. See, Barth, *CD* II/2, 127.

Suffice it to say, his treatment will not be found satisfactory by those for whom the necessities of logical plausibility constitute deal-breaker criteria for the faithfulness and truthfulness of Christian theology. And this is simply because these are not Barth's criteria. Indeed, they cannot be, given his belief that the content of God's engagement with the world and so of the Church's faith, confession and proclamation, and so of Christian theology, is the *living* and *personal* reality that is Jesus Christ, wherein God and the creature encounter each other in an event of address and response for the sake of a history of loving and responsible reciprocity. Barth is willing to let the wreckage of logical contradiction stand unresolved as witness to what must in the last analysis be the mystery of this encounter. The mystery of which is not simply due to the incomprehensibility of divine nature, or to the origin and nature of sin, but due to the event of personal encounter itself. For Barth, theology is about something that *happens*—what has happened and what will happen—about the ongoing history of the living God's Word and action to and for the creature and the creature's response. As such it is about that which is radically contingent and so cannot be reduced to—or be expected to play by the rules of—rational, logical necessity.

The Pietist strands of Evangelicalism are capable of greater sympathy with—or at least lesser offense at—Barth here, given their own privileging of the experience of personal encounter over the strict impersonal rigor of doctrinal proposition.[28] Though, as we will see, there is no shortage of offence in that camp when all is said and done.

Second, there is in fact a shadow of divine rejection in Barth's doctrine of election, albeit a highly qualified one. God's election of Godself to be only for the creature in Jesus Christ, including as it does the election of the creature to be only for God, does entail the rejection of an alternative possibility: the possibility of enmity between God and the creature. This is the divine No that is entailed in, yet also bracketed by, the divine Yes. God rejects from all eternity the possibility of ever being a God directed against the creature. Good news indeed! But God also rejects, in this very decision, the possibility that the creature set itself against God. This is somewhat more foreboding news. For it is precisely this rejected possibility—the possibility of enmity with God, of creaturely rejection of God's loving overture—that the human creature chooses, every time, each and every one.[29] Barth acknowledges, then, that in as much as the creature chooses to live under the shadow of what God has rejected in electing them to a relationship of loving fellowship, attempting to claim for themselves this possibility rejected by God, the

---

28. For example, see Thorne, *Evangelicalism and Karl Barth*, 72.
29. Rom 3:23

term "rejected" can be theologically applied to them. And consequently, it is applicable to all.

Third, we know that the creature elected in the election of Jesus Christ is the rejected sinner, because The Elect, Jesus Christ, is elected "to suffer and die."[30] As *the* elect, Jesus Christ is the one who stands in for sinners, for the rejected, becoming *the* rejected on their behalf, taking all the destructive consequences of their choice to live the life of the rejected upon himself so that these consequences may not finally fall on them. Because Jesus Christ is elected to be the rejected, in our place—and so to suffer eternal damnation and hell—we are the rejected who, precisely as rejected, have been elected: "the Elect who stands at the head of the rejected elects only the rejected."[31] And this is true for each and every one. For "every man is rejected," and "as such," the "predestinate."[32] This enables Barth to boldly conclude that "in so far ... as predestination does contain a No, it is not a No spoken against man." In as much as it does "involve exclusion and rejection, it is not the exclusion and rejection of man."[33]

The news of our election in Jesus Christ, decided and disclosed from all eternity, reaches us as always already the creature who is rejected, who has opted for the rejected possibility of autonomy and alienation over against God and so is living in contradiction to our true identity as God's creature elected to fellowship and communion. The universality of election in Jesus Christ, then, is twice confirmed. *All* are elected precisely to the extent that *all* are rejected. There is no one rejected who is not also—precisely *as* rejected—*elected*. And there is no one elected who is not so only as the elected *rejected*.

Barth draws two rather radical conclusions from this:

a. As we have already seen, according to what is eternally decided, disclosed and accomplished in the election of Jesus Christ, the terms elected and rejected cannot finally be separated from each other theologically, employed to signify two absolutely separate groups of human beings, as the objects of two different eternal divine decisions. Both election and rejection—including all scriptural witness to election and rejection, and to the elected and rejected—receive their theological meaning only as they are fulfilled in the One Jesus Christ.[34]

30. Barth, *CD* II/2, 122.
31. Ibid., 123.
32. Ibid., 316.
33. Ibid., 166.

34. This conviction with regard to scriptural witness is grounded in Barth's understanding of how Scripture is the Word of God in his doctrine of revelation. He asserts

b. This means that the way in which we are *all* both rejected and elected is strictly and *irreversibly ordered* according to what is accomplished not only in the eternal decision that is Jesus Christ but in his very real *history*; that is, according to the movement of death to resurrection.[35]

For Barth, everything that our status as rejected sinner means for us is comprehended in the cross of Jesus Christ. Meaning that it is that which *has been judged* in that event. And everything that our status as elected means for us is comprehended in the resurrection of Jesus Christ that follows decisively upon the judgment of the cross and stands as the irrevocable—because actual—*future* of the judged. The elected, then—as the elected rejected—"is always the one who was dead and is alive again (Luke 15:7)."[36]

As decided, disclosed and accomplished in Jesus Christ, then, every creature's identity as elected (the *elected* rejected), while real and actual in Jesus Christ, never simply becomes ours to possess—never passes into our hands as a new "nature" over which we have proprietary ownership. It is always only ours in openhanded expectation, received as an already secured future awaiting fulfillment. Likewise—and most troubling to the evangelical heart—every creature's identity as the rejected (the elected *rejected*) can only ever be a past that has run its course. Their rejection has already been "born and cancelled by Jesus Christ."[37] It has "reached its goal," the "execution" of God's judgment upon it having been fulfilled such that "eternal damnation" can no longer "be their concern."[38] Rejection, then, has no future and so cannot be a genuine eschatological future awaiting the creature as final destination and ultimate meaning.

As pertains to the doctrine of election, then, the witness of the Church to each and every member and each and every neighbor "consists in this:

---

that Jesus Christ, as the living personal Word of God, is the content of all Scripture when it becomes the Word of God for and to us in the event of revelation, wherein it becomes the vehicle for Jesus' self-testimony in the power of the Spirit and so God's self-giving self-communication. Thus, nothing in the Bible can have any meaning for the Church independent of that given it as testimony to the living history of Jesus Christ and what is accomplished and communicated therein. This event-of-personal-address-oriented view of Scripture as the Word of God finds some resonance with Pietist traditions, but has been one of the key pillars of polemic critique for Reformed Orthodox inerrantists.

35. "Everything happens according to this basic and determinate pattern." Barth, *CD* II/2, 8.

36. Ibid., 124.

37. Ibid., 306.

38. Ibid., 319.

that [the] choice of the godless man is void; that he belongs eternally to Jesus Christ and therefore is not rejected, but elected by God in Jesus Christ."[39]

While we pause to catch our breath in the wake of this remarkable interpretation of election as unsurpassable and irrevocable good news, we might note amidst our disorientation that, as opposed to Reformed Orthodoxy as Barth's conclusions about the universal consequences of election appear to be, he seems to get there in a very Reformed way: it is the sovereignty of divine decision that finally, eternally determines the eschatological future of the creature.[40] And this appears to leave no room for the genuinely self-determining creaturely response of belief or unbelief that is so precious to the Arminian and Pietist traditions, making Barth just as objectionable to them on these particular grounds—never mind that everyone might get in—as Reformed Orthodoxy.

As I hope to now show in concluding this all too brief—yet too long!—sketch of the pivotal movements of Barth's doctrine of election, the former observation with regard to sovereignty is indeed accurate, but the latter observation with regard to creaturely response is not. An inaccuracy no doubt the symptom of disorientation brought about by the vision of a bankrupt hell.

Creaturely Response

"Between the Being of the Elect and His Life as Such"—an Eschatological Openness[41]

"The choice of the godless man is void" in the face of eternal divine decision. For Barth, the human being cannot finally, absolutely determine herself to *be* the rejected—to *exist* apart from and outside of Jesus Christ—and so secure divine rejection as her ultimate reality and eternal judgment as her irrevocable future. But "there is something," Barth insists, "that is *not* decided in the word of promise."[42] And that something is precisely the creaturely response to the news of her or his irrevocable election to fellowship with God as beloved child, partner, friend—a response represented by Barth as the choice, the creaturely decision, to believe or not to believe. The human being "may refuse to . . . believe," and so live "in conflict with his election." Or "he may . . . believe" and so live a life "corresponding to his election."[43]

---

39. Ibid., 306.
40. Ibid., 9.
41. Ibid., 321.
42. Ibid., 324. Emphasis mine.
43. Ibid., 321, 324.

And this decision to believe, for Barth, constitutes a real "transition" within the creaturely sphere, from living the life of the rejected to living the life of the elected.[44] For Barth, the sovereign, comprehending and irrevocable electing decision in Jesus Christ is not in competition with or the eclipse of genuine creaturely decision. Rather, it occurs as the "theonomy of God which wills and decrees as such the autonomy of man," taking "historical form . . . as a human electing in which man can and should elect and affirm and activate himself."[45]

There are two things to note here:

a. This creaturely decision, word, and action marks a very real fork in the road; it marks a real distinction, making a real difference—with very real consequences—within the creaturely sphere.

b. Because this difference between believing in one's election and refusing to believe in one's election is decided as, in, and by the "adoption of an attitude which this subject [i.e., the human creature] adopts," it is a decision constituting a genuine act of creaturely self-determination.[46] It is a decision, word, and action of "real subjectivity," such that Barth can say quite plainly that "to believe in Jesus . . . means to be elected."[47]

Because that which is decided by God does not decide everything for and about the creature, but calls him or her to a genuine creaturely response, Barth understands the doctrinal content of election to point to and call forth an event that cannot be contained within "any mere 'statement'" of the doctrine itself, but as "a summons" must and can occur as the real, open history between God and the human creature.[48] The doctrine of election articulates the event of corresponding divine and human decision for fellowship and communion that has occurred in Jesus Christ, and awaits—indeed, elicits, calls forth—human response to and confirmation of that event, in another event. This is why Barth says (and performs!) that the propositional form of doctrinal statement in the doctrine of election cannot avoid crossing over at some point to the prophetic and homiletic first-person address of proclamation: Thou! You are the elected rejected in Jesus Christ! This news is about, for and addressed to you. What say you?[49] The divine-human event of mutual election that has occurred in the Person and history of Jesus Christ still

---

44. Ibid., 322.
45. Ibid., 180.
46. Ibid., 324.
47. Ibid., 322, 127.
48. Ibid., 324.
49. Ibid., 323–24.

awaits this further event of election: the human yes to this proclamation; the creaturely decision to live in accordance with their true being. Election happens. It has happened once for all yet is ever waiting, pursuing, calling, to happen again in creaturely affirmation.

This affirmation of the creaturely decision to believe or to refuse to believe in response to the divine decision as genuinely determinative of one's creaturely status as elected or rejected—at least within a certain theological use of those terms—rings with a decidedly Arminian and Pietist note. But of course, things are immediately complicated. This affirmation entails a both/and, a now-yet-not-finally. This is due to the fact that the theological terms of election—determined for Barth as they are by the *divine-human* Person, reality and history of Jesus Christ—have a double reference. They constitute the language of a *double* predestination. They refer to both divine and creaturely decision, word and action in their qualitatively different natures and spheres; distinct natures and spheres that are nevertheless genuinely related and engaged in a history of interpersonal interaction and encounter taking place in the event of call and response.

The creaturely decision in response to the divine-human event and summons that occurs in the election of Jesus Christ, then, is *both* genuinely determinative of a distinction within the creaturely sphere which can be appropriately signified—within certain qualified limits—by the terms elected and rejected; *and* yet not finally and eschatologically determinative in as much as that creaturely sphere is bounded on all sides by divine decision, word, and action. And this bounded-ness marks the "certain qualified limits" to which the terms elected and rejected can be used appropriately to signify self-determination within the creaturely sphere.[50]

The key to this both/and in Barth's rendering of the self-determining agency of the creaturely decision in relation to divine election can be found in the distinction marked by Barth between the "being" of the elected creature (the elected rejected) and the "life" the elected creature chooses to live in relation to that "being." Barth puts it this way:

> Between the being of the elect and his life as such there lies the event and decision of the reception [or rejection] of the promise. It is not for his being but for his life as elect that he needs to hear and believe the promise. Not every one who is elected lives as an elect man. Perhaps he does not yet do so. Perhaps he

---

50. This "bounded-ness" of the creaturely by divine sovereignty and freedom is a fundamental Reformed instinct; the nature and goal of this divine sovereignty and freedom as personal relation and interpersonal encounter of love and forgiveness is a fundamental Pietist instinct. SUCH that Barth can both be read as doing Reformed theology in a Pietist key; or doing Pietist theology in a Reformed key.

> does so no longer. Perhaps he does so only partially. Perhaps he never does so. In so far as he does not do so yet or any longer, or does so only in part or never, he lives as one rejected in spite of his election. These are the possibilities of the godless man as such. And it is the godless man . . . who is the object of God's gracious choice.[51]

Occurring between the being of the elect and the life of the elect, the decision to believe or refuse to believe can determine the latter but cannot determine the former.

It is necessary here to briefly unpack the nature of this distinction between the being and life of the creature as Barth is employing it here, in order to better focus our attention upon that to which he is drawing it and avoid the distraction of a tantalizing—and common—confusion on this point: that Barth is trafficking in Platonic, Gnostic, Marcionite, Arian—take your pick—metaphysical dualism.

First, it is clear that a genuine qualitative distinction between God and the creature, between the respective natures and spheres of activity proper to both of them, is being assumed here.[52] Creaturely "being" is precisely that which is properly the business of God *as God*. It is what God gives, maintains, determines beyond the reach and capacity and responsibility of the creature. Consequently, only divine action can determine our ontological status, our fundamental, true being and nature. We cannot create ourselves, our nature, our being. As creatures we do not determine our own ontological horizon, the sphere of possibilities that constitutes the creaturely sphere. *But*, we *are* given a genuine creaturely sphere of responsibility and activity—entailing real creaturely consequences—with regard to how we live *in relation to* who we in fact *are*, in accordance with or in conflict with our true being. The important thing to note here is that the qualitative distinction

---

51. Barth, *CD* II/2, 321.

52. The "fact" of one's "being" the elect "transcends" one's own choice to live as the elect, to live in accordance with one's election. This "fact" of one's "being" elected—the elect—most properly "happens to" and not "in" us, is not part of our "human nature," either as general anthropological possibility or as divine gift of new redeemed nature that passes into my possession and control. Barth, *CD* II/2, 321. Reformed Orthodoxy tends to see this kind of paradoxical logic as irretrievable self-contradiction and so evidence of the failure of Barth's theological method, given their assumption that God reveals Godself and God's redeeming activity in a way commensurate to human knowledge and understanding, at least in a redeemed state. For his part, Barth assumes the reality of the divine-human history—a history of divine righteousness and mercy encountering and overcoming the resistance and brokenness of a sinful world—that is the subject matter of dogmatics is itself paradoxical mystery that can only be faithfully addressed and witnessed to by such paradoxical logic.

between God and the creature does not eclipse or eliminate the latter but establishes and preserves the integrity of the sphere proper to it in genuine and very real difference from the divine. For Barth, this can only be seen as a problem—as unjust divestiture or expropriation of creaturely reality—if the creature desires a share of what is properly divine capacity and activity; that is, if the creature is not content to be a creature but rather aspires to play god.

Second, this qualitative distinction does not exist in abstraction; it is not assumed or asserted as a necessary metaphysical or ontological principle with which Christian theology must begin and to which its statements must be subject. It is assumed and asserted here within the context of a doctrine of election itself determined very specifically by a confession of the divine-human Person, reality and history—the concrete *event*—that is Jesus Christ, i.e., the accomplished occurrence of divine decision, Word and action for fellowship and communion that is met with a corresponding and affirming human decision, word and action in Jesus Christ in the power of the Holy Spirit. That is to say, the qualitative distinction between God and the creature and their respective spheres of action cannot be abstracted from the more fundamental assumption and assertion of a genuine interpersonal relationship of engagement and encounter, of summons and response—that is, a very real *history*—between God and the creature and their respective spheres; indeed, a history in which the creaturely sphere is inhabited by God for the sake of a specific relation of fellowship and communion between God and the creature in their very difference. Consequently, the qualitative distinction here is not primarily between divine and human essence or their metaphysical nature as such, e.g., between the infinite and the finite. It is between the nature, reach and dimension of divine and human spheres of decision, word and action. This distinction is not then conceived by Barth here as a "static" metaphysical, ontological or cosmological dualism, or in terms of the necessary dialectic of an historical process. It is the assumption of a very real and contingent history of interpersonal encounter and engagement between God and the human creature *in their qualitative difference*—in which the integrity of creaturely reality and action as well as of divine reality and action is preserved—that requires the distinction between creaturely being (as properly the work of God's activity) and living (as appropriate to the creaturely sphere) in this context.

Third, Barth can be seen to demonstrate the extent to which Christian theology must be nimble in its employment of the theological terms and categories of elected and rejected. They must be used differently in relation to what can be and is properly decided and accomplished by God and what can be and is properly decided and accomplished by the creature. The trick, of course, is that these two spheres of decision, word and work are genuinely different. And this difference must be honored theologically by deploying these terms and categories in different ways in order to witness to the difference of these spheres in the living history of their interpersonal interaction with one another. It is just this that Barth is attempting to do. In his words, the creature's "rejection can be *attributed* to him . . . *only* as a threat hanging over him, just as his election can be *ascribed* to him *only* as the promise given to him."[53]

Finally, it is worth noting here that believing, for Barth, is not fundamentally the cognitive assent to propositional statements, or even the confession of a creed. It is the concrete *living of a life*. Furthermore, the living of a life is constituted primarily as bearing witness, as giving testimony. Consequently, Barth states that while the human creature who chooses to live in conflict with her or his election—that is, to live *as if* she or he were rejected—"has no right to *be* this [the rejected] man," she or he nevertheless "may *represent* this man."[54]

This service of representation, of bearing witness, means that the life of those who refuse to believe bears witness to and reminds the believer that their true being as the elect is always properly determined as the elected *rejected*. They, from first to last—notwithstanding the very real transition from a life of unbelief to belief within the creaturely sphere—stand in solidarity with the unbelieving neighbor as the rejected who have, from before the foundations of the world, been elected in Jesus Christ. Alternatively,

---

53. Barth, *CD* II/2, 321. The creaturely decision to believe or not to believe, precisely as a fully genuine creaturely decision, does not and cannot determine or change the already accomplished fact of one's election as such—the fact that one has been, and so *is*, the elected (rejected). The fact that he chooses "no" does indeed "conflict with his election, but it cannot annul it, because it is not to be sought or found in Him, but is grounded in Jesus Christ" (ibid.). The critical question for the Arminian-Pietist strands is whether and when the creaturely choice to endure in the refusal to believe, the choice to continue living in conflict with one's election—even up to and with one's dying breath—finally constitutes an eternal enduring and continuing such as to render null and void one's *being* as the elect by and through one's *living* as the rejected. For Barth, the answer is clear: the creature can live in conflict with her election until and with her dying breath, but even then "cannot reverse or change the eternal decision of God"; she "cannot possibly deny or annul the gracious choice of God" (ibid., 316). For Barth, this active conflict and the choice to endure within it has no final eschatological future, such that as long as the creature chooses to endure in it, and is capable of enduring in it, no duration can ever be long enough to outrun and outstrip her true eschatological future. Such decision and endurance is always in the face of a future that contradicts it and awaits it as its own-most possibility and truth; a future that cannot be annulled by any amount or length of persistence in enduring in active conflict with one's election—even into eternity itself.

54. Ibid., 316. Emphasis mine.

in and by their response of belief, those living the life of the elect in the creaturely sphere bear witness to those living as if they were rejected. They bear witness to the latter's true being: in living the life of the rejected they are always, from before the foundations of the world, the *elected* rejected. Precisely as rejected, as godless, they are the elect—forgiven sinners elected to be friends and partners of God. And therefore their rejection—the final, eschatological consequences of their choice to live a life in conflict with their true identity—is rendered void. She or he "belongs eternally to Jesus Christ and therefore is not rejected, but elected."[55]

Barth believes, then—in striking resonance with the Arminian and Pietist strands—that the theological employment of the terms rejected and elected, as categories marking a real distinction between human creatures resulting from genuine self-determining subjective agency, is appropriate and necessary. But precisely because this is a distinction resulting from genuine *creaturely* self-determination, the theological provenance, scope and dimension of these terms so employed cannot ultimately be ontological, metaphysical or eternal. Their provenance, scope and dimension are necessarily ontic, temporal, historical and hermeneutical. As such they bear witness to a situation that necessarily remains eschatologically open. The final word over the creature's existence, the creature's being, is not the creature's to pronounce, possess or control.

So again, Barth can be seen to think and work betwixt and between the Reformed Orthodox and the Arminian-Pietist strands of Evangelicalism. The Arminian-Pietist tendency identifiable in Barth, regarding genuine creaturely self-determination in relation to the theological categories of elected and rejected, is nevertheless inhabited by a Reformed instinct. Or, put the other way round, it emerges and occurs within a Reformed frame. Consequently, in its very distinction from Reformed Orthodoxy in the direction of the Arminian-Pietist strands at this point, Barth's doctrine of election remains, simultaneously, distinguishable from the latter in the direction of the former. With the result being, to my mind at least, doctrinal witness to a Gospel entailing better news than either can muster or bear under their own steam.[56]

---

55. Ibid., 306.

56. Not only has God determined in Jesus Christ to be only for and with us sinners, from and to all eternity, such that the "ontological" sphere, meaning, and horizon of the creature is bounded by this decision and action of the Creator such that they are determined as the elected rejected, the forgiven sinner, whose judgment has been fully executed and fulfilled on the cross and so is behind them with the resurrection to new life as friend and partner with God their only true, real future. God does all this out of the desire for a genuine human decision, word, and action in response to this divine decision, word, and action; that is, God desires a genuine creaturely partner. In Barth's

Final Assessments: Barth and the Future of Evangelical Theology

If Evangelicalism is to be considered as an historical and theological phenomenon that includes and is indeed substantively characterized by the vast array of Arminian and Pietist Christianities, rather than being identified solely with Reformed Orthodoxy, then Barth clearly appears to be more in line with Evangelicalism than his Reformed Orthodox critiques have traditionally allowed. Generally speaking, we have seen Barth's resonance with Arminian-Pietist strands of Evangelicalism to be located in a radically personalist, dynamic—event and address oriented—understanding of revelation, and of the entire mode and purpose of God's relation to creation. This, in distinction from a fixed, mechanical inerrancy and a necessary unfolding of abstract divine decree. More specifically, with regard to the doctrine of election, his Christocentric reading allows Barth to register as evangelical precisely to the extent to which he appears to believe that the gospel news is truly good. That is, Barth registers as evangelical in precisely those places that Arminian-Pietist strands of Christianity have always been horrified by the classical positions of Reformed Orthodoxy on election and predestination and the way they appear to radically limit the goodness of the Gospel and the God who is said to encounter us there; for example, in limited atonement and the inability of the creature to determine their own response to God's decision, word and work on their behalf. From Arminian and Pietist points of view, the way in which Reformed Orthodoxy's commitment to divine sovereignty and the objectivity of its eternal decrees over against the creaturely sphere limits the gracious will of God and condemns certain creatures to the hell of eternal damnation from the outset constitutes a radical distortion of the good news of the Gospel. In this light, Barth's doctrine of election appears to recover an evangelical joy in the news to be proclaimed, i.e., that in Jesus Christ God wills that and has made provision for all to be saved. And in recovering this joyful news, Barth recovers the very reason for proclaiming it: to call forth joyful creaturely response and conversion, the creaturely turning from the life of the rejected to the life of the elect.

For their part, the Reformed Orthodox will no doubt fail to be impressed. They will most likely remain convinced that the Arminian-Pietist strands of Christianity themselves, with their (from the Reformed

---

words, the news of one's election is "very different from any mere 'statement,' and has its specific weight and true meaning in the fact that it is a summons (originating in Jesus Christ, the eternal World of God . . .) which has as its aim the decision which each one of those summoned makes himself—or rather, himself is" (*CD* II/2, 324).

perspective) overly emotional, subjective and experiential conversionist revivalism, are a rather embarrassing cultural distortion of proper Evangelicalism. Their critique of Barth, in other words—though based on a misreading of Barth as too "subjective"—is often of a piece with their critique of Pietism.

However, while being better news than and so perhaps more evangelical in spirit relative to Reformed Orthodoxy, Barth's doctrine of election is nevertheless still not properly evangelical from Arminian and Pietist points of view. And this is precisely due to Barth's Reformed commitment to divine sovereignty and the objectivity of divine decision, word and work over against the creaturely sphere. Ironically, the horrifying mischief of sovereign election at work here, in the hands of Barth, is not the eternally decreed consignment of poor helpless creatures to an eternal future of damnation from before the foundations of the world. Quite the contrary. It is the prospect that eternal damnation as an eternal future might be cancelled altogether. As we have seen, atonement, for Barth, is not only unlimited in breadth. Because it is the eternal decision, Word and work of divine sovereignty, it is also unlimited in efficacious actuality.

Alas, then, dear reader. Do not be mistaken by Arminian-Pietist horror at the employment of divine sovereignty by Reformed Orthodoxy. If they are appalled that divine sovereignty should consign some to hell from all eternity, they are just as likely to be appalled at the possibility that it might do just the opposite, consigning all to mercy, forgiveness and resurrection in the history that has occurred between God and the human being in Jesus Christ. So while Arminian and Pietist Evangelicalisms may want the Gospel to be better news than is available in the hands of Reformed Orthodoxy's deployment of divine sovereignty, that does not mean they can tolerate the possibility that it might be as good a piece of news as takes shape in the hands of Barth's deployment of that same theological theme.

For the Reformed Orthodox, then, the real problem with Barth's theology as seen through the lens of the doctrine of election is not that he is too personalist and subjective rather than properly objective, but that he grants objectivity to the wrong things. Or, put differently, he assigns the wrong content to a proper Reformed commitment to the objectivity of God's eternal divine decree over the subjective sphere of creaturely response. The problem from this point of view is that Barth identifies the *living inter-personal reality of Jesus Christ*, together with the history of incarnation and reconciliation between God and sinners that takes place in him in the power of the Spirit, as the objective content of God's primal, eternal sovereign decree. This objectivity *of living personal reality* cannot then be simply identified with, and possessed in and through, propositional statements and logical necessity. (And, worst of all, it means the objective reconciliation of all.)

The Arminians and Pietists see the problem differently—Pietists especially, given their suspicion of the apparent impersonal fixity of abstraction of propositional statements and logical necessity. The problem from this point of view is that Barth is too objective where he should be subjective. He identifies the living personal reality of Jesus Christ, together with the history of incarnation and reconciliation, etc., as the *objective content of God's primal, eternal sovereign decree*. This *objectivity* of living inter-personal reality cannot then be simply identified with, and possessed in and through, the internal subjective agency and experience of the creature. (And, worst of all, it means the objective reconciliation of all.)

As I suggested early on, these objections have different centers of gravity within inherited doctrinal structures, corresponding to the differences and conflicts between these traditions—that is, corresponding to the ways in which they think each other is unfaithful to an evangelical hearing, believing and proclaiming of the Gospel. In the light cast by Barth's doctrine of election, however, one catches a glimpse of a shared, pan-evangelical anxiety—an anxiety inherent in and central to the historical and theological phenomenon of modern Evangelicalism no matter whom gets proprietary rights over the term. It is the anxiety that eternal damnation may not, in the end, be *anybody's* eschatological future and final destination.

If Evangelicalism requires that somebody *must*—of *necessity*, either due to eternal divine decree or divine righteousness in the face of sinful creaturely agency—suffer eternal damnation, then Barth will never be evangelical enough for evangelicals. And, of course, he will be extremely reassured and gratified by his exclusion from those ranks. If, however, Evangelicalism is indeed about good news, and the news is to be truly and wholly good—the best news the human being, individually or collectively, could ever hope to hear—then to this extent neither Reformed Orthodoxy nor Arminian or Pietist traditions are evangelical enough. And Barth points a way forward to a possible future wherein they might be. *If* they—if *we*—can only be converted from the seemingly intractable need for someone to burn.

Bibliography

Boesel, Chris. *Risking Proclamation, Respecting Difference: Christian Faith, Imperialistic Discourse, and Abraham*. Eugene, OR: Cascade, 2008.

Bolich, Gregory C. *Karl Barth and Evangelicalism*. Downers Grove, IL: InterVarsity, 1980.

Gibson, David, and Daniel Strange, eds. *Engaging with Barth: Contemporary Evangelical Critiques*. New York: T. & T. Clark, 2008.

Hunsinger, George, ed. *Karl Barth and Radical Politics*. Philadelphia: Westminster, 1976.

Thorne, Phillip R. *Evangelicalism and Karl Barth: His Reception and Influence in North American Evangelical Theology*. Allison Park, PA: Pickwick, 1995.

11

God Says What the Text Says
Another Look at Karl Barth's View of Scripture
Frank D. Macchia

God Himself now says what the text says. The work of God is done through the text. The miracle of God takes place in this text formed of human words.[1]

God says what the text says? The above quote could very well have come from one of Karl Barth's evangelical critics. Is it really Barth who wrote such startling words? The popular assumption concerning Barth's view of Scripture has typically been that the Bible for Barth is not in any objective sense the Word of God but rather *becomes* God's Word *only* when it means something *to us*. The objective content of the biblical words supposedly meant little to Barth; the only thing that mattered was the encounter with God that occurs as the text is proclaimed. The popularity of this misconception is what makes the above quote from Barth so tantalizing.

I intend to show that the evangelical view of Barth mentioned above is a distortion. The above quote has Barth saying the opposite, namely, that God says precisely what the text says! Of course, Barth will develop this point with nuanced complexity but not to the point of losing the point's essential validity. Barth will strive to protect the freedom of the Word of God revealed in and through the Bible but not in ways that leave the Bible's verbal content behind. Let us thus seek to understand Barth's view of Scripture *on*

1. Barth, *CD* I/2, 532.

its own terms before we readdress the accuracy of his critics. We will begin with a few preliminary remarks.

Preliminary Remarks

The Liberal tradition has typically viewed the Bible as symbolic of an ancient community's experience of God. Modern persons were then challenged to draw wisdom from these ancient symbols of faith but they were also considered free to reject some of these symbols as culturally irrelevant. The Fundamentalist tradition thus emerged in protest to what they considered to be a Liberal "pick and choose" mentality when it came to Scripture. The Liberals allegedly wanted to accept from the Bible that wisdom which they were already convinced was valid to begin with. So the Liberals were thought to peer into the Bible as a pool of water to observe their own reflection. In protest to this Liberal view of Scripture, Fundamentalists accepted the Bible as a series of propositions revealed directly by God and beyond any possibility of error. Others challenged this view of Scripture through appeal to traces in the Bible of cultural attitudes considered today to be oppressive.

Barth rejected both Liberal and Fundamentalist stereotypes. Over against the Liberals, Barth insisted that the Bible is quite literally God's Word in the churches and is not simply a symbolic expression of human faith or experience. Moreover, the chief subject matter of Scripture is not human faith, morality, or experience of God. This chief subject is rather God's address to humanity, particularly, as revealed in God's free and gracious turn to sinful humanity in Christ. For Barth, "revelation does not differ from the person of Jesus Christ nor from the reconciliation accomplished in Him. To say revelation is to say 'the Word made flesh.'"[2] The Bible then is not symbolic of human experience; it is a living *witness* to God's gracious address to humanity that becomes in this witness the very voice of this address, the very Word of God to the churches. Over against the Fundamentalists, however, Barth noted that the Bible is literally God's Word but as a fallible witness that is birthed and sustained as God's Word by God's gracious turning to humanity in Christ and by the Spirit. The Bible is not an object of our control, as though we could "freeze" the relationship between the scriptural words and the living God who self-reveals,[3] or as though the living God is "buried" within an ancient text as in a stone mausoleum.[4] The Bible is God's

---

2. Barth, *CD* I/1, 119.
3. Ibid., 124.
4. Barth, *CD* I/2, 683.

Word in its very content but only by the gracious address of God to humanity to which this Bible was born, and is now sustained, as *witness*.

Barth thus developed his understanding of Scripture with two fundamental assumptions in mind:

1. The Bible speaks as the Word of God in the churches (contra the Liberals);
2. The Word of God is free of human mastery or control (contra the Fundamentalists).

How will Barth explain the coherence of these two fundamental assumptions? I will explain how he does this through a series of six explanatory points.

Six Explanatory Points

First, Barth is adamant that the Bible is God's authoritative Word in the churches only within God's free self-disclosure to humanity, or only in the sense that God makes the Bible revelatory. Barth clearly identified the Bible as revelation or as the Word of God: "Scripture as the original and legitimate witness of divine revelation is itself the Word of God."[5] The Bible is the witness to revelation, "which itself belongs to revelation."[6] But the Bible is also God's Word "to the extent that God causes it to be His Word, to the extent that He speaks through it."[7] God alone is the Lord of revelation. The Bible is continuously dependent on the divine self-disclosure to be the Word of God, in part, because the Bible was born from the power of that self-disclosure and is by nature its obedient servant and medium. God is thus not bound to Scripture, Scripture is bound to God ("He is not bound to it but it to Him"[8]). The Bible is thus God's Word as an ongoing *event* in which God freely turns to us as God has turned decisively to us in Jesus Christ.[9] The Bible is a staff "which commands and sets moving and points the way" but only as "moved by a living stretched-out hand just as the water was moved in the Pool of Bethesda that it might thereby become a means of healing."[10] The Bible is thus the authoritative Word of God in the churches

---

5. Ibid., 502.
6. Ibid., 501.
7. Barth, *CD* I/1, 109.
8. Ibid., 139.
9. Ibid.
10. Ibid., 111.

for Barth, but not in a way that makes revelation an object accessible to human mastery and control or that reduces revelation to a set of ancient words written on a page. Revelation in and through the Bible is always God's free and gracious turning to humanity.

Second, the divine decision to speak through the Bible involves the Bible's content as Scripture. Again, Barth wrote, "God Himself now says what the text says. The work of God is done through the text. The miracle of God takes place in this text formed of human words."[11] The Bible is not for Barth merely a transparent medium for God to speak to the churches. Rather, for Barth, Scripture as a written witness is involved in its unity with revelation and in the authority that it exercises in the churches. Concerning the biblical author, Barth wrote, "On the written nature of the Canon, on its character as *scriptura sacra*, hangs his autonomy and independence, and consequently his free power over against the church."[12] Apart from the Bible, "the Church is not addressed; it is engaged in dialogue with itself."[13] Thus, "the Church cannot evade Scripture. It cannot try to appeal past it directly to God, to Christ or to the Holy Spirit. It cannot assess or adjudge Scripture from a view of revelation gained apart from Scripture and not related to it."[14] The Bible as a written text thus has authority over all subsequent witnesses, even as it stands in essential unity with proclamation in the event of God's Word.[15]

The Bible imposes itself on the church "in virtue of this its content."[16] Barth even wrote that "in the event of God's Word revelation and the Bible are indeed one, and literally so."[17] This reference to the *literal* identification of the Bible with revelation is not to be overlooked, for it refers to the Bible's specific content as a text written in a given time and place. Therefore, in discerning revelation "we are tied to these texts."[18] Revelation is not behind or above the biblical text but in and through it.[19] Indeed, as Barth wrote, "if a biblical text in its literalness as a text does not force itself upon us, or if we have the freedom word by word to shake ourselves from it, what meaning is there in our protestation that the Bible is inspired and the Word of God?"[20]

---

11. Barth, *CD* I/2, 532.
12. Barth, *CD* I/1, 104.
13. Ibid., 105.
14. Barth, *CD* I/2, 554.
15. Barth, *CD* I/1, 102.
16. Ibid., 108.
17. Ibid., 113.
18. Barth, *CD* I/2, 492.
19. Ibid., 494.
20. Ibid., 533.

God speaks through the particulars of the biblical text, for "God does reveal Himself in statements, through the medium of speech, and indeed human speech. His Word is always this or that word spoken by the prophets and apostles and proclaimed in the Church. The personal character of God's Word is not, then, to be played off against its verbal or spiritual character."[21]

The inspiration of the Bible is indeed *verbal* inspiration for Barth, for the biblical authors "have heard His voice as we cannot hear it, as we can hear it only through their voices. And that is their *theopneustia*."[22] The verbal inspiration of the Bible means that "if God speaks to man, He really speaks the language of this concrete human word of man."[23] Barth can thus write of the "objectivity of the inspiration of the Bible."[24] God speaks through the Bible but in ways informed by this text's verbal witness and not as some vague, mystical encounter. Barth is clear on this point: "God Himself now says what the text says."[25] Indeed, "we do have to abide by the human word" of Holy Scripture.[26] If the Church would see and hear Jesus Christ, "it is directed and bound to Holy Scripture."[27]

Third, the content of the Bible is one with revelation precisely as witness, or as it abandons any significance for itself and points beyond itself to this revelation. Since the core of the Bible's content is a witness to revelation, the Bible *is* God's Word precisely in its function as witness *to* God's Word. As witnesses to revelation, the authors of Scripture point beyond themselves to something (revelation) they are *not* in themselves apart from God. *Their unity with revelation is a unity in distinction.* They "do not speak or write for their own sakes, nor for the sake of their deepest inner possession or need; they speak and write, as ordered, about that other."[28] Thus the Bible of necessity (by its very nature) reveals God *indirectly*, not by providing symbols of human experience of God (as the Liberals typically held) but rather by pointing the reader to God's gracious self-giving, God's address to humanity. In pointing to revelation, the Bible points to "the life of God turned to us, the Word of God coming to us by the Holy Spirit, Jesus Christ."[29] Yet, in pointing to revelation, the Bible ends up offering this revelation to us, for in

---

21. Barth, *CD* I/1, 137–38.
22. Barth, *CD* I/2, 506.
23. Ibid., 532.
24. Ibid., 534.
25. Ibid., 532.
26. Ibid., 533.
27. Ibid., 583.
28. Barth, *CD* I/1, 112.
29. Barth, *CD* I/2, 483; see also 512–13.

pointing beyond itself to revelation, the text "sets it before us."[30] The Bible is one with revelation by claiming nothing for itself and everything for this revelation, by pointing to it in obedient witness. The Lord alone speaks in revelation, so the Bible is revelation in obedient witness to this speaking. The distinction and the unity between the Bible and revelation is thus not a philosophical dialectic that Barth imports from the outside, but rather it comes from a penetrating insight into the very content of the Bible as a self-effacing witness.

Barth is of course convinced that all of the voices of the canon struggle to bear this burden of pointing to God's gracious turning to sinful humanity. The Bible in this witness is thus "a chorus of very different and independent but harmonious voices. An organism which in its many and varied texts is full of vitality in the community."[31] In this varied witness to grace, in the very content of this Bible, God freely speaks this grace to others. The Bible *is* God's Word in *pointing to* God's Word. The Bible has its "being in this becoming."[32] In the very content of the Bible as witness, the Bible as God's Word ends up being analogous to the incarnation of the Word in Jesus (the supreme act of revelation), who was God's Word precisely as the one who gave all as the faithful witness.[33] The Scripture thus mimics the kenotic Christ, though only analogously. Therefore, Barth notes that God's self-disclosure in the Word become flesh in Jesus opened up the possibility of an inspired witness among biblical authors that would also be revelation by witnessing obediently to it. He wrote that the "divine Word became the Word of the prophets and apostles by becoming flesh."[34] In fact, as Bruce McCormack has persuasively argued, Barth developed between 1927 and 1934 his classic threefold structure of the Word of God (Christ, Scripture, and Proclamation) as an essential unity of distinct modes, such as one would have analogously in the Trinity. The Bible in the event of revelation is thus objectively the Word of God in its essential unity with God's self-disclosure in Christ.[35]

Fourth, Barth did not disparage exegesis in the service of hearing the Word of God through the text, since God allows "the prophets and apostles to say again here and now to us what they said there and then."[36] Barth only

---

30. Ibid., 463.
31. Barth, *CD* IV/2, 674.
32. Barth, *CD* I/1, 110.
33. This is not to deny the uniqueness of the incarnation, something that Barth supported. This is why I've carefully chosen the term *analogy*, a similarity in difference.
34. Barth, *CD* I/2, 500.
35. McCormack, "Being of Holy Scripture," 55–75, esp. 58.
36. Barth, *CD* I/2, 533; Barth's original statement was not in italics.

insisted that the exegete seek to follow by God's grace where the text is pointing in its witness. So long as the reader is concentrated on the biblical author's spirituality or faith rather than on the author's witness to God's address to us, he or she does not yet understand the Bible. Historical-critical investigation into the particularities of a text as they relate to a text's history or to an author's influences do not yet reach the treasure of the Bible as Scripture, for the author is pointing beyond himself to the self-revealing God. Historical-critical investigation has a "rightful place" for Barth as an intellectual preparation (prolegomena) for hearing precisely what God is saying to the church.[37] Indeed, "no honest and unprejudiced reader of the Bible can ignore the historical definiteness of the Word."[38] But apprehension of the witness of the text should pierce by God's grace to the text's spirit "which is the Eternal Spirit."[39] This Spirit of the text is not a vague, mystical encounter but rather a penetration beyond the particularities of its words and its author's situation into the essential matter (*Sache*) to which this text in all of its particularity is seeking ultimately to bear witness. But the particular meaning of the words is still vital in discerning the Spirit of the text that struggles to expression through them. Barth asked early on, "Is there any way of penetrating the heart of a document—of any document!—except on the assumption that its spirit will speak to our spirit through the actual written words?"[40]

Barth was discouraged early on, however, by the timidity of biblical commentators to penetrate theologically into the witness of the biblical texts. He was irritated by their satisfaction with relatively peripheral matters of language and history. He was critical of commentaries that were confined to "a rendering of the Greek words and phrases by their precise equivalents, a number of additional notes in which archeological and philological material is gathered together, and a more or less plausible arrangement of the subject-matter in such a manner that it may be historically and psychologically intelligible from the standpoint of pure pragmatism."[41]

Hearing the Spirit through the text involves more. Understanding Paul, for example, "involves more than a mere repetition in Greek or in German of what Paul says: it involves a reconsideration of what is set out in the Epistle until the actual meaning of it is disclosed."[42] It means following

---

37. Barth, *Epistle to the Romans*, 1.
38. Barth, *CD* I/2, 468.
39. Barth, *Epistle to the Romans*, 1.
40. Ibid., 18.
41. Ibid., 6.
42. Ibid., 6–7.

Calvin's example of rethinking the whole of the Epistle and wrestling with it "till the walls which separated the sixteenth century from the first become transparent!"[43] Indeed, hearing the Spirit speak in the text means that the "conversation between the original record and the reader moves round the subject-matter, until a distinction between yesterday and to-day becomes impossible."[44] The words of the text are never abandoned in this penetration to the core of the Bible's witness to revelation, for "the Word ought to be exposed in the words."[45] The words remain the guide to the Word. The words of the text are mined for their theological voice, the voice that God as the eternal Subject of revelation will speak. Barth describes this process as discerning in spiritual fashion what is spiritually intended in the text.[46] As Brevard Child's notes, Barth thus rediscovered the theological voice and witness of the Bible at a desperate time for the church (in between the wars), creating fertile soil for the rise of the biblical theology movement.[47]

Of course, exegesis and interpretation always threaten to make the Bible captive to human ideology, thus doing damage to the Bible as a free text. This is why exegesis must always "remain open on all sides" for the sake of a free text.[48] No exegesis or reading of Scripture is entirely adequate or final, because the prophets and apostles continue to bear witness to God's Word through their human words penned long ago. For the Bible to cease doing this is for it to cease being Scripture. There was never a time when the Scriptures were anything other than this. There is no essence to the Scriptures other than this. There is no other way for the Scriptures to *be* God's Word than to *become* God's Word in witness to God's self-disclosure. This witness is central to the Bible's content as well as the secret to understanding the ongoing impact of its words today as God's Word.

Fifth, it is thus not accurate to say that the Bible is the Word of God for Barth only when we experience it as such. Barth in fact goes out of his way to deny such a conclusion. Notice his clear denial:

> The confession that the Bible is God's Word is a confession of faith, a statement of the faith which hears God Himself speak through the biblical word of man. To be sure, it is a statement which, when venturing it in faith, we accept as true even apart from our faith and beyond all our faith and even in the face of

---

43. Ibid., 7.
44. Ibid.
45. Ibid., 8.
46. Ibid., 19.
47. Childs, *Biblical Theology in Crisis*.
48. Barth, *CD* I/1, 106.

our lack of faith. We do not accept it as a description of our experience of the Bible. We accept it as a description of God's action in the Bible, whatever may be the experiences we have or do not have in this connection.[49]

Barth clearly does not accept the confession of the Bible as God's Word to be "a description of our experience of the Bible" but rather a description of "God's action in the Bible." Barth really believed that God speaks and acts through this biblical text today in correspondence with the self-disclosure that originally gave rise to the text to begin with and that forms the core of the text's actual witness.

We can refer here to Barth's "objective pneumatology" or to Barth's conviction that the Spirit in speaking to us cannot be collapsed into human subjectivity or experience.[50] As Barth wrote, "The witness of Holy Scripture is therefore the witness of the Holy Spirit."[51] In this unified witness of Spirit and text, we are not just speaking of our *experience* of the divine Word, "but its actual presence."[52] What governs the voice of Scripture is the divine self-giving in Christ and not our experience of this: "The presence of the Word of God is not an experience, precisely because and as it is the divine decision concerning us."[53] Of course, our reception of the Spirit's witness is always colored by human subjectivity, and our interpretations of the Bible always threaten to take the Bible captive, but Barth is confident that the Spirit's speaking through the text "is objective enough to emerge victorious from all the inbreaks and outbreaks of man's subjectivity."[54] The Spirit witnesses to our spirits that we are children of God (Rom 8:15–16); so also does the Spirit witness to us (to our subjectivity) through the words of the biblical text for Barth.[55] Of course, the Bible must continuously become God's Word by God's grace in fulfilling the witness for which it was written. The same grace that encountered the biblical authors when they wrote in obedient witness freely sustains the text continually as the Word of God to the churches. But Barth is clear that the "reference to this 'continually,' of course is not to human experience, as though our reaction to this event or our attitude to it could be constitutive for its reality and content. The refer-

---

49. Ibid.
50. See Thompson, *The Holy Spirit in the Theology of Karl Barth.*
51. Barth, *CD* I/2, 538.
52. Ibid., 533.
53. Ibid., 532.
54. Ibid., 534.
55. Barth referred early on to the Spirit's speaking to our spirits "through the actual written words" of Scripture (*Epistle to the Romans*, 18).

ence is to the freedom of God's Word."⁵⁶ The text is tied from its inception in essence and function to the freedom of the Spirit's witness, which is the freedom of God's turning to us in grace.⁵⁷

Though the divine speaking through the biblical words provokes rich experiences of God, Barth is clear that no experience can adequately grasp it. This is why the divine speaking cannot be reduced for Barth to a human experience or to the sum total of all experiences in the church. To the contrary, this divine speaking through the text grasps us and our limited grasping back is only possible "when and as the Bible grasps at us."⁵⁸ In the voices of the Scriptures, it is the God incarnated in Christ, the God "with us" "that grasps us in recollection (Christ come in the flesh) and hope (Christ yet to come)."⁵⁹ The inspiration of the Bible (which involves for Barth the Bible's ongoing revelatory nature and function) is thus sustained by the unfathomable power of the Holy Spirit: "It is not our faith but the power of God that underlies the inspiration of the Bible."⁶⁰ The Spirit is Subject in both the objective speaking and corresponding subjective experience of the hearers, for the Spirit also seeks a correspondence of obedience between the text and the hearer.⁶¹ The correspondence between the obedient text and the Spirit's voice is thus ideally to analogously be represented in the obedience of the hearer to the voice of God heard in the words of the text.⁶²

Those who argue that Barth reduces revelation to an experience have difficulty explaining his repeated insistence that human experience and understanding fall short of the biblical witness. Scripture for Barth is autonomous and independent of all exegesis in its authority over the church.⁶³ It is thus Christ as the chief subject matter of the Bible and not human experience that provides the hermeneutical key and source of authority when it comes to the Bible: "To say that Jesus Christ rules the Church is equivalent to saying that Holy Scripture rules the Church. The one explains the other, the one could only be understood through the other."⁶⁴ Indeed, as mentioned earlier, "The Bible says all sorts of things, certainly; but in all this multiplicity and variety it says in truth only one thing—just this: the name

56. Barth, *CD* I/1, 117.
57. Barth, *CD* I/2, 528–29.
58. Barth, *CD* I/1, 109.
59. Ibid., 120.
60. Barth, *CD* I/2, 534.
61. Ibid., 538.
62. Ibid., 543.
63. Ibid., 583.
64. Ibid., 693.

of Jesus Christ, concealed under the name Israel in the Old Testament and revealed under His own name in the New Testament."[65] Relying on our own, we can miss this core witness of Scripture entirely. Indeed, if one "sees only an empty spot at the place to which the biblical writers point . . . there can be no question of a legitimate understanding of the Bible by this reader."[66] In other words, the Bible can by God's grace be pointing as it is read and proclaimed but much of the church can still be looking the other way.

Sixth, the Bible is not perfect as an obedient witness, meaning that its unity with revelation is ultimately a miracle of grace. Even as an obedient witness inspired by God, the Bible is imperfect and inadequate without God's ongoing action to involve the reader in God's gracious self-giving. No human word has the power to "smite us in our existence."[67] Only God can do that. The Bible as a finger pointing to revelation is crooked and inadequate, in need of the divine Spirit at both its inception and in fulfillment of its own nature and role as revelation. Barth notes that "we call the Bible the Word of God only when we recognize its human imperfection in the face of its divine perfection, and its divine perfection in spite of its human imperfection."[68] The fallibility or weakness of the Bible covers the entirety of Scripture as a finite medium, for the authors "can be at fault in any word, and have been at fault in every word."[69] The Bible is not a book of infallible oracles that gives us revelation directly but a fallible human word that points beyond itself through its concrete witness to God's gracious self-disclosure. Thus, we may take offense at the Bible, even at its theological assumptions.[70] As a human witness, "the Bible is vulnerable. At every point it is the vulnerable word of man."[71]

This is the point in Barth's view of Scripture that is perhaps most difficult for many evangelicals to accept. Yet, others have appreciated Barth's help in recognizing how the Bible, despite its limitations as an ancient human text, can transcend these limitations in its witness *by* God's grace *to* God's grace. Regardless how one comes out on this matter, it is important to recognize how Barth qualifies his assumption concerning the fallibility of the biblical text. First, it is important to note that the fallibility of the Bible is for Barth only one side of a dialectic of distinction and unity. Just

---

65. Ibid., 720.
66. Ibid., 469.
67. Barth, *CD* I/1, 141.
68. Barth, *CD* I/2, 508.
69. Ibid., 530.
70. Ibid., 507.
71. Ibid., 512.

as the Bible is both distinct from and one with revelation for Barth, so also is the Bible distinct from and one with divine infallibility. Though in its humanity the Bible bears the limitations of human speech and culture, it becomes one in its witness with infallible revelation by God's grace. I thus agree with McCormack that Barth holds to a "dynamic infallibilism" with regard to the Bible.[72] Second, Barth considered it arbitrary and problematic to relegate inspiration to only the parts of the Bible that we favor[73] or to play some voices of the Bible over against others.[74] He maintained rather that biblical authors "belong to revelation" and "spoke by the Spirit what they knew by the Spirit" and are, therefore, worthy of respect in "all their words."[75] He refused to follow Bultmann in seeking to distinguish between those texts that reflect the Spirit of Christ and those that offer alien spirits in the Bible. For Barth, all texts bear alien elements but struggle in their essential witness to point to the Spirit of Christ.[76] Third, Barth held that we do not have the capacity to sit in judgment over the biblical text from our own limited vantage points in order to determine with certainty where the Bible is right and where it is wrong. Not only does Barth never do this in his writings but he was against it in principle.[77] With regard to the biblical authors, it is thus "better to speak only about their capacity for errors."[78] We should for the sake of understanding a biblical author's essential witness dare "to accept the condition of utter loyalty," for "to make an oration over a man means to speak over his body, and that is to bury him finally, deeper and without hope in his grave."[79] For Barth, it is important to note further, this loyalty "does not exclude a criticism of the letter by the spirit, which is, indeed, unavoidable," for it is "precisely a strict faithfulness which compels us to expand or to abbreviate the text, lest a too rigid attitude to the words should obscure that which is struggling to expression in them and which demands expression."[80] This does not mean that we can access this "spirit" through any other means than by a careful allegiance to the words. Again, Barth notes that "if a biblical text in its literalness as a text does not force itself upon us, or if we have the freedom word by word to shake ourselves

---

72. McCormack, "Being of Holy Scripture," 73.
73. Barth, *CD* I/2, 517–18.
74. Ibid., 509.
75. Ibid., 517.
76. Barth, *Epistle to the Romans*, 16–17.
77. Barth, *CD* I/2, 531.
78. Ibid., 508.
79. Barth, *Epistle to the Romans*, 18.
80. Ibid., 18–19.

from it, what meaning is there in our protestation that the Bible is inspired and the Word of God?"[81] Implied here, however, is that for Barth the Bible is self-correcting, granting us from the vantage point of its essential witness the wherewithal to see precisely how this fragile and weak text can reach by God's grace to be the Word of God in the churches.

Concluding Remarks

In conclusion, there are a myriad of critical questions that can be posed in response to Barth's complex view of Scripture but limited space will not allow for much exploration here. For example, can we speak of a "capacity" for theological error in the Bible and, yet, stop short of making any specific mention of them? And if we are free to mention them, at which point do we stop and who can then stop us? Barth's implication that the Bible is self-correcting is helpful here but needs to be developed. How, for example, do we avoid playing some biblical expressions off against others, as Barth seemed to want to avoid? Or, do we follow the specific biblical expressions to their essential witness and then from the vantage point of that witness recognize the limitations of the language that got us there?

Moreover, Barth's preoccupation with the historical-critical method (understandable given the exegetical methods current in his time) did not offer him many conceptual tools for understanding more precisely how the witness of Scripture as a sacred text or canon specifically mediates the miracle of revelation or how exegesis creatively occasions this miracle. For example, a number of theologians in the so-called postliberal tradition, such as George Lindbeck and Hans Frei, have attempted to clarify or to expand on Barth by showing precisely how the biblical text as a cultural-linguistic reality (Lindbeck) or as narrative (Frei) draws one to the diverse particulars of God's gracious self-giving to humanity and the human response called for in the text. Rhetoric, narrative, canon-conscious redactions, or cultural-linguistic insights into the text (among others) have been variously used to clarify and grant greater specificity to the vital role of the text in pointing by God's grace to its chief subject matter in the divine self-disclosure. In the midst of this flurry of options, I can almost see the grand old man puff on his pipe, smile, and remind us not to become so preoccupied with the function of the text that we fail to sit in wonder at the miracle of the divine address that confronts us in and through it.

Still, the text in all its concreteness and specificity is indeed involved in God's free self-disclosure for Barth. If anything, Barth was too hesitant to

---

81. Barth, *CD* I/2, 533.

grant human experience much of a role in how the Bible speaks as the Word of God to the churches. I found myself wanting to balance his discussion by talking about how a diversity of experiences within various contexts grants eschatological expansiveness to the voice of the Spirit through the text. Of course, all such experiences are fallible and some require significant correction, even rejection. Yet, Barth's confidence in the power of the Spirit to constantly or eventually break through such limitations and call the churches to repentance and renewal is surely helpful in this context. Regardless of how Evangelicals may want to criticize Barth on multiple sides, they can no longer argue that for Barth the Bible is only God's Word as we (and in the sense that we) experience it as such. Even if the reader remains convinced that this is the necessary implication of Barth's view of Scripture, he or she should at least concede that this was not Barth's view of the matter and that he struggled clearly and fiercely to oppose it.

Bibliography

Barth, Karl. *The Epistle to the Romans*. Translated by Edwyn C. Hoskyns. New York: Oxford University Press, 1977.

Childs, Brevard S. *Biblical Theology in Crisis*. Philadelphia: Westminster, 1970.

McCormack, Bruce. "The Being of Holy Scripture is in Becoming: Karl Barth in Conversation with American Evangelical Criticism." In *Evangelicals and Scripture: Tradition, Authority, and Hermeneutics*, edited by Vincent Bacote et al., 55–75. Downers Grove, IL: InterVarsity, 2004.

Thompson, John. *The Holy Spirit in the Theology of Karl Barth*. Allison Park, PA: Pickwick, 1991.

12

The Church as "Witness"

Karl Barth and the Missional Church

Kyle A. Roberts

> Mission is not primarily an activity of the church, but an attribute of God.
>
> —DAVID BOSCH[1]

KARL BARTH'S INFLUENCE ON modern ecclesiology has been palpable and extensive. For what may be obvious cultural and historical reasons, his imprint is less discernible in conservative evangelical traditions, although interest in the relation between Karl Barth and American Evangelicalism has grown. A curious recent phenomenon within contemporary Evangelicalism, however, has been the prevalence of conversations around "missional theology" and "missional churches." Ironically, the origin of these conversations and the turn to "missional" language in understanding the nature and vocation of the church has been traced to Karl Barth. This essay aims toward a renewed appreciation of this genealogy, along with some suggestions regarding the appropriation of Barth's "missional ecclesiology" in the context of the American evangelical church today.[2] By reasserting this genealogy and by offering a detailed (though selective) reading of Barth's ecclesiology, I hope to encourage a renewed impetus for the *missional theology* and *missional church*

---

1. *Transforming Mission*, 390.
2. I realize that "evangelical" is a deeply contested identity marker. My working definition of "Evangelicalism" will be provided below.

movement to (more broadly) claim Barth as a theological source. Further, I intend to explore how Barth's theology might impact the missional church's understanding of its vocation in the world. The implications are many for rearticulating a robust theology of the church as *witness* to God's reconciliation with the world through Jesus.

In setting forth my argument, I hope to commend as a unifying theme Barth's understanding of witness as applied to the nature and task of the church in the world. Theological focus on the concept of witness could be instrumental in helping evangelicals formulate an ecclesiology that is both faithful and relevant today. Barth's ecclesiology, hammered though it was on the anvil of a different time and place, is well suited for a reinvigorated conversation around the unique vocation of the church in a post-Christian, pluralist, tumultuous, and fragmented world. His material, both in *The Epistle to the Romans* and in *The Church Dogmatics*, offers a deep and rich tapestry for developing a theological vision for the church in the context of the world—a definition of *church* that, while not being anti-institutional, contains within itself the seeds for a constant critique of institutionalism and the continual temptation to reduce the gospel to a pale version of the New Testament's proclamation. I intend to show that Barth's theology of the church's vocation as witness takes shape in two forms relevant for contemporary ecclesiology: (1) the witnessing church is *missional* and (2) the witnessing church is *eschatological*. As a by-product of exploring the connection between Barth's theology of the church as witness, the essay attempts to contribute to the discussion regarding the relationship between Barth's *Romans* and *CD*. Witness, with its underlying ecclesiological and eschatological aspects, exemplifies a strand of theological continuity between the so-called early and late Barth.

The Missional Church and the Identity of Evangelicalism

We have encountered several contested terms that require clarification: *Evangelical/Evangelicalism* and *missional*. Articulations of Evangelicalism are legion and span from theological definitions (i.e., core, shared, doctrinal convictions) to historical/sociological ones (descriptive summaries of the varieties of communal/denominational evangelical expressions, from its post-Reformation and Anabaptist beginnings) to its contemporary manifestations (as largely British and American socio-cultural phenomenon). Even given all its variations, as Kimlyn Bender points out, it is difficult to avoid working under a prevalent understanding of evangelical, which he describes as a "post-World War II phenomenon with roots in American Puritanism, Pietism, and revivalism" and as defined theologically in relation to Bebbington's quadrilateral: (1) biblicism, (2) conversionism, (3) crucicentrism, and (4) evangelism.[3] And yet, one must keep in mind that Evangelicalism is a very diverse movement, comprising individuals and communities with overlapping but distinct ethical values, theological perspectives, and denominational heritages. Moreover, "movement," as Bender points out, is an apt term; it is a dynamic, changing constellation whose identity is always in flux. Within that movement, the phenomenon now known as the *missional church* has ascended in popularity and influence, deeply impacting many individual churches, denominations, para-church organizations, seminaries and book publishers.[4]

Like "evangelical" and "Evangelicalism," understandings of "missional" are legion. Nonetheless, there are some clearly overlapping themes and constants across the spectrum of those who embrace the term. A well-received definition comes from the seminal text *Missional Church*, written by participants in the North American "Gospel and Our Culture Network." Darrel Guder writes,

> The ecclesiocentric understanding of mission has been replaced during this century by a profoundly theocentric reconceptualization of Christian mission. We have come to see that mission is not merely an activity of the church. Rather, mission is the result of God's initiative, rooted in God's purposes to restore and heal creation. "Mission" means "sending" and it is the central biblical theme describing the purposes of God's action in human history.[5]

Craig Van Gelder, also a participant in the network and a contributor to that volume, has recently suggested four themes prevalent in the North American "missional church" literature:

1. "God is a missionary God who sends the church into the world";
2. "God's mission in the world is related to the reign of God";
3. "The missional church is an incarnational (versus an attractional) ministry sent to engage a postmodern, post-Christendom, globalized context," and;

---

3. Bender, "Church in Karl Barth," 181.

4. For example, Baker, Eerdmans, InterVarsity, and Zondervan each has established a series dedicated to the topic of missional church.

5. Guder, "Introduction," 4.

4. "The internal life of the missional church focuses on every believer living as a disciple engaging in mission."[6]

Primarily, the missional church identifies itself as "sent," on behalf of God (who is "missionary" by nature); its vocation is defined by its "sent-ness" and its primacy is relativized by its place within God's greater plan of reconciliation with the world.

While a "missional" understanding of the church's vocation has been prevalent within Catholicism and mainline Protestantism and in the ecumenical missions movement of the mid-twentieth century (as we will see), evangelicals have only relatively recently embraced the *missional* turn.[7] Yet within the evangelical church-world today, many pastors, denominational and ministry heads, and church planters identify with the movement. This may explain why evangelicals are also only recently beginning to develop a robust theology to undergird their emphasis on the *praxis* of mission. Bender suggests that Barth and evangelicals share a sense that church is defined, at least in large part, by the centrality of mission and evangelism. Where they differ, he says, is that "for evangelicals mission is often thought of as what the church *does*, whereas for Barth's *actualistic* ecclesiology mission is what the church *is*."[8] But it should be noted that the rise of the missional church movement within Evangelicalism is changing this understanding. Evangelicals who identify with the missional movement are exhibiting an increased understanding that God, and God's mission, defines the church, rather than the other way around. Nonetheless, there are still expressions of the evangelical missional church that have not caught on to the full implications of the kind of theological shift that Barth's ecclesiology can inspire.[9]

Apart from notable exceptions, the contemporary literature related to the missional church has been written more by practitioners and missiologists more than by biblical, systematic, or constructive theologians. It should be noted that the thinker who left the most indelible impression on the contemporary missional church movement was missionary Lesslie Newbigin, who became a theologian in his later years. His writings evidence a deep theological understanding of the nature of the church and are informed by years of missionary experience.[10] Other leaders in the move-

6. Van Gelder and Zscheile, *Missional Church in Perspective*, 4.

7. For the story of evangelical reluctance to embrace the *missio Dei*, see McIlvaine, "What Is the Missional Church Movement?" 89–106.

8. Bender, "Church in Karl Barth," 200.

9. This will be further addressed below.

10. Newbigin was a missionary and influential church leader in India for many years. When he returned to Great Britain after his retirement, and upon his perception

ment who have articulated the intersection of theology and mission for a renewed ecclesiological understanding include Craig Van Gelder, Darrell Guder, Alan Roxburgh, John Franke, and others affiliated with the "Gospel and our Culture" network. More recently, Paul Chung's work has argued for "mission" as a basis for a constructive theology.[11] Christopher Wright has put forth a compelling biblical theology of mission, which he describes as a "missional hermeneutic" (a common term in the missional movement).[12] There are an increasing number of works that bridge the chasm between theory and praxis and that put forth a sophisticated blend of theology and missiology.[13] Many of these works pay homage to Barth's early influence on the missional turn. Nonetheless, there appears to be space for a fresh visitation of Barth's theological ecclesiology in the context of the missional movement. The most theologically sophisticated treatments of the missional church have been—and continue to—emerge from mainline denominational perspectives. These thinkers are already notably indebted to Barth.[14] Yet, as Keith Johnson notes, many evangelicals have a ready-made point of contact with Barth's ecclesiology that might prove beneficial toward a theological dialogue: they possess an intuition about the purpose of the church as not an *end in itself*, but as possessing a vocation to exist on behalf of those outside the church (I grant that "evangelicals" also exist within the mainline church; I have in mind here of the definition of Evangelicalism given earlier).[15] Furthermore, they sometimes exhibit default openness toward a

---

of a widespread nominalism in Western cultural Christianity, he took up the task of theological writing. His most influential works are *Foolishness to the Greeks*, *The Open Secret*, and *The Gospel in a Pluralist Society*.

11. Chung, *Reclaiming Mission as Constructive Theology*.

12. Wright, *Mission of God*, 39.

13. See, for example, Van Gelder, *The Ministry of the Missional Church*; Van Gelder and Zscheile, *The Missional Church in Perspective*; Roxburgh and Boren, *Introducing the Missional Church*; Roxburgh, *Missional*; and Hirsch, *The Forgotten Ways*. Nonetheless, as Paul Chung points out, if the missional church movement hopes to be a major influence upon theological disciplines more generally (as a practical theology that galvanizes other theological voices around the centrality of mission), it needs to be more attentive to academic biblical studies, hermeneutics, etc. See Chung, *Reclaiming Mission as Constructive Theology*.

14. The clearest example of this, as I hope to show, is that of Darrell Guder, one of the founding participants in the North American Gospel in Our Culture Network and contributing author to the influential *Missional Church: A Vision for the Sending of the Church in North America*. Guder, along with Craig Van Gelder and others, was instrumental in articulating the distinctive nature of the "missional church" in America.

15. Johnson, "Being and Act of the Church," 201–26. In his conclusion he writes, "For all our problems, the strength of Evangelicalism lies in the reality that the task of proclaiming the word of the gospel to the world is ingrained in our theological DNA.

broader Christian ecumenism, which is likely tied to their sense of vocation as *missional*. A "rediscovery" of Barth could accomplish a renewed attention to the theological nature of the church and a more holistic understanding the gospel within the more "pragmatic" and conservative evangelical wings of the missional church movement.

"Witness" as Unifying Theme

Through what immediately follows, and before we probe the two aspects of the church as witness in Barth, I will explore the continuity between the ecclesiology of the 2nd edition of *Romans* and its "mature" development in the *CD*. The conceptual link between the two is Barth's view that the vocation of the church is to witness to the gospel in and for the world. Admittedly, the "mature Barth" declared at points that his earlier, more radical critiques of the church and Christianity in *Romans* were a bit over-stated. In his lecture on "The Humanity of God," presented in 1956, Barth stated, "One of the exaggerations of which we made ourselves guilty around 1920 was that we were able to see the theological relevance of the church properly only in its character as negative counterpart to the Kingdom of God, then so fortunately rediscovered by us." And yet, a few sentences later, Barth insisted on maintaining "the note sounding ultimately through the whole Bible of the judgment beginning at the house of God."[16] Barth's reminder of the Bible's ominous warning about ecclesial judgment puts into clear context the consistent threads and themes between *Romans* and the *CD*. These reveal an unbroken conviction for Barth that the church, as subservient to the kingdom, is a transitional instrument whose primary task is to witness to God's reconciliation with the world. Whenever and to the extent that it forgets or neglects this role, it is no longer the church of the crucified and resurrected Christ.

The Witness of the Church in Romans: The "Fall of the Church Is Not the End"

The centerpiece to *Romans,* or the core assumption of his early theology lies, Barth noted, in Kierkegaard's "infinite distinction between time and eternity." The problem driving Barth's early theology was that of explicating the difference between creation and the Creator, or between God and

---

Mission is who we *are*—*it* is what 'counts' for evangelicals" (226).

16. Barth, *God, Grace, and Gospel*, 50. Cited in Torrance, *Karl Barth*, 92–93.

humanity. This infinite difference creates ontological and existential problems, which can only be addressed by God's initiating act. The church is not a refuge from this problem; rather, its existence draws attention to it. The church, along with all creation, thus cannot avoid being a negative side of the dialectic: part of the "No" to God's "Yes."

The church is a human response to the divine; as such it is "the endeavor to make the incomprehensible and unavoidable Way intelligible to men."[17] The Gospel is preached in, to and from the church, but the Gospel is fundamentally in "opposition" to the church; thus, whenever the Gospel is proclaimed, it "dissolves the Church, and the Church dissolves the Gospel."[18] God reveals Godself through the medium of concrete, creaturely realities; thus, even in the proclamation of the gospel in the church there is always a "divine incognito."[19] As a medium of divine revelation, the church, according to Barth,

> is the place where the eternity of revelation is transformed into a temporal, concrete, directly visible thing in this world. In the Church, the lightning from heaven becomes a slow-burning, earth-made oven, loss and discovery harden into a solid enjoyment of possession; divine rest is changed into human discomfort, and divine disquiet into human repose.[20]

The task of the church to proclaim the gospel means that the church is a parable, or a storied, metaphorical witness to God's reconciliation.[21] When the church fails to recognize the parabolic nature of its speech about God and the vast gulf between the divine and the creaturely, it begins to serve itself rather than God and the gospel.

The church seeks to understand, comprehend, and proclaim God's revelation. Recognizing its epistemological and theological limitations in mastering God, due to the bridge between finitude and infinitude, it rejects God. The "catastrophe" which that rejection occasions enables divine reconciliation.[22] The church can recognize the impossibility of apprehending divine revelation and can be "impaired" (as an institution) by this realization without fatal effect, because the kingdom of God supersedes the church. "The contrast between the Church and the Kingdom of God is infinite. And no man can escape the condemnation involved in this contrast, for we all

---

17. Barth, *Epistle to the Romans*, 332.
18. Ibid., 333.
19. Ibid.
20. Ibid., 332.
21. Ibid., 333.
22. Ibid., 403.

stand within its context."[23] The kingdom lies in front of (while encompassing) the church as the eschatological mystery, evoking hope and faith in the face of hopelessness.

This line of thought raises, for Barth, a question: if the role of the church is essentially parabolic, subservient and transitory, why should we not dissolve the church altogether and dismiss it as a curious historical phenomenon? If the kingdom of God is greater than the church, if revelation cannot be captured and mastered by it, and if it tends toward self-deception and idolatry, why should we not simply set it aside? Barth's answer to his own question is that the church brings to light both the problem and the answer (the No and the Yes). The difference between humanity and God is the problem. The church, which "causes us to be disturbed," brings that problem to light; the Gospel, which is carried along imperfectly through the church, is the answer. Thus the positive is rendered through a negative: "The Church is that visibility which forces invisibility upon our notice, that humanity which directs our attention toward God."[24] This all means that we should not "hold ourselves aloof from the Church or break up its solidarity; rather, participating in its responsibility and sharing the guilt of its inevitable failure, we should accept it and cling to it."[25] We must "use our tools" in the service of the church for the proclamation of the Gospel. Essential to "clinging to" the church, however, is to recognize that the church "means suffering and not triumph."[26]

The mode of the church's existence in the world is suffering and voluntary death to self. As the church undertakes to hear the Word in community, it confesses and commits to the death of "all that is human . . . in order that it may live unto God."[27] In this way, it lives in the light of God's eschatological promise: "In the midst of the possibility of the Church lies the impossible possibility of God."[28] Thus the mission of the church, as Barth details it in *Romans*, is to witness to the impossible possibility of God through the "impossible possibility of the man of faith."[29] As such, the church exists as "no more than an imprint, a signpost and an intermediate station, a reminder and a negation."[30] The church, then, is fundamentally paradoxical

23. Ibid., 413.
24. Ibid., 337.
25. Ibid., 334.
26. Ibid.
27. Ibid., 345.
28. Ibid., 374.
29. Ibid., 375.
30. Ibid.

in its role in God's economy. The church, as sign, a parable, or a *witness* to God's reconciliation, is necessary in its fragility as a transitional movement toward the eschatological kingdom. As Barth puts it, "Only when the end of the blind alley of ecclesiastical humanity has been reached is it possible to raise radically and seriously the problem of God."[31] The church is a medium through which God is made known in human history, but this does not mean that God *needs* the church, or that God (or the kingdom) is subservient to the church. Indeed, "God does not belong to the Church."[32] When the transitional, instrumental nature of the church is finally and completely recognized, the gospel will achieve the prominence and reach it deserves.

In the midst of this ambiguous and somber picture of the church lies a hopeful point: it is precisely because of its guilt, its transience, and its negative instrumentality that it plays a central role in God's economy of revelation, salvation and reconciliation in the world. The way forward, then, is not in "demanding some new 'reformation,'" a "new movement of reform or of some school of thought" but to hope for the "impossible possibility" of the miracle of faith.[33] The task of the church is to be obedient in witnessing to the paradoxical reality of God's grace as manifest in the life, death and resurrection of Christ.[34] The church's witness is a testimony to the narrative of Jesus Christ, from crucifixion (the "end of the church") to resurrection, which exemplifies its eschatological transformation. The church experiences, Barth observes, a "perpetual collapse." It is through its catastrophic failure that room is made for the possibility of God. Barth concludes with a hopeful tone: "rejection is not the final word either for humanity as a whole or for the Church."[35] And so, "the fall of the Church is not the end."[36]

---

31. Ibid., 337.

32. Ibid., 339.

33. Ibid., 379–80.

34. "Forgiveness cannot be proclaimed to the world save through the capitulation of the Church. On the one hand, therefore, the world is the mirror in which the Church recognizes its own humiliation and its own promise. On the other hand, the Church is the mirror required by the world, if it is to perceive its own relation to God." Ibid., 405.

35. Ibid., 406.

36. Ibid., 403.

The Witnessing Church in the *Church Dogmatics*: The Church as "Impossible Possibility" and Unnecessary Necessity

In the *CD*, Barth insists that the church is called to witness to God's reconciliation with the world. It does this in and through the power of the Holy Spirit, who creates the communities called *church*, in response to the form of revelation in the Word, Jesus Christ. For Barth, the church is not, in the first place, an institution; rather, it is particular, localized fellowships of individuals together committed to Christ and to witnessing to the Gospel in the world. Barth provides a concise definition of the church as the "community of those to whom Jesus Christ has entrusted the word of reconciliation."[37] The church is a particular worshipping community, gathered together by the reconciling action of God in Christ through the Spirit, which is committed to solidarity with the world. The true church, he says, exists *for* the world.[38] The task of the ecclesial community is to confess Christ and the Gospel, which he defines as the "good, glad tidings of Jesus Christ."[39] The church's vocation is to witness to God's "Yes" in Jesus Christ: "It has no other task beside this."[40] Every new expression of the church in every new context shares this task.

Jesus, as the *primary* Witness about which the church testifies, encounters humanity as mediator in the form of "the Slain and Crucified of Golgotha."[41] God represents himself to us in the form of this suffering servant:

> The Jesus who lives and is among us in our time is the One who is still harassed and forsaken, accused and condemned, despised and smitten. He has already fought and won as such, but He still does so as the true Witness, unmasking the falsehood of our time and therefore of us all. It would not be our time, this strange era *post Christum,* if He could be present in it otherwise than as the Man of Sorrows. To be sure, He is God's Hero, rescuing the world from its woes. But He is God's Hero in this form, the mighty Warrior in His very weakness.[42]

---

37. *CD* IV/3.2, 693.
38. Ibid., 780.
39. Ibid., 800.
40. Ibid.
41. Barth, *CD* IV/3.1, 777.
42. Ibid., 393.

The inescapable implication, for Barth, is that the community of God should reflect the cruciform life of Jesus in its own life together and in its solidarity with the world. The church proclaims God's presence within the world as "the presence of the Crucified."[43] To witness to the crucified one is to point to the reality of the Word through the presence of the Holy Spirit on the strength of the promise of God manifested in the resurrection of Christ.[44]

As with *Romans,* in the *CD* the church is proclaimed to be a "provisional representation of the whole world of humanity justified in Him."[45] The church is the name for that community of people whom God allows to "live as His servants, His friends, His children, the witnesses of the reconciliation of the world with Himself as it has taken place in Jesus Christ . . ."[46] This means that while the church is of necessity visible, it must not glorify itself.[47] As the body of Christ, the church exists as the "earthly-historical form of His existence."[48] The consistency, or overlap, between the "witnessing Church" in *Romans* and the *Dogmatics* can be described in terms of two crucial aspects of the church's vocation in the world: *missional* and *eschatological.*

The Witnessing Church Is Missional: The Vocation of the Church Is to Be for the World

The prominence of *missional* language (e.g., "missional theology" and the "missional church") is commonly traced to the emergence of the influential phrase *missio Dei* and to the locating of motivation for mission in the nature and being of God (in particular, the *Trinitarian* God). In several of these genealogies, Barth is listed as an early influence in this turn. There is debate regarding precisely when and how Barth introduced the concept, but most point to a lecture he gave at a mission conference, published as, "*Die Theologie und die Mission in der Gegenwart.*"[49] Barth's early emphasis on the notion of *actio Dei* (he did not use the term *missio Dei*, but the idea was similar), and his grounding of the impetus for missions in the nature of God's Trinitarian character and action, was influential on subsequent discussion of

43. Ibid., 395.
44. Ibid., 420.
45. Barth, *CD* IV/1, 643.
46. Ibid., 650–51.
47. Ibid., 658.
48. Ibid., 662.
49. Barth, "Die Theologie und die Mission in der Gegenwart," 204.

mission and later ecumenical missions and social justice developments in the World Council of Churches.[50] As the Father sends the Son and the Spirit into the world to reconcile it, so God sends the Church into the world to announce and continue the project of reconciliation.[51] *Missio Dei* language was initiated in 1934 by missiologist Karl Hartenstein (who reflected on Barth's theology), and became solidified after a 1952 missionary conference in Willingen, Germany, which focused on Barth's Trinitarian theology of mission.[52]

It is noteworthy that Barth's ecclesiology and theology of mission was deeply influenced by the Pietist pastor-theologian Christoph Blumhardt (and his father, Johann), who believed that the gospel of Christ must be understood not just as a message of inward, individual salvation but as the good news that God's reconciliation of the world includes profound, positive social transformation. The gospel implicates and transforms the social sphere no less than the private and the individual. God's mission for the world (which involves the church as an instrumental witness) is concrete, social and holistic.[53]

While Barth introduced to missiology the theological notion of God's nature as a "missionary God," Georg Vicedom was most responsible for the widespread use of the term *missio Dei*.[54] Vicedom's text referenced Barth's *Dogmatics* at several places to support the notion that the church is "sent" into the world to be a witness to the kingdom of God. The church's mission hinges upon, and is derivative of, God's nature and action. While the details are disputed, the general thrust of this genealogy of missional language has become more or less established in the literature. Barth stands at the origin of the modern turn to missional theology and the missional church movement.[55] The turn to mission, as Hodemaker notes, provided a

50. Hoedemaker suggests that Barth's *actio Dei* was reiterated and given the terminology of *missio Dei* by Hartenstein in 1934. He cites Schwarz, *Mission, Gemeinde und Oekumene*, 130. See Hoedemaker, "The People of God and the Ends of the Earth."

51. "Karl Barth begins his great essay on the calling of the Christian community with a fundamental consideration of 'the people of God in world history.' Here he indicates that neither mission nor church is a starting point in theology: What is at issue is the structure of God's witness concerning himself. The Christian community is a provisional form of a calling that is extended to all humanity." Hoedemaker, "People of God," 160–61.

52. Hodemaker argues that it was Hartenstein's commentary on Willingen (1934) that gave import to the term *missio Dei*. See also Chung, *Reclaiming Mission*, 112–15.

53. For the influence of Blumhardt on Barth's theology of mission, see Chung, *Reclaiming Mission*, 106. For a full-length treatment, see Collins Winn, *"Jesus is Victor!"*

54. Vicedom, *The Mission of God*.

55. It should be noted that John Flett attempts to problematize this "received

Part III—Renewing Christian Doctrine

rationale for the church to relate positively to the world and to culture and grounded mission in Trinitarian theology, giving the church a more robust understanding of the diversity of God's presence and action in the world through the agency of Christ and the Spirit.[56]

As pervasive as "missional" language currently is in evangelical church life, it is difficult to imagine that, as we have previously noted, evangelicals once looked with suspicion upon the phrase *missio Dei*. Evangelicals have not always embraced the turn to a *missional* approach for both theological and cultural reasons. Many evangelicals feared that embracing the term would lead to an uncritical alliance with a "social justice" and ecumenical movement.[57] They feared association with mainline liberal, contextual and ecumenical wings of the church, which had enthusiastically embraced *missio Dei*. Yet, through the positive influence on evangelicals by influential voices such as the Anglican missiologist Lesslie Newbigin and the aforementioned founders of the "Gospel and Our Culture Network," missional theology and the missional church movement have become a part of the DNA of a young, vibrant evangelical church planting and church reform movement. Its influence can be seen in both more progressive (e.g. the "Emergent Church") and more fundamentalist (e.g., the Southern Baptist Convention and the Acts 29 church planting network) elements of contemporary Evangelicalism.

Many evangelicals are currently embracing a wider (more holistic) view of the gospel than their twentieth-century predecessors. But the temptation is always latent within conservative Evangelicalism—with its typical emphasis on individual salvation and escapist eschatology—to reduce the gospel to a pale version of the New Testament. This tendency can be illustrated even in the missional church movement itself. In 2011, Ed Stetzer, a Southern Baptist missiologist and prominent voice within the conservative wing of the evangelical missional movement, gathered a group of like-minded pastors and missional leaders who composed a "Missional Manifesto." The document contains ten "affirmations." The "Gospel" affirmation of the document reads as follows:

> We affirm that God, who is more holy than we can imagine, looked with compassion upon humanity made up of people

---

history." He attributes the historical problems to Hoedemaker and to David Bosch. However, Flett's description of the problems are themselves unconvincing and, interestingly, he nowhere mentions the role of Vicedom's work. The details of the history notwithstanding, Flett agrees that Barth's conceptuality of God as an acting God and his Trinitarian activity in connection with mission has a good deal to say to the task of mission. See Flett, *The Witness of God*.

56. Hodemaker, "People of God," 164–65.

57. See McIlvaine, "What Is the Missional Church Movement?"

who are more sinful than we will admit and sent Jesus into history to establish His kingdom and reconcile people and the world to Himself. Jesus, whose love is more extravagant than we can measure, gave His life as a substitutionary death on the cross and was physically resurrected thereby propitiating the wrath of God. Through the grace of God, when a person repents of their sin, confesses the Messiah as Lord, and believes in His resurrection, they gain what the Bible defines as new and eternal life. All believers are then joined together into the church, a covenant community working as "agents of reconciliation" to proclaim and live out the gospel.[58]

Note that the affirmation clearly defines "the Gospel" as a message of penal substitutionary atonement for individual salvation from God's wrath. The death of Christ is applied to individuals who accept that gospel and repent; these redeemed people then form the church, which "lives out" the implications of the gospel (via social justice, acts of service, etc.). This is a striking example of the bifurcation of individual salvation (atonement through penal substitution) and the nature and vocation of the church, or what Darrell Guder (drawing upon Barth), calls "Gospel reduction." Its emphasis on the sinfulness of humanity ("more sinful than we will admit") obscures the positivity of creation and undermines the potential scope of the reconciliation with creation, which God has already begun in Christ.

In terms of application to evangelical ecclesiology, Barth's insistence on the Church as *witness* to the reconciliation of God with the world is a prophetic and timely one. It calls for a holistic understanding of the gospel, for a reuniting of the "soteric" and the "ecclesial" elements of Christianity[59] and for a shift from an ecclesiocentric to an "ec-centric" mode of existence (an outward-looking and positive view of the world in the vocation of the church).[60] This means that the church is not an end in itself; it is a means—and a deeply flawed one at that—to hearing and the voice of God and proclaiming what is heard. The church is called simply to announce and *witness to* God's reconciliation with the world.

---

58. Stetzer et al., "Missional Manifesto," para. 9.

59. On the capacity of Barth's theology to reunite the soteric and the ecclesial, see Bender, "Church in Karl Barth," 196–97.

60. Healy, "Karl Barth's Ecclesiology Reconsidered," 293. Cited in Johnson, "Being and Act," 225.

The Problem of Gospel Reduction:
Barth and the Continuing Conversion of the Church

In his important work *The Continuing Conversion of the Church*, Darrell Guder utilizes Barth's theology of witness as a key to unpacking the implications of missional theology for urgent task of the church in the world.[61] He argues that mission is the summative concern of the New Testament, as it "defines comprehensively the missional calling of the church in the New Testament."[62] The community of God exists as a "sign of God's redemptive purposes in the world."[63] In its role as sign, the church itself is not the goal or aim of mission. Rather, the identity and purpose of the church hinges on God's greater redemptive plan for the cosmos.[64]

For Guder, the reduction of the gospel to individual salvation and to the individual benefits of salvation prevents the church from fulfilling its biblically defined mission in the world.[65] Guder suggests, borrowing from Barth, that the reason for this reduction of the gospel lies in the human temptation to seize control of one's life and of God.[66] A genuine conversion of the church requires the recognition of this temptation for control and it requires genuine repentance from Gospel-reductionism. True witness should incorporate the horizontal, vertical and social/communal dimensions of the calling of Christians and of the church in proclaiming and living out the gospel.

Reduction of the gospel can be countered by an understanding of "the definition of Christian existence as witness."[67] Guder explains that for Barth, "the essence" of the vocation of the Christian and the church is "that God makes them His witnesses."[68] To focus on witness is to subordinate the Christian and the church to the freedom, sovereignty and grace of God. Only God can bring about his mission in the world and only God can bring about the kingdom of God. As Guder writes,

> The call to Christ must be a call to his mission. The reason Christians are formed into communities is because of God's work to make a people to serve him as Christ's witnesses. The

---

61. Guder, *The Continuing Conversion of the Church*.
62. Ibid., 53.
63. Hays, "Ecclesiology and Ethics in 1 Corinthians," 33.
64. Bosch, *Transforming Mission*, 178.
65. Guder, *Continuing Conversion*, 151.
66. Ibid., 131–32.
67. Ibid., 131.
68. Ibid.

congregation is either a missional community—as Newbigin defines it, "the hermeneutic of the gospel"—or it is ultimately a caricature of the people of God that it is called to be.[69]

Similarly, Richard Bauckham has suggested recently that the most contextually appropriate and potentially fruitful biblical notion for the church to follow today is *witness*. As he notes, the idea of witness is "non-coercive"; it does not depend on the "rhetorical power" of persuasion or one's ability to win arguments. Rather, it involves a whole life lived in testimony to God's truth. He concludes: "In our time witness is likely to be the main contender for truth against the various manifestations of the will to power."[70]

The breadth of enthusiasm for the missional church and for missional theology today raises the prospect of a wide diversity of understandings and applications of the term. This suggests that the contribution of a major theologian like Karl Barth, who himself contributed to the emergence of the shift, is necessary. In a competing array of perspectives and voices, the theologian who was most historically significant in advancing the turn to missional theology should not be forgotten today. His development of the theological concept of the church as *witness* and his insistence that to understand the vocation of the Christian and the people of God as a parable, a sign, and a symbol of reconciliation, of unity, of justice and of ecumenicity must continue to stand as central to what it must mean for the evangelical church to definite itself as *missional*.

Evangelicals seem to engage Barth's work time and again—with more or less understanding and appreciation. My sense is that, in this time in the history of Evangelicalism and in particular within ecclesiology, the church would benefit from Barth's ecclesiological guidance. The church exists in a seemingly tense situation in America. We exist in a tenuous, brittle world; an increasingly post-Christian and postmodern (some might say, "post-postmodern"), in which the patience for plurality and difference, characteristic of postmodernism, is being joined by new hostilities and by an increased hardening of divergent, opposing perspectives. Furthermore, society as a whole seems to be lessening in its respect for and hopefulness toward the church as a positive change-agent in society. As Christianity loses its grip on political power and social capital, it should develop an attitude of a cautious hopefulness, rather than dismay and resignation. In God's economy, a loss of social power and prestige can make way for reconciliation and life. *The fall of the church is not the end.*

69. Ibid., 136.
70. Bauckham, *Bible and Mission*, 99–100.

The Witnessing Church Is Eschatological: The Church as the "Impossible Possibility of God"

For Barth, the vocation of the church in the world is to witness to the discernible but elusive presence of the kingdom. As such, ecclesiology and mission is incomplete without eschatology. In fact, only eschatology provides the logic and structure for biblical ecclesiology and mission. William Stacy Johnson, who highlights the centrality of *witness* in Barth's theology, points out that, for Barth, justification (and the union with Christ it occasions) is "not something presently visible in believers." By definition, the witness points beyond oneself. Thus, the witness does not sufficiently illustrate in himself or herself that to which they point.[71] Just as there is always an aspect of hiddenness in the revelation of God in Christ, so there is also a hiddenness of God's work of salvation in believers. This hiddenness is a consequence of the fact that salvation as reconciliation is a dynamic, changing, eschatologically-determined process which creates an "ec-centric" existence. For Johnson, an implication of this is that

> Christ's work was never simply to focus people on his own person for his own sake, but to realize and actualize the existence and freedom of others. Similarly, the life of the Christian in Christ is to display a parallel dynamic. The Christian never exists to realize some static "union with Christ" for the Christian's own benefit, but the Christian lives dynamically "from out of the center," or "ec-centrically" . . . union with Christ is not an end in itself but a dynamic calling towards the other.[72]

Johnson emphasizes that, for Barth, salvation (and the Church) is never to be seen as an end in itself. The Christian is always called to witness to the reality of Jesus Christ, who as the primary Witness mediates the reality of the kingdom in the world. Christians—and the church—participate as "a sign of God's action on behalf of all people" in the in-breaking, eschatological reign of God.[73]

The eschatological nature of the church's vocation can be seen in Barth's dialectical tension between the church of Jacob (the invisible church) and the church of Esau (the visible church). The church of Jacob is the sphere of God's agency of reconciliation and salvific action in the world. The church of Jacob is God's historical address to humanity; this justifying grace of God is "invisible" and yet tangibly experienced by real persons in history.

---

71. Johnson, *Mystery of God*, 147. Johnson refers the reader to *CD* IV/3.2, 540–54.
72. Ibid., 54.
73. Ibid., 148.

The church of Esau is humanity's fallible, imperfect, but actual response to God's salvific initiation. As such, the church of Esau is the visible, concrete reflection of the possibilities latent in the church of Jacob.[74] The dialectical conjunction of the church of Esau and the church of Jacob means that while they are identified together, participation in the church of Esau is as "a sign, a dialectical witness, an expression of faith, an impress of revelation, an arrow shot from the other bank, a pointer to the church of Jacob, to God's free grace."[75] The tribulation inherent to the church lies in its challenge to exist in the tension created by the dialectic of Jacob and Esau. This tension is inescapable and is eschatologically oriented. But, for Barth, "That is the hope of the Church." That is, the church's hope lies precisely in its eschatological orientation, not in its (visible) successes or failures as the (visibly manifested) church of Esau.

Barth's eschatological definition of the church is a distinguishing marker in the ecclesiastical landscape, as some scholars have recently pointed out. Nicholas Healy defends Barth's ecclesiology against critiques raised in Stanley Hauerwas' *With the Grain of the Universe*.[76] There, Hauerwas suggested that Barth did not sufficiently focus on the distinctive kind of people and practices the appropriation of the gospel should create. Healy countered by pointing out that Barth's ecclesiology has to be understood in light of his eschatology, in which God's apocalyptic, redemptive action in the world is always primary and our (human) response, even in the church, is always fractured, transient, and elusive when attempting to define it categorically. The church is called to witness to the gospel. This focus relieves the pressure on the church to sustain itself *as an institution*. Most importantly, perhaps, the church defined as witness, in Barth's sense, can never rest on its own laurels or assume that its own practices are consistent with God's call on the church in its present context in light of God's Christocentric, eschatological kingdom. For Healy, the eschatological reality of the kingdom precludes any settled decisions about what counts as adequate church practice. It calls for a "theologically adventurous" approach to witness, mission and church.[77]

Hauerwas emphasizes the importance of Christian communities living as "communities of character," fleshing out the patterns and practices distinct to Christian discipleship. For Healy, on the other hand, a Barthian theology of witness insists on avoiding the temptation to draw attention to the practices of a community (howsoever laudable and potentially consistent

---

74. O'Grady, *Church in the Theology of Karl Barth*, 22.
75. Ibid.
76. Healy, "Karl Barth's Ecclesiology Reconsidered."
77. Ibid., 297.

with the New Testament they might be), shifting the focus to the ineffable, apocalyptic, in-breaking of the kingdom of God. Ultimately, then, for Barth (on Healy's account), witness is the "declaration, explication and application of the Gospel," which is Jesus Christ.[78] "It is not, or not in the first instance, a particular kind of life."[79]

This discussion has recently progressed via the work of Nate Kerr, who analyzes both Barth and Hauerwas with respect to their view of the relationship between Christology, apocalyptic, and history.[80] While Kerr shows appreciation for Barth's apocalyptic Christology, which he finds most profound in the *CD*, he argues that Barth ultimately fails to ground it in the ebb and flow (and flux) of history. Barth's alternative to Troeltchean idealism, in Kerr's view, is simply an atemporal, metaphysical idealism from the other side of the coin. He critiques Hauerwas in the same vein as does Healy: Hauerwas' insistence that the church embody the claims of Christ and the gospel through distinct social practices places the priority (in Kerr's view) on ecclesiology rather than on the apocalyptic Christ who is Lord over history. Hauerwas' view of the church as distinctive *polis* strikes Kerr as an overly static and "overdetermined" metaphor: appropriation of the Christ-event cannot be reduced and universalized by any particular, localized set of practices (e.g., pacifism).[81]

For Kerr, the church only ever emerges in response to the missionary reaction to the apocalyptic event of Christ. The church is not, ultimately, the result of mission. As the missionary response to the event and person of Christ, it should have within it no self-preserving tendencies or self-serving aims. Hauerwas, in his response to Kerr, affirms that Kerr's "stress on mission as the necessary condition for the church to be the church is meant to ensure that Jesus is not made captive to the church."[82] Hauerwas empathizes with this concern and yet finds something lacking in Kerr's aversion to specificity. What counts as Christian practice? What does it mean to be a "witness" to the Gospel and to Christ? As Hauerwas puts it,

> I confess I simply find it hard to understand, or better, to have a sense of what mission might look like for Kerr. He says that mission is a "sending" of the Spirit by which we are gathered into the priestly work of God's perfect agape. But surely mission so understood begs for exemplification. Too often I simply do

78. *CD* IV/3, 843.
79. Healy, "Karl Barth's Ecclesiology Reconsidered," 296.
80. Kerr, *Christ, History, and Apocalyptic*.
81. Ibid., 106.
82. Hauerwas, "Beyond the Boundaries," 63.

not understand the significance of the alternatives Kerr thinks crucial to distinguish our positions . . . there remains an abstract character to Kerr's position that betrays his stress on the particular.[83]

In one sense, it seems that Kerr and Hauerwas are not too far apart. Kerr affirms Hauerwas' notion that "witness" necessitates a lived, social embodiment of the Gospel in concrete particularity. Hauerwas affirms Kerr's concern that the apocalyptic Christ not be supplanted by the *ecclesia*. However, on the whole, it seems that Kerr's emphasis is more consistent with the Barthian approach to *witness* I have attempted to articulate in this essay. If the identity of the church is determined in relation to a specific set of practices, or a "community of character" that can be articulated categorically, then the temptation is present to identify the redemptive work of God with the activity of the church; thus, the church's "forms of life" can become institutionalized and can give in to an impulse toward self-sustaining preservation (its practices are assumed to be sufficient to proclaim and witness to the kerygma; they thereby become unquestionable). On the other hand, to retain Barth's dialectical ecclesiology is to preclude any settled sense that what the church is currently doing is identical with what God's agency with respect to the reconciliation of creation.

This distinction bears directly on the missional church movement. It is theologically appropriate, following Barth, for the church to understand itself, primarily, as a community which is "sent" into the world and which takes its identity from its vocation to be witnesses to Christ and the gospel for the sake of the world. Its understanding of and practice of the gospel should be holistic and social (exemplifying that Christ came to reconcile whole persons and whole communities, not just to provide an eternal individual salvation). Moreover, the church needs to be ever mindful that it is not *itself* God's agent of reconciliation (or at least not primarily so), but it exists as a witness to that reconciliation in Christ. This means that whatever specific conglomeration of practices a community undertakes (acts of service, evangelism, community development, hospitality, etc.), it must bear in mind that these actions are subservient to the reconciliation of God which has already taken place in Christ.

Furthermore, in the context of our increasingly post-Christian world, in a situation in which particularity and contextuality is ever in flux, the historical and living Christ is by necessity appropriated in diverse and dynamic ways—reflecting the plurality and difference of a global world that seems

---

83. Ibid., 65, 67.

to be cracking at the seams, awaiting its redemption.[84] Emphasis on the church as *polis* and as *habitable world* as could be utilized (despite the sure protests of Hauerwas) for a continuing program of "Christianity as culture," in which the distinction between the apocalyptic Christ and the particularities of human culture is collapsed, and one localized, contextual way of living the gospel is universalized. This collapsing of Christ and culture was of course endemic to colonial mission and continues to be manifested in Constantinian forms of church. This is not what Hauerwas wants, of course, but Kerr and Healy are right to re-focus attention on the apocalyptic Christ who gives birth to mission, which gives birth to the church, which is instrumental for gospel and kingdom. Christians and local churches must still raise questions about the criterion and the extent to which their individual and corporate lives and practices reflect the in-breaking kingdom of God. Indeed, if there is anything that can be "universalized" in Barth's ecclesiology as applied to the missional church, it is that being a church involves a holistic and social understanding of the gospel. As Paul Chung notes, "In the light of Trinitarian mission and reconciliation, Barth's missional theology becomes more holistic, dynamic, and socially and critically engaged in the public sphere."[85] This understanding of the gospel, ecclesiology, and mission creates possibilities for engagement in a post-colonial world that might otherwise have been prohibitively destructive.

The danger comes when universally extrapolating a particular community's contextual understanding of *missional* practices. Questions of faithfulness can only be raised and assessed by those people and communities living in obedience to the True Witness, the Crucified One, and in the light of God's, fresh and ongoing reconciliation with the world in the power of the Spirit.

Conclusion

In sum, I reiterate that Barth's ecclesiology, as the *witnessing church*, offers to contemporary evangelical theology and church practice a great deal of substance for reflection. The evangelical church is consistently prone to the very sorts of temptations and failures that Barth's ecclesiology pointedly addresses. Barth's "church as witness" provides theological inspiration for the church to creatively and prophetically address its own health and faithfulness with respect to its vocation in the world. While specific, detailed criterion may be lacking in Barth for such assessment, there are

---

84. Rom 8:19–22.
85. Chung, *Reclaiming Mission*, 109.

profound—if implicit—pointers to the kind of values and dispositions the church ought to embrace, practice and model in contemporary society. Some of these values and dispositions include: a deference to the kingdom over the church, an expectation of newness over the same, an openness to ecumenical Christian fellowship, a concern for justice and righteousness in society and in the church (and an understanding that these concerns are components of a holistic gospel), and a desire for solidarity with the world outside the church. These things will matter as much or more to the witnessing church than preserving its own power, institutional strength, social status, doctrinal purity, or epistemic certainty. The witnessing church will consist of local communities who are willing to critique, deconstruct and reconstruct themselves in the face of the penetrating grace and reconciling mercy of God's future. In short, a Barthian ecclesiology calls the church to be both *missional* (understood in a holistic, social sense) and *eschatological,* or externally focused and forward-looking, grounded on the hope in God's completed reconciliation in Christ.

Bibliography

Barth, Karl. *The Epistle to the Romans.* Translated by Edwyn C. Hoskyns. London: Oxford University Press, 1933.

———. *God, Grace, and Gospel.* Translated by J. Strathearn McNab. Edited by T. F. Torrance and J. K. S. Reid. Edinburgh: Oliver and Boyd, 1959.

———. "Die Theologie und ide Mission in der Gengenwart." *Zwischen den Zeiten* 10 (1932) 190–215.

Bauckham, Richard. *Bible and Mission: Christian Witness in a Postmodern World.* Grand Rapids: Baker, 2003.

Bender, Kimlyn. "The Church in Karl Barth and Evangelicalism." In *Karl Barth and American Evangelicalism*, edited by Bruce L. McCormack and Clifford B. Anderson, 177–200. Grand Rapids: Eerdmans, 2012.

Bosch, David. *Transforming Mission: Paradigm Shifts in Theology of Mission.* Maryknoll, NY: Orbis, 1991.

Chung, Paul S. *Reclaiming Mission as Constructive Theology.* Eugene, OR: Cascade, 2012.

Collins Winn, Christian T. *"Jesus is Victor!": The Significance of the Blumhardts for the Theology of Karl Barth.* Eugene, OR: Pickwick, 2009.

Flett, John G. *The Witness of God: The Trinity, Missio Dei, Karl Barth, and the Nature of Christian Community.* Grand Rapids: Eerdmans, 2010.

Guder, Darrell. *The Continuing Conversion of the Church.* Grand Rapids: Eerdmans, 2000.

———, et al., eds. *Missional Church: A Vision for the Sending of the Church in North America.* Grand Rapids: Eerdmans, 1998.

Hauerwas, Stanley. "Beyond the Boundaries: The Church Is Mission." In *Walk Humbly with the Lord: Church and Mission Engaging Plurality*, edited by Viggo Mortensen and Andreas Østerlund Nielsen, 53–69. Grand Rapids: Eerdmans, 2010.

———. *With the Grain of the Universe: The Church's Witness and Natural Theology; Being the Gifford Lectures Delivered at the University of St. Andrews in 2001.* Grand Rapids: Brazos, 2001.

Hays, Richard B. "Ecclesiology and Ethics in 1 Corinthians." *Ex Auditu* 10 (1994) 31–43.

Healy, Nicholas. "Karl Barth's Ecclesiology Reconsidered." *Scottish Journal of Theology* 57 (2004) 287–99.

Hirsch, Alan. *The Forgotten Ways: Reactivating the Missional Church.* Grand Rapids: Brazos, 2009.

Hoedemaker, L. A. "The People of God and the Ends of the Earth." In *Missiology: An Ecumenical Introduction*, edited by A. Camps et al., translated by John Vriend, 157–71. Grand Rapids: Eerdmans, 1995.

Johnson, Keith L. "The Being and Act of the Church: Barth and the Future of Evangelical Ecclesiology." In *Karl Barth and American Evangelicalism*, edited by Bruce L. McCormack and Clifford B. Anderson, 201–26. Grand Rapids: Eerdmans, 2012.

Johnson, William Stacy. *The Mystery of God: Karl Barth and the Postmodern Foundations of Theology.* Louisville: Westminster John Knox, 1997.

Kerr, Nate. *Christ, History, and Apocalyptic: The Politics of Christian Mission.* Eugene, OR: Cascade, 2009.

McIlvaine, W. Rodman. "What Is the Missional Church Movement?" *Bibliotheca Sacra* 167 (2010) 89–106.

Newbigin, Lesslie. *Foolishness to the Greeks: The Gospel and Western Culture*. Grand Rapids: Eerdmans, 1986.

———. *The Gospel in a Pluralist Society*. Grand Rapids: Eerdmans, 1989.

———. *The Open Secret: An Introduction to the Theology of Mission*. Grand Rapids: Eerdmans, 1978.

O'Grady, Colm. *The Church in the Theology of Karl Barth*. Washington, DC: Corpus, 1968.

Roxburgh, Alan. *Missional: Joining God in the Neighborhood*. Grand Rapids: Baker, 2011.

Roxburgh, Alan, and Scott Boren. *Introducing the Missional Church: What It Is, Why It Matters, How to Become One*. Grand Rapids: Baker, 2009.

Schwarz, Gerold. *Mission, Gemeinde und Ökumene in der Theologie Karl Hartensteins*. Stuttgart: Calwer, 1980.

Stetzer, Ed, et al. "Missional Manifesto." http://www.edstetzer.com/missional-manifesto/.

Torrance, Thomas F. *Karl Barth: An Introduction to His Early Theology, 1910–1931*. Edinburgh: T. & T. Clark, 1962.

Van Gelder, Craig. *The Ministry of the Missional Church*. Grand Rapids: Baker, 2007.

Van Gelder, Craig, and Dwight J. Zscheile. *The Missional Church in Perspective*. Grand Rapids: Baker, 2011.

Vicedom, G. F. *The Mission of God: An Introduction to a Theology of Mission*. Translated by Gilbert A. Thiele and Dennis Hilgendorf. St. Louis: Concordia, 1965.

Wright, Christopher, J. H. *The Mission of God: Unlocking the Bible's Grand Narrative*. Downers Grove, IL: InterVarsity Academic, 2006.

13

Jesus Christ as the One and Only Sacrament

Kurt Anders Richardson

Karl Barth, twentieth-century church father of evangelical Protestantism, contributed to the renewal and reform of Christian theology (*semper reformandum*) by refreshing and deepening its foundations in the revelation of God in Christ. It is important to be clear about both of these dimensions: renewal and reform; the former which reinvigorates and the latter which corrects and extends. What Barth had to assert about sacraments and their theology was as much the latter as the former. After a century of largely abortive reform in Liberal theology, Barth offered his work on the basis of Trinitarian centering upon Christ and Scripture, maintaining the Reformed tradition of covenantal, soteriological, and eschatological thinking. It was in light of this re-centering that he appealed at various key points in his *Church Dogmatics* for reform of doctrine. This took place certainly in his understanding of election and most definitely in his understanding of sacraments. What would unite the two was the distinction between divine and human action in both and so also the ethical implications of both.

Although Barth readership and scholarship has grown massively, his reception is perhaps strongest among critically open evangelicals, especially of the Reformed traditions, but also very much among Anglicans; then Baptists, Pentecostals, and a host of others. Through the second half of the twentieth century, among Protestant readers and scholars, there was certainly a rivalry between Barthians and Tillichians. On balance, the trends went postliberal and evangelical—Barth and his paradigm "won," so to speak. This is not to say that the outcome could have been taken for granted. Mainline theological institutions began seeing a drastic reduction in influence, the vast majority of students studying in evangelical contexts and in those post-liberal places that warmly welcomed more moderate versions of the same. Two of the great students of Barth, Thomas Torrance and Eberhard Jüngel, not to mention a host of others who were far more Barthian than Tillichian, also helped tip the balance. But it was Jüngel especially, the leading Lutheran theologian in Germany who contributed decisively to understanding Barth as he wished to be understood: profoundly committed to Reformed ecumenicity in theology, and *semper reformandum*—"always reforming"—in church and theology. Jüngel realized Barth's centering upon the doctrine of election and its decisive implications for understanding the distinctions between divine and human actions, particularly in terms of the sacraments; or more precisely, of Jesus Christ "the One and only sacrament." The reforming propositions on Baptism that Barth laid out *CD* IV/4 appear based upon vast segments of theological reasoning and exposition from II/2 onward. This essay is an endeavor to capture some salient aspects of this theological development in *CD*. This chapter tries to highlight what Barth thought the sacramental was about, namely, the reconciled relationship of the risen and contemporaneously present Lord Jesus Christ with his church and vice versa. Barth approached reform in sacramental theology the same way he embraced the basic mandate of dogmatics, such that necessary exposition simultaneously requires consideration from the perspectives of every other major doctrine. Barth's controlling center was his Christology even when accused of the rather odd and impertinent "fault" of "christomonism."[1] Reform in sacramental theology required no less Christ-centeredness than in any other doctrine.

In the massive two-part *CD* I, Barth lays out the founding principles and inherent method of his theology. The language of sacrament is strongly present in terms of Baptism and Lord's Supper and always in the context of proclamation and communal confession of faith in Christ, often, in very Reformed ways. *CD* II has a profound impact on the grounding of Baptism and Lord's Supper because of the ethical implications of the doctrine of

---

1. In expressing his determination "to hold fast at all costs and at every point to the Christological thread" throughout the *CD*, Barth responds briefly to this "recent reproach" (*Vorwurf*) in the preface to *CD* III/3, xi: "my question to those who are dissatisfied is whether with a good conscience and cheerful heart Christian theology can do anything but seriously and finally remember 'Christ alone' at each and every point. And I am rather concerned to find that, in spite of Church, Pope, Mary, sacrament and other impedimenta, some Roman Catholic friends seem to understand me remarkably well, whereas that not very pretty slogan [christomonism] emanated from the mouths or pens of prominent (and not 'Liberal') Evangelicals" (cf. *KD* III/3, v).

election. Indeed as a result of his work here, the rest of the *CD* is vitally determined in its theological modeling of divine action and of human action on the bases of divine and human freedom. In creation and revelation, the human being has been elected to a creaturely freedom of being. The result of the doctrine of election is to distinguish clearly that which belongs to God and that which belongs to the human.

Sacramentally, Barth's thinking here is the death of human beings in the atoning death of Christ, all based upon his representation of us in the incarnation. At the same time, also based upon election, the human embodies creaturely autonomy that is its very own, in order to reflect the true livingness of being in the image of God. There is nothing mediated or synergistic about human action; all of it belongs to the created integrity of being human. And the same is said of Christ and his active dying upon the cross for us. Therefore, the self-offering called for in the "reasonable service" (Rom 12:1) of the Christian is not a "repetition or representation of that event, or even of an actualisation which has still to be effected" which "needs no completion or re-presentation," that is the death of Christ. Everything performed in Christian living: confession, suffering, repentance, prayer, humility, works, "baptism, too, and the Lord's Supper can and should attest this event but only attest it."[2] Barth declares that there is no preparatory, no supplemental "other" event(s) which lends anything to the death of humanity in the death of Christ. As such, it "is the one *mysterium*, the one sacrament, and the one existential fact before and beside and after which there is no room for any other of the same rank."[3] Our death in Christ's death is the one true sacrament, that is, mediation of the full incorporation and reception of the benefits of Christ's representation of us. On Golgotha Christ's death for humanity takes place as the effective intervention in which he "actually took away sinful man, causing him to disappear." Sin is not just pardoned or removed, but the sinful person itself. As God's faithful love achieved its goal in Jesus Christ for humanity, "it had in fact to have the form of the consuming fire of His wrath, burning down to the very foundation, consuming and totally destroying the man himself who had become the enemy of God." The cross absorbs and eradicates all that had been "against us" in its "for us" event which is "the conversion of man and the world to God."[4] This event has been established in

> the decision and act of God which has taken place actually, irrevocably, and with sovereign power. It is a completed fact, to

2. *CD* IV/1, 296.
3. Ibid.
4. Ibid.

which nothing can be added by us in time or in eternity, and from which nothing can be taken away by us in time and in eternity. It is something that we have to see and read like an opened page which we have no power to turn, like a word which we cannot go beyond dialectically, making it equal with some other word, and thus depriving it of all its force.[5]

Jesus Christ obediently suffered judgment and death instead of us, and Barth is emphatic that there is nothing else above or beyond this event that can be added. The death of Jesus has directly "overtaken us" as "the event of atonement . . . as the decisive and controlling aspect . . ." It is on the basis of the unsurpassable completeness of the atonement in Christ, indeed, the very nature of its end and new beginning that counts for Christ himself as the one and only sacrament.

What then is sacramental reasoning? In a very basic way it is the new being and status of covenantal relations in Christ, that the personal knowing of "Him is identical with knowing the power of His resurrection (Phil. 3:10)."[6] Indeed, this knowledge is "surely the only basis for sacramental reasoning." This knowledge is, in the first instance, that which is witnessed and memorized (μνημονεύειν) as we move toward the assured future resurrection as the new basis of life in this world. The wounds of Christ in the post-resurrection appearances of Jesus (cf., John 20:25ff.), the one who was the Crucified, as now present to us as to his disciples forevermore. Resurrection, Barth argues, "was a second act of justice after the first to the extent that it was the divine approval and acknowledgment of the obedience given by Jesus Christ, the acceptance of His sacrifice, the proclamation and bringing into force of the consequences, the saving consequences, of His action and passion in our place."[7] Crucial here are the soteriological consequences of the resurrection which justified him as "the Representative of all men" (Rom 4:25).[8] To be in this relation with Christ and his wholly justified condition is to exist continuously and irrevocably in sacramental relation with him. The accomplishment of this subjectively, is by the life-giving Holy Spirit (John 6:63; 2 Cor 3:6) who is also "the κύριος" (2 Cor 3:17) within the Trinity and external as the world's Creator and Reconciler, source of truth, our witness and our help, the love of God conveyed to our hearts (John 14:17; 15:26; 16:13; 1 John 4:6; 1 Cor 2:10; Eph 3:5; Rom 8:26, 16; 5:5). Barth makes much of the disciples' original witness to the resurrection which was their

---

5. Ibid.
6. Ibid., 297.
7. Ibid., 298, 305.
8. Ibid., 306.

beholding of glory, hearing, and handling of the Word made flesh (John 1:14; 1 John 1:1). What Barth means by the presence of Christ to humanity in faith, and also means sacramentally, is rooted fundamentally in what was experienced originally and now always after with the resurrected Christ.

The sharing in Christ that is accomplished by his full representation has its far greater reality in the "exaltation" of human being, since he is the "true" man whose life "from below" accomplished the world's reconciliation with God. The entire event accomplished by Christ, Barth contends, is based upon three aspects: the divine election of grace, the historical fulfillment of the incarnation, and Jesus' resurrection and ascension as the basis of revelation.[9] Keeping in mind Barth's extensive arguments in *CD* II/2, election in Christian theology is reckoning with "the eternal beginning of all the ways and works of God" in Jesus Christ and his true humanity upon and around which all that is contingent and historical will revolve, unfold and find resolution. The humanity of the Son, therefore for Barth, is

> the primary content of God's eternal election of grace, i.e., of the divine decision and action which are not preceded by any higher apart from the trinitarian happening of the life of God, but which all other divine decisions and actions follow, and to which they are subordinated. As a history which took place in time, the true humanity of Jesus Christ is, therefore, the execution and revelation, not merely of *a* but of *the* purpose of the will of God, which is not limited or determined by any other, and therefore by any other happening in the creaturely sphere, but is itself the sum of all divine purposes, and therefore that which limits and determines all other occurrence.[10]

God's eternal election is the election of Jesus Christ and simultaneously the self-election of the Son to be the rejected and resurrected man for all humanity—which he calls "the very depth of the secret of God's grace": "that He elected this so strangely merciful exchange."[11] This is the place where Barth affirms double predestination, that is, the triune work of the Son, determined to assume humanity's reprobation and exaltation with its all-encompassing effects. In this perspective of election "everything else, all God's other purposes and therefore all occurrence, proceed . . . directly in the history of His incarnate Word . . . the unfolding [from below] of that which is enfolded [from above] in this eternal divine decree"[12] as the one

---

9. *CD* IV/2, 31.
10. Ibid.
11. Ibid., 32.
12. Ibid.

in whom are all things: true God and true man. Barth is thinking quite profoundly along key biblical lines (e.g., John 1:1–14; Col 1:15–20) where the pre-existence of the Son who comes into the world as man, does so in "the way in which, Jn. 6:51, 'the living bread which came down from heaven' is equated with 'my flesh, which I will give for the life of the world.'"[13] This is the revelation of the primal election of the Son who is God's covenant partner for us as "the basis of all reality," "the root of all Christian knowledge and thinking."[14] The outcome and foundation of all being, history and knowledge under the created conditions of God: "God *man* and the Creator *creature!* . . . an event which is *sui generis*, and distinct from all others."[15]

The focus here is on revelation and Barth neatly formulates: "He who is by the Holy Spirit is also known by the same Spirit." This he refers to as the "self-exposition" of God by God and our participation in this as "the event of the *testimonium Spiritus sancti*." But suddenly, Barth points out, that this "is not for everyone, but only for those to whom this *testimonium* is given as they ask for it."[16] The subjective knowing of the objective knowledge of God in Christ is the result of prayer. Since the divine act in the incarnation as ground of being and knowledge it is the Holy Spirit who discloses this "the great Christian mystery and sacrament beside which there is, in the strict and proper sense, no other."[17] Here we have the determinative language and statement by Barth on sacrament, next to which there is precisely and properly, "no other." This is "the inconceivable actually" taking place in this man, according to all proclamation, revelation and conception, but remaining every bit the sole mystery that it is. It is "the reconciliation of the world with God in relation to reconciled man . . . [who] is originally the man Jesus."[18] In Jesus, the humility of God has become supremely appropriate, grace manifest in this event, "in His mode of being as the Son." The full implications of this, the *assumptio carnis* is the will "to co-exist as the Creator with the creature," far beyond dispensing grace and mercy to creatures.[19] In this event, it is entirely "without cause or merit or co-operation on the part of the creature. Mankind itself has not produced Jesus Christ as the realisation of one of its possibilities."[20] The anthropology of salvation is

---

13. Ibid., 34.
14. Ibid., 35.
15. Ibid., 37f.
16. Ibid., 39.
17. Ibid., 40.
18. Ibid., 41.
19. Ibid., 42.
20. Ibid., 45.

entirely what humanity is and become in the elect humanity of Christ which is God's "new creation" (cf., 2 Cor 5:17; Gal 6:15). Barth sees no creaturely cooperation here, even in the case of Mary where her only confirming but not completing or fulfilling *fiat mihi* ("let it be to me") "is grounded in the resolve and promise of God." Humanity on its own is never capable of "providing a point of contact." Indeed, since the event is the incarnation, Barth regards the capacities of the human as useless and in any case contributing nothing to the glory of God.[21] And yet it is all *pro nobis*, for us, in that he not only became a man, Jesus of Nazareth,

> but the *humanum*, the being and essence, the nature and kind, which is that of all men, which characterises them all as men, and distinguishes them from other creatures. It is not the idea of the *humanum*, in which *per definitionem* this could exist in real men either never and nowhere or only always and everywhere. It is the concrete possibility of the existence of one man in a specific form—a man elected and prepared for this purpose, not by himself, but by God (this is the point of the election and calling of Israel and Mary). But in this form it is that which is human in all men. It is the concrete possibility of the existence of a man which will be like the concrete possibility of the existence of all men and in the realisation of which this man will be our Brother like ourselves.[22]

The event of the incarnation makes him is one with and among us in every way with "finally no less than the universal relevance and significance of His existence for all other men."

The humility of God that is the event of the incarnation of the Son, fulfilled solely in the man Jesus "as this One ἐφανερώθη ἐν σαρκί (1 Tim 3:16) . . . the confessedly (ὁμολογουμένως) great mystery, *the Christian sacramentum*"[23] properly to describe the mystery. What is it about the incarnation that makes it "the Christian sacrament"? Barth avers that all aspects of the matter

> rest on the "hypostatic" union, i.e., the union made by God in the *hypostasis* (the mode of existence) of the Son . . . on the direct unity of existence of the Son of God with the man Jesus of Nazareth . . . He does this by causing His own divine existence to be the existence of the man Jesus. This hypostatic union is

---

21. Ibid.

22. Ibid., 48f., which Barth acknowledges also "by the term *anhypostasis*, the *impersonalitas* of the human nature of Christ" and then "the positive concept of *enhypostasis*."

23. Ibid., 50.

the basis and power of the *nativitas Jesu Christi*, of the secret of Christmas, which as such is accompanied by the sign of the miraculous conception and birth of Jesus Christ (*C.D.*, I, 2, § 15, 3), yet which is not grounded in this miracle, but in the fact that it is (ὁμολογουμένως μέγα) event.[24]

What is crucial here is, as he writes, not the miracle but the event. All that the man Jesus is from above and all that he is from below is the sacramental reality in which and from which we participate and confess by faith everything of the grace of God in the new being and new creation in Christ.

As Barth reasons about incarnation and sacrament, he is very careful in making a comparison of the unity of person that is uniquely in Jesus Christ and the unity of soul and body that is every human being. Barth rejects "an obvious temptation to compare the *unio hypostatica* in Jesus Christ with what the older dogmatics called the *unio sacramentalis*, i.e., the concurrence, on the basis of the divine institution and a divine act, of a divine and human, an outward and inward, a visible and invisible operation and reception of grace in the 'sacramental' actions of baptism and the Lord's Supper."[25] Barth also points to the parallel controversies with the Reformation on the sacramental as well. He concedes that a comparison is acceptable but only "so long as we realise that there is no sacramental union and unity at all as distinct from the unity of God and man in their unity as it is grounded and achieved in Jesus Christ."[26] He goes on to point to the Church's ceasing to make this point regarding the incarnation,

> the mystery of Christmas, the one and only sacrament, fulfilled once and for all, by whose actuality it lives as the one form of the one body of its Head, as the earthly-historical form of the existence of Jesus Christ in the time between His ascension and return . . . the giving and receiving of this one sacrament, whose actuality it has to attest in its proclamation and therefore in baptism and the Lord's Supper, but whose actuality it cannot represent or repeat in any other way either in its preaching or in baptism and the Lord's Supper . . . [Catholic and Protestants retained this move which unfortunately required the presupposition that] the Church itself is a kind of prolongation of the incarnation. If this presupposition is not legitimate, then we can only say that the true *unio sacramentalis* is the *unio personalis* in

---

24. Ibid., 51.
25. Ibid., 54–55.
26. Ibid.,. 55.

> Jesus Christ, and that the comparison is therefore left hanging in the air.²⁷

What Barth here equates is sacrament and person of Jesus Christ. This is not to say that baptism and Lord's Supper have been sublated, but that they are at most derivatively sacramental.

Barth finally sums up the entire matter: "The fact that the existence of God became and is also in His Son the existence of a man—the *unio hypostatica* as the basic form of the Christ-event—seems to dispense with formal analogies altogether, according to the general drift of our discussion."²⁸ Finally, Barth sums up the utter inappropriateness of any analogy or analogizing when it comes to the incarnation:

> With a strange, one-sided, self-glorious spontaneity, we have to do here with the work and action of the faithfulness and omnipotence and mercy of God Himself, which has no ground of reality except in Himself, or ground of knowledge except in His self-revelation. We have seen that in His work and action God is primarily true to Himself; that He can do this work as the eternal Son of the eternal Father. But not even in the being of the triune God is there any analogy for the fact that He does actually do it. We cannot deduce and understand it even from that point, as though God were under a necessity to do it. In relation to God as to man it can be acknowledged and recognised and confessed only in the light of the fact that this event has actually taken place between God and man, that it is a real fact grounded in the free and eternal counsel of the divine will and accomplished in the divine omnipotence. The incarnation of the Word is this fact, without precedence, parallel or repetition either in the divine sphere or (much less) in the human, natural and historical creaturely sphere. The incarnation of the Word is the great "Thus saith the Lord" to which theology can give only the assent that it has heard it and understood it as such, from which all reflexion which seeks and discovers analogies can only

---

27. Ibid. Barth here enters upon extensive refutation of an equation or correspondence with *unio mystica*, "mystical union" that is the subject of much religious speculation over many centuries, reacting particularly to Donald Baillie in his use of the Chalcedonian definition. Comparing it to the problem with the *unio sacramentalis correlation before us, all of it so erroneously generalizes*: "Anything and everything can pass for what it calls divine sonship." Fascinatingly, here Barth inserts a similar cancellation as above: "we may even reverse the statement and say that the *unio personalis* of Jesus Christ is itself alone the true *unio mystica*—which means again, of course, that any comparison between them is left hanging in the air" (57).

28. Ibid., 57.

derive, but to try to subject which to analogies either in earth or heaven is quite nonsensical.²⁹

Existence as in Christ, whether the church or individually, is in virtue of his existence and cannot exist apart from him. Indeed, together they are "*totus Christus*—Christ and Christians." This is not according to some "divinisation of the Church or the individual Christian which Jesus Christ has only to serve as a vehicle or redemptive agency" since "He is the Subject present and active and operative in His community."³⁰ In our context here, this is also because he as "the Subject of atonement and therefore of incarnation, Jesus Christ, is the Son of God."³¹

Barth is never far from the Reformed view of corporate remembrance as the point of interaction and integration in the life of the church and discipleship:

> in more than one demand of Jesus Himself in the Gospels that His words should be remembered (Lk. 24:6; Jn. 15:20, 16:4); in the account of the Last Supper in Luke (22:19, cf. 1 Cor. 11:24f.), especially with the formula: "This do in remembrance of me" (εἰς τὴν ἐμὴν ἀνάμνησιν); and indirectly in the curious saying concerning the anointing in Bethany (Mk. 14:9): "Verily I say unto you, Wheresoever this gospel shall be preached throughout the whole world, this also that she hath done shall be spoken of for a memorial of her." Since "we cannot speak of the Gospels as monuments to the memory of this man, and therefore of the fact that He was present" . . . He refers to the tense of Christian remembrance, a "'perfect' to which they look back [that] is not a 'preterite' . . . not 'past.' The Lord whose memory they enshrine is not a dead Lord. He is not only unforgettable for the community, but it thinks of Him as the One who still is what He was. It is not the community, but He Himself who sees to it that He is not forgotten.³²

Far beyond forgotten, he is present continuously with them and in a very evangelical way, Barth always keeps this promise in close connection to his reasoning:

> Hence the pregnant request of the disciples who went to Emmaus (Lk. 24:29): "Abide with us: for it is toward evening, and the day is far spent." Hence the sayings in Jn. 6:56 and 15:4 about

29. Ibid., 57–58.
30. Ibid., 63.
31. Ibid., 65.
32. Barth, *CD* IV/2, 163.

His abiding with those who abide with Him. Hence Mt. 18:20: "Where two or three are gathered together in my name, there am I in the midst of them." Hence Mt. 28:20: "Lo, I am with you alway, even unto the end of the world." Hence the even more comprehensive Mk. 13:31: "Heaven and earth shall pass away: but my words shall not pass away." And it may well be that fundamentally we have to place in the same category, and need not try to explain in detail, the bewildering changes between past and present forms in narration which are so characteristic a feature of the style of the Fourth Gospel. When we read the Gospel records we cannot abstract from the fact that what is narrated on the basis and as the content of the knowledge of the community was the existence of a man who as they see it lives and speaks and acts to-day no less than yesterday (Heb. 13:8).[33]

The ever present one, Jesus Christ, brings to the community and to the believer his sacramental reality, of which proclamation, baptism and Lord's Supper, and Confession, sum up the recognition and proper engagement with this already fully present reality.

When we take these later statements by Barth, with those much earlier in the *CD* on Lord's Supper a number of points come into their proper orientation. In discussion of the hypostatic union of God and humanity in Christ, the personal presence of God is already of central importance. This gracious presence of God in the incarnation extends continuously in proclamation, "sacrament (. . . the outward creaturely sign of word and elements), and with God's gracious presence in the hearts of those chosen and called by faith."[34] Through this relation, speech, water, bread and wine are "inseparably bound to God" as "believing many may live . . . inseparably bound to God" on account of this continuous gracious presence. These elements are part of the ancient "sign-world" where kerygma, baptism and Lord's Supper, have been ordained, become "sign-giving" (*Zeichengebung*) with the Church as manifestation or visibility of the messianic: "the language of the incarnate Word." Each of these is profoundly attached to the action of the Church "till he come" (1 Cor 11:26) "at the end of our time." They are "signs of the New Testament" instituted beginning with the apostolate. Barth acknowledges that this becomes "the point at which the Evangelical conception of the Church diverges abruptly from the Roman Catholic and also the Modernist Protestant." This is because the entire theological substance here is reflective solely of "the act of the objective revelation of God . . . an act in the existence of Jesus Christ as very God who is also very man. So,

33. Ibid., 164–65.
34. Barth *CD* I/2, 226.

too, the act of sign-giving by which the objective revelation comes to us is an act in the existence of these signs as they were given us once and for all at the inauguration of the apostolate."[35] And this reality has nothing to do with office or ecclesial institution but the renewal of the objective reality by God in each successive generation of "fresh recognition of revelation, an act which devolves upon the Church of every age." And the valid recognition of the institution of the apostolate is its concrete expression in Holy Scripture from which proceeds "the exercise *pure* and *recte*, i.e., in accordance with Scripture, of preaching and the administration of the sacraments."[36] Barth is also cautious to say that while the "signs of revelation" are "always made new" for the Church that lives in time "there is no new revelation," just as there are "no new signs."[37] In this way, and only this way, objective revelation brings subjective reception of revelation into alignment.

Interestingly, we do not have to look only to Barth's later foundational material on Christ as the one and only sacrament. Early on he highlights the point that the original concept *sacramentum* (μυστήριον) was much more comprehensive in meaning (cf. the usage of Tertullian and Cyprian) where it denoted "the mysteries of the faith as such."[38] He can certainly quote also his Protestant sources for the language of "means of grace" as "fruits of redemption" seeing the entire church itself sacramentally. He pays close attention to Calvin's metaphors (e.g., *Instit*. IV 14, 5f.) to signify sacraments as "seal-impressions, or paintings, or reflections of the divine promise of grace; they are supporting pillars of faith, or exercises (*exercitia*) to develop certainty about the Word of God." These figures are just as suited to the more comprehensive concept of sign-giving, which belongs to revelation and mediates objectively to the human subject."[39] Barth consistently interprets sacraments in *CD* I according to the mediation of the subjective reception (sign-giving) of revelation. These are the external, visible, above all "sensible" (including "audible") signs of baptism and Lord's Supper: "symbols and actions which are visually apprehensible," part of a continuum of signs that includes human words (cf. Augustine, *In Joann. tract.* 45, 9). All this corresponds to the divine intention to create visible signs, the Church containing the "*symbola externa*" instituted by Christ himself. There are visible things of the sacrament "in its narrower sense are *elementa*, i.e., elements of

---

35. Ibid., 227–28.
36. Ibid.
37. Ibid., 228.
38. Ibid.
39. Ibid.

a spatially extended, corporeal nature, water, bread and wine."[40] Barth sees as a consequence an extraordinary distinction, according to appearance, of the sacrament in comparison to general sign-giving by God. He also places emphasis upon the sacrament as "an *actio sacra*." But it is just as much "instituted by Christ as a sign of the *res sacra*." They signify the divine grace in Christ in *sanctificatio or iustificatio*, of applying the objective reconciliation through those who minister these signs. Preaching supplies the general context which sacraments "merely underline" and to which they belong. They are the enactment of the sign-giving pointing to reality, to an event, namely, "the event of the entry of this Creator into our history,"[41] which is absolutely nothing to interpret when it comes to the presence of God in Christ, the action of God Almighty, Maker of heaven and earth. The other side at this stage for Barth can give emphasis, "in a way which preaching can never do, the sacrament underlines the words σάρξ and ἐγένετο."[42] In them there is the "divine sign-giving [*göttlichen Zeichengebung*] as the objective side of the Church," a "quality in divine sign-giving is its special feature as compared with preaching and its special feature in the whole life of God's people assembled to form the Church." All in "the very simple fact that in the Church baptism must always be administered and the Lord's Supper celebrated. By this fact it is reminded that, since it is the reality of revelation, the subjective reality of revelation necessarily has an objective side."[43]

Getting to the heart of the matter of "divine sign-giving," Barth asserts that the form of revelation is itself "something of the nature of a sacrament" as stemming from both natural elements and human action. Thus, biblically "John the Baptist is the prototype of all sign-giving" which is "attestation . . . in distinction from and in relation to Christ when he describes himself as him that baptises with water" (cf. John 3:4; Eph 5:26ff.; Titus 3:5) in contrast to Christ's "inner work of the Holy Spirit."[44] Barth is working with a profound correspondence here. As in John 6:52–58 Jesus speaking, "eating and drinking unto eternal life," a radical realism is in view. The "objective witness" (*objektive Zeugnis*) to be received in the sacrament means that it is conceived *pars pro toto*. Revelation is conveyed through this "living and concrete way, as a creative event in history" for our reception and application. Revelation therefore comes to us just like a sacrament possessing "the

---

40. Ibid., 230.
41. Ibid.
42. Ibid. Cf. Vogel, *Das Wort und die Sakramente*, 6f.
43. Barth, *CD* I/2, 231.
44. Ibid; "inneren Werk des Heiligen Geistes."

objective quality of grace."⁴⁵ Because revelation is always also a matter of salvation and vice versa: "It is no mere matter of the water in baptism or of the bread and wine in the Lord's Supper." The Holy Spirit enlivens these things for their purpose in the revelation-salvation nexus. Baptism is necessary but not an "automatic necessity" since we cannot "tie God" to our actions. As such, baptism is a command to be acted upon. In the water of baptism and in the bread and wine of the Lord's Supper, "the sign of the concrete, living, creatively active lordship of God" is established and recognized.⁴⁶ This is the case since what happens in the signs of Scripture is "exactly the same as what is involved in the water of baptism and in the bread and wine of the Lord's Supper."⁴⁷ Baptism "as an objective testimony pronounced upon us" corresponds to the authoritative prophetic and apostolic word on account of the Incarnate Word and vice versa, "just as we are fed with bread and given wine to drink in the Lord's Supper."⁴⁸ Baptism and the Lord's Supper bind us as tokens of the life giving Word which is mediated by the words of the prophets and apostles. Just as their words do this indispensably as "means of grace" (*Gnadenmittel*) so also do the sacraments. Objectively "the Church is sacramental" as an extension of the analogy of baptism and the Lord's Supper because: "The sphere of subjective reality in revelation is the sphere of sacrament."⁴⁹ Like preaching, the sacraments are those signs and events by which objective revelation is "reaching man," appropriated subjectively for the life and maintenance of faith in the church. And yet this only takes place because the Holy Spirit is revelation in its subjective reality. The Spirit is the one by whom "the person and work of God are manifest" as we begin and end with Holy Scripture, the medium of both objective and subjective revelation.⁵⁰ This does not mean the objective and subjective revelation are identical of course—they are not reversible either—but it does mean that the signs, by which revelation comes to humanity, while inseparable, are

45. Ibid; "so als schöpferisches Ereignis in der Geschichte, kommt die Offenbarung zu uns und will sie empfangen und aufgenommen sein: so wie sie sich in besonderer Betonung dieses ihres objektiven Gnadencharakters im Sakrament darstellt" (*KD* I/2, 252).

46. Ibid; "die Aufrichtung und Erkenntnis des Zeichens der konkreten, leibhaften, schöpferischereignishaften Gottesherrschaft."

47. Ibid.

48. *CD* I/2, 232; "wir leben in der Weise vom Wort der Propheten und Apostel, das heißt von der auf ihr Zeugnis begründeten Verkündigung und wiederum durch diese Verkündigung von der Gnade des Wortes Gottes, wie wir im Abendmahl mit Brot gespiesen und mit Wein getränkt warden" (*KD* I/2, 252–53).

49. Ibid; "der Raum der subjektiven Wirklichkeit der Offenbarung ist der sakramentale Raum" (*KD* I/2, 253).

50. Ibid., 232–33.

equally ordained and as signs reversible. Since the Holy Spirit is the subjective reality of revelation these signs, either in the objective or subjective conveyance are inseparable from the living, triune God.

As a human acquires faith because of the revelation of Jesus Christ, Barth is emphatic that it is not for mere private interests. "Real revelation puts man in God's presence" (*die den Menschen vor Gott stellt*) who is "for us" and as recipients takes us up into revelation of the living presence of God that is event in every case, since revelation and salvation are inseparable.[51] And of course as Barth continuously emphasizes, in subjective revelation there is no additional truth or second revelation beyond objective revelation. The revelation in its objective reality is solely in Christ, by which human beings are adopted by God and where Christian self-recognition is acquired by the Holy Spirit and through that Spirit caught up in this revelation.[52] Barth describes this as being "in Christ by Christ," that is, "in God by God." Revelation is thus always soteriological:

> "In Christ" means that in Him we are reconciled to God, in Him we are elect from eternity, in Him we are called, in Him we are justified and sanctified, in Him our sin is carried to the grave, in His resurrection our death is overcome, with Him our life is hid in God, in Him everything that has to be done for us, to us, and by us, has already been done, has previously been removed and put in its place, in Him we are children in the Father's house, just as He is by nature. All that has to be said about us can be said only by describing and explaining our existence in Him; not by describing and explaining it as an existence which we might have in and for itself. That is why the subjective reality of revelation as such can never be made an independent theme. It is enclosed in its objective reality.[53]

The Holy Spirit is God convincing us of this and we come to exist for revelation and, most importantly, become "free for it." This happens, as Barth cites, what for him is a highly important passage, Calvin on the *modus percipiendae Christi gratiae* (*Instit.* III 1) where Christ himself, by the Holy Spirit, is proclaiming to the human being and aiding the human being as the *arcana operatione Spiritus*—the secret, inner work of the Spirit.[54]

In this way "our receiving the grace of Jesus Christ is necessarily that it concerns this *locupletatio*, the occupation by Him of the empty space which

---

51. Ibid., 237.
52. Ibid., 239–40.
53. Ibid., 240.
54. "durch das im Geheimnis sich vollziehende Werk des Geistes" (*KD* I/2, 262).

is ourselves."⁵⁵ Revelation, since it is soteriological, never remains in its *extra nos*, "outside us" objective dimension as we are in our condition separated from him, since his presence would have no bearing upon us. Revelation is always communication, the imparting of the grace revealed in him so that it is always "with us" as well. Barth is emphatic about Christ's presence to us: "He has to become our own. He has to dwell in us" (cf. Eph 4:15; Rom 8:29; 11:17; Gal 3:27): "*Communicatio* of grace is *communicatio* of Christ Himself" so that He and we become, in Calvin's expression, a coalesced unity.⁵⁶ This is efficacious grace that is the divine intention of revelation and thus the fruit of participation in the grace of Christ. Christ who was born and died for our sakes, "that came by water and blood" (1 John 5:6; cf. John 19:34; as connected since the ancient Church with baptism and the Lord's Supper). The Spirit's sanctifying work in this light is purification and cleansing. All of this corresponds with the original appearing of Jesus Christ through the apostolic witness and the signs of their visible testimony chosen by God in their preaching, along with baptism and the Lord's Supper, "they are the language of the incarnate Word."⁵⁷ Barth is clear that Christ's incomparable authority is not a possession of the Church, nor even the living apostolic testimony of the Twelve.

> What does not cease is the extension of the Church's work on the basis of its witness to Christ: the proclamation of Christ by the preaching of Christ, the institution of baptism, and the festival of the Lord's Supper; and the gathering of the people out of all nations by this proclamation. That is the new and simplified and concentrated sign-world of the New Testament. The Church, the body of Christ, and therefore Christ Himself exists and exists only where there are the signs of the New Testament, that is,

---

55. "um die Besetzung des leeren Raumes, der wir selbst sind, durch ihn" (*KD* I/2, 263).

56. Ibid; "Communicatio der Gnade ist die communicatio Christi selbst, sie besteht also darin, daß er und wir nicht mehr zwei, sondern eins sind: daß wir cum ipso in unum coalescimus. Das ist's, was im Glauben an das Evangelium geschieht. Aber das Evangelium wird vielen verkündigt, ohne daß sie glauben und also ohne daß das geschieht. Geschieht es doch, dann ist das eben jenes Geheimnis der Wirksamkeit des Geistes, die arcana Spiritus efficacia. Durch sie kommt es zum frui, zur Anteilnahme an Christus und seiner Gnade. So ist Christus „gekommen in Wasser und Blut" mit uns solidarisch geworden und für uns gestorben (1. Joh. 5, 6 vgl. Joh. 19, 34; die alte Kirche hatte sicher nicht Unrecht, wenn sie diese Stellen mit Taufe und Abendmahl in Beziehung brachte!) . . ."

57. Ibid., 226.

preaching, baptism and the Lord's Supper, in accordance with their institution fulfilled at the inauguration of the apostolate.[58]

Ultimately, Barth concludes, communion with Christ supersedes everything so that "we must look at Christ Himself."

Barth enters in upon nothing less than a discussion of biblical piety at this point: "It is only when we look in this direction that we can answer the very relevant question: Have I the Holy Spirit?" His answer is straightforward, that it is not according to human "seizure," "but only by Christ," according to "divine seizure," and then "we can have it for ourselves only by continually turning to Him" (as he cites, John 6:37).[59] Practical theological concern is the direction but according to bases in "Church and Holy Scripture and preaching and the sacrament."[60] As hearers, there is concern with really hearing and doing the Word. For Barth it is a matter of "true preaching" intent on being rather "rigidly" scriptural or baptismal, or of the Lord's Supper, rather than verbal content from someone's experience, i.e., of faith in Christ who died and rose again for each one of us. This is so that preaching is not about any one person's ("ambiguous") experience in order to make it part of the gospel message, since Jesus Christ is "the source of all true and proper experience."[61] This is the mode and content of the subjective side of revelation: receiving Christ, the incarnate Word himself, through the "outpouring" of the Holy Spirit. This is "the divine act of lordship, the mystery and the miracle of the existence of God among us, the triumph of free grace."[62] The fact of this receiving, Barth concludes, must be insisted upon in proclamation repeatedly. A certain clarity becomes apparent at the point and Barth asserts it simply enough, that everything belongs to grace in Christ and yet faith in Christ is truly faith based upon the gifts of the Holy Spirit grounded in him and direct by him.

---

58. Ibid., 227. What is particularly noteworthy here is the nonnecessity of using the term *sacrament*.

59. Ibid; "Und gerade echte und rechte Verkündigung der subjektiven Möglichkeit der Offenbarung, gerade rechte Predigt vom Heiligen Geist der Pfingsten wird nicht im Hinweis auf unser eigenes oder anderer Menschen Ergriffensein, sondern im Hinweis auf das göttliche Ergreifen und damit wiederum auf Christus selbst bestehen" (*KD* I/2, 272).

60. Ibid., 249; "Die Kirche, die heilige Schrift, die Predigt und das Sakrament werden also doch wieder die Kriterien sein, nach denen praktisch allein gefragt werden kann."

61. Ibid; "die Quelle echter und rechter Erfahrung, das heißt eben zu Christus."

62. Ibid., 250; "von der Fleischwerdung des Wortes in Christus zu sagen ist: göttlicher Herrschaftsakt, Geheimnis und Wunder der Existenz Gottes unter uns, Triumph der freien Gnad."

Baptism and Lord's Supper in Barth are then extensions of the means of proclamation under the reality of the Holy Spirit for effecting the subjective reception of revelation: "only in His name, in the revelation and reality of His person."[63] In precisely this way, the action of the Holy Spirit affects the response of faith: "summoned to faith in Him, to the recognition and acknowledgment of the repentance which He has completed for it, and therefore to the repentance in which the bearing away of sin which He has accomplished becomes recognisable and real for the world"[64]—of which baptism and Lord's Supper are the visible signs of awakened faith in the believer. Barth draws from Matt 28:19-20, where the μαθητεύσατε, "teaching them," is explanatory of the βαπτίζοντες αὐτοὺς εἰς τὸ ὄνομα τοῦ πατρὸς καὶτοῦ υἱοῦ καὶ τοῦ ἁγίου πνεύματος, "baptizing them in the name of the Father and of the Son and of the Holy Spirit."[65] The world is to learn the gospel from the apostles and to be baptized "into the revelation and reality of the mercy of the triune God" which is "the recognition and acknowledgment of the free grace." And also the τηρεῖν, "to observe," that is, "the maintaining, proving, guarding, defending, maintaining intact, of a form which cannot be controlled either by men or by the apostles, but is given with the thing itself, with the Gospel ["the rule of faith"], and therefore by Jesus Christ; by the One who has taken away their sin by the repentance which He has completed on their behalf." Teaching and baptism are "directly connected, in substance"[66] with Christ himself in the concluding words: "Behold, I am with you always, even to the end of the world"—and Barth giving his own paraphrase of the words of the Lord: "You may rely in every age on the power of My authority in which I send you forth."[67] The continuous presence of Christ with his disciples and all who "confess Him before men . . . through the presence of Jesus Christ, immanent in . . . word and work"[68] is the source of their power as they teach in his name (cf. Luke 24:49). In spite of the many failings of the apostles, Jesus maintained them and assured them of the glory yet to be revealed in him so that "the institution of the Lord's

---

63. Barth, *CD* II/2, 434.

64. Ibid.

65. Which is the basis of the "baptismal analogy" of the Holy Trinity and really the most reliable, since its assertion is so simple: the being of the one eternal God corresponds with the reality of the three eternal persons named. Baptism is acknowledgment of the divine giving of grace: "Erkenntnis und Anerkennung des göttlichen Gnadengeschenkes" (*KD* II/2, 481).

66. Ibid., "zu diesem Taufen und Lehren inhaltlich schlechterdings an den gebunden ist."

67. Ibid., 434.

68. Ibid., 235.

Supper speaks of the strongest possible affirmation and confirmation of the fellowship between Jesus and the apostles."[69] Barth describes the Lord's Supper as "the real institution of the apostolate." The apostles' connection to Christ is their calling and mission resulting in their empowerment to proclaim the gospel.[70]

The Lord's Supper brings Christians into focus the new relation of self-examination with regard to the Law of God and human action (cf. 2 Cor 13:5; Gal 6:4; 1 Cor 11:28). In the presence of God as Judge there takes place "our public and solemn participation in the communion of the body and blood of Christ."[71] The "self-knowledge correspondent to the action of the Lord's Supper, which is the good will of God to man, inviting him to partake in this sacrament and expecting him at the table of the Lord" is "spiritual nourishment" by which we say of Jesus Christ: "I am His, and He is mine."[72] It "is the constant renewal of the community as the body of Christ, and of each of its members as such." As such, according to Barth, these acts connected with participation in confrontation with Christ and the personal reflection arising from it is the basis of all Christian ethical inquiry.

It is in this ethical connection that the "objective obligatory work of all to all" takes place in confession, corporate and individual, for mutual consolation and edification.[73] In the "human response to the Word of God" as "the common word of all" confession is the "first element in public worship": recitation of the creed, singing, "decisively in free witness, bound only to its object, as the Word of God is proclaimed and published and taught and preached and heard by the community according to the commission of its Lord." When a community does this, it is thereby "constituted as a fellowship of confession" in "answer to the Word of God . . . a matter of witness to Jesus Christ . . . He who wills that they should be spoken . . . He Himself is present where they are spoken and heard by those whom He has gathered."[74] In the performing of "the liturgical act of confession" the gathering achieve much more than mere speech but the "where two or three are gathered together in the name of Jesus they will mutually recognise and acknowledge that they are those who are gathered by Him as their one Lord, and regard and receive one another as brothers because they are all brothers

---

69. Ibid.
70. Ibid., 445.
71. Ibid., 641.
72. Ibid.
73. Barth, *CD* IV/2, 700.
74. Ibid.

of this First-begotten."⁷⁵ As to the composition of this community, Barth is again straightforwardly evangelical: they are those "awakened by the quickening power of the Holy Spirit, and therefore a saint, and as such a member of the communion of saints" as the basis of true communion in Christ and crucially among them, in mutually trusting relation of belonging.⁷⁶ They are tasting together the salvation that is in Christ, accepted as the baptized, "in the frame of mind in which they came to baptism,"⁷⁷ beginners in the knowledge of Christ confessing together. It is "the presence in the midst of the One who has brought them together" as a "fellowship of baptism," "the sign . . . act of obedience undertaken in perfect confidence."⁷⁸ Together they strengthen one another continually in their common work. And this they do

> where He Himself presides as Lord and Host . . . eating of one bread and the drinking from one cup, of the common nourishment of them all, because it is He, Jesus Christ, who brings them to it, who invites them . . . who is Himself, indeed, their food and drink . . . He strengthens and upholds them in their existence as His body and its members, and therefore to eternal life in the concealment and glory of God. He constitutes Himself their preparation to attain this . . . the event of His own life is reflected and repeated in the event of the Supper (as in that of confession and baptism). In remembrance of Him there takes place here and now exactly the same as took place there and then between Himself and His first disciples, immediately prior to His death and resurrection.⁷⁹

Every Lord's Supper is a "reflection and imitation"⁸⁰ of the original Lord's Supper and that on account of his continuous presence ever constitutes the participants as *communio sanctorum* ("communion of saints") in Jesus' name. They are then enabled to pray the "Our Father" together as prayer "with the One by whom they are united and who is Himself present in the midst—their predecessor in prayer."⁸¹ In this prayer as they pray "Jesus ranges Himself alongside His disciples, or His disciples alongside Himself, taking them up with Him into His own prayer." The "we" of the prayer is the

75. Ibid., 700–701.
76. Ibid.
77. Ibid., 702.
78. Ibid.
79. Ibid., 703.
80. Ibid.
81. Ibid., 705.

sign of the attachment of Lord to people and people to Lord as one community. "Prayed in fellowship with Him, it is never in vain." Indeed, "The community is constituted as it prays."[82] Thus confession, baptism, Lord's Supper, prayer form a continuum of acts by which the Lord's relationship as "Head of the community . . . [demonstrates] His own presence and lordship in its assembling for divine service."[83] All of this is conducted according to "the Scripture principle" that establishes the exclusive right of the Lord to determine these acts in union with himself: "He is their law; He, the One who is attested in Holy Scripture" who is "present and active in divine service" as its law[84] for the Church. Scripture is the normative source for the commands which constitute the Church as they declare his presence in applying the same Scripture. He in his Lordship assembles the community and through each act nurtures it to eternal life.

Barth has in *CD* IV dispensed with the terminology of "sacrament" for anything other than the incarnate, risen, ascended and everywhere present Lord Himself. And yet there is no lessening of significance:

> The eternal life to which the community is strengthened and preserved in the Lord's Supper is the glorification of the whole of human life. Thus the Church order to be derived from the eucharistic action will necessarily embrace, protect and claim the life of the community and its members as it is now lived in its totality and therefore at one and the same time in its physical and spiritual nature. It will aim at the living fellowship of Christians in both spheres. In each respect it will make the strong responsible for the weak, the healthy for the sick, the rich for the poor. It will make Christians answerable for one another and for the continuance of the community, outwardly no less than inwardly. It will claim the help of all in both spheres. And it will promise help to all in both spheres. It will remind the community that what is lawful and right in the Lord's Supper is lawful and right everywhere: fellowship in heavenly and therefore also in earthly things; the *communion* of the *sancti* in and in respect of the *sancta*.[85]

Crucial here for Barth, the "axiomatic certainty" is "Jesus's presence" (*Jesu Gegenwart*), the *Realpraesenz* as God and man which cannot be limited to the so-called sacraments (astoundingly expressed) but experienced in

---

82. Ibid.
83. Ibid., 706.
84. Ibid; "referred wholly and utterly to Holy Scripture."
85. Ibid.

Kurt Anders Richardson—Jesus Christ as the One and Only Sacrament

the totality of Christian fellowship where "two or more are gathered in my name" and simply because Christians have the Spirit and are led by the Spirit.[86] Indeed, nothing hierarchical as well can be fashioned for this community, since all are brothers and sisters of the one Christ. All have the same need, the same task, the same access, none has precedence or claim over the other, but all are equally under Him, the true guide and actual, not institutional authority. Leadership in this context is practical and of humble service of true community.

The real presence of Christ to and in the community of Christians who have identified with him in every way (Barth cites the baptismal text, Rom 6:1–11) means that the celebration of the Lord's Supper is a true act of remembrance and of genuine tradition ("wirkliche Erinnerung und echte Uberlieferung"). This is not a "Christ mysticism" or a "Christ ethic" but because of the leading of the Spirit who actualizes the personal promises of Christ to be with Christians as in the *locus classicus* of evangelical theology, Matt 18:20.[87] For Barth, this is precisely the new life in the Holy Spirit that has been promised and realized in Christ in the life of Christians. The Incarnation is the sacrament of Christian union with God: "Jesus in der Inkarnation, wir Christen im Sakrament—wirklich mit Gott vereinigt warden."[88] His constant presence with them and indeed, their life in him who is the one true sacrament constitutes the nature of grace whose only means is the incarnate Lord himself[89]—the gift and the Giver are one and the same and cannot be limited in any way to a single moment in the church ritual and action.

What then do we have with Barth's view of sacrament? Everything rests on the sacramental mystery in what he claims is its original sense: the presence of the incarnate Word in Jesus Christ (*Christus praesens*) in intimate relation with the Church, his body, both corporate and individual. The Church is constituted by and experiences the contemporaneity of Christ, as Barth continuously argues along the evangelical appeal to Matthew 18:20. Even early in the *CD* where he is using "sacrament" in a traditionally Reformed way to refer to baptism and Lord's Supper, what Christ is doing as

---

86. *KD* III/2, 561ff.
87. *CD* III/2, 564.
88. *KD* III/3, 474.
89. Throughout the *CD*, Barth refers to the Roman Catholic view of sacraments as *ex opera operato* (mere performance of the sacrament by the clergy) and that this view disqualifies their performance as such as sacraments; marriage, for instance, is not a sacrament since it does not mediate grace, ref. to the *locus classicus* of Eph 5:32, pointing out that Augustine did not regard it as such, and Peter Lombard explicitly denied it; cf., e.g., *CD* III/4, 122ff; *KD* III/4, 136.

Part III—Renewing Christian Doctrine

the representative humanity of the Son of God as revelation itself and our subjective participation in that revelation, looms far larger than that which is communicated by the elements of these signs. Along with all the acts of Christian worship and obedience beginning in confession, baptism and the Lord's Supper "bear witness" and only so.[90] Indeed, for Barth, much of the thinking in Christianity has been ideologized and mythologized according to nineteenth-century models of "religionism . . . liturgism, sacramentalism . . . even existentialism."[91] Finally, it is the historical Incarnate Christ that is the one and only sacrament to which baptism testifies and is itself (baptism) not a sacrament at all.[92] At this point, at the end of the *CD*, Barth has pressed the principle and necessity of reform to the furthest extent he is able, based upon the Christological principle that is the heart of the NT and, as he is contending, the trajectory of the tradition.

---

90. Cf., *KD* IV/1, 325.

91. "... humanistischen Religionismus, den uns das 19. Jahrhundert hinterlassen hat, und angesichts all des Ekklesiastizismus, Sakramentalismus, Liturgismus—aber doch auch Existenzialismus" (*KD* IV/1, 583).

92. "Die Taufe antwortet auf das eine 'Mysterium,' das eine 'Sakrament' der Geschichte Jesu Christi, seiner Auferstehung, der Ausgießung des Heiligen Geistes: sie selbst ist aber kein Mysterium, kein Sakrament" (*KD* IV/4, 112).

Bibliography

Vogel, Heinrich. *Das Wort und die Sakramente.* Munich: Kaiser, 1936.

14

Eschatology from Basel to Azusa Street
The Voices of Karl Barth and Pentecostalism in Dialogue

Peter Althouse

ANY DIALOGUE BETWEEN SWISS Protestant theologian Karl Barth (1886–1968) and Pentecostalism is fraught with difficulties from the outset. Barth was born 10 May 1886 in Basel Switzerland, commenced his theological education under some of the best Protestant Liberal intellectuals of his day, and pastored for ten years in Safenwil. He taught in Münster (1925–30) and then in Bonn, where he wrote the first part of *Christian Dogmatics*, a project he later abandoned. In 1935 Barth was dismissed from his German teaching position for having participated in the drafting of the Barmen Theological Declaration, and he finally settled in Basel where he would remain for the rest of his life. The University of Basel offered Barth the opportunity to write his magnum opus, *Church Dogmatics*.[1] In all, Barth was afforded the highest education and conducted a professional career as pastor and university professor.

During the same period, a grass-roots revival occurred in the United States and abroad. In 1906, a revival broke out in Los Angeles, California, at the Azusa Street Mission under the leadership of African-American Holiness preacher, William J. Seymour.[2] On the surface, this small revival looked like

---

1. Webster, "Introducing Barth," 2–8.

2. See Robeck, *The Azusa Street Mission & Revival*. American Pentecostal scholarship revolves around whether the ministries of Charles F. Parham (Topeka, 1901) or William H. Seymour (Azusa, 1906) constitute the origins of Pentecostalism. However, recent scholarship is questioning the primacy of Azusa Street for Pentecostal origins.

many of the other revivals that had cropped up in the nineteenth and twentieth centuries, only subsequently to wane and sputter out. Like many other revivals in the history of the Wesleyan Methodist, Holiness and American revivalist traditions, Azusa Street exhibited ecstatic manifestations, somatic expressions, bodily healing, along with conversions, recommitments to Christ, and calling into ministry and mission work. What Azusa Street and the Pentecostal movement was most known for, however, was its practice of *glossolalia*, incomprehensible audible vocalizations simply called "speaking in tongues," "unknown tongues," or just "tongues." Patterning itself after apostolic Christianity as depicted in Luke-Acts, the participants of Azusa Street believed that the outpouring of the Spirit on the day of Pentecost in which believers were baptized and began to speak in other tongues (Acts 2:1–4) was likewise occurring at Azusa Street as the "latter rain" outpouring of the Spirit ushering in the second coming of Christ. "This is that" was shorthand for describing the Azusa Street outpouring as the Spirit's free movement among God's people, empowering Christian workers to prepare for the great "harvest of souls," which was believed to be God's final calling before establishing the divine kingdom on earth. The Pentecostal revival quickly spread along evangelical networks: camp-meetings, periodicals, preaching tours, etc. The details are not essential, except to say that while the rest of the Christian world basically ignored, or criticized, Pentecostal exuberance the movement on the whole continued to grow, expand, mutate (which constituted new expressions and growth), until finally in the second decade of the twenty-first century, Pentecostal-Charismatic Christianity influences many areas of Christianity over the entire globe.

The difficulty with engaging in a dialogue between Barth and Pentecostalism is the theological, social, political, and cultural distance that stands between the two. One the one hand, Barth's theology could be used to speak to issues to strengthen the burgeoning Pentecostal theology. This is certainly a worthy and valuable approach in which a premier, highly-educated theologian speaks to a populist movement lacking theological sophistication. There is some evidence that Barth may have even known about Pentecostalism through a relationship with Pentecostal ecumenist David du Plessis, and even noted that "we want to praise and thank God that there is a

---

Azusa Street was neither the first such revival nor the only one associated with the Pentecostal movement. Allan Anderson points to revivals both contemporary and prior to Azusa: Edward Irving's Catholic Apostolic Church (1830); Johann Blumhardt (ca. 1850s); Russia and Armenia (1855 and 1880); Wales (1904), Korea (1903), India (1905–7), China (1908), and Toronto (1906). See Anderson, *Introduction to Pentecostalism*, 24, 35–37, 172–73. Significantly, the Blumhardt revival had theological influence on Barth. Nevertheless, Azusa Street has taken on symbolic significance.

Pentecostal Movement," but he was uncomfortable with the glorification of success in mass evangelistic campaigns. For Barth, this was merely another example of secularization.³

On the other hand, Pentecostalism as a whole is an eclectic movement, borrowing its theology from multiple traditions and piecing them together in a patchwork fashion. Certainly much of the writings and doctrinal developments of the early movement has an eclectic feel and were written as guidelines, not as confessions of faith. Moreover, Pentecostal scholars cannot agree on a theological core that can be used to define the movement. How does one go about defining the theology of a movement as diverse as Pentecostalism?

For the most part, Pentecostalism has been defined by its most distinctive doctrine, the baptism in the Holy Spirit, the theological meaning ascribed to the practice of *glossolalia*. However, this doctrine is neither uniform nor universal in that Pentecostals around the world often highlight other areas such as healing or dreams and visions. Even though the Charismatic Renewal and Independent Charismatic movement engage in *glossolalic* utterances, they are less willing to attach the practice to a doctrine of Spirit baptism. For the Charismatic Renewal in particular, baptism in the Spirit is associated with the initiation of faith and *glossolalia* or other spiritual gifts are further expressions in the Christian faith, a position more in line with Barth and historic Christianity on the whole, as we shall see. Keith Warrington therefore makes a distinction between Pentecostals who affirm the doctrine of the baptism in the Spirit with the "evidence of speaking in tongues" as a dogmatic formula, and Pentecostals who affirm the Spirit's enabling presence in the experience of tongues to which they ascribe theological meaning.⁴

Donald Dayton has noted, however, that a truncated focus on *glossolalia* distorts the theological landscape of the Pentecostal movement. Instead, four theological themes have formed the *gestalt* of early Pentecostal theology. Known as the full or fourfold gospel, early Pentecostals proclaimed that Jesus Christ is Savior, Healer, Baptizer in the Holy Spirit, and Coming King.⁵

3. Macchia, "Karl Barth Meets David du Plessis," 5–6.

4. Warrington, *Pentecostal Theology*, 95–96. See also, Schner, "The Appeal to Experience."

5. Dayton, *Theological Roots of Pentecostalism*, 21–22. Wesleyan Pentecostals assert a fivefold gospel, which follows Wesley and the Holiness movement to highlight sanctification as a fifth component in the full gospel, but Dayton argues that the fourfold model better articulates Pentecostal theology. The fourfold model also better aligns with Barth's theology, as will become clear, in which sanctification as an activity of the Spirit is the means by which the objective work of Christ is subjectively applied to the believer.

Central to the fourfold gospel is a fifth element that integrates the other four: *Jesus Christ is* the one who saves, heals, baptizes by giving the Spirit, and who is coming to reign. Dialogue between Barth and Pentecostalism is possible then along the lines of the full gospel. I will take the eschatological theme of the coming of Christ as my organizing principle, with the caveat that for Barth and Pentecostals Jesus Christ *is* the beginning and the end of all theological articulations and the Spirit mediates Christ and his kingdom to the world.

The Character of Christian Hope in Barth's Eschatology

Eschatological hope was a theological concern for Barth early in his career. In *The Epistle to the Romans* Barth writes: "If Christianity be not altogether thoroughgoing eschatology there remains in it no relationship whatsoever with Christ. Spirit which does not at every moment point from death to new life is not the Holy Spirit . . . Redemption is invisible, inaccessible, and impossible, for it meets us only in hope."[6] In part, Barth's eschatology was a counterpoint to the theological Liberalism of his day. In reaction to modernity's faith in human optimism and progress as the means for transforming human life and society, Barth calls the church back to its roots, "to the impossibility of redemption apart from the cross, apart from dying, apart from waiting for God in hope."[7] Barth rejected a self-authenticating natural theology in favor of a Christ-centered view of divine revelation.

On this point, Jürgen Moltmann criticizes Barth's "theology of crisis" as epiphanic—confusing the promise of eschatological hope with eternal presence. The eternal breaks into history and in doing so collapses time into no-time. Moltmann insists that the breaking in of eternity into history forces human history into its final crisis. "If eschatology has to do with the presence of eternity in the moment, and therefore with this limitation and abolition of time, then the problem of 'the delay of the *parousia*' collapses on its own accord. For this problem resulted from 'consistent eschatology' and its 'experiences of disappointment' in history."[8] In other words, in order to explain the delayed *parousia* in the apostolic church time itself is abolished in the presence of an eternal God. For Moltmann, though, the difficulty with Barth's eschatology is that the future is no longer relevant:

---

6. Barth, *Epistle to the Romans*, 314.
7. Bolt, "Exploring Karl Barth's Eschatology," 210.
8. Moltmann, *Coming of God*, 14.

> If *eschaton* means eternity and not End-time, then eschatology has no longer anything to do with the future either. Its tension is not the tension between present and future, the "now already" and "not yet"; it is the tension between eternity and time in past, present and future. When Jesus proclaims that the kingdom of God is "at hand," he is not looking into the future in the temporal sense; he is looking into the heaven of the present. The kingdom does not "come" out of the future into the present. It comes from heaven to earth . . .[9]

On first blush, Moltmann's critique of Barth emerges from a concern for social, political, and ecological liberation in which the eschatological inbreaking of the kingdom from the future transforms the present, and addresses the concern of the eternal presence; and therefore the proclamation of a "realized eschatology" passively accepts the world as is, despite its sinful realities.[10] Indeed, Moltmann places Barth in the company of Rudolph Bultmann, Paul Althaus, and C. H. Dodd as theologians with similar eschatological interests. Moltmann's criticisms of Barth have to do with his fear that Barth undermines the "yet-to-be-realized" work of Christ and highlights the "not-yet-concluded" character of revelation in *CD* IV/3.[11] However, a more nuanced reading of Barth, especially in *CD* IV, suggests a complex inaugural eschatology that places emphasis on future consummation, but centered on God's revelation in Christ Jesus, whose own coming is the realization of the coming of the eschatological kingdom. With Barth, the eschatological kingdom is not a speculative rendition of futuristic scenarios as with much of North American dispensational premillennialism, but is, as with everything in Barth's theology, about Jesus Christ. "Genuine Christian eschatology is one that is consistently and thoroughly about Christ alone."[12] Before addressing the Christological center of Barth's eschatology we need to look at the contours of the Christian hope of Barth's eschatology.

On the whole, Barth saw the problem of eschatology as one of the relationship between time and eternity. From the human perspective there is a before and after, past and future, but from God's perspective all chronological time is simultaneous, because it is a created reality and God's equivalent. For the early Barth, the eschatological character of salvation is the eternal inbreaking as simultaneous occurrences in past, present, and future, though this is only a problem from a human perspective which is

---

9. Ibid., 15.
10. Ibid.
11. Webster, *Barth's Moral Theology*, 84 n. 21.
12. Bolt, "Exploring Karl Barth's Eschatology," 217.

limited to temporality. The eternality of the divine perspective is not bound by chronological time. Barth highlights the tension between time and eternity in Rom 3:21: "*But now* directs our attention to time which is beyond time, a space which has no locality, to impossible possibility, to the gospel of transformation, to the imminent Coming of the Kingdom, to affirmation in negation, to salvation in the world, to acquittal in condemnation, to eternity in time, to life in death—*I saw a new heaven and a new earth: for the first heaven and first earth are passed away.*"[13] Barth picks up this eschatological theme in the last volume of *Church Dogmatics*. The problem for Barth is that modernity has absolutized the concept of time and that Christian theology has a responsibility to critique any concept that subordinates the sovereign freedom of God. Modern intellectuals thought of time as an "absolute reality" in which the conditions of time "are not subject to any condition. They are infinitely constant relationships, orders and forces, and as such presuppositions to which we are wholly and always subject. They are the indestructible walls of our prison. Our supposedly free action is only within these walls whose significance is simply to be walls, so that our existence can have no other significance than to be existence within them. Enclosed within them, we are not merely not yet redeemed but totally unredeemed."[14]

Absolute time, argues Barth, is a "concept of time without God" (*CD* III/2, 552), but there can be no deified time "rivaling God and imposing conditions on Him. There is not a God called Chronos" (*CD* III/2 456). Time is not "eternal in every 'moment'" nor a technological chronology in the "idea of endless progress" (*CD* III/2 516).[15] "The true God is not the 'Infinite One' at all. By revealing himself, he disputes the very 'idea of the infinity of time.' By clinging to this idea, we not only miss God but also ourselves in our being in time, and thus we generate a deformed time for ourselves."[16] Barth criticizes modern time because it posits absolute time without God. For Barth, God is the Eternal One who has time. In order for God to reveal God's self in time God must be the Lord of time. "If by the statement, 'God reveals himself—is meant the revelation of an event. That means it also includes an assertion about a time proper to revelation. If stated with reference to this, it is equivalent to the statement 'God has time for us.'" Barth's concept of time here is intimately related to God's revelation in Jesus Christ, so that no time is "gained independently of revelation itself."[17] "In fact it is

13. Barth, *Epistle to the Romans*, 92.
14. Karl Barth, *CD* IV/3.1, 338; as quoted in Busch, *Great Passion*, 264–65.
15. Busch, *Great Passion*, 265.
16. Ibid.
17. Barth, *CD* I/2, 45.

an illegitimate anthropomorphism to think of God as if He did not eternally have time, and therefore time for us, in virtue of His eternity.... If this were so, if this and therefore abstract non-temporality were the truth about eternity, it would be far too akin to time, indeed it would be only an image in the mirror of our reflection."[18] Time and eternity conceived as polar opposites is a modernist notion reminiscent of Feuerbach's image of God as merely a reflection of human self-willing.

> Feuerbach would wish us only to perceive and acknowledge that the name of "God," in which all man's highest, worthiest and most beloved names are concentrated, actually first sprang from the human heart, and that religion is thus in the deepest sense concerned with man himself; he would have us perceive and acknowledge that with God it is a question of man's own will for life, and not of a second, different thing in opposition to it. "God, as the quintessence of all realities or perfections, is nothing else but the quintessence, comprehensively summarized for the assistance of the limited individual, of the qualities of the human species, scattered among men, and manifesting themselves in the course of world history."[19]

God is free, constant and eternal, and therefore has power over time. Moreover, because the triune God can experience time there is a genuine duration of beginning, succession and end, as threefold but inseparable.[20] God is supra-temporal (both pre-temporal and post-temporal), co-temporal, and in-temporal, or rather God was and will be, both past and future clothed in God's eternality. "He gives *us* time by creating and preserving time. He takes time to Himself *for us* by Himself becoming temporal."[21]

For Barth, time is conceived in this threefold but interconnected manner and is contingent on the God of creation who created time. The later Barth makes room for Christian hope, arguing that the inbreaking of the kingdom is a divine event rather than a human accomplishment. The inbreaking of the kingdom "is absolutely unexpected and inconceivable. It comes down directly from above and beaks through the level of all that has taken place thus far. It thus demands and creates freedom for human thought and volition in a new dimension."[22] The kingdom introduces the *novum* into the world that is given in creation. For Barth, this inbreaking is

---

18. Barth, *CD* II/1, 612; as quoted in Busch, *Great Passion*, 268.
19. Barth, *Protestant Thought*, 521.
20. Busch, *Great Passion*, 269.
21. Barth, *CD* II/1, 618; as quoted in Busch, *Great Passion*, 269.
22. Barth, *CL*, 235.

a radical and total break in which the kingdom turns the world on its head, so to speak:

> The kingdom is revealed in this call [to discipleship]; the kingdom which is among the kingdoms of this world, but which confronts and contradicts and opposes them; the *coup d'état* of God proclaimed and accomplished already in the existence of the man Jesus.... But always, it will set forth the kingdom of God drawn near, and therefore the greatest, the only and definitive break in the world and its history as it has already taken place in Jesus Christ and cannot now be healed.... But in this onslaught it is a matter of God's destruction, accomplished in the existence of the Son of Man, of all the so-called "given factors," all the supposed natural orders, all the historical forces, which with the claim of absolute validity and worth have obtruded themselves as authorities.[23]

Although the kingdom is already here in this world through Christ, it cannot be created, achieved, accomplished, or established through any human activity or work, but the sole activity of God. "It is not men, or any man, who can make the break with these given factors and orders and historical forces.... It is the kingdom, the revolution, of God which breaks, which has already broken them. Jesus is their Conqueror."[24]

In the section titled "Thy Kingdom Come" in *The Christian Life*, Barth fleshes out his view of the kingdom. The coming kingdom is not to be thought of as something happening solely in the future but is already inaugurated in the Christ event.

> The future, the world to come, the last thing to which the petition undoubtedly looks, has already encountered those who call upon God in it here in the present, in this world. It already stands before their eyes, knowable and known by them, as the first thing. It is before them as they know it to be already behind them.... Thus it is already an event here and now but is still to be awaited then and there. They are near to it but distant.... Both as future, world to come, and last thing—but also as present, this world, and first thing—it is the new thing of God which is not in their hand or power, so that even as it takes place before their eyes they must call upon God for it to take place.[25]

---

23. Barth, *CD* IV/2, 543–544.
24. Ibid.
25. Barth, *CL*, 247.

For Barth, the coming of the Lord is "for the justification and redemption of individuals in judgment; for the end and new beginning of the cosmos; for the kingdom as the last thing corresponding to the first which was in the counsel of God before all times. . . . For everything was really to be expected from the risen Jesus. He could not possibly be known only as the One who has come and was present. As the One who had come and was present He had necessarily to be known also the One who comes."[26] The coming kingdom is the coming of Jesus Christ in time, the future *parousia* of Christ found in his proclamation.[27] The Easter event, both the cross and resurrection of Christ Jesus, is the dawning of the new creation and peace on earth in which the kingdom is both present and future.[28]

However, Barth includes Pentecost in the unfolding of the kingdom. In the Easter event the disciples looked forward to "the future of his completed history,"[29] but integrally related to the Spirit's outpouring. Hopeful expectation "still takes place in Christians up to our own day, in virtue of the gift and in the doing of the work of the Holy Spirit. . . . Without reference to Easter and Pentecost, it is impossible to give an answer, at least in the New Testament sense, to the question of the possibility of the turning which took place for and in the New Testament community from the past history of Jesus Christ and the coming of God's kingdom to their future."[30] What was fulfilled in Christ at Easter and made real to the apostolic community in Pentecost is the promise of its future fulfillment. The One who has come and the one in whom we believe is the One in whom we hope in eschatological expectation.[31]

Easter, Pentecost, and *eschaton* then constitute a threefold eschatological continuum, which constitute the last days.[32] Barth writes,

> According to the New Testament, the return of Jesus Christ in the Easter event is not yet as such His return in the Holy Ghost and certainly not His return at the end of the days. Similarly His return in the Easter event and at the end of days cannot be dissolved into His return in the Holy Ghost, nor the Easter event and the outpouring of the Holy Spirit into His last coming. In all of these we have to do with the one new coming of Him who

---

26. Barth, *CD* III/2, 487.
27. Barth, *CL*, 249.
28. Ibid., 237.
29. Ibid., 255.
30. Ibid., 256.
31. Busch, *Great Passion*, 283.
32. Bolt, "Exploring Karl Barth's Eschatology," 224.

> came before. But if we are to be true to the New Testament, none of these three forms of His new coming, including the Easter event, may be regarded as its only form. The most that we can say is that a particular glory attaches to the Easter event because here it begins, the Easter event being the primal and basic form in which it comes to be seen and grasped in its totality.[33]

The problem of the delayed *parousia* is overcome as a misunderstanding when one realizes that there is a threefold eschatological coming of Christ. Easter and Pentecost constitute the first two forms of the *parousia* and nourish Christian hope as anticipation. They point to a third form, which in the consummation and final *parousia* of Christ, which will be at the end of time because "there is no history in time that can end except in him."[34] For Barth, the unity of the threefold *parousia* reflects the perichoretic unity of the triune God, whose work in reconciling the world in Christ in the *parousia* (i.e., threefold presence) is the work of each of the triune persons acting in perichoretic unity as Creator, Reconciler, and Redeemer, or to use more traditional language Father, Son, and Holy Spirit.[35]

One final point before moving on is that the eschatological fulfillment of the kingdom includes more than human beings and a world defined by their social and political interactions, but conveys the "new creation." Through the death and resurrection of Christ, the old passes and the new has come, but not through its annihilation but through healing.

> The old, the former thing, has passed away: the new has come, has grown, has been created. It is "in Christ"—the Crucified and Risen—and Christ is in it. In his death its death and that of the world is, in fact, already past, and in His life its own life and that of the future world is before it. . . . This means that the event of the end of the world which took place once and for all in Jesus Christ is the presupposition of the old man, and the event of the beginning of the new world which took place once and for all in Jesus Christ is the goal of the new man, and because the goal, therefore the truth and power of the sequence of human existence as it moves towards this goal.[36]

The new creation will not destroy the old for it was deemed "good" by God. Rather, the new will destroy the dark and chaotic powers that threaten

---

33. Barth, *CD* IV/3, 294.
34. Busch, *Great Passion*, 284–85.
35. Bolt, "Exploring Karl Barth's Eschatology," 224.
36. Barth, *CD* IV/1, 311–12.

Part III—Renewing Christian Doctrine

creation.[37] Yet the new is not merely a return to some idyllic pre-Adamic state. God's creation is an external expression of the covenant that will find its completion in the *eschaton* at which point the chaotic powers that threaten creation will be destroyed. Thus all creation will be made new as the coming *parousia* conquerors all opposing and corrupting forces.[38]

The Eschatological Future of Christ

The character of Christian hope and its eschatological consummation in the kingdom to come is not an abstraction of a general future for humanity, but Jesus Christ's eschatological *parousia* in whom the people of God and all creation will participate in divine glory and thus rightly named God's kingdom. Christ is the one who will bring about the eschatological day as a sovereign act in which the history of the messianic Christ is taken up into the day of the Lord.

Barth's Christological affirmation is that "Jesus Christ *is* our hope—that what Christians mean by 'hope' receives its substance from Jesus Christ. For Jesus Christ is no mere 'means or instrument or channel,' the mediating occasion of 'some general gift': rather, he is 'the One in whom the Christian is summoned to hope.' More specifically, Jesus Christ is our hope because in him is the promise of the world's future, a promise which is at the same time a summons to acts of witness to that future."[39] For Barth, "The proclamation of the kingdom of God by Jesus, however, is not the proclamation of a reality and differing from himself as its Proclaimer, from his being and life. In the history of his prophecy, the reality and truth of the kingdom are not just indicated in the sense that there is a coming somewhere behind and above his own words and works and suffering and death, he himself being merely a precursor."[40] Jesus does not merely announce the kingdom that is to come, but *is* his kingdom in which he as the full manifestation of God is fully present.

> The mystery of the proclamation of Jesus Christ himself, however, is that in officiating as the prophet and preacher of the gospel of God (Mk. 1:14), of the King and Lord of his kingdom, he himself is the Son of God, so that his person and work and word cannot be distinguished from the person and work and word of God; and God's kingdom is his, the kingdom of the Son no less

---

37. Barth, *CD* III/1, 109–10.
38. Busch, *Great Passion*, 281.
39. Webster, *Barth's Moral Theology*, 83; cf. *CD* IV/1, 116.
40. Barth, *CL*, 249–50.

than the Father.... Not just in virtue of his coming but... 'in, with, and under' (cf. Luther's Large Catechism) his coming, the kingdom of God comes in full present reality.[41]

For Barth, this means that in the eschatological glory of Christ salvation reaches its fullness. Jesus Christ is the eschatological focus.[42] The kingdom's "presence and influence characterise the creation which in the death of Jesus Christ and in virtue of His resurrection from the dead is already reconciled to God, but is not yet redeemed and consummated by His coming in glory, i.e., in His final, definitive and universal revelation."[43] Instead of focusing on some futuristic scenario, Barth maintains that "we must concentrate strictly on the one thing by which Christian eschatology distinguishes itself from all other possible eschatologies, on the *one* person, the *new* person, in whom God 'was and is and is to come' (Rev. 4:8)."[44] "Jesus Christ is the Prophet who knows and proclaims the will of God which is done in His existence. The Synoptic statement that 'the kingdom of God is at hand,' materially identical with the Johannine 'I am'... is the sum and substance of His prophetic message and therefore of the knowledge mediated by Him."[45]

The eschatological cannot simply mean "the end" or "the last things" as the final stage of the *parousia*, but is the "reconciliation accomplished and fulfilled" in Christ's death through which his time has come and brought an end to all other times. According to Barth, world time has passed in the death of Christ, but has brought the dawn of God's time through which humanity is reconciled to God.[46] Yet the old world continues to exist and so we experience the end of our time as not yet. Thus there is a future dimension in eschatology, "wholly dependent on and comes from the 'End' manifest in the death of Jesus Christ. Clearly this cannot mean that it is simply Christ's 'past somehow prolonged into and determining the present,' but it is Jesus Christ himself who, in the power of his reconciling life, is our Future, the Coming One. We can therefore say that the eschatological perspective is based on the Christological and means quite simply the Coming Again of Jesus Christ as the One who came."[47]

---

41. Ibid., 250.
42. Bolt, "Exploring Karl Barth's Eschatology," 217.
43. Barth, *CD* IV/3, 165–86.
44. Barth, *Letters, 1961–68*, 235, as cited by Bolt, "Exploring Karl Barth's Eschatology," 218.
45. Barth, *CD* IV/3, 180–81.
46. Ibid., 295.
47. Thompson, *Christ in Perspective*, 126–27.

Christian hope does not draw its sustenance then from some abstract vision of the future or from potentialities of human possibilities, but from a definitive past in Christ, who is the future hope of the world. "Hope in the promise of God is, as it were, circumscribed on the one side by the finished work of Jesus Christ (focused in the resurrection as the climax of the incarnational and paschal mystery) and on the other side by the coming parousia."[48] The life and history of Christ culminating in his death and resurrection constitute hope for the world, but shapes true reality awaiting its consummation. The *parousia* is the coming again, the full revelation and manifestation of the power of the finished work of Jesus.[49]

> Jesus Christ defines our time as the time between his resurrection and his return, and therefore, as the time of promise. As the time of promise, it is therefore the time in which hope is not only one possible attitude among many dispositions of humanity, but the human attitude and action which is most in accordance with how things really are in the world. Hope is required of us because hope corresponds to what really *is*. And reality, what really *is*, is constituted by Jesus' history—constituted as a history reconciled to God and therefore appointed to hope for its full redemption in the coming manifestation of Jesus' glory.[50]

Thompson is only partially correct, however, when he claims that from our perspective the eschatological events of the resurrection and *parousia* are two events, but for the eternal God is one single event.[51] There is a threefold form of the eschatological *parousia*, which takes its bearing from the death and resurrection of the Easter event, the outpouring of the Spirit in the event of Pentecost, and the final consummation of the event of the *parousia*. All are manifestations of the revelation of Christ by the Spirit of God.

The Eschatological Orientation of Christ's Saving Work

For Barth, divine action is primarily saving action, "directed to the articulation of God's purposes for and realizing salvation." All other theological loci are "'grounded and determined in the fact that God is the God of the election of His grace' (*CD* II/2, 14)."[52] In reaction to abstract attempts to

---

48. Webster, *Barth's Moral Theology*, 83.
49. Thompson, *Christ in Perspective*, 127.
50. Webster, *Barth's Moral Theology*, 84.
51. Thompson, *Christ in Perspective*, 127.
52. Gunton, "Salvation," 143–44.

relate Christology to soteriology, Barth determines to develop a theology of reconciliation in the concrete person and work of Christ. As Gunton states, "The person of Christ is his saving work, so that an adequately articulated Christology will also be a theology of salvation."[53]

Although Barth prefers the doctrine of reconciliation over soteriology as his organizing principle, he rejects the traditional terminology established in Protestant dogmatics because it is concerned only with "a temporal sequence, in which the Holy Spirit does His work here and now in men," which divided the *ordo salutis* in justification, sanctification, vocation, regeneration, conversion, union and glorification.[54] However, Barth makes a distinction between objective soteriology (justification, sanctification, and calling), on the one hand, and subjective soteriology (faith, love, and hope), on the other. Moreover, reconciliation is thoroughly Christocentric, corresponding to the hypostatic union. Jesus Christ as "very God" notes the humiliation of God in Christ and establishes his priestly office. Christ as "very man" notes his exaltation and establishes his kingly office. The former corresponds to justification and the latter to sanctification. Jesus Christ as the "God-man" is unique and establishes his priestly office and relates to calling. "The downward [humiliation] and upward [exaltation] of Jesus Christ involved in this one divine action the justification and sanctification of man, i.e., the divine verdict and the divine direction."[55] Thus Barth argues, "The action of God in His reconciliation of the world with Himself in Jesus Christ is unitary. It consists of different 'moments' with a different hearing. It accomplishes both the justification and the sanctification of man, for it is itself both the condescension of God and the exaltation of man in Jesus Christ. But it accomplishes the two together. The one is wholly and immediately with the other."[56]

Subjective soteriology (faith, love, and hope) as outlined in IV/3 denotes the application of the work of Christ in the believer, which has an as "yet-to-appear" quality corresponding to the objective work finished in Christ (justification-faith, sanctification-love, calling-hope). The objective takes place in Christ but must be appropriated for the believer through the hearing of the Word. It is definitely not a human work. Barth states,

> When we say justification, sanctification and calling, on the one side we are already expanding the relevance of what was done in Jesus Christ, but on the other we are explaining only

---

53. Ibid., 144.
54. Barth, *CD* IV/2, 502.
55. Klooster, "Aspects," 8.
56. Ibid.

the objective relevance of it and not its subjective apprehension and acceptance in the world and by us men. We might say, we are dealing with the ascription but not the appropriation of the grace of Jesus Christ, or with what has taken place in Him for the world as such, but not for the Christian in particular. In the Christian there is an appropriation of the grace of Jesus Christ or with what has taken place in Him for the world as such, but not for the Christian in particular. In the Christian there is an appropriation of the grace ascribed to all men in Jesus Christ, a subjective apprehension of what has been done for the whole world in the happening of the atonement.[57]

The common appellation leveled against Barth is that he has confused the atonement and justification,[58] and correspondingly applied objective activity of God in the event of the cross to all, thereby opening himself up to accusations of universalism. Space does not permit a full discussion of this debate except to say that his emphasis on the appropriation of grace by the particular Christian suggests otherwise. The objective and subjective parts in Barth's soteriology resists universalistic claims. Instead, Barth "sought to take with full seriousness the biblical teaching which affirmed that election is 'in Christ.' And that 'in Christ' takes us to the very heart of God, which is saving being."[59] "God is none other than the One who in his Son or Word elects Himself, and in and with Himself elects His people."[60]

Because Christian hope is centered in and through Christ Jesus, salvation is conceived as an eschatological work in which Christ's redeeming and reconciling activity culminating in his death and resurrection finds its fruition in the *eschaton*. "Jesus Christ is the beginning, middle and end of God's electing and saving action, so that any account of Barth's theology of salvation must either begin here or, in some way, bring this into the centre. Salvation, eschatologically considered, means the completion of the purpose of election which takes its origin in the very eternal being of God."[61] Through Christ, the human being is pardoned and receives new status, but this status stands in proleptic tension with the eschatological future. "I was and still am the former man: man as wrongdoer. . . . But I am already and will be the latter man: the man whom God has elected and created for

---

57. Barth, *CD* IV/1, 147.
58. See Gunton, "Salvation," 148.
59. Ibid., 145.
60. Barth, *CD* II/2, 76.
61. Gunton, "Salvation," 145.

himself . . . the man who is not unrighteous but righteous before God."[62] Pardon is an eschatological reality of justification that is already spoken in the present with the double meaning that the human race as a whole has received a new status before God in the Christ event, but that this new status is also appropriated by the believer as an act of God in which we participate in the new life of Jesus' holiness, i.e., sanctification.[63] "What happens to Jesus, especially in the resurrection, is his coronation (*CD* IV/2, 292), but it is one that involves us all, in a movement that corresponds to it . . . But it is partly by anticipation. 'In Jesus Christ a Christian has already come into being, but in himself and his time he is always in the process of becoming' (*CD* IV/2, 307)."[64]

The Eschatological Work of the Spirit

At this point, it is important to note explicitly what has until now been implicit: the activity of the Spirit in the work of salvation, first in relation to Jesus Christ, and then to the incorporation of believers into Christ through the Spirit awaiting eschatological redemption.[65]

> The Holy Spirit liberated and commanded them to turn to that beginning and in so doing to turn to this end, thus entering into the Easter event and no less definitely and certainly than the first disciples seeing Jesus and God's kingdom in the future of his history and therefore in his revelation as the Son of God and the Lord of all creation. Apart from the Holy Spirit, apart from being liberated and empowered by him, no one has called Jesus Lord and no one can (1 Cor. 12:3). The Holy Spirit is the *forward* which majestically awakens, enlightens, leads, and impels, which God has spoken in the resurrection from the dead, which he has spoken and still speaks to the world of humanity; *forward* to the new coming of Jesus and the kingdom. The Spirit is the *Holy* Spirit because, coming from the Father and the Son, he is God himself in the same act in which in the Easter event he confessed his complete work in the history of Jesus Christ with the promise that he will confess it again universally and definitively.[66]

---

62. Barth, *CD* IV/1, 544.
63. Gunton, "Salvation," 148–50.
64. Ibid., 150.
65. Ibid., 152. Gunton believes Barth insufficiently emphasized the role of the Spirit.
66. Barth, *CL*, 256.

For Barth, as we have seen, the eschatological outworking of divine revelation is qualified by a threefold form incorporating the Easter, Pentecost and Consummation events, all of which are understood as "moments" in Christ's *parousia*. His threefold form allows him to include the activity of the Spirit in the *parousia* of Christ, not as an independent agent working for the eschatological, but in bringing forth Christ's kingdom reign.

Philip Rosato claims that the *parousia* is "one divine event which unfolds in three progressive stages: the resurrection of Jesus Christ, the promise and impartation of the Holy Spirit and the final coming of Jesus Christ in glory."[67] Each form is itself an eschatological event, but that the middle form is the time of the Spirit's work in and for the Christian community, a time of transition and therefore provisional, looking to its ultimate in the final glorification of Christ. The outpouring of the Spirit is therefore an important theological focus for Barth. It is the event that inaugurates the church as Christ's body and community of God, but in an eschatologically dynamic sense. The outpouring of the Spirit is a pledge that the community is with Christ in transition from the cross and resurrection to the final revelation of Christ. The Spirit mediates Christ to the community, guaranteeing that the ultimate is already at work in the community, and through the community to the world. The community finds its relational life through the Spirit, who mediates the divine encounter between God and humanity as well as one with another through the lordship of Jesus Christ, the God-man, who is the true image of godly relationship.[68]

George Hunsinger argues that for Barth "revelation," "reconciliation," and "redemption" are inseparable and take place in the history and work of Christ, but in their outworking over time is the saving work of the Spirit. Revelation imparts reconciliation, while reconciliation makes the truth of revelation known. Redemption, however, is the future of reconciliation so that reconciliation is redemption's ground and content, while redemption is reconciliation's goal. As a work of the Spirit, redemption is the "consummation of all things," "resurrection of the dead," and "eternal life in communion with God." From the perspective of redemption, the work of Christ serves the work of the Spirit, whereas from the perspective of reconciliation, the work of the Spirit serves the work of Christ.[69] "The presence and power of the Spirit are understood to attest what the incarnate Word of God has done for our salvation apart from us (*extra nobis*) (cf. *CD* IV/1, 211–83) and to mediate our participation in it by faith (*participato Christi*) (cf. *CD* IV/2,

---

67. Rosato, *Spirit as Lord*, 116.
68. Ibid., 116–18.
69. Hunsinger, *Disruptive Grace*, 178.

518, 526–33, 581–84). The Spirit who enabled Christ alone to accomplish our salvation as a finished work there and then is the very Spirit who enables us to participate in it and attest to it here and now."[70]

Thus the Holy Spirit works salvation in and through the believer and community of faith. Before moving on, however, a few words need to be said about Barth's theology of baptism with the Spirit since this doctrine will pertain to Pentecostal notions of the Spirit's work. The entire volume of *CD* IV/4 is devoted to two doctrines: baptism in the Spirit and baptism in water. Barth's theology of Spirit baptism is understood as the moment in the initiation of faith when the Spirit establishes "the epitome of the entire Christian life, founded on the divine turning toward human beings."[71] The Spirit witnesses to and makes present the resurrection of the crucified Christ as an objective reality now made real in us by a divine change.[72] "When he [God] is heard and received, when human beings are renewed and awakened to their new life in him, when they respond in obedient gratitude to his grace, this takes place as the work of the Holy Spirit. The *telos* of *de jure* participation in Christ is de facto participation in Christ, and the Holy Spirit is the teleological power of this transition."[73] The baptism of the Spirit, for Barth, is the act of God on and in the new believer that initiates that person to new life, placing her in the family of God so that she may participate in God.

According to John Webster, Barth's theology of Spirit baptism is multidimensional. Baptism of the Spirit is first the work of the Spirit in founding the Christian life and is always and integrally bound up in the perfect work of Christ. The two are inseparable. Secondly, Spirit baptism effects grace. "Baptism with the Holy Spirit is effective, causative, even creative action on man and in man."[74] Thirdly, because Spirit baptism has brought divine change in the human it deserves our unconditional gratitude. Fourthly, Spirit baptism has ecclesial dimensions in which the new Christian "discovers himself to be the companion, fellow and brother of these others, bound to them for better or for worse."[75] Finally, baptism with the Holy Spirit is eschatological. When one is baptized by the Spirit one is oriented toward the future, not as a journey of progress, but one who exists in miraculous newness in anticipation of the future revelation of Christ.[76] Moreover, baptism of

---

70. Ibid., 181.
71. Richardson, *Reading Karl Barth*, 183.
72. Webster, *Barth's Ethics of Reconciliation*, 139–40.
73. Neder, *Participation in Christ*, 82.
74. Barth, *CD* IV/3.1, 34.
75. Ibid., 37.
76. Webster, *Barth's Ethics of Reconciliation*, 140–44.

the Spirit is sacramental, with the proviso that for Barth this is understood predominantly as an act of Christ, and only secondarily as ecclesial. "Barth ascribes to Spirit baptism a sacramental quality, but this is precisely because the Spirit is the Spirit of Christ, whose sole gracious agency is consistently affirmed by Barth."[77] Thus for Barth, Spirit baptism is an unmediated divine act whereas water baptism is our obedient response to divine grace.[78] Christ is the sacrament of God and the Spirit mediates Christ to the world and to us through the baptism of the Spirit, thereby affecting the transition to participate in Christ.[79]

These last two points are of interest and, as we will see, are taken up by Pentecostal Frank Macchia in order to construct a Pentecostal theology of Spirit baptism. Barth clearly ascribes baptism of the Spirit to the initiation of faith as a divine act, but also sees its final completion in the *eschaton*. In the context of his threefold eschatology baptism with the Spirit also coincides with the outpouring of the Spirit. In a way analogous to the threefold but unified *parousia* can we speak of differing "moments" along the eschatological continuum of Spirit baptism? If so, then potential space is created for a theological framework for the Pentecostal doctrine of Spirit baptism, not as a separate act of grace, but as a threefold act of divine change and divine sending, already instilled in the believer and the church but not yet realized in its fullness. The problem of subsequence is ameliorated in that from our perspective God acts in different moments in time, but from God's perspective there is one act from Easter, through Pentecost, to the final consummation. The benefit for Pentecostal theology is it brings unity to Spirit baptism as an experience of power and/or purity, and the reception of the Spirit in Christian initiation and its sacrament of water baptism, thereby affirming the one Lord, one faith, one baptism credo of Eph 4:5. Moreover, and in conjunction with the prior point, if Spirit baptism is sacramental in nature, that is, the Spirit mediates the presence of God to the community of faith in and through Christ, then the Pentecostal emphasis on Spirit baptism and its *glossolalic* indicator points to God acting by the Spirit of Christ in the body of Christ, creating, sustaining and empowering the community for acts of service in the world as a sign of the kingdom.

---

77. Richardson, *Reading Karl Barth*, 193.

78. On this last point, Richardson critiques Webster's historic Reformed Anglican position on infant baptism, because Webster insists that Barth's view of adult baptism as obedient confession is logically inconsistent. However, Richardson argues that Barth's position is entirely consistent within the span of *CD* as a whole, in order to argue that Barth can make potential contributions to Baptist, Pentecostal, and Charismatic theologies. Richardson, *Reading Karl Barth*, 177–208.

79. Neder, *Participation in Christ*, 83.

Constructive Approaches to Pentecostal Eschatology

As we turn to Pentecostal eschatology a number of caveats need to be expressed up front. The first is that Pentecostalism as a movement is diverse. Although much of the Pentecostal movement has been influenced by popular versions of fundamentalist dispensationalism with its sevenfold understanding of history, insistence of a secret Rapture that takes the true church out of the world, the unfolding seven year Tribulation, coming of the Antichrist, and Battle of Armageddon, it is not altogether clear whether early Pentecostals or Pentecostal intellectuals hold to such a view. My own research into early Pentecostal eschatology suggests that the "latter rain" eschatology of the early movement was more diverse and that the charismatic outpouring of the Spirit at the dawn of the twentieth century was viewed as the penultimate anticipation of the coming King preparing the church and its workers for the manifestation of the kingdom. Early Pentecostals were as willing to talk about the second coming in covenantal or inaugural terms as dispensational.[80] When dispensational terminology was used it as often referred to a threefold dispensation stemming from John Wesley and especially John Fletcher's theology, as to the sevenfold dispensation of Fundamentalism.[81] Even into the middle years as fundamentalist dispensationalism was taking root in at least one Pentecostal denomination, the Assemblies of God, dispensational eschatology had to be modified to make room for the activity of the Spirit in all the charismatic dimensions; otherwise Pentecostalism would have to adopt the cessation of the Spirit's gifts that is core to dispensational theology.[82] A new generation of Pentecostals has emerged that is engaging the theological issues of the day, rejecting dispensationalism in favor of an inaugural eschatology of promise-fulfillment, inauguration-completion, or the already-not yet of the kingdom. As such, contemporary Pentecostal intellectuals, at least, have rejected the futuristic focus of fundamentalist dispensationalism as incoherent in Pentecostal theology and are attempting to reinterpret the tradition in light of current biblical and theological scholarship.[83]

With such a diverse movement how can we engage in a dialogue between Pentecostal eschatology and the theology of Barth? Walter Hollenweger has suggested that the first decade represents the "heart" of Pentecostal

---

80. Althouse, *Spirit of the Last Days*; Althouse, "'Left Behind'—Fact or Fiction"; Myland, *Latter Rain Covenant*, 1ff.

81. Dayton, *Theological Roots of Pentecostalism*, 51–52, 149–53.

82. Jacobsen, "Knowing the Doctrines of Pentecostals," 91.

83. See Althouse and Waddell, *Perspectives in Pentecostal Eschatologies*.

spirituality, rather than its "underdeveloped infancy."[84] Consequently, if one keeps to its heart then newer streams of Pentecostal thought and life are legitimate expressions. Certainly the movement has entered a "new intellectual stage" in which Pentecostal theologians take their bearings from the "heart" of Pentecostalism and not from specific doctrinal assertions made by denominational authorities.

Starting from Hollenweger's appraisal, Church of God theologian Steven Land constructively reworks Pentecostal eschatology with an eye to Barth's theology of prayer as well as Moltmann's theology of hope. Proposing an inaugural rather than dispensational understanding of the kingdom, Land claims,

> The coming and mission of Jesus and that of the Spirit was couched in the language of promise and fulfillment in such a way that fulfillment carried an overflow or residue of promise which had personal and global historical implications. Each "already" of fulfillment carried within it the "not yet" of consummation. The waiting for Christ became waiting in Christ for his return. The waiting for the promised Spirit became waiting in the Spirit for the time when, by the Spirit, God would be all in all.[85]

Unfortunately the tension between the already/not yet has often been resolved prematurely in either an otherworldly escapism, such as fundamentalist dispensationalism's fascination with a "secret Rapture" that will snatch the remnant church out of this world and therefore abdicates the church's responsibility to this world as a sign of the kingdom, or a this-worldly accommodation in which the kingdom is aligned with the values and structures of this world but in a way that the church loses its prophetic voice.[86]

When turning to Pentecostal theology, Land argues that a Trinitarian view of the kingdom's inbreaking is such that "the presence of God who, as Spirit, is the agent of the inbreaking, soon-to-be consummated kingdom," which is "Christocentric precisely because it is pneumatic," and the Pentecostal soteriology of justification, sanctification and Spirit baptism integrates "righteousness, love and power in this apocalyptic movement of spiritual transformation."[87] Through apocalyptic passion the full gospel (in Land's case the fivefold gospel) integrates the presence and activity of Christ and the Spirit in the work of justification, sanctification, Spirit baptism and healing, which awaits its completion in anticipation of the eschatological

---

84. Hollenweger, *Pentecostals*, 551–52.
85. Land, *Pentecostal Spirituality*, 15.
86. Ibid.
87. Ibid., 23.

reign. Moreover, with the shift from postmillennialism to premillennialism in the broad contours of evangelical Christianity at the turn of the twentieth century, and the corresponding shift from a focus on love to power, from gradual to instantaneous views of personal and social transformation, Christ was not separated from the Spirit, but rather there was an infusion of the two.[88]

In other words, Land is adamant that Pentecostal theology has not shifted, or at least need not shift, to a focus on the Spirit by minimizing Christ, but that the focus on the Spirit brings Christ to his rightful place in the forefront of the saving activity of God, because the Spirit reveals Christ. However, Land's Christology is typical of Pentecostalism on the whole in its emphasis on the "work" of Jesus in salvation. In Pentecostal circles, this functional Christology which emphasizes the victory of Christ in his overcoming of sin and helplessness through the "supernatural" inbreaking of Jesus in concrete history has the tendency to ignore the ontology of Christ—Jesus Christ, the God-man, is fully God and fully human. The danger within Pentecostal and evangelical circles is a docetic tendency, which emphasizes the divinity of Christ who acts in miraculous victory, but in a way that minimizes his humanity in the incarnation and therefore the role of creation as the outworking of God's covenant. Barth's Christology is important here because he clearly establishes the objective reality of Christ's hypostatic being in condescension and exaltation, but in a way that does not prioritize natural theology over revelation of the Word. In other words, Barth's theology could help Pentecostals strengthen their Christology, while maintaining their accents on the eschatological relevance of theology and enervation of life and the church through the work of the Spirit.

Assemblies of God theologian Frank Macchia, likewise contemplates the role of eschatology in Pentecostalism and its relation to the Pentecostal distinctive of Spirit baptism. Macchia is perhaps most influenced by Barth's theology among Pentecostal theologians, having studied at the University of Basel under Jan Milic Lochmann and, like Barth, found a common interest in the kingdom theology of Pietist pastors Johann and Christoph Blumhardt. Barth commits an entire chapter of *Protestant Theology in the Nineteenth Century* to the theology of Johann Christoph Blumhardt, despite the fact that he was a pastor rather than a theologian, and makes extensive reference to Blumhardt in *CD* IV.[89] The use of the Blumhardts is significant because it suggests a Pentecostal influence on Barth. With an emphasis on healing and revival, the Blumhardts are considered by some scholars to be the be-

---

88. Ibid., 63.
89. Barth, *Protestant Theology*, 629–39; cf. *CD* IV/3.1, 168–71.

ginning of the Pentecostal outbreak in Europe.[90] Macchia, however, draws from the Blumhardts' theology of the kingdom to argue that the kingdom is already partially present in history in the incarnation, death and resurrection of Jesus Christ, but that we must wait its coming in the future. However, the Blumhardts included that outpouring of the Spirit in Pentecost as an inbreaking of the kingdom, which bestowed divine gifts, bringing victory over darkness, healing and liberation.[91] Johann also developed a theology in which "Jesus is Victor" after a two-year "battle" to exorcise evil spirits and bring healing to a woman named Gottliebin Dittus. From the battle came a theology of healing, which recognized human bondage and suffering in which Jesus and a new outpouring of the Spirit could bring healing and liberation.[92] Thus Easter, Pentecost and the final *parousia* were "moments" in the eschatological "last days" and our responsibility to Christ and his kingdom demanded both patient "waiting" for the kingdom to come as a sovereign act of God, and "hurrying" to spread the kingdom through help for the suffering and healing for the sick.[93] Yet healing included within it a cosmic dimension in which all creation would be redeemed.[94]

Curiously, the threefold unfolding of the kingdom in which Jesus Christ is victor is adapted by Barth, especially as he works out his theology of reconciliation in *CD* IV. Macchia uses the Blumhardts' eschatology to rework Pentecostal eschatology in which the kingdom is both present and future, in order to develop a social ethic of liberation and ecological responsibility in the cosmic renewal of creation as a function of healing and liberation, and especially to include the outpouring of the Spirit as the means by which the kingdom, as both present and future, comes. In *Baptized in the Spirit*, Macchia shifts away from his earlier stance on the priority of eschatology as the lens through which to interpret Pentecostalism and identifies the doctrine of Spirit baptism as *the* Pentecostal distinctive which is then eschatologically conceived.[95] The emphasis on the outpouring of the Spirit as an eschatological event in the Blumhardts and in Barth provides him with the framework to rework Spirit baptism. However, while giving priority to Spirit baptism, he redefines the Pentecostal doctrine along an eschatological plane of the already but yet-to-come baptism of the Spirit, which is not exhausted by Christian initiation or church essence. Barth, as with much of

---

90. Moltmann, "Foreword"; Anderson, *Introduction to Pentecostalism*, 24, 30.
91. Macchia, *Spirituality and Social Liberation*, 73–74.
92. Ibid., 64–69.
93. Ibid., 88–90.
94. Ibid., 82–83.
95. Macchia, *Baptized in the Spirit*, 11–18.

historic Christianity, sees the initiation of faith as the baptism of the Spirit, the pouring out of the Spirit into the life of the new creature. For Barth, the baptism of the Spirit is followed by the sacrament of water baptism, which is the obedient human response to God's gracious election.[96] Importantly, for Macchia, Spirit baptism "points to redemption through Christ as substantially pneumatological and eschatological . . . given at Pentecost but fulfilled in the final act of salvation at Christ's return," allowing the church "to participate in, and bear central witness to, the final sanctification of creation."[97] Spirit baptism is the foundational doctrine that connects Christian initiation as the act of Christ, the Pentecostal outpouring of the Spirit as the presence of the kingdom already, and the final consummation of the kingdom of God. New life in Christ "allows one to participate already in a Spirit baptism that is yet to come. It is always present and coming, energizing and encountering. The Pentecostal belief in the connection between Spirit baptism and sanctification, on the one hand, and between Spirit baptism and the latter rain of the Spirit at the end of the age, on the other. . . ."[98]

Macchia strengthens his pneumatological position further by arguing that the Spirit is the kingdom. Drawing on Gregory of Nyssa, Macchia asserts, "the Son is the King and the Spirit is the kingdom in the fulfillment of the Father's will. Through Christ as the Spirit Baptizer, the Spirit brings creation into the Kingdom of the King by indwelling all things with divine presence so as to deliver creation from the reign of death unto the reign of life."[99] Thus, the kingdom and the new creation is future in a way that impinges on the present and brings meaning to the past. One can see hints of Barth when Macchia says, "This ongoing transformation involves a sense of continuum abiding in God and God in us as God indwells us penultimately as a foretaste of the final indwelling of all things. Decisively inaugurated in the life, death and resurrection of Jesus, the kingdom of God becomes the dynamic within history through the outpouring of the Spirit that is directed toward the divine indwelling in all of creation so that all things might be conformed to Christ's image."[100] Spirit baptism becomes critical in this eschatological construal. Spirit baptism is a "liberating force," "the renewal of creation," "anticipation of the final victory," "the will of the Father to indwell the creation through the Spirit . . ."[101]

96. Richardson, *Reading Karl Barth*, 182–85; cf. *CD* IV/4, 33–34.
97. Macchia, *Baptized in the Spirit*, 86.
98. Ibid., 87.
99. Ibid., 91.
100. Ibid., 97.
101. Ibid., 106–7.

As with Land, the kingdom is fundamentally a Christocentric reality:

> The kingdom of God is also the kingdom of Christ, because he is the one who is the incarnate Word and the chief bearer of the Spirit. He inaugurates the kingdom of God in his person and work as both the sanctified Son and the charismatic Christ. The transformative power of the kingdom, therefore, has a *Christoformistic* goal and direction. The field of the Spirit and of the kingdom is the field of the risen and ascended Christ's increasingly diverse presence. It is also the field of the crucified Christ, meaning that it is realized among us in the power of the risen Christ as we bear one another's burdens and reach out to others in solidarity with suffering victims everywhere.[102]

Jesus Christ is God incarnate, who as the suffering servant offering himself so that the eschatological reign of God may dawn in time, is also the eschatological King coming from the future to liberate creation from its bondage, instilling seeds and signs of the kingdom through the inbreaking activity of the Spirit who is poured out so the Christ may reign. To be baptized in the Spirit is to be baptized in, with, and by Christ so that we too may participate in and participate with God's liberative reign.

In one sense, Macchia appropriates Barth's threefold *parousia* in order to include the outpouring of the Spirit at Pentecost, when the disciples were baptized in the Spirit, as an eschatological event in the soteriological outworking of Christ's reconciliation. This is a major correlation that includes the outpouring of the Spirit as a significant event as the sending of the Spirit by Christ and the work of the Spirit to bring the world and all creation into the eschatological glory of Christ's reign. Macchia's work has made initial proposals for constructing, and has potential for further construction of a Pentecostal doctrine of Spirit baptism in an ecumenically nuanced way, which is able to highlight the event of Pentecostal as theologically important for our understanding of the person and work of Christ seeking eschatological fulfillment in the future. Curiously, the earlier Pentecostal view in the Assemblies of God was that "speaking in tongues" is the "initial physical sign" of the "*consummation* of the baptism in the Holy Spirit."[103] This articulation is, in my opinion, pregnant with eschatological meaning. Spirit baptism occurs in the initiation of faith (as with Barth and historic Christianity), but is fulfilled or consummated by the physical act of *glossolalia*. This view is a more open stance on the doctrine than current revisions that see it merely in evidentiary language. Macchia's view that baptism in the Spirit is

---

102. Ibid.
103. See Althouse, "The Ecumenical Significance of Canadian Pentecostalism."

indicative of the initiation of faith and a secondary act in empowerment is a faithful and theologically nuanced reading of the movement without holding to the problematic position of two acts of grace in the believer. However, Macchia also proposes a future eschatological fulfillment in which baptism of the Spirit sanctifies all creation as the eschatological fulfillment of Christ's *parousia*. As with Barth, Spirit baptism is seen as "moments" in time from a human perspective, but is one unitary act of grace from God's eternal perspective.

One final comment is that Barth, along with much of Reformed theology, is sorely lacking in a pneumatological foundation for dogmatics. Barth was acutely aware of this at the end of his life. Pentecostal theology has brought the person and work of the Spirit to the fore in much of Christianity, and it has the potential, at least, of rehabilitating the pneumatological lack, through the construction of a richer and more robust theology of Spirit—not as either Christ or the Spirit, but as both Christ and the Spirit. Constructing a richer pneumatology would necessarily include the eschatological focus—the kingdom for which the Spirit is working in order for the glorification of the Father and the Son.

Conclusion

Dialogue between Barth and Pentecostalism has the potential to nourish a mutual understanding of the fullness of the gospel of Jesus Christ. Barth's Christocentric focus on the Word shapes his entire theological project, but at the end he begins to think about the Spirit and how a theology of Spirit can sharpen his theology. Volume IV of the *CD* focuses predominantly on the saving work of faith, love and hope in which the Spirit mediates Christ to the world. The eschatological activity of Christ by the Spirit is through the threefold *parousia* of Easter, the outpouring of the Spirit at Pentecost and the final *parousia* at the end of time. The Pentecostal "full gospel" is likewise centered on Christ, in which the Spirit sent by Christ works to save, baptize, heal and manifest Christ's kingdom both now and in the future *parousia*. Although Pentecostals have been influenced by fundamentalist dispensationalism, the inaugural eschatology of Barth is helpful in allowing them to construct an eschatology that accents the role of the Spirit in the eschatological outworking of Christ. It also points to the Spirit's eschatological work in the saving activity of Christ as the redeeming and reconciling work of Christ through faith, love and hope. Baptism is both Christological and pneumatological in that Spirit baptism initiates the new creature into the body of Christ but for Pentecostals suggests further outworking of the

Spirit's activity for purity and power. Pentecostals also emphasize bodily healing and while Barth is aware of this through the healing ministry of the Blumhardts, he also draws out the implications of their healing theology to see creation itself as the locale of divine healing. In the end, the juxtaposition of Barth and Pentecostal theology is mutually beneficial for both partners and offers opportunities for further dialogue.

Bibliography

Althouse, Peter. "The Ecumenical Significance of Canadian Pentecostalism." In *Winds from the North: Canadian Contributions to the Pentecostal Movement*, edited by Michael Wilkinson and Peter Althouse, 55–78. Leiden: Brill, 2010.

———. "'Left Behind'—Fact or Fiction: Ecumenical Dilemmas of the Fundamentalist Millenarian Tensions within Pentecostalism." *Journal of Pentecostal Theology* 13 (2005) 187–207.

———. *Spirit of the Last Days: Pentecostal Theology in Conversation with Jürgen Moltmann*, edited by Peter Althouse, 9–60. New York: T. & T. Clark, 2003.

———. "Toward a Theological Understanding of the Pentecostal Appeal to Experience." *Journal of Ecumenical Studies* 38 (2001) 399–411.

Althouse, Peter, and Robby Waddell, eds. *Perspectives in Pentecostal Eschatologies*. Eugene, OR: Pickwick, 2010.

Anderson, Allan. *Introduction to Pentecostalism*. New York: Cambridge University Press, 2004.

Barth, Karl. *The Epistle to the Romans*. Translated by Edwyn C. Hoskyns. London: Oxford University Press, 1968.

———. *Letters, 1961–1968*. Edited by Jürgen Fangmeier and Hinrich Stoevesandt. Translated and edited by G. W. Bromiley. Grand Rapids: Eerdmans, 1981.

———. *Protestant Theology in the Nineteenth Century: Its Background and History*. Translated by Brian Cozens and John Bowden. Grand Rapids: Eerdmans, 2002.

Bolt, John. "Exploring Karl Barth's Eschatology: A Salutary Exercise for Evangelicals." In *Karl Barth and Evangelical Theology: Convergences and Divergences*, edited by Sung Wook Chung, 209–35. Grand Rapids: Baker Academic, 2006.

Busch, Eberhard. *The Great Passion: An Introduction to Karl Barth's Theology*. Translated by Geoffrey W. Bromiley. Grand Rapids: Eerdmans, 2004.

Dayton, Donald W. *The Theological Roots of Pentecostalism*. Grand Rapids: Asbury, 1987.

Gunton, Colin. "Salvation." In *The Cambridge Companion to Karl Barth*, edited by John Webster, 143–58. Cambridge: Cambridge University Press, 2000.

Hollenweger, Walter J. *The Pentecostals*. Translated by R. W. Wilson. Minneapolis: Fortress, 1972.

Hunsinger, George. *Disruptive Grace: Studies in the Theology of Karl Barth*. Grand Rapids: Eerdmans, 2000.

Jacobsen, Douglas. "Knowing the Doctrines of Pentecostals: The Scholastic Theology of the Assemblies of God, 1930–55." In *Pentecostal Currents in American Protestantism*, edited by Edith L. Blumhofer et al., 90–107. Urbana: University of Illinois Press, 1999.

Klooster, Fred H. "Aspects of the Soteriology of Karl Barth." *Bulletin of the Evangelical Theological Society* 2 (1959) 6–14.

Land, Steven J. *Pentecostal Spirituality: A Passion for the Kingdom*. Sheffield: Sheffield Academic, 1993.

Macchia, Frank D. *Baptized in the Spirit: A Global Pentecostal Theology*. Grand Rapids: Zondervan, 2006.

———. "Karl Barth Meets David du Plessis: A New Pentecost or a Theater of the Absurd?" *Pneuma: The Journal of the Society for Pentecostal Studies* 23 (2001) 5–8.

Part III—Renewing Christian Doctrine

———. *Spirituality and Social Liberation: The Message of the Blumhardts in the Light of Württemberg Pietism*. Metuchen, NJ: Scarecrow, 1993.

Moltmann, Jürgen. *The Coming of God: Christian Eschatology*. Translated by Margaret Kohl. Minneapolis: Fortress, 2006.

———. "Foreword." In *Spirit of the Last Days: Pentecostal Theology in Conversation with Jürgen Moltmann*. New York: T. & T. Clark, 2003.

Myland, D. Wesley. *Latter Rain Covenant*. Billings, MT: A. N. Trotter, 1910.

Neder, Adam. *Participation in Christ: An Entry into Karl Barth's Church Dogmatics*. Louisville: Westminster John Knox, 2009.

Richardson, Kurt A. *Reading Karl Barth: New Directions for North American Theology*. Grand Rapids: Baker Academic, 2004.

Robeck, Cecil M. *The Azusa Street Mission & Revival*. Nashville: Thomas Nelson, 2006.

Rosato, Philip J. *The Spirit as Lord: The Pneumatology of Karl Barth*. Edinburgh: T. & T. Clark, 1981.

Schner, George P. "The Appeal to Experience." In *Theology and Sexuality: Classic and Contemporary Readings*, edited by Eugene F. Rogers, 23–44. Malden, MA: Blackwell, 2002.

Thompson, John. *Christ in Perspective: Christological Perspectives in the Theology of Karl Barth*. Grand Rapids: Eerdmans, 1978.

Warrington, Keith. *Pentecostal Theology: A Theology of Encounter*. New York: T. & T. Clark, 2008.

Webster, John. *Barth's Ethics of Reconciliation*. Cambridge: Cambrige University Press, 1995.

———. *Barth's Moral Theology: Human Action in Barth's Thought*. Grand Rapids: Eerdmans, 1998.

———. "Introducing Barth." In *The Cambridge Companion to Karl Barth*, edited by John Webster, 2–8. Cambridge: Cambridge University Press, 2000.

Contributors

William J. Abraham (DD [h.c.], Asbury Theological Seminary, 2008; DPhil, Regent's Park College, Oxford University, 1977) is Albert Cook Outler Professor of Wesley Studies at Southern Methodist University's Perkins School of Theology. He is an ordained elder in the United Methodist Church and the author of numerous works, including *Crossing the Threshold of Divine Revelation* (2007) and *Canon and Criterion in Christian Theology* (1998).

Peter Althouse (PhD, University of St Michael's College at the University of Toronto) is Professor of Religion and Theology at Southeastern University, Florida. He has authored *Spirit of the Last Days: Pentecostal Eschatology in Conversation with Jürgen Moltmann* (2003) and *The Ideological Development of Power in Early American Pentecostalism* (2010), and coauthored, with Michael Wilkinson, *Catch the Fire: Soaking Prayer and Charismatic Renewal* (2014).

Kimlyn J. Bender (PhD, Princeton Theological Seminary) is Associate Professor of Theology at George W. Truett Theological Seminary of Baylor University. He is the author of *Karl Barth's Christological Ecclesiology* (2013) and coeditor of *Theology as Conversation: The Significance of Dialogue in Historical and Contemporary Theology* (2009).

Chris Boesel (PhD, Emory University) is Associate Professor of Christian Theology at Drew Theological School. He is author of *Risking Proclamation, Respecting Difference: Christian Faith, Imperialistic Discourse, and Abraham* (2008). He played varsity basketball for the Faith Academy Vanguards in Manila, Philippines, in 1979–80.

Eberhard Busch (ThD, University of Basel) was Professor of Reformed Theology at the University of Göttingen from 1986 to 2002. He worked as an assistant to Karl Barth from 1965 to 1968. He serves on the editorial board for the *Gesamtausgabe*, the collected works of Karl Barth, and is the author or editor of numerous works, including *Karl Barth: His Life from Letters and*

Autobiographical Texts (1976), *Karl Barth and the Pietists* (2004), and *The Great Passion: An Introduction to the Theology of Karl Barth* (2010).

Stina Busman Jost (PhD, Princeton Theological Seminary) is assistant professor of theology and culture at Bethel University in St. Paul, Minnesota. She earned a PhD in Religion and Society at Princeton Theological Seminary and has authored articles appearing in the *Princeton Theological Review*, as well as presenting at the annual Center for Barth Studies theological conference in Princeton, New Jersey. She is on the advisory board for the Gospel and Our Culture Network, and author of *Walking With the Mud Flower Collective: "God's Fierce Whimsy" and Dialogic Theological Method* (2014).

Christian T. Collins Winn (PhD, Drew University) is Professor of Historical and Systematic Theology and Chair of the Biblical and Theological Studies Department at Bethel University in St. Paul, Minnesota. His areas of research include the theology of Karl Barth, the history of Pietism, political theology, eschatology, and interfaith dialogue. He is author or editor of six volumes, including *"Jesus Is Victor!" The Significance of the Blumhardts for the Theology of Karl Barth* (2009) and, with Roger Olson, *Reclaiming Pietism* (forthcoming). He is coeditor of the Blumhardt Series and is an ordained minister in the American Baptist Churches (USA).

Terry L. Cross (PhD, Princeton Theological Seminary) is Dean of the School of Religion and Professor of Systematic Theology at Lee University (Tennessee). He is the author of *Dialectic in Karl Barth's Doctrine of God* (2001), and has worked with the Barth translation group at Princeton Theological Seminary to provide English translations of Barth's German and French conversations from 1959 to 1967 (*Gespräche*). Currently, he is working on an ecclesiology from a Pentecostal perspective.

Donald W. Dayton (PhD, University of Chicago) taught theology and ethics at North Park University, Northern Baptist Seminary, Drew University, and Azusa Pacific University before his retirement in 2006. He is the author or editor of numerous volumes, including *The Theological Roots of Pentecostalism* (1987); *The Variety of American Evangelicalism* (2001), with Robert K. Johnston; and *(Re)Discovering an Evangelical Heritage* (2014), with Douglas Strong.

John L. Drury (PhD, Princeton Theological Seminary) is Assistant Professor of Systematic Theology at Indiana Wesleyan University and an ordained minister in The Wesleyan Church. He is author of *The Resurrected God: Karl Barth's Trinitarian Theology of Easter* (2014).

Contributors

Peter Goodwin Heltzel (PhD, Boston University) is Associate Professor of Theology and Director of the Micah Institute at New York Theological Seminary. He is the author of *Resurrection City: A Theology of Improvisation* (2012), *Jesus and Justice: Evangelicals, Race and American Politics* (2008), and most recently, *Faith-Rooted Organizing: Mobilizing the Church in Service to the World* (2013), with Alexia Salvatierra. His edited volumes include *Mobilizing for the Common Good: The Lived Theology of John M. Perkins* (2013), with Charles Marsh and Peter Slade; and *Evangelicals and Empire* (2008), with Bruce Ellis Benson. An ordained minister in the Christian Church (Disciples of Christ), he serves as Associate Pastor of Evangelism at Park Avenue Christian Church. Inspired by Karl Barth's *Church Dogmatics*, he is currently writing a systematic theology that demonstrates the relevance of prophetic Christianity for the growing global movement for justice.

Joel D. Lawrence (PhD, Cambridge University) is the Senior Pastor of Central Baptist Church, St. Paul, Minnesota, and Faculty Associate at Bethel Seminary, St. Paul, Minnesota. His doctoral work at Cambridge focused on the theology of Dietrich Bonhoeffer. Lawrence is a Fellow of the Center for Pastor Theologians, Oak Park, Illinois, serves as the cochair of the "Bonhoeffer: Theology and Social Analysis" group of the American Academy of Religion, and is the bibliographer for the International Bonhoeffer Society English Language Section. Lawrence is the author of numerous articles and book chapters, as well as *Bonhoeffer: A Guide for the Perplexed* (2010).

Frank D. Macchia (ThD, University of Basel) is Professor of Christian Theology at Vanguard University. He was president of the Society for Pentecostal Studies and for more than a decade editor of the society's journal, *Pneuma*. He has also served on the Faith and Order Commission of the National Council of Churches. His most recent book is titled *Justified in the Spirit: Creation, Redemption, and the Triune God* (2010).

James Nelson (PhD, University of Aberdeen) was Professor of Theology at North Park University in Chicago. He received his PhD from King's College at University of Aberdeen, Scotland.

Kurt Anders Richardson (DTh, University of Basel) is an evangelical and Reformed theologian; co-founder of Society for Scriptural Reasoning and of the Comparative Theology Group in the AAR. He specializes in comparative and confessional theology as a professor of applied anthropology in the Graduate Institute of Applied Linguistics in Dallas where he co-leads the graduate program in Abrahamic Studies. He is the author of *Reading Karl Barth: New Directions for North American Theology* (2004).

Contributors

Kyle A. Roberts (PhD, Trinity Evangelical Divinity School) is Associate Professor of Public and Missional Theology at United Theological Seminary of the Twin Cities in New Brighton, Minnesota. Roberts is a Kierkegaard scholar, having published essays on Kierkegaard's use of the Bible and his influence on modern theology. He has also published essays on existentialism, Pietism, and the connection between eschatology and spirituality. His recent book is *Emerging Prophet: Kierkegaard and the Postmodern People of God* (2013); he is currently co-authoring a theological commentary on the gospel of Matthew.

Index

Arminian, 162–63, 166–76, 180, 182, 185–89

Baptism, 35, 72–73, 86, 96–98, 132, 144, 231–32, 237–52, 255–57, 271–79

Blumhardt, Christoph Friedrich, 12–13, 47, 50, 132–36, 139, 142–44, 217, 275–76, 280

Blumhardt, Johann Christoph Friedrich, 12, 50, 132–36, 139, 142–44, 217, 275–76, 280

Bultmann, Rudolph, 17, 26, 45, 52, 75, 80, 202

Calvin, John, 5–6, 8, 49, 72, 76, 81, 93, 95, 132, 198, 241, 244–45

Church, xxi–xxii, 7, 15, 21, 29, 35, 38–41, 46–60, 105, 112–13, 115, 118–28, 130–143, 150, 153–60, 164–79, 192–204, 206–27, 237–51, 273–77

Ecclesiology, xvii, xxi–xxii, 11, 56, 58–59, 121–23, 125, 130–135, 138, 142, 206–11, 217–27
Volkskirche, 38
Ecclesiolae in Ecclesia, 55–56, 140
Conventicle, 57

Election, xix, xx–xxii, 5, 8, 52, 91, 100–101, 118–19, 125, 162–63, 166–89, 230–236, 244, 266–68, 277

Double Predestination, 169, 176, 178, 182, 234

Predestination, xv, 169, 176 178, 182, 187, 234

Eschatology, xvii, xxi, 50, 60, 98, 134, 169, 172, 179–80, 182, 185–86, 189, 204, 207, 213–18, 222–23, 227, 254–79

Epistemology, ix, xvii–xviii, 16, 151, 154, 157–60, 167, 173

Ethics, xvii, 5, 72, 78, 81–82, 99, 135, 141, 170–171, 208, 230–231, 248, 251
Social Ethics, xvii, 40–41, 99, 131–42, 217–27, 248, 255, 258, 263, 275–76
Social Justice, 24, 40–41, 60, 117, 132–43, 141–43, 217–27

Evangelism, 5, 10, 39–40, 70, 126, 208–9, 225, 285

Francke, August Hermann, 47, 49, 59, 63

Gospel, 7–8, 30, 34–36, 40–41, 101, 106, 110, 118, 141–42, 156–62, 163–75, 187–89, 208, 210–227, 239–40, 246–48, 256–59, 279

Grace, xvi, 5, 8–13, 25–27, 31–36, 61, 73–74, 84, 93–94, 97–100, 124, 156–57, 196–203, 214, 219–23, 234–37, 241–47, 251, 268, 271–72, 279

Index

Holy Spirit, 11, 15, 29–32, 52–53, 72–73, 76–80, 86–88, 92–101, 108, 119, 122, 125, 128, 131–42, 153, 164–70, 184, 192–204, 215–18, 224, 226, 233, 235, 242–51, 255–57, 262–63, 266–80
    Pneumatology, xvii, 199, 279
Human Agency, 162, 167, 182, 186, 189
    "decision of faith", 34–36, 86, 97, 119, 157, 175
    Appropriation of salvation, xxi, 10, 92, 268

Jesus Christ, xviii, xix–xxii, 8–9, 11–13, 16, 23–24, 27–36, 38–41, 50–52, 60–61, 69–88, 91–101, 102, 108–13, 115–28, 131, 134–42, 153, 155–56, 163–89, 192–96, 200–202, 214–16, 219–20, 222, 224–27, 230–51, 255–79
    Christology, 4, 8–9, 11–12, 16, 52, 61, 71, 76, 108, 113, 134, 136, 169, 224, 231, 251–52, 258, 264–65, 267
    Christocentric, 4, 8–9, 11–12, 16, 27, 50, 52, 60–61, 123, 130, 142, 167–68, 173, 187, 200–201, 223, 230, 257–58, 265, 267, 274, 278
    Christomonism, 12, 97, 167–69, 231
Joseph, Josephology, xxi, 117–28
Justification, xvii, 5–8, 27, 58, 69, 75–76, 84, 93, 96, 102–5, 108–9, 112, 222, 262, 267, 268–69, 274

King, Jr. Martin Luther, 133, 140–141
Kingdom of God, xxi, 23–24, 38–41, 50, 60, 92, 101, 123, 130–143, 211–14, 217, 219–20, 222–27, 255, 257–65, 269–79
    Parables of the Kingdom, 138–41, 212–14

The Lord's Supper, 94, 144, 231–32, 237–52

Eucharist, 38, 250
Communion, xx, 83–86, 90, 130, 141, 178, 181, 184, 246–50, 270

Mary, Mother of Jesus, xxi, 117–24, 127, 236
Methodism, 13, 80, 103
Missiology, 210, 217
Mission, 40, 56, 59, 208–10, 213, 216–17, 220, 226
Missional, xxii, 206–11, 216–21, 225–27
Moltmann, Jürgen, 257–58, 274, 276

"New Birth", xv–xvii, xix, 30
Conversion, xviii, xix, 5, 22, 24, 26–28, 35–37, 39, 50, 71, 78, 93, 98, 100, 104, 108, 163, 187, 220

Orthodoxy, 5–6, 10, 14, 165
    Lutheran, 62, 165
    Protestant, xiii–xiv, xvii, xix, 14, 62–63, 103, 110, 165
    Reformed, xiii, xxii, 62, 162–63, 165–67, 169, 174–75, 180, 186–87

Prayer, xxi, 131–32, 135–39, 141–42, 149–54, 156–60
    The Lord's Prayer, 131–32, 134–39, 141–42
    Petition, 131–32, 135–37
Pentecostalism, xxii, 254–57, 273–74, 279
Pietism, xvi–xvii, xx, xxii, 5, 9–13, 20–33, 35, 37–38, 40–41, 45–54, 56, 58–63, 87, 95, 103, 132–35, 140, 165, 188, 208
    Erweckungsbewegung, 5, 20
    Gemeinschaftsbewegung, 10, 20
    Neupietismus, 5, 10

Reconciliation, 27, 33, 39, 31, 71, 76, 78, 91–94, 96–101, 108–10, 117, 134–35, 143, 189, 192, 212,

214–15, 217, 219, 221–22, 225, 265, 267, 270, 278
Atonement, 5, 87, 169, 172, 174, 176, 187–88, 219, 233, 239, 268
Resurrection, xix, xx, 16–18, 73, 97, 113, 134, 138, 141, 179, 188, 214, 233–34, 266, 268–71
Revelation, 16, 31–32, 47, 51, 53–54, 113, 153, 155–56, 158, 160, 167, 171, 173, 187, 192–96, 198, 200–203, 212–14, 234–35, 241–47, 252, 267–59, 265–66, 270–271

Sacrament, Sacramental, 6, 73, 230, 237–43, 245–52
Sanctification, 24–29, 100, 103–6, 108–9, 267, 274, 277
Holiness, 93, 98, 100, 269
Schleiermacher, Friedrich, 10, 15, 46, 61, 155
Scripture, xv–xviii, 13–16, 26–27, 49, 52–57, 60, 102, 107, 112–13, 116–17, 128, 136, 150, 153, 155, 191–204, 241, 243, 246, 250
Inspiration, 15, 52–53, 106, 195, 200, 202
Inerrancy, xv–xvi, 13, 52–53, 167, 187

and Holy Spirit, 15, 52, 195, 199–200
Sin, 33–36, 41, 86–87, 104, 110, 128, 142, 169, 176–77, 179, 186, 219, 232
Soteriology, xviii, 11–12
apokatastasis ton panton, 33
Cosmic Salvation, 10, 91, 96, 276
Objectivism, xvii 10, 16, 22, 28, 31–32, 68, 86, 267
Subjectivism, 31, 68, 79–80, 267
Universalism, 268
Spener, Philipp Jakob, xvi, 47, 51, 53–58, 64, 140

Tholuck, August, 60–61, 70

Wesley, John, 63, 103–4, 273
Wesleyan, 102–7, 112–13
Witness, xxi, 16, 40, 99, 108–13, 123, 125, 131, 134, 141, 143, 185–86, 207, 211, 214–17, 219, 223–27, 242, 248
of Scripture, xxi, 164, 178, 192–203
Testimony, xxi, 102–13, 214, 221, 245

Zinzendorf, Nicholaus Ludwig von, 12, 27, 50–52, 59, 72, 82

www.ingramcontent.com/pod-product-compliance
Lightning Source LLC
Chambersburg PA
CBHW021651230426
43668CB00008B/586